SCIENCE ANNUAL

A Modern Science Anthology for the Family

2002

SCIENCE ANNUAL
2002

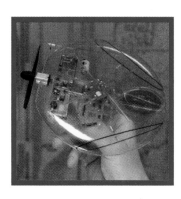

STAFF

CONTRIBUTORS

ERIC ADAMS, Associate editor, *Air&Space/Smithsonian* magazine
LIGHT AND MAGIC

WAYNE P. ARMSTRONG, Biology professor, Palomar College, San Marcos, CA
STINKERS OF THE PLANT WORLD

JAMES A. BLACKMAN, Professor of pediatrics, University of Virginia, Charlottesville, VA
WEST NILE VIRUS

OLAF BOEBEL, Marine research scientist, Graduate School of Oceanography, University of Rhode Island, Kingston, RI
OCEANOGRAPHY

BRUCE BOWER, Behavioral sciences editor, *Science News*
BUILDING FROM BABY BABBLE

JOE BOWER, Contributor, *Audubon* magazine
THE DARK SIDE OF LIGHT

GUY C. BROWN, Biochemist and a Royal Society research fellow at the University of Cambridge in England; author, *The Energy of Life: The Science of What Makes Our Minds and Bodies Work*
SPEED LIMITS

MALCOLM W. BROWNE, Science writer, *The New York Times*
REFINING THE ART OF MEASUREMENT

CHARLENE BRUSSO, Freelance writer; member, New England Science Writers; Science Fiction Writers of America
ASK THE SCIENTIST: PHYSICAL SCIENCES
CHEMISTRY

SIRI CARPENTER, Science writer, *Monitor on Psychology*, a publication of the American Psychological Association (APA)
BEHAVIORAL SCIENCES

VICKI CROKE, Columnist, *The Boston Globe*; author, *The Modern Ark: The Story of Zoos*
THE WORLD'S MOST ELUSIVE CARNIVORE

JEFFREY S. DEAN, Contributor, *Scientific American Discovering Archaeology* magazine
coauthor, ARTIFICIAL ANASAZI

KATE DOUGLAS, Editor, *New Scientist* magazine
CLAW-TO-CLAW COMBAT

CASSIA B. FARKAS, Freelance writer and editor living in New Canaan, CT
ENDANGERED SPECIES
SEISMOLOGY
ZOOLOGY

DAVID E. FASTOVSKY, Professor and Chair, Department of Geosciences, University of Rhode Island, Kingston, RI
GEOLOGY
PALEONTOLOGY

ROBERT C. FIERO, JR., Senior network specialist, Cummings and Lockwood
coauthor, COMMUNICATION TECHNOLOGY

GLENN FLEISHMAN, Freelance writer and contributor to *The New York Times, Fortune, Wired, Business 2.0*, and former columnist for *The Seattle Times*
THE WEB WITHOUT WIRES

PETER FRIEDERICI, Journalist, *National Wildlife* magazine
COLORLESS IN A WORLD OF COLOR

PETER GARRISON, Author, pilot, and amateur airplane builder whose columns appear regularly in *Flying* magazine
MICROSPIES

DEBBIE GARY, Air-show pilot and freelance aviation writer based in both Atlanta and Houston
SPACE-SHUTTLE IMPERSONATOR

SUE GEBO, Consulting nutritionist based in West Hartford, CT; author, *What's Left to Eat?*
NUTRITION

JOSIE GLAUSIUSZ, Associate editor, *Discover* magazine
JOINING HANDS: THE MATHEMATICS OF APPLAUSE

JESSICA GORMAN, Chemistry/materials-science editor, *Science News*
MAKING STUFF LAST

GEORGE J. GUMERMAN, Contributor, *Scientific American Discovering Archaeology* magazine; professor, University of Arizona, Tucson
coauthor, ARTIFICIAL ANASAZI

DAVID HART, Science writer, San Diego Supercomputer Center (SDSC) at the University of California in San Diego; author, *The Cross-Platform Mac Handbook, Mac OS X Web Server Handbook*
COMPUTERS
ELECTRONICS
MATHEMATICS

ROBERT HENSON, Freelance journalist and writer/editor at the University Corporation for Atmospheric Research in Boulder, CO
METEOROLOGY
THE YEAR IN WEATHER

T.A. HEPPENHEIMER, Frequent contributor to *American Heritage of Invention & Technology* magazine
WHAT EDWARD TELLER DID

MARGUERITE HOLLOWAY, Freelance journalist specializing in environmental and science reporting; contributing editor to *Scientific American* magazine.
CUTTLEFISH SAY IT WITH SKIN

SUSAN HORNIK, Senior editor at *Time* magazine in Hong Kong
FOR SOME, PAIN IS ORANGE

MICHAEL KERNAN, Former reporter/editor for the *Washington Post*; contributor to *Smithsonian, National Geographic,* and *Life* magazines; author, *Lost Diaries of Frans Hals.*
HOW SQUIRRELS FLY

JILL LEE, Member of the agricultural-research service information staff for *Agricultural Research* magazine
RESTORING A NATIONAL TREASURE

CALVIN LIEBERMAN, Contributor, *American Heritage of Invention & Technology* magazine; he worked in the scrap and solid-waste fields for more than 60 years and is a consultant on environmental and legislative issues, with an office in Toledo, OH
CREATIVE DESTRUCTION

CONTENTS

FEATURES

HUMAN SCIENCES 116

PAST, PRESENT, AND FUTURE 146

FEATURES

PHYSICAL SCIENCES

TECHNOLOGY

REVIEWS

FEATURES
2002

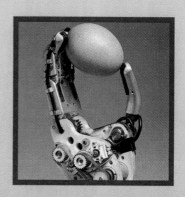

ANIMALS AND PLANTS

■ARIZONA'S SONORAN DESERT SUPPORTS SPECTACULAR FLORA AND FAUNA, INCLUDING THE WESTERN PATCH-NOSED SNAKE, SHOWN HERE SLITHERING THROUGH A BLOOMING BARREL CACTUS. THANKS TO ITS MUTED STRIPING, THE SNAKE DOES NOT STAND OUT AMONG THE SPINES AND FLOWERS, AND MAY BE ALL BUT INVISIBLE TO POTENTIAL PREY.

CONTENTS

THE WORLD'S MOST ELUSIVE CARNIVORE

by Vicki Croke

We are hiking in silence, at a fast clip, up a nearly vertical ridge in Madagascar's Ampijoroa National Park. It's 7 o'clock on a winter morning, but the temperature is already approaching 100° F (38° C)—a wall of heat through which we struggle to carry our gear and gain some traction from the sandy soil. Overhead, stands of baobab and rosewood trees rise more than 60 feet (18 meters) into the sky, opening out into an airy, inviting canopy. Down here, the forest is a tangle of lianas, shrubs, and saplings. We are scratched and bruised and desperate for a sign—any sign—of our quarry.

For a week now, we have hiked more than 20 miles (32 kilometers) a day, frequently off trail, in search of the island's most elusive animal: a carnivore little known to science and unknown to most of the world. The Malagasy people call it a fossa (pronounced FOO-sa), and tell bedtime stories of it snatching babies from cribs, extinguishing campfires, and killing coopfuls of chickens with its flatulence alone. "Be good," parents tell their children, "or the fossa will get you." (Even worse, they say, you could be reincarnated as one.) Scientists call it *Cryptoprocta ferox* with taxonomic exactitude, but they know little about it; many have spent years in Madagascar without even getting a glimpse of the animal. Only one thing is certain: on an island often described as an Eden, distinctly lacking in natural violence, the fossa is a striking anomaly. Although it weighs less than a cocker spaniel, pound for pound, it may be the deadliest carnivore on the planet.

Today, as usual, Luke Dollar is leading our team. And, as usual, he is frustrated. A graduate student in ecology at the University of Tennessee, Knoxville, Dollar has radio-

Madagascar's predatory but elusive fossa (left) has been misunderstood and needlessly feared by humans; only now are its secrets being revealed. With squirrel-like agility, fossas use their long, slender tails for stability and balance when climbing (right).

collared two fossas already. But they have a hunting range of 12 miles (19 kilometers), and in this forest, Dollar's equipment has a range of barely 2 miles (3 kilometers). Sometimes, when he holds the rubbery antenna aloft, loud, promising *tocks* come over the receiver. But deep ravines and impassable ridges can block transmission, and even the best signals turn to static.

Still, this morning feels different. Last night, something attacked one of the 25 traps Dollar had set up around camp, mutilating one of the live chickens he uses as bait. Although the attacker got away, shreds of evidence suggest it was a young female fossa named Tasha. She will probably return. Now, as we approach the traps and the telemetry signal grows more insistent, Dollar quietly gives a high five to Pierrot, his Malagasy assistant. Pierrot takes off to check the traps, but we continue upward, following Dollar's instincts as much as the signal.

Five minutes later, our pulses racing, we stand stock-still at the crossroads of two trails in the heart of the forest. Seventy yards (64 meters) away, in the dim light of the deep woods, a shape as long and low and dark as the shadows emerges. For just a moment, it hesitates at the forest's edge, peering in either direction. Then it floats across the open path and disappears.

SHROUDED BY LEGEND AND MYTH

Dollar first heard of the fossa in 1994, while working as a research assistant in the Ranomafana rain forest in southeastern Madagascar. He was tracking some red-bellied lemurs, he remembers, when his telemetry equipment picked up an odd signal. Its frequency suggested that it was coming from a collar worn by a lemur named Stanzi, but Stanzi's collar hadn't been working in years. Intrigued, Dollar tracked the signal to its source, stopping where the signal seemed to be strongest. There, on the ground, amid a few clumps of lemur fur and

carnivore scat, he found the shredded remains of Stanzi's collar. Its battery wires had been reconnected by a powerful chomp. When the Malagasy field assistants saw this, they whispered only one word: "fossa."

From that moment on, Dollar dedicated himself to the study and conservation of an animal he had never seen. He began by returning to the United States and thumbing through every animal encyclopedia and wildlife journal he could find. He discovered that the fossa had been first seen by Westerners in 1833, but that they had noticed little about it other than its taste for blood. In 1874, *Johnson's Natural History* noted that the fossa is "ferocious and sanguinary in the highest degree." Twenty-three years later, *The Antananarivo Annual* went even further: "When at large, [the fossa] is justly dreaded, and from its mode of attack, appears to be like an immense Weasel, but preying on the largest animals, Wild hogs and even Oxen."

After that, for nearly a century, biologists kept mum. In the 1970s, a reclusive Frenchman named Roland Albignac wrote about captive fossas and observed them in the wild. And today, there are 55 fossas in captivity worldwide, 13 of them in a zoo in Duisburg, Germany. But biologists have yet to sort out some basic issues of fossa gender, and the animal's behavior in the wild is even more of a mystery. In the United States, only the San Diego and the San Antonio zoos have fossas in their collections.

The prevailing ignorance is understandable. Tracking carnivores is tough in any setting—and in the forests of Madagascar, it is close to impossible. Even short trips through the forest can leave one slashed by sharp branches or burned by "itchy vines." The air is full of sweat bees, lapping up precious moisture from any exposed skin.

Nearby Lake Ravelobe is full of parasites and 14-foot (4-meter) Nile crocodiles, and the ground may be covered in terrestrial leeches. Medical care is primitive, cholera outbreaks frequently occur, and chloroquine-resistant malaria is rampant.

At the age of 26, Dollar has lived through all of these miseries and more. And yet, every year, after a few obligatory months in the United States to gather school credits and grant money, he bolts back to the island, slipping comfortably into this ancient world of taboos, forests, and ever-so-complicated modes of transportation. Dollar has trapped and radio-collared 16 fossas and examined hundreds of samples of their droppings. He knows how they look, how they sound, and how they smell (musky, with a hint of rancid meat). There may be times when he even knows how they think.

The payoff has been a biologist's bonanza. So little is known about the fossa, and so much of what is known has been incorrectly recorded, that nearly everything Dollar documents is new to science. Figures on fossa weights, for instance, tend to be based on zoo specimens and therefore exaggerated, and the fossa diet is only dimly understood. Until Dollar noticed that the animal's scat sometimes smelled fishy, no one knew that fossas eat fish. Until he tracked them during the day, biologists assumed the animals were nocturnal. But they are cathemeral: hunting and napping with no set schedule.

Inevitably, science has been able to strip the fossa of some of its mystery and power (even the most vicious fossa, we now know, couldn't possibly kill a cow). But Dollar's work has also demonstrated the fossa's pride of place. The animal is the linchpin of Madagascar's ecosystem, he believes, filling the same role that lions, cheetahs, and leopards combined do in Africa. Although there are seven other native carnivore species on the island, the fossa is largely credited with keeping lemur populations in check. And it rules not just the dark forest of Ampijoroa, but the ring of trees that completely surrounds this otherwise denuded 1,000-mile (1,600-kilometer)-long island.

Unfortunately, we still don't know how many fossas there are, exactly how they hunt

Native Forest Formations

Lowland rain forest

Mid-altitude montane rain forest

High-altitude montane rain forest

Western dry deciduous forest

Southern subarid thorn scrub

Evergreen uapaca woodland

Fossa distribution

Ankarafantsika
Ampijoroa
Tsimaloto

Zahamena

Ranomafana

Previously classified as a feline because of its catlike molars and sleek body, the fossa (above) is now thought to be a closer relative of the mongoose. Fossa researcher and graduate student Luke Dollar (right) returns to camp with sedated Tasha—a female that his team had been tracking for several weeks.

and breed in the wild (although a fossa pair was filmed mating in a tree), or how habitat loss affects their numbers. The island's ecology depends on a mystery, it seems—one that Dollar is doing his best to unravel.

CHEWING THE FAT AT CAMP

One evening early in this trip, Dollar and I sat down together at a greasy wooden table next to a corrugated shack. In our hands were bottles of orange Fanta and Three Horses beer, coated in congealed blood from the zebu meat next to which the bottles were stored. On our plates was a supper fit for a French penal colony: zebu stew with shards of bone, and rice with rocks. Over the years, Luke has destroyed four molars on such fare, and tonight, the photographer, Roy Toft, bit down with a sickening crunch.

After several months in Madagascar, Dollar had lost his usual 20 pounds (9 kilograms), and had the rangy look and stoic attitude of someone who's roughing it. He wore sandals and tank tops set off by traditional Malagasy wraps called *lambas*—perfect garb for the role of intrepid explorer.

When I asked how he would classify fossas biologically, he laughed. "I guess I'd still call them killing machines," he said, in his relaxed Alabama accent. "It is equipped to take anything it would encounter in its natural environment." The fossa is as agile as a squirrel, using its long, powerful tail for balance when leaping from branch to branch. Yet the fossa's muscle is closer to that of a clouded leopard, its only rival in arboreal athleticism. "It's like a small puma," Dollar said, "with the tenacity of a mongoose."

The comparison is apt. Most biologists, noting the shape of the fossa's skull and its low-slung body, classify it as a member of the mongoose family. But for years, it was classified as a feline because of its catlike molars and overall shape. Either way, the animal's hybrid appearance and dual citizenship offer a glimpse of how the two families' common ancestor might have looked and behaved many millions of years ago.

As Dollar talked, the camp mascot—a tame brown lemur named Piper—leaped up onto his lap for a scratching. In the wild, a fossa's face is often the last thing a lemur sees. But no one has ever seen the killing occur. Biologist Clare Hawkins, who has captured an astonishing 43 fossas, believes the animal hunts alone and that it stalks its

Even "killing machines" need to take a break every now and then. It was originally believed that fossas were strictly nocturnal. But studies of their behavior have shown that the creatures sleep or eat whenever the mood strikes them.

prey like a cat. "There is absolutely no nervousness," she says. "They just get on about their business." Because Dollar often finds the remains of a kill near trees where lemurs gather to rest, he suspects that fossas strike sleeping lemurs or ones that are just waking up from afternoon naps.

"The fossa is capable of explosive speed," Dollar says excitedly. The attack must be straightforward in the extreme: "Wham! Face first, head bite, then front claws slashing the stomach and eviscerating. Puncturing the cranium and crushing the jawline in one bite. Front claws opening the body cavity." Given the chance, a fossa will "eat anything with a heartbeat: lemurs, reptiles, chickens, fish, wild pigs."

EVEN PARADISE NEEDS A KILLER

Madagascar has no truly venomous snakes or big cats, no bears or wolves. Yet even paradise needs a killer or two. Predators keep prey populations in check, which saves plants from being overgrazed. As the lemur's worst nightmare, the fossa helps maintain the island's blissful natural balance.

But for how long? Since humans first arrived here 1,500 years ago, 17 species of lemur have died out, as well as multitudes of other species. What remains clings to a mere 10 percent of the island's original undisturbed wilderness. Flying over Madagascar or driving through it, one can't help but see the pitiful state of the environment: miles of scraggly crops where forests used to stand, eroded hillsides where natural wonders once lived. The island looks naked, scarred, battered, and burned.

What's left may be the single most precious, most species-rich area in the world. Eighty-three percent of the wildlife on Madagascar is unique, including 8,000 of its 10,000 plant species and two-thirds of the planet's chameleon species. Still, if the island's health depends on the fossa's brutal care, then that is a precarious balance indeed. Although the World Conservation Union (IUCN) has long listed the fossa as vulnerable, they have recently changed the creature's status to endangered. Dollar guesses that there may be fewer than 2,000 of the animals left. But how varied are their physiology and behavior? How stable are their populations? Answering those questions may take years.

Dollar's work, helped along by volunteers from the Earthwatch Institute, has shown that fossa density in Ampijoroa is surprisingly low. In three weeks in 1998, in the neighboring forest of Tsimaloto, Dollar

The young fossa's playfulness belies its true nature. Zoologists estimate that fewer than 2,000 of these remarkable predators remain on Madagascar.

caught three fossas in live traps and documented another three with motion-sensitive cameras. Given the similar terrain and lemur life here, he had expected to trap 10 to 20 in three months. By project's end, he would catch only two.

Dollar's conclusion is sobering: although fossas live in every kind of woodland on the island—from montane rain forest to dry deciduous forest—they may not always be able to stay put. "As soon as there's any habitat disturbance, fossa fall out," he says.

In Ampijoroa, lemur researchers aren't the only ones combing the forest. Local honey cutters chop down whole trees to collect nectar-filled hives; loggers search for rare woods; poachers kill rare animals. One day, I saw a local park guardian collecting firewood in the forest, against park rules. On another day, a poacher appeared from the forest. "I don't have anything," he protested, hurrying off. We soon discovered his 6-foot (2-meter) blowpipe stashed under some brush. When Dollar pressed his mouth to one end and exhaled, a rusty 6-inch (15-centimeter) dart fell to the ground. The dart had lemur fur on it.

As Slick as Root-Beer Taffy

Today, on our last day in camp, it seems as if our own hunting will be less well rewarded than the poacher's. Although we glimpsed the fossa this morning, we weren't able to catch it. Even so, Dollar isn't ready to give up. He hikes back up the trail one last time to check the traps. Within minutes, the camp is roused by cries of "Fossa! Fossa!" Dollar strides into the clearing carrying Tasha's limp, sedated form.

Up close, the fossa is even more spectacular than she seemed in the forest that morning. As sinewy as a mountain lion and as slick as root-beer taffy, she has enormous paws and a long tail that dangles below Dollar's cradling arms. Her fur is a dark chocolate with black highlights, her underbelly bears a creamy blaze, and even though she has just killed and eaten an entire chicken, she is spotlessly clean.

From all around the camp, staff members and volunteers, villagers and their children, converge around the battered table where Dollar has laid his prize. He removes the thick red, white, and blue leather collar, number 448808, and puts the channel out of service. Then he and a veterinary volunteer measure everything measurable.

This terror of the forest weighs only a bit over 14 pounds (6 kilograms). Her other measurements, though typical for a fossa, seem equally tame. Her canines are 0.6 inch (1.5 centimeters) thick. Her neck circumference is just a tad over 9 inches (23 centimeters). Chest circumference: 13 inches (33 centimeters). Full body, no tail: 28 inches (71 centimeters). Full body with tail: 56 inches (142 centimeters). Heart rate: 140 beats per minute.

Once the blood and tissue samples have been taken and the study is complete, the carnival begins. Everyone wants to pose with the fossa, and so she is passed from hand to hand, photographed by one instant camera after another. It is a discomforting scene, but I can't help joining in. As the forests of Madagascar and other Edens fall, and as species after species tumble toward extinction, we yearn to hold on to the survivors a moment longer—to touch something wild and mysterious before it disappears.

And yet, even as we hold the fossa in our arms, we know its true nature has eluded us. It is floating through the trees even now: a rumor, a shadow, a story to tell children. A shape as ephemeral as smoke. ◢

RESTORING A NATIONAL TREASURE

by Jill Lee

Each year, nearly 600,000 tourists come to see the cherry blossoms in Washington, D.C., bringing revenue to the local economy and taking home photographs and memories of a spectacular show offered by some of the nation's most cherished trees. And soon, visitors will have the U.S. National Arboretum in Washington to thank for the gift they will undoubtedly enjoy—500 cherry trees propagated from the original Yoshino trees presented by Japan to First Lady Helen Taft in 1912.

Unfortunately, though, even the best-tended trees do not live forever. Yoshino cherry trees live an average of 40 years, and spring 2001 marks the 89th year of bloom for the surviving trees that surround Washington's Tidal Basin—more than twice their expected life span. Sadly, it is estimated that only 125, or a mere 4 percent, of the original trees from Japan remain.

HELPING HANDS UNITE
Fortunately for all visitors and residents of the historical city, arboretum horticulturist Ruth L. Dix has grown new trees, *Prunus x*

yedoensis, from cuttings taken from the Yoshinos over the past two years. These original trees were a thank-you gift to President William Howard Taft for his support of Japan during the 1905 Russo–Japanese War, when he was U.S. secretary of war.

"We really didn't have a program to propagate replacements from the original trees. We just maintained the population from commercial nurseries," says Robert DeFeo, the National Park Service's chief horticulturist for the National Capital Region. In the 1930s, William Clarke of the W.B. Clarke Nursery in San Jose, California, presented to Washington a seedling selection of Yoshino trees that bear pink flowers called Akebono (meaning daybreak) for planting around the city's Tidal Basin.

The Park Service keeps the Tidal Basin completely covered in springtime pinks and

Every spring, thousands of tourists visit the Tidal Basin in Washington, D.C., to see the flowering Yoshino cherry trees, a gift from Japan in 1912. The few original trees that remain have been blooming for 89 seasons—more than twice their typical life span.

whites through its "Blossoms in Our Future," a successful tree-donation program, which receives contributions—often given as memorials—to replace dying trees with American nursery stock. But DeFeo and the Park Service understand why people become passionate about historic trees such as the Yoshinos.

In an article in the *Washington Post*, retired arboretum botanist Roland M. Jefferson stressed the need to save the surviving cherries. Jefferson collected, evaluated, and tried to preserve the Yoshinos' genetic material, in a project he conducted with the head of the arboretum's shrub-breeding program, the late Donald R. Egolf.

When the *Post* article appeared, arboretum director Thomas S. Elias and National Park Service officials decided to ensure the survival of the remaining original cherry-tree lines. "Tom Elias was great," DeFeo recalls. "He called me up and said, 'Just let us know what we can do.'" Elias put DeFeo in touch with Margaret R. Pooler, a geneticist in the arboretum's Floral and Nursery Plants Research Unit. In no time, Pooler and DeFeo decided they should start taking cuttings from the historic survivors right after cherry-blossom time.

Complications pushed back their start date, however, to early summer—close to the end of the optimal time for cuttings. But Pooler knew that if the cherry trees could be propagated, Ruth Dix could do the job. Dix had already propagated cherry trees successfully from the original 1912 gift trees at the U.S. Naval Observatory.

TOO FEW OR TOO MANY?

It took two attempts to bring the cherry trees to Washington nearly 90 years ago. Disappointingly, the first shipment was diseased and had to be destroyed. The second contained 3,020 trees—mainly Yoshino and

U.S. National Arboretum researchers ensure regeneration of the trees that adorn Washington's landscape and symbolize a friendship between two nations.

some later-blooming Kwanzan—far more than the famed Tidal Basin's border could ever accommodate. "The trees were too crowded, so they replanted some at additional Washington landmarks, such as the Supreme Court, U.S. Naval Observatory, and Library of Congress," says DeFeo, who used to work with Jefferson at the arboretum. "The library did not even know what they had until Roland found the records and told them."

Those little-known plantings provided researchers with a means of differentiating original trees (such as those near the Jefferson Memorial, above) from later replacements around the Tidal Basin, and were an invaluable second source of original material for future propagation.

"We couldn't be too choosy," says Dix of her time gathering cuttings at the Tidal Basin. "For any living thing, renewal and regeneration get harder as it ages—and these trees had already lived twice their normal life span."

WILLING AND ABLE SUPPORT

Cost was a significant factor in the propagation effort, which included DNA fingerprinting by Pooler to help confirm the trees' identity. The project was financed in part by

the J. Frank Schmidt Family Charitable Trust established by J. Frank Schmidt & Son Co., a wholesale grower of shade, flowering, and ornamental trees in Oregon.

"The cherry trees in Washington, D.C., are a national treasure," says Jan Schmidt Barkley, who chairs the trust, which supports horticultural research and education across the country. "The nursery industry and the public have benefited from the U.S. National Arboretum's work. We have been happy to give back by underwriting the propagation effort."

The nursery is also testing new cherry-tree hybrids developed by Pooler and her predecessor, Egolf.

"It is exciting to us that Dr. Pooler is working on cherry breeding; it's very important to the nursery trade," says J. Frank Schmidt's horticultural expert, Keith Warren. "We are evaluating several of her new cherry cultivars here in Oregon. We feel her work has great potential."

Cherry trees have the beauty and compact size many urban gardeners like, but they are vulnerable to insects, diseases, and flooding, Warren says. "That's why Pooler's work to toughen these trees up is so valuable." Stronger trees require less fertilizer and pesticides. Warren is aware that woody ornamentals are important not only to his company, but also to the economic well-being of his state. For Oregon, nursery crops are a primary moneymaker. "Last year, in terms of dollars earned, they brought in more than barley, wheat, or cattle," he says.

This genetic research will become even more important with the rapidly growing environmental-horticulture industry. But while Pooler's efforts may focus on new ornamental cherry hybrids, she is also exploring the genetic value of the 1912 trees. Those still living may be extremely well suited to city life—another potentially marketable trait.

AT THE ROOT OF GOOD CUTTINGS
Most people think of taking cuttings as simply breaking off plant stems and placing them in water. Saving antique cherry trees, however, requires much more effort, and Dix has years of experience.

"You look for the most juvenile new growth," she explains. "Many people think the top of a tree is the best place for cuttings, but that's not always the case."

Dix performed the delicate task of transforming hundreds of cuttings, carefully wrapped in wet towels and stored in an ice chest, into 500 healthy trees. First, she cut them into smaller parts. Then she inflicted a wound on the stem at the base of the cutting—a process that actually creates more surface area for the rooting hormone to penetrate. Afterward, she planted the cuttings and placed them on a greenhouse bench equipped with an automatic-misting system. All of Dix's work paid off with an 80 percent success rate. "You always feel so exhilarated when you see your cuttings take root," says Dix. "Plus, it makes you feel really good to be part of preserving history."

TOUGH LOVE FOR TREES
But as the trees grew, Dix had to turn from tender loving care to tough love. Most cherry trees have weak apical dominance: basically, the process by which hormones "instruct" one branch to become the main stem of a tree. Some cherry trees would be happy enough just being cherry bushes. Because of this characteristic, Dix had to cut off stray, straggling branches and stake the trees to bamboo poles to nurture them into upstanding members of the Tidal Basin community. The new trees will be a welcome addition, but they do present DeFeo with a challenge. Genetic authenticity is great, but too little genetic diversity in a planting of trees makes them vulnerable to diseases and pests.

"The guideline is to plant less than 10 percent of the same species, 20 percent of the same genus, or 30 percent of the same family," says DeFeo. "But I'm working with 100 percent species similarity, so I need all the diversity I can get."

Pooler's DNA work will help uncover the answer to what remains a question—whether the trees have subtle genetic differences. It will also confirm DeFeo's hunch that there are some genetic differences in the trees, and will help him plan which trees might need extra protection in the future. ◤

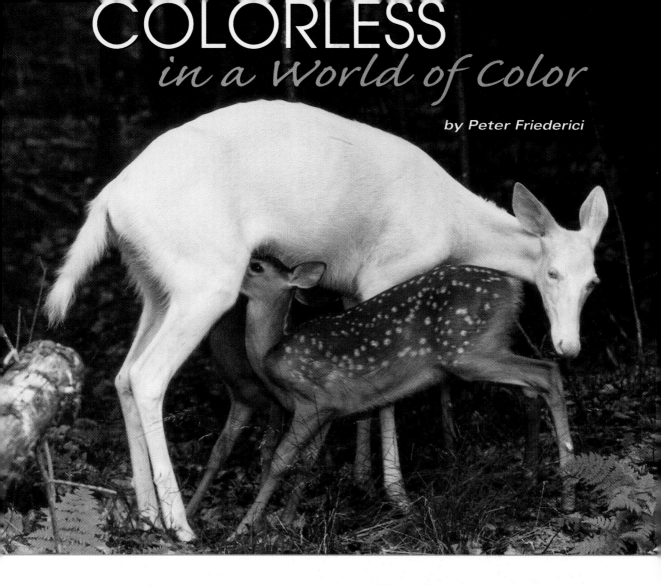

COLORLESS
in a World of Color

by Peter Friederici

Snow-white coloration, pink eyes, and ruby-colored pupils distinguish albino animals from the norm. Their offspring may appear normal.

It was in west-central Wyoming where Dick Baldes recently saw something extraordinary. A resident of the expansive Wind River Indian Reservation, he was accustomed to seeing white-tailed prairie dogs that range in the area's short-grass prairies. But he had never seen prairie dogs like these: about a dozen snow-white, pink-eyed crea-tures scattered amid the hundreds of ordinary, earth-colored animals.

Baldes had worked for a number of years as a biologist for the U.S. Fish and Wildlife Service, and he knew this sighting was a rare occurrence. So he photographed and video-taped the white creatures for three weeks. Then, seemingly overnight, the animals vanished. It wasn't too difficult for Baldes to guess why.

"From a distance, you can't see the brown prairie

Their conspicuous whiteness makes albinos vulnerable to predators, especially in sparsely vegetated habitats. Airborne predators may become confused by unpigmented prey, and instead pursue more familiar looking animals.

dogs, but the white ones stood out like sore thumbs," he says. "They must have been pretty vulnerable to aerial predators."

RARE PHENOMENON

The unusual prairie dogs were examples of a recurring phenomenon that is quite rare in nature. In a wide array of species—including humans—individuals occasionally are born lacking a normal complement of skin, fur, feather, or scale pigments. As a result, part or all of their typical coloration is conspicuously absent.

Most people know such animals as "albinos," which are distinguished not only by their pure-white skin or fur, but also by their pink eyes. The pinkness comes from blood vessels that are normally colored, but in this case are unshielded by other pigment. Not all paler-than-usual animals are albinos, however. Some lack pigment everywhere except their eyes—a phenomenon biologists call "leucistic." Other animals that are partly white and partly colored are labeled "partial albinos," as, for example, a black raven with some white feathers.

FOR BETTER OR WORSE

Because albinism occurs unpredictably in the wild, it is difficult to study. But in recent years, scientists have gained new insight into the lives of albino animals. And in some cases, biologists have found that, for better or worse, albinism is sometimes closely linked to human activities.

Albinism and its variants have been recorded in an astonishing array of animals, including more than 300 species of North American birds and such diverse creatures as whales, snapping turtles, salamanders, and freshwater snails. It results from several factors, the most common of which is genetic. A gene that forms in the production of pigments mutates and fails to function properly. The resulting mutation can be passed down, generation to generation.

Since albinism is usually recessive, however, it generally manifests in offspring only when both parents carry the mutated genes. That's one reason why the phenomenon remains rare. Mammalogists have estimated that about 1 in 10,000 births results in a true albino. In a recent study of more than 30,000 wild birds that were examined after they were temporarily captured in mist nets in Southern California, only 17—or about one-eighteenth of 1 percent—displayed any degree of albinism.

STUDIES EN MASSE

Occasionally researchers have pinpointed particular causes for such color aberrations. Ornithologists have documented, for example, scattered cases in which birds grew white feathers following a sudden shock or injury, or as a result of old age. In the

Ukraine, where the Chernobyl nuclear-power-plant accident in 1986 caused large-scale radioactive contamination, barn swallows subsequently showed a much higher rate of partial albinism than did other, uncontaminated populations. The rate of partial albinism among swallows near Chernobyl jumped from 0 percent before 1986 to 15 percent in 1991.

Lack of normal pigmentation has also been seen occasionally en masse in amphibians such as toads and salamanders. Last summer, Oregon biologist Jay Bowerman found thousands of unusually pale individuals in a population of western toad tadpoles. "Approximately 1 percent of the tadpoles appeared to be virtually white," he says. "They appeared to lack any black or dark pigmentation." In the Oregon lake where Bowerman studied the creatures, the normal-colored tadpoles continued to develop and completed metamorphosis, while the white tadpoles did not progress beyond the early leg stage.

The scientist observed that white tadpoles remained healthy even though they did not transform into adulthood. He surmises that the phenomenon could have resulted from a genetic mutation that disrupted the production of both hormones and pigments needed for metamorphosis. Eventually the white tadpoles in the lake disappeared, leading him to suspect that they were far easier for predators to find than were the darker tadpoles.

LIABILITY VS. ASSET

Albinos face many obstacles. Some albino birds, for instance, have brittle feathers that may be worn away more quickly than usual. Lacking a full set of eye pigments, true albinos often have poor eyesight and are very sensitive to sunlight. What's more, in many social species, odd-looking individuals are not accepted by their peers.

Researchers have observed shunned albinos among species as disparate as ravens, barn swallows, and red-winged blackbirds. In studies of Adélie penguins in Antarctica, Jun Nishikawa of Japan's Ocean Research Institute found that albino birds are frequently shunned and, because of such ostracism, are less likely to reproduce and pass on their genes.

High visibility, poor eyesight, and sensitivity to light can make albino animals' chances for survival precarious at best. Furthermore, the albino's peers may shun the pale creature, making mating and reproduction unlikely.

The specific mutation that results in deficient pigmentation remains comparatively rare because it manifests itself in offspring only when both parents carry the problem genes.

eastern screech owls in enclosures containing one brown and one albino mouse, the owls generally pounced on the albinos. So did shrikes, but only when dense vegetation was present in the study area, thus allowing the brown mice to camouflage themselves better than the albinos.

When Kaufman repeated the experiment with shrikes in open areas, the avian predators captured more brown than albino mice. This led him to conclude that visually oriented predators use a particular search image. In areas with sparse cover, where both types of mice were highly visible, shrikes pounced on the brown mice they most readily recognized from past hunting experiences. The odd coloring apparently helped protect the albinos.

ENVIRONMENTAL EFFECTS

In the early 1990s, a group of researchers from Miami University in Ohio trapped an albino meadow vole during a field study. By mating that male with darker, naturally colored wild females, and then mating the resulting young with one another, the team produced more than 100 albinos. These were released, along with the darker voles, in a grassy enclosure.

"I had read several articles about how conspicuous animals get picked out of a population first," says Gary W. Barrett, an ecologist who oversaw the study and is now affiliated with the University of Georgia. "We wanted to test that hypothesis under experimental field conditions." The researchers found that the albinos had a greater rate of survival during late fall and early winter. The reason, say the scientists, had a lot to do with the quality of habitat.

The effects of predation on albinos apparently vary according to the animals' habitat and the type of predator. In the 1970s, University of Georgia researcher Donald Kaufman conducted a series of experiments with normal-colored and albino mice to see whether predators preferentially chose one or the other. When Kaufman released captive barn owls and

The main predators on the test plots were raptors, which were stymied in their pursuit of both types of voles by dense, matted grasses, under which the voles could easily tunnel and hide. Later the researchers recaptured many of the albinos and darker voles and released them in a field where cover was

Visitors to Olney, Illinois, are greeted by almost ubiquitous images and references to white squirrels, by far the community's most celebrated group of residents. Olney's white squirrels descend from two pairs of gray squirrels released in 1902. Many of Olney's normal-colored squirrels carry the albino gene.

sparse. The following year, they found quite a few naturally colored meadow voles but no albinos. "This work lends credence to the importance of quality habitat for conspicuous small mammals," says Barrett.

TOWN MASCOTS

Sometimes the increased conspicuousness that comes with albinism can work to an animal's advantage. That, at least, is the case in the southern Illinois town of Olney, where two pairs of albino gray squirrels were released in 1902.

The creatures soon multiplied into hundreds, and they became the community's beloved mascots. Today, the town's official flag and police cars are adorned with pictures of a white squirrel, and fines are imposed on any automobile drivers who run over the revered animals.

Currently, about one-sixth of the community's squirrels are albino, and half of its normal-colored squirrels carry the gene for albinism that can produce more white off-

spring. "There are some albinos in the woods outside of town, but hawks, owls, and coyotes attack them," says John Stencel, a biologist at Olney Central College who conducts a local albino-squirrel census each fall. "They're more susceptible because they're easily seen in the woods." But in town, he observes, increased visibility can be a plus because motorists tend to see a white squirrel more readily than a gray one.

To help protect the animals, authorities have put up "squirrel crossing" signs throughout the community and instituted a leash law for outdoor cats. Local Boy Scouts have also mounted squirrel nest boxes in areas where there are not enough large trees to provide natural cavities.

Still, the scientist fears that the albinos may disappear entirely within the next 20 years or so. "They go in cycles," he says, "and we've been seeing over the long term a drop in their numbers." He notes that any small, isolated population is more likely to disappear through chance events—such as disease or storms—than is a large one.

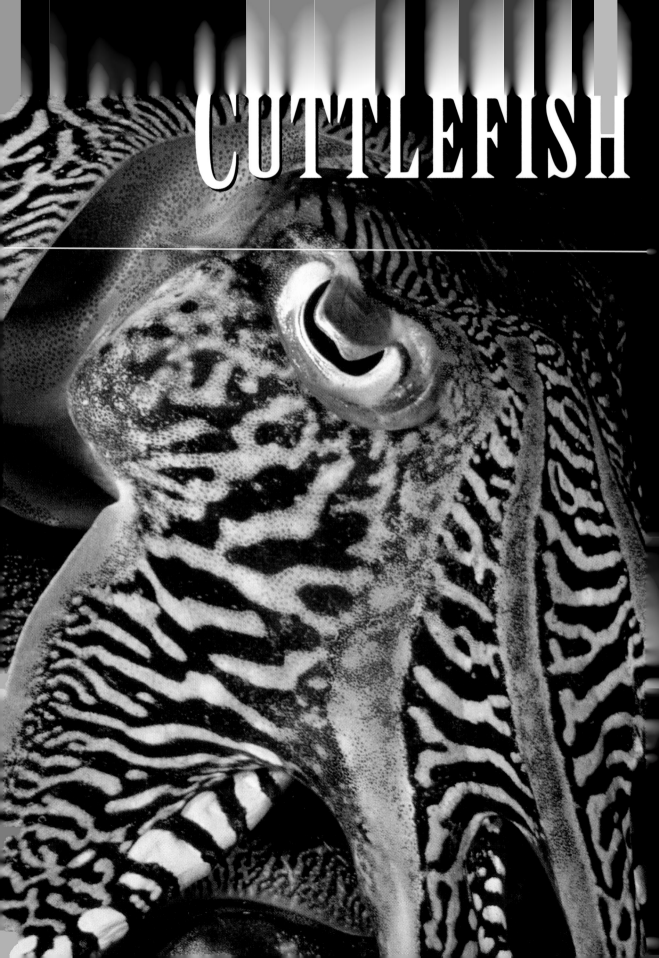

CUTTLEFISH

SAY IT WITH SKIN

by Marguerite Holloway

A fleet of tiny creatures swim the length of a shallow tank at the Marine Biological Laboratory at Woods Hole, Massachusetts, passing above yellow sand, then brown sand, then variegated pebbles, and finally a bed of white shells. These newly hatched animals, each no larger than a thumbnail, undergo instant and seemingly magical transformations as they travel the route; their skin color shifting from yellow to a tasteful khaki, to mottled black and white, to a uniform soft white. These young creatures are cuttlefish, and they are masters of disguise.

A single cuttlefish can become speckled, ocellate, stippled, lineate, whorled, black, white, brown, gray, pink, red, iridescent—all in different combinations and all in less than a second. It can hold zebra stripes for hours or send waves of color flickering across its skin. It can make half its body white while the other half displays lines. Its skin can pucker into riffles and spines and bumps, then suddenly go smooth as polished stone. And that's just the common cuttlefish (*Sepia officinalis*); each of the 100 or so other species has its own repertoire of quick changes.

SURPRISE, SURPRISE

Cuttlefish are highly advanced invertebrates, a distinction that they share with several cephalopods, a class of mollusks that includes squid and octopuses. But while cuttlefish are closely related to these other ink-spurting, color-flexing creatures, they remain more mysterious, largely because they are for the most part so hard to observe in their natural habitats. Researchers have

From striped to iridescent, from bumpy to polished or puckered, cuttlefish (left) have the almost magical ability to transform their skin's color and texture.

No larger than a thumbnail when hatched, cuttlefish grow rapidly, with some species—such as Sepia apama—*reaching an impressive 3 feet in length.*

recently ventured into the field with high-tech equipment, but most of what we know about cuttlefish still comes from the laboratory. There, often clustered together in glass tanks, these cephalopods—probably solitary by nature—continue to yield surprises. Scientists have found that cuttlefish can detect water motion in the same way that fish do, that their large eyes (with *W*-shaped pupils) can see polarized light, and that their reproductive behaviors and modes of communication are quite complex.

Cuttlefish range enormously in size from the 2-inch (5-centimeter) *Metasepia pfefferi* to the 3-foot (1-meter)-long *Sepia apama*. But all have eight arms and two tentacles, the latter usually remaining retracted unless the cuttlefish is feeding. As with other cephalopods, cuttlefish seem to grow quickly, mate once, and then die—most live for no more than 18 months. Like squid and

Cuttlefish have nearly panoramic vision, thanks to their ability to move their eyes to compensate for the position of their bodies. Their mysterious W-shaped pupils may allow them to see backward and forward at the same time.

octopuses, cuttlefish have a funnel for jet propulsion, but unlike the other two, they also have an internal, oval-shaped bony chamber that fills with gas. The result is that, as well as being able to swim and squirt backward and forward, they can gracefully hover, rise, and fall.

Transformation is handy whenever danger looms. A threatened cuttlefish might assume menacing color patterns or raise its arms in a defensive posture.

MOLLUSK MORSELS

Found in tropical and temperate oceans everywhere except in the Americas, cuttlefish favor mostly nearshore environments such as coral reefs, mangrove swamps, and fields of sea grass and algae. Although they are an important source of food for many people, no data have been compiled on whether they have been endangered by overharvesting, and demand for them has been growing in Asia and the Mediterranean. Still, even if they cannot always escape nets, cuttlefish can stay hidden from their other predators: sharks and teleosts (a range of bony, jawed fish). This ability probably evolved between 370 million and 190 million years ago, when teleosts began taking over coastal environments and forcing some mollusks into deep water, where hydrostatic pressure made their shells cumbersome. So the cephalopods (with the exception of the chambered nautilus) shed their shells and slowly moved back to compete with, and to avoid, the fish.

PERFORMING PAPILLAE

The secret to the cuttlefish's capacity to fade into the background lies in several special types of muscle groups and cells: papillae, which allow the animals to deform their skin so they can assume the texture of seaweed or a bumpy rock; chromatophores, which contain pigment; and two kinds of reflecting cells, iridophores and leucophores, which influence color. In the common cuttlefish—the most extensively studied species because it is rather easily found in the eastern Atlantic Ocean, the English Channel, and the Mediterranean Sea—the chromatophores are yellow, red, orange, and dark brown to black, with a density of about 30,000 per 1 square inch (6 square centimeters). The muscles that are around these sacs of pigment expand or contract in response to "messages" sent from the brain as it processes visual information—all happening with extreme swiftness; chameleons, on the other hand, control coloration through hormones traveling in the blood—a much slower process.

Iridophores are made of stacks of very thin layers of chitin that diffract (cause interference patterns in) light, giving rise to a shimmering array of blues, greens, and silvers. Recent research conducted by Roger T. Hanlon of the Marine Biological Laboratory suggests that iridophores also may be under indirect neural control, primarily through the action of the neurotransmitter acetylcholine. Leucophores, found in some cuttlefish species, are flat, branched cells that reflect colors.

RICH REPERTOIRE

The mesmerizing array of hues and patterns resulting from these specialized cells is important not only for hiding but for communication. Cuttlefish, as well as squid and octopuses, have a rich repertoire of signals for defense, hunting, reproduction, and warning—and perhaps for types of communication not yet understood. In *S. officinalis,* for instance, the so-called "intense zebra" display warns other males to stay away. This and other dermal changes are often accompanied by a complex set of postures and arm movements. Hanlon and his colleague John B. Messenger of the University of Sheffield in England have described 54 components of the common cuttlefish's "vocabulary," including such postures as Drooping Arms, Flanged Fin, and Wrinkled First Arms.

Deciphering this vocabulary has been challenging—and has just become more so. Watching female cuttlefish choose mates, Jean G. Boal of the University of Texas Medical Branch (UTMB) at Galveston recently made the discovery that females tended to shy away from those males making aggressive zebra displays. Instead, the females seemed substantially more interested in males that

Cuttlefish mate only once during their brief lives—most individuals live only 18 months—and then die even before their tiny eggs (top) hatch.

had just mated, which suggests that the females were responding to a chemical cue from the male. Sure enough, Boal and Sherry Painter, also at UTMB, found that cuttlefish recognized a pheromone that Painter had recently isolated from a marine snail, a cephalopod relative. "Mollusks, in general, use pheromones to coordinate their behavior because they are not all that mobile," explains Boal. "It serves as a communicator over much longer distances than visual signals could ever work."

HAVE WE MET?

Boal's studies have also revealed that cuttlefish cannot recognize each other individually. If, say, a male encounters another male and responds aggressively, he'll repeat the behavior after swimming around the tank and bumping into the same male a minute later. "I talked to many people who were very disappointed: 'Oh, cuttlefish are stupid, huh?'" Boal recalls, laughing. Cuttlefish probably live far apart in the wild, except when they gather en masse to mate, so they have no real need to recognize individuals: "If two males have a fight," says Boal, "the loser can leave and is not likely to bump up against that male again. He has a whole blooming ocean out there." And because cuttlefish, like almost all cephalopods, die before their eggs have hatched, there is no reason for them to have the capacity to recognize their young.

SAVVY SWIMMERS

The question of intelligence is what attracted Boal to cuttlefish in the first place. "No matter how you measure it," she points out, "their brain is larger than an octopus brain." Her current experiments on learning suggest that both cephalopods do well with spatial learning; cuttlefish seem to learn their way around a maze with the same facility as octopuses. Such savvy comes as no surprise to cuttlefish aficionados, who can sit entranced in front of a tank for hours, feeling the creature's curiosity or (making allowances for the perils of anthropomorphism) what seems to be its passing interest in the human observer. "I think that's part of the allure of cuttlefish," says John W. Forsythe, a biologist at UTMB's National Resource Center for Cephalopods in Galveston, a sort of Cuttlefish Central that supplies the animals to aquariums and researchers all over the world. "They're really interactive. They're looking at you as much as you're looking at them."

AWESOME PREDATORS

The reverie is broken. It's feeding time in Galveston. As Forsythe begins to toss large frozen shrimp into the tank, a *S. pharaonis* swims forward, its eight arms all touching one another so that together they look almost like an elephant's trunk. Slowly, two tentacles appear, stretching almost lazily toward a shrimp until, with staggering speed, they shoot out to their full extent and grab the prey, pulling it back into a beaked and hungry mouth. Mealtime continues fast and furious; the tank is clean within minutes. "They're the most awesome predators. I'm very thankful they don't get to be 6 feet [2 meters]," says Forsythe, adding that if crabs had been on the menu, the waters would have roiled.

Cuttlefish are indeed perfectly honed hunters. Everything about their physiology enhances their search for shrimp, crabs, and fish; their huge eyes, for instance, are as sophisticated as those of vertebrates. Although they seem unable to see in color (unlike most of the fish that feed on them), their eyes can detect polarized light, allowing them to easily locate transparent or camouflaged prey. Thirteen or 14 muscles control their eyes, while humans' eyes are controlled by only six, and octopuses' by seven. The extra muscles allow cuttlefish to see pretty much everything, because they can move their eyes to compensate for the position of their bodies, and can cause their lines of vision to converge for optimal perception of depth. Why they have *W*-shaped pupils remains a mystery, however; Forsythe suspects it allows them to see backward and forward at the same time.

Cuttlefish can sense movement in other ways. Bernd U. Budelmann of UTMB's Marine Biomedical Institute has determined that cuttlefish have tiny hair cells that detect the directional flow of water, enabling them to sense and interpret changes in currents or water movement up to 60 feet (18 meters) away. And they are also outfitted with statocysts (organs similar to the vestibular structure, or inner ear, in vertebrates), which allow them to maintain their orientation. So whether they're swimming forward, jetting in reverse, or just hovering, cuttlefish can figure out which way is up. "They're like cats—built to right themselves," explains Forsythe. And then, with some of the fervor that cuttlefish seem to evoke, he blurts out, "They're so cool!"

Where the Spitting Cobras Play

by Joe Slowinski

Although it has been more than 10 years since Myanmar abandoned its disastrous "Burmese Road to Socialism"—an official policy of strict isolationism and self-reliance—this Southeast Asian country remains comparatively remote and largely unknown to the outside world. It is also a very impoverished land, without adequate infrastructure, and quite bureaucratic—all of which makes it one of the hardest places for a foreign scientist to work. Since the British relinquished control in 1948, few of us have ventured to Myanmar.

But these challenges have only served to whet my appetite. Two reasons for spending time there quickly become apparent to anyone who has ever visited the country. First, Myanmar is a visually stunning place. Ancient gilded pagodas sprinkle the landscape; the enormous Irrawaddy (Burmese: Ayeyarwady) River cuts through the middle of the country, unconstrained by dams or levees; jungle-clad mountains form a continuous, horseshoe-shaped barrier around the country, isolating it from neighboring India, China, and Thailand. Second, the people are unbelievably friendly, and crime is virtually unknown.

HANKERING FOR HERPETOFAUNA

But what really drew me to Myanmar were the reptiles and amphibians—its herpetofauna. Along with the rest of the flora and fauna, Myanmar's herpetofauna is one of the least studied in Asia. Many new species await discovery.

My project, supported by the National Science Foundation (NSF), has two parts: a general survey of the amphibians and reptiles, and an ambitious training program aimed at providing Burmese biologists with the necessary skills for conducting their own biodiversity surveys. The first component is important to our efforts to understand the composition and evolution of the Southeast Asian herpetofauna. The second is critical because biodiversity surveys will provide baseline data needed for making wise conservation decisions—something Myanmar, like the rest of Southeast Asia, badly needs.

I have always been interested primarily in snakes, especially venomous ones. I currently study members of the family Elapidae, which includes such highly dangerous species as cobras, coral snakes, and sea snakes. With 37 species, Myanmar is particularly rich in venomous snakes.

SNAKE SHOPPING

In February 1998, accompanied by herpetology colleagues Jens Vindum and Carol Spencer from the California Academy of Sciences, I arrive on my second trip to Myanmar. First, we travel south of Mandalay to visit a wholesale snake operation, whose

shaped mark—the "monocle"—on the back of its neck, clearly visible when the animal spreads its hood in response to a perceived threat. The king cobras in Myanmar are banded. Yet this cobra is patternless.

There is another big difference: This is a spitting cobra. It is capable of spraying its venom directly at the eyes of a predator, and its aim over a short range—6 feet (2 meters) or so—is unnervingly accurate. If the victim's eyes are not immediately flushed with water, blindness may result. Spitting adds a whole new dimension to snake catching!

For a herpetologist, finding a new species is always exciting; for me, finding a new cobra species is the ultimate discovery. We buy a couple of the spitting cobras, but for specimens acquired this way, there is always doubt about their original locality.

HUNTING IN DRESSES AND FLIP-FLOPS

We arrange for employees to take us out searching for other cobras. That night, we drive south. We assume our guides are taking us to a thick forest, and are surprised when we stop alongside some fallow cotton fields—bare dirt everywhere and no trees. How can there be snakes here?

Soon our guides begin catching large Russell's vipers (*Vipera russelli*), which lie curled in the fields. This species is considered Myanmar's most dangerous snake—it kills more than 1,000 Burmese a year—yet our guides snag them with homemade tongs, made by connecting two flimsy bamboo rods. And they do it dressed in *longyis*, a sarong-like garment, and cheap sandals. Jens expresses his admiration for men who can catch large and deadly snakes wearing nothing but "dresses and flip-flops."

After two hours, we have caught 15 snakes: four Russell's vipers and an assort-

A Burmese spitting cobra assumes a threatening position in front of herpetologist Joe Slowinski (above). The newly identified species, discovered by Slowinski in 1998, lacks the patterning characteristic of the monocled cobra (right).

stock finds use in Chinese traditional medicine. Although illegal in Myanmar, the snake trade continues to thrive in the region around Mandalay. We have come to see if we can purchase any valuable snake specimens.

I get excited when a dark-brown cobra, which we are told was caught locally, is brought out. I see immediately that it is distinct from the two known cobra species in Myanmar—the monocled cobra (*Naja kaouthia*) and the king cobra (*Ophiophagus hannah*). The monocled cobra has a circle-ment of other species. Unfortunately, this night, and the rest of the monthlong trip, passes without a cobra sighting.

VEXING VERIFICATION

Back in the United States, with the help of cobra expert Wolfgang Wüster at the University of Wales, I begin researching whether or not the spitting cobras we purchased are a new species. Based on coloration, anatomic characteristics, and a comparison of its DNA to that of other Asian cobras, we determine that this is indeed a new species. We begin to write a formal description, but I am vexed by the fact that our only specimens were purchased from snake collectors, and therefore lack reliable locality data.

In pursuit of an exact identification, I presently return to Myanmar and head straight for the Mandalay area, where, accompanied by a driver and translator, I travel west to Monywa. It is brutally hot, well over 100° F (38° C), but this is typical May weather in the central dry zone. This area receives much less rainfall than the rest of the country, and the natural vegetation is an open, scrubby savanna. In this heat, the snakes spend their days deep in rodent holes, and hunting them is a waste of time. So we travel north, stopping at each village to interview the inhabitants about the local cobras. Everyone has stories to tell about a relative or friend who was killed by a snake within the past several years. At one village, we are told that a cobra was killed the night before, but no one seems to know where the carcass is. Come back later, they say.

ON THE ROAD AGAIN

We return at night, when the temperature has dropped to the level where snakes become active. In these remote parts, for-

eigners are rare, and my presence quickly attracts almost the entire village, which encircles us, uncomfortably close. The villagers have found the cobra carcass and bring it to us. It is the new spitting cobra; that's the good news. But terribly mangled from machete blows and highly decomposed, it is useless as a specimen.

Before dejection can set in, a woman across the village starts screaming "*mwe mwe*"—Snake! Snake! I run toward the cries, accompanied by 100 villagers. We reach a small hut, where a terrified family has a small spitting cobra cornered in the back of their home. After some awkward thrusts, I

Villagers have grown accustomed to scaly critters slithering into their homes, coiling in the farm fields, and even resting on well-traveled roads.

snag it with my snake tongs and secure it in a cloth bag. Finally!

All of this is hugely entertaining to the villagers crowded around, who laugh and move forward to shake my hand. I shake many hands. Then I ask them to take me out into the fields to look for more specimens. But instead of to the fields, I am led from hut to hut. At each hut, *tody*, a weak moonshine of fermented palm sap, is brought out in ceramic bowls. I soon realize that rather than help me find cobras, the villagers have

Illegal snake-trading operations thrive in Southeast Asia. Captured snakes, secured in cloth bags (left), are stored in warehouses until shipped to China and elsewhere.

BULL'S-EYE!

Following several productive snake-catching nights in a row, it is time to photograph and videotape our bounty. Snakes do not lie quietly waiting to be photographed; they prefer to crawl away. After several hours of tedious still photography, we pull out the cobra we had caught two nights ago for some video footage. I wear protective sunglasses, but suddenly the cobra darts between my legs, looks up, and lets loose with a barrage of venom. Because of the angle, some of the venom hits my eyes. I feel an instant, intense burning pain. I yell for water. Within seconds, Dong is pouring water liberally into both of my eyes, but minutes later they are still burning. Our driver suggests that I try a local folk remedy. I am laid on a bench, and the juice from tamarind leaves is squeezed into my eyes. More searing pain! This hurts even worse than the venom. I bolt upright, yelling in agony, and pour more water into my eyes, which are now ruby red.

After several hours pass, my vision is fine, and I feel completely recovered. Did the tamarind juice work? I don't know.

taken this opportunity to begin a village-wide party. After downing several bowls, I set out in search of more cobras.

I shake numerous hands and climb into the car. Not more than 75 yards (68 meters) away, we encounter a Russell's viper stretched out on the road. It is not hard to understand why snakebites are such a big problem in central Myanmar. Venomous snakes are as common in and around villages as they are in more-remote areas.

A TREASURE FROM THE DRY ZONE

Snake hunters confirm that this new cobra is restricted to the central dry zone of Myanmar. Back at the academy, Wüster and I complete our manuscript describing the new cobra, which is already scheduled for a journal publication. Meanwhile, I make plans to return to Myanmar, this time accompanied by academy photographer Dong Lin.

We decide to begin in Pakokku, in the central dry zone. As night falls, we hit the road to look for snakes. Road cruising is one of the most effective ways to find snakes, especially in hot, dry areas, because snakes often seek the warmth of pavement as the temperature drops. After an hour or so, we encounter a brown snake stretched across the center of the road. As I walk toward it, it rears up and spreads its patternless hood—a sign of the new cobra.

BACK FOR SECONDS

I have been back to Myanmar several times, and have collected a number of interesting amphibians and reptiles, including several new species. I have also captured additional specimens of the new cobra I like to think of as mine. Reports from experienced Burmese snake collectors of a rare, second species of spitting cobra in the country, one that has a spectacle-shaped hood mark, have also lured me to return. Several additional hunts for the second spitting species have proved fruitless. As of now, this elusive—and perhaps even mythical—creature still belongs to the world of the unknown.

STINKERS OF THE PLANT WORLD

The flowers of carrion plants, such as that of the "stinking corpse lily," Rafflesia arnoldii, lure insects by emitting a stench not unlike that of decaying flesh.

by Wayne P. Armstrong

A typical flower may be stereotyped as a colorful, sweet-smelling structure that attracts insects. A variety of insects generally find its showy petals and fragrance irresistible, and the reward for their pollination service is a carbohydrate-rich, sugary nectar secretion from a lovely blossom. While this scenario fits the majority of flowers, some peculiar exceptions exist. Among the most remarkable are carrion flowers—showy blooms with a stench of rotting flesh that entices flesh- and feces-lov-ing insects to visit. These plants belong to a variety of different and unrelated families, and include some of the largest and most bizarre flowers on Earth.

WHAT ARE THEY?

Unlike the fragrant blossoms that attract bees, butterflies, and moths, carrion flowers depart from the stereotype. Instead, these flowers simulate the odor of a rotting carcass, and therefore attract "carrion insects," such as beetles and a variety of flies. Not

especially when a flower's male anthers release pollen several days after the female stigma is no longer receptive. When the insects are freed, they receive a thorough dusting of fresh pollen that they will carry to another plant.

GNAT TRAPPER

One of the classic insect-trapping carrion flowers is the Dutchman's-pipe, *Aristolochia clematitis*, a European member of the birthwort family (Aristolochiaceae). The striking, tubular flower of Dutchman's-pipe is held upright when it emits its foul odor. Small gnats land on the vertical upper calyx surface, but then slip down through the floral tube and into the inflated "pipe chamber," where slippery wax granules dot the inner surface. Dense, downward-pointing hairs in the floral tube prevent the gnats from climbing out. During their involuntary stay, the gnats receive rations of nectar. Several days later, when the flower's anthers release pollen, the stalk bends, the trapping hairs wilt, and the flower tilts horizontally. The pollen-laden gnats are freed, but most likely only to fly into another trap. There are about 350 species of *Aristolochia*, mostly in tropical regions of the world. Many species have ingenious insect traps and emit malodorous, even nauseating, stenches when their blossoms first open.

only do these flowers smell like dead animals, but their petals are typically flesh-colored and often densely covered with hair. Their overpowering stench is caused, in part, by putrescine and cadaverine, aptly named amine compounds derived from the amino acids ornithine and lysine.

Carrion insects—defined as those that are attracted to and feed on feces, rotting flesh, and other decaying organic matter—also lay their eggs amid such putrid-smelling deposits. Carrion flowers are unknowing masters of deception. They, too, can lure such insects by virtue of their odor. The flowers benefit by being pollinated, but the fate of the hapless insects is dismal. Unlike typical insect-pollinated flowers, most carrion flowers do not waste precious energy rewarding their pollinators with nectar. Consequently, the deceived insects and their maggot offspring perish from lack of any suitable food.

In some carrion flowers, insects, tempted by foul odors, are drawn into dark openings that lead to a flower's putrefying interior; there, they become trapped among the floral organs. This event ensures cross-pollination,

SICKENING STENCHES

Some of the most notorious carrion flowers belong to the milkweed family (Asclepiadaceae), diverse plants characterized by their milky-white sap. Several South African succulent genera—including *Stapelia*, *Caralluma*, and *Huernia*—resemble spineless, sprawling cacti with strange, starfish-shaped flowers. The flesh-colored, hairy blossom of *Stapelia gigantea*—usually 8 to 10 inches (20 to 25 centimeters) across—exudes a sicken-

ing stench. Fringes of soft white hairs on the reddish-brown petals superficially resemble a layer of mold growing on rotting matter—at least when seen through the compound eyes of carrion insects. Occasionally grown in Southern California, these curious flowers attract flies and maggots when they are in full bloom during the warm summer months.

Some other bizarre carrion flowers belong to the arum family (Araceae). This large tropical family contains many popular cultivated genera, such as *Anthurium, Caladium, Philodendron,* and *Dieffenbachia.* Like the common garden calla *Zantedeschia aethiopica,* the small, unisexual flowers are packed along the base of a vertical, central spadix. The spadix emerges from a vase-shaped or funnel-like modified leaf, or spathe, which is often brightly colored. Probably the best-known North American species is the skunk cabbage *Symplocarpus foetidus* of the eastern United States. A showy western skunk cabbage, *Lysichiton americanum,* has a somewhat musky odor, but not nearly the marked degree of offensive stench of its eastern counterpart.

The European relatives of the skunk cabbage, the lords-and-ladies arum, *Arum maculatum,* and the dragon arum, *Dracunculus*

A Stapelia gigantea milkweed (left) lures insects into its flower trap; flies and maggots find its malodorous stench and flesh-colored, hairy petals particularly appealing. The brightly colored blossoms of the skunk cabbage (below), a member of the arum family, use a decidedly musky bouquet to draw unwary bugs.

A south African milkweed resembles a spineless, sprawling cactus; its peculiar starfish-shaped blossoms are irresistible to flesh- and feces-loving insects.

vulgaris, also emit decidedly putrid odors. They are definitely not recommended for presentation as a gift bouquet!

The spadix, or floral, fleshy spike of some aroids—any plant belonging to the arum family—generates substantial heat during cold weather. In fact, the temperature of the spadix can be up to 54° F (30° C) higher than a cool air temperature of 50° F (10° C). This heat may stimulate the activity of pollinators and help to vaporize the stench of the flowers. The heat-production mechanism may involve the male flowers packed around the spadix. In some species in which the upper part of the spadix is sterile (flowerless), the heat production appears to be in the cells of this sterile tissue. The cells in these flowers rapidly oxidize lipids and carbohydrates, thus releasing heat.

Another unique member of the arum family, *Helicodiceros muscivorus,* is native to the rocky Mediterranean islands of Sardinia and Corsica. It has an ingenious fly trap as well as a stench reportedly as strong as a rotting sheep carcass. Blowflies are lured into the pungent aperture at the base of its funnel-like spathe. Behaving as they would inside a real carcass, the flies force their way into the blossom's neck, past the spadix, and down into a pitch-dark chamber. Carrying pollen from another plant, they inadvertently pollinate the receptive female flowers at the base of the chamber. Like the doomed gnats that get caught in the Dutchman's-pipe, blowflies are soon unable to escape from the chamber due to a dense rosette of stiff hairs. The flies remain trapped until the male flowers above the stiff hairs begin to release pollen. Then the barricade of hairs wilts, and the flies are able to get away, though not before being dusted with pollen.

TOO CLOSE FOR COMFORT?

The most awe-inspiring carrion-flower aroid is the well-named corpse flower, *Amorphophallus titanum*, also known as the "krubi," which is native to tropical Asia. In 1937, an impressive specimen bloomed at the New York Botanical Garden. As is typical, its show all began with a seed that developed into a dormant tuber; in this case, the tuber measured 6 feet (2 meters) in circumference and weighed more than 100 pounds (45 kilograms). It eventually flowered, producing a spadix more than 8 feet (2.4 meters) tall. The giant spadix emerged from a huge pleated spathe more than 4 feet (1.2 meters) tall and 4 feet across. Technically, the blossom is an inflorescence, or cluster of flowers around the base of a spadix. It has been said that the enormous inflorescence of *A. titanum* generates such an overwhelming smell that people have been known to pass out from taking a whiff.

ENDANGERED SMELLERS

A related family of parasitic flowering plants, the Rafflesiaceae, includes the "stinking corpse lily," *Rafflesia arnoldii*, (which is not actually a lily at all). It's the world's largest individual flower and truly a wonder of the Plant Kingdom. This rare and endangered species occurs only in the rain forests of Sumatra and Borneo in the Malay Archipelago. Unlike most flowering plants, it has no leaves or stems, and grows endoparasitically within the woody stems of its host vine, *Tetrastigma* sp., a relative of the grape.

You might walk right past a *Tetrastigma* vine without ever knowing that a complete *Rafflesia* plant was living inside its stem. Occasionally, a large flower bud resembling a pale-orange cabbage breaks through the bark of the host vine and expands into an enormous blossom of up to 3 feet (1 meter) in diameter that can weigh perhaps 25 pounds (11 kilograms). The gigantic unisexual flower has five fleshy red lobes (sepals) spattered with raised white spots.

The foul-smelling blossom attracts the usual carrion insects, which shuttle the pollen from male to female flowers. When a female flower ages and becomes mushy, it may contain up to 4 million slimy seeds that are dispersed by a variety of animals—from ants, tree shrews, and squirrels to the feet of wild pigs and Asian elephants. If a seed becomes lodged in a moist crevice of its host vine, the seed germinates and penetrates the host tissue, where it proliferates into a network of microscopic filaments of cells. These funguslike networks of vascular tissue eventually give rise to a mammoth blossom that pushes out through the host stem, making *Rafflesia* one of the most intriguing and unusual of plants. But the chances of a seed finding a host vine are slim, and massive deforestation has further decreased the odds of this remarkable event occurring. Indonesia and Malaysia have begun to recognize the value of this plant, and for that reason, ecological preserves are being established in both Asian countries.

FLORISTS NEED NOT WORRY

Strange flowers that entice carrion insects by their putrid fragrances are some of nature's most fascinating—and successful—experiments in evolution. They represent some of the oddest examples of floral diversity. And although the carrions include some of the largest, showiest, most unique, and most mysterious blossoms in the world, one fact about them is known for certain: they are a poor choice for a floral arrangement!

THE TRUTH ABOUT
WOODCHUCKS

by Sy Montgomery

For every creature on Earth there is a purpose, according to a lead article of the New England Pumpkin Growers Association's newsletter. But its editor, Hugh Wiberg, clearly doesn't believe it. "Someday, maybe," he writes, "someone will explain to me the 'purpose' of woodchucks."

To Wiberg, the woodchuck, like the despised squash beetle, is simply one more obstacle standing between him and the 1,000-pound (450-kilogram) record-break-

The pudgy critters known as woodchucks (or ground-hogs) pass their days feasting on vegetables and flowers and furiously digging sometimes-gaping holes.

ing pumpkin of his dreams. Similar dark thoughts plague gardeners of more-ordinary ambitions, as ripening vegetables suddenly vanish—and woodchucks grow rounder.

WAGING WAR ON WOODCHUCKS

But a woodchuck is on its own schedule. By July of each year, the animal begins to accumulate the protective 0.5-inch (1.3-centimeter) layer of fat that will sustain it for winter hibernation. A particularly hungry woodchuck in a single day may eat the equivalent of one-third of its body weight. Since a big 'chuck can weigh 15 pounds (7 kilograms), that's a lot of prized veggies.

And then there are woodchuck holes. With entrances 6 inches (15 centimeters) across, the burrows run 25 to 30 feet (8 to 9 meters) long and plunge 2 to 5 feet (0.6 to 1.5 meters). Digging one entails the removal of 700 pounds (318 kilograms) of subsoil—and the cavity left behind can topple a moving tractor. The woodchuck, it is often said, "eats to give himself the strength to dig holes, and then will dig holes to give himself an appetite"—none of which endears him to gardeners or farmers. Ironically, it was the farmers and early settlers who made the woodchuck the ubiquitous animal that it is today—one of the most frequently spotted mammals in North America.

Before the arrival of European settlers, woodchucks were not particularly numerous; they kept to the woods, and they were generally admired. The Eastern Abenaki Indian tribe of present-day Maine considered the woodchuck their maternal ancestor, a wise grandmother who taught them to fish, hunt, and build canoes.

As European arrivals cleared their wooded territory, woodchucks adapted. Because farmers planted plenty of food and exterminated most of the woodchucks' natural predators—wolves, cougars, and lynx—the animals thrived in this new, open habitat, where their numbers have been recorded as high as 39 per 1 square mile (2.6 square kilometers). Today, the only predators woodchucks must be wary of are hawks, dogs, people, and automobile drivers.

Even though woodchucks had not brought this population explosion on themselves, farmers declared war on the animals. In 1883, for instance, New Hampshire established a Legislative Woodchuck Committee, which pronounced the animal "absolutely destitute of any interesting qualities," and set a bounty of 10 cents for every animal killed. Other states followed suit. Today, while there is no bounty on the critters, the war on woodchucks continues.

REDEEMING ROTTEN REPUTATIONS

Naturalist Meade Cadot thinks it is time to rehabilitate the woodchuck's reputation. First, he would just stop calling the critter a woodchuck—or even its other name, the groundhog, of February fame. "Really, it is a marmot," says the professor from Antioch New England Graduate School. And marmots are not vermin, he says.

The *Marmota monax*, as it is known in Latin, is one of North America's five species of marmots, members of the squirrel family—albeit exceptionally fat ones. The other marmots all live out West, not in vast open fields but among rolling hills and rocky mountains, where they enjoy the respectable reputation of "watchable wildlife."

The eastern marmots, if they are not nibbling away at your garden, are just as engaging. Ask Genie Ferguson, the booking agent for the three plump woodchucks of Drumlin Farm Wildlife Sanctuary in Lincoln, Massachusetts. They make numerous public appearances at schools, camps, and nursing homes for Traveling Audubon Ark's wildlife-education programs. "All three woodchucks are booked every day," Ferguson says—sometimes twice a day. "Kids think they are adorable, like a giant guinea pig or hamster," remarks Diane Barker, caretaker to the stars at the sanctuary.

CLOWNING CLIMBERS

Even if the Audubon Ark doesn't stop at your neighborhood, it is likely that wild woodchucks will. You will find them forag-

The woodchuck inadvertently gained an ideal habitat when early settlers cleared woods, planted crops, and exterminated the animal's natural predators.

Every February 2, woodchuck watchers flock to the official Groundhog Day ceremony in Punxsutawney, Pennsylvania, to see whether "Phil" will cast a foretelling shadow.

ing at the edge of fields, nibbling the grass along median strips, chomping on dandelions and daisies in parks. Sometimes you will see one holding a choice morsel in both hands, like a child who is clutching a big apple. You can then watch them wash their faces with their dexterous, long-fingered hands. During the warmest part of the day, you might see one basking in the sun or sleeping on a stone wall, a fallen log—or even propped atop a fence post.

Woodchucks are surprisingly capable climbers. They can scramble over fencing as well as burrow under it, and they can make their way up low trees to reach fruit. They can swim, too. But in summer, such athleticism is seldom called for—other than to stand up periodically on hind legs for a better view. In this position, many observers have remarked, the 'chuck looks like a portly senator about to make a speech.

If the creature sees something particularly alarming, it might give a shrill whistle (indeed, the woodchuck is also called a whistle-pig) and dive down the nearest hole.

A Snooper's Fate
A woodchuck seldom ventures more than 50 yards (46 meters) from its burrow. Each adult has a summer and a winter burrow, some with three to five entrances (sometimes called plunge holes). In fact, woodchucks are the architects of most of the big holes you find in woods and fields. Fastidious housekeepers, the pudgy creatures renovate burrow entrances several times a week. Evidence of fresh digging indicates that a burrow is currently occupied.

The surest sign that a burrow is inhabited is an angry 'chuck rocketing out—so do not go poking into those holes. It is best not to annoy a woodchuck, as certain dogs and other woodchucks can attest to. A missing tail is often evidence of a run-in with another male. Rivals try to grab an opponent by the tail and flip an offguard individual; a tail

is often lost in the process. Those teeth can also do a number on a dog, and they are not usually aimed at the dog's back end.

Unlike other marmots, woodchucks do not reside in large colonies underground. Rather, like fortunate suburbanites, they live in single-family dwellings, or burrows. Some researchers have reported finding two-parent households, but family usually means mom and four to six babies—until mom abandons the kids or drives them off (this happens in the Northeast in July, when there is plenty of food).

"They have lots of individual personality," says Janet Wright, a mammalogist at Dickinson College in Carlisle, Pennsylvania. "Some are real sweeties; some are very nervous; some are aggressive." She knows because she has live-trapped hundreds of them, spraying each with a different-colored pattern for easy recognition.

Chucking Wood
Wright is studying woodchucks' social structure and how it might affect their susceptibility to disease. But she has also pondered a more pressing question: "How much wood could a woodchuck chuck if a woodchuck could chuck wood?"

She consulted a student whose interest lay in the shapes of the muscles of mammals. The woodchuck's limbs, the student reported, are adorned with exceptionally strong muscles for pulling back, but are not that great for throwing forward. "So if woodchucks are going to chuck any wood at all," concludes Wright, "they are going to chuck it backwards."

Bird Courtship:
The
Dance
of Life

by Michael McKeever

Some of the most beautiful dance per-formances in the world are never seen by human audiences. Across the globe, birds strut and present themselves, dancing and prancing, through courtship rituals as ancient as time itself. Some sketch intricate and elaborate patterns in the dust or on leaf-dappled forest floors, while others perch on branches and offer themselves with an allur-ing song or with simple movements as sub-tle as shadows.

Some of these rituals appear to our eyes aggressive and vainglorious. There are birds who puff out feathered chests at mating time and strut about like schoolyard bullies;

on the other hand, there are those who appear humbly demure during courtship. The black-headed gull (*Larus ridibundus*), for example, is named for its mask of dark feathers, intended to intimidate other birds. But when courting, both male and female black-headed gulls turn their heads away so as not to frighten their mate.

There are even birds who, like millions before them, bear small gifts, usually prof-fering bits of food to entice a mate. Bower-birds of Australia and New Guinea go so far as to pour their energy into constructing fanciful bowers, or dwellings. These fussy, feathered homemakers, decorate their bow-ers with everything from pebbles to cast-off bottle caps. Other species posture and dance with a grace that, combined with spectacu-lar plumage, enchants observers.

Sixteenth-century European explorers did some of their own enchanting. Newly returned from their travels, they astounded European courts with feathers from a variety of birds, including birds of paradise and peacocks, and other flashy birds. As clerics held iridescent feathers in their hands, they wondered if the Garden of Eden lay far to the south. Truly, they speculated, only in Eden could such beauty be found.

BEGIN THE BEGUINE

Like the feathered creatures that had so impressed early explorers, the beauty of the male argus pheasant—*Argusianus argus*, of the Phasianidae family—can touch just about any traveler's sense of wonder. Originating in the jungles of Sumatra, Borneo, and the Malay Peninsula, it is during the argus pheasant's mating season that the real purpose of the male's wondrous plumage becomes readily apparent.

The male argus first creates a stage that will best show off his feathered glory and give him plenty of room to properly present himself to a mate. In preparation for display (a particular behavior during mating season), he clears the ground of debris and pushes back any crowding plants. Then, every so often, he announces his presence with a piercing call that can be heard well into the distance. Should a female argus pheasant investigate the commotion, the awaiting male dances around her, enticing her to mate. The dance comes to a spectacular conclusion as the male raises his wing feathers and forms a shimmering halo upon which patterns of countless "eyes" appear. As the bird turns this way and that, his tail's eyes seem to dance in and out of the now-huge circle of feathers.

It is no wonder that the argus pheasant was named after Argus, the 100-eyed watchman from Greek mythology. The story goes that when Argus was killed, Queen Hera memorialized her loyal servant by spreading his eyes on the tail of her sacred peacock, one that shared the argus pheasant's distinctive eyespot pattern.

A SIGHT TO BEHOLD

"Much of what we know about birds that offer elaborate displays, we have learned from birds in captivity," says David Rimlinger, curator of birds at California's San

Birds often use flamboyant feathers or enticing "dances" to impress a possible mate. A magnificent bird of paradise vies for a female's attention by puffing out his chest and quivering his long, curlicue tail feathers (top). Bulwer's wattled pheasant (center) fans his snowy white plumage during courtship. The need to mate is particularly urgent for the dwindling numbers of dazzling Blyth's tragopans (right), among the most handsome of all pheasants.

A male bird of paradise fluffs his tail to charm the smaller female (right). Temminck's tragopan's blue wattle—ordinarily almost entirely concealed under his beak (facing page, bottom)—flares out into a stunning blue banner during courtship, as two "horns" sprout on his head (below).

Diego Zoo. "Some displays, such as those of the tragopans, would be extremely difficult to see in the wild. Others, like certain birds of paradise and manakins, use traditional sites year after year and thus are more predictable, but even these species don't usually allow observers a close look. It is a privilege for our visitors to witness these remarkable displays."

While some species adopt a rather leisurely attitude about their displays, others announce their intentions with quick flashes of color or rapid movements. For example, the five species of tragopans, indigenous to the mountain vastness of Central Asia, are among the most beautiful of pheasants. However, the quickness of their displays and remoteness of their habitat makes watching them in their native habitat difficult at best.

Fortunately, the tragopans adapt well to zoo life, permitting firsthand study and enjoyment without interested observers having to endure extreme treks into rough territory. To get a good look at the strikingly colorful Temminck's tragopan (*Tragopan temminckii*), one need only look up into tree branches, where the brightly colored bird, like all tragopans, spends much of its time. Its mating call is a good directive, too—there is never a question of when mating time has arrived for this spe-

cies. Zoo visitors are likely to hear a series of loud clicking sounds from within a Temminck's tragopan's enclosure. These peculiar sounds signal that the male's display is in progress. And what a display it is!

Popping out from behind a log or a rock, the male tragopan presents himself to a resident female. His blue wattle, normally tucked neatly under his beak, enlarges and spills down onto his breast in a cascade of red, white, and blue colors. His plumage rises outward, white spots standing out like cotton puffs on a bed of reddish feathers. Simultaneously, twin fleshy blue "horns" rise not unexpectedly from his head, and his clicks synchronize perfectly with the up-and-down flapping of his colorful wings.

Raising his body to its full height, beak downward and hissing, he offers himself during mating. His whole display is astonishingly brief—from beginning to end it lasts perhaps a mere 30 seconds or so. Moments later, the male's fleshy "horns" lie flat once again, while his brilliantly colored wattle returns to its normal size.

Most of the time, the watching female appears to be quite unimpressed. Sometimes the male rushes toward her after the display, as if demanding a reaction, but she runs away. If the time is right, however, the coy female allows mating to occur.

A Fragile Hold on Life

In 1870, visitors to the London Zoo in England were fascinated by a pheasant never before seen by the public. The Blyth's tragopan (*Tragopan blythii*) had been brought from the dense mountain forests of northeastern India. Still found there, as well as in northwestern Myanmar and southern Tibet, Blyth's tragopan is one of the rarest pheasants on Earth. In 1995, it was estimated that the bird's population numbered fewer than 5,000.

The male's face is colored the bright yellow of a van Gogh sunflower, with black bands moving up from the beak and back from the eyes along its wine-red head. As with other tragopans, it undergoes an amazing transformation during courtship as its brilliantly colored wattle spreads downward across its breast, and fleshy "horns" rise upward. But for the endangered Blyth's tragopan, courtship takes on a special urgency, as the species maintains its fragile hold on life.

A Pompous but Precarious Existence

The Bulwer's wattled pheasant (*Lophura bulweri*) makes its home deep in Borneo's tropical forests. Unfortunately, these forests, beset by logging and clearing for agriculture, grow smaller year by year. But fortunately, four preserves have been set aside as protected areas for the rain forest's fragile ecosystem. In these safeguarded refuges and in a handful of zoos, the Bulwer's wattled pheasant continues its precarious existence on Earth. Sadly, it has been estimated that there are fewer than 50 of these birds in zoos and aviaries around the world.

A harsh screeching call signals the beginning of the male's courtship posturing, and it soon becomes spectacularly evi-

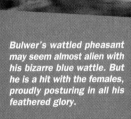

Bulwer's wattled pheasant may seem almost alien with his bizarre blue wattle. But he is a hit with the females, proudly posturing in all his feathered glory.

BUNDLES FROM PARADISE

It is no wonder that 16th-century explorers were awestruck by the magnificent bird feathers they brought back to Europe. In 1521, returning from their historic round-the-world voyage, Ferdinand Magellan's crew displayed several preserved specimens that intrigued the world. Because of the beauty of the plumes, and because the feet of the specimens had been removed, observers speculated that these birds never landed, but flew eternally in heavenly skies. Long ago, science literally brought such speculation down to Earth. But the lovely name given to the explorers' extraordinary discovery from a strange land more than five centuries ago has remained: birds of paradise.

There are numerous species of birds of paradise, each markedly different. In build, they range from little more than starling-sized to stout and crow-sized, adorned with a feathery tail up to 1 yard (1 meter) long. In plumage, they range from funereal black to a painter's palette of brilliant colors.

The courtship rituals of these birds are as varied as their colors. A male Salvadori's bird of paradise (*Paradisaea raggiana salvadorii*), with its blue beak and green-and-yellow head, flails his wing feathers and tail plumes into a splendid fan. Similarly, the magnificent bird of paradise (*Diphyllodes magnificus hunsteini*) male puffs out his chest and quivers his long curlicue tail feathers. The superb bird of paradise (*Lophorina superba feminina*), with his iridescent-blue breast shield, fluffs his black neck feathers into a huge cowl.

But whatever their plumage—and whether they perform, pose, or strut—birds in courtship draw on the same timeless theme: the eternal dance, the one that ensures that life will go on. ◩

dent why the Bulwer's wattled pheasant is also known as the white-tailed wattled pheasant. Its dark-feathered body transforms, haloed by an impressive fan of snowy-white tail feathers. The bird's tail fan is a wonder, with its nearly 32 feathers, twice the number grown by other pheasants. The pheasant produces them in abundance; when they molt and drop off, they are quickly replaced. As the pheasant's white tail feathers rise up, the brilliant blue wattle about its head expands, moving backward toward its tail and downward over its purplish breast. The bird's eyes, with their red irises, gleam like scarlet rubies against the contrasting blue wattle. Body erect on stiffened legs, the male prances around the female, first displaying his one side, then quickly turning to display his other. His long and rigid bottom tail feathers rake the ground as he turns this way and that.

High in the verdant mountains of New Guinea, the forest's human inhabitants appear to mimic the choreography of such a bird's instinctive dance. When a group of these people gathers for celebration or ceremony, male warriors bedeck themselves with seashells and boars' tusks, coloring their bodies with clay and jungle dyes in an exhibition of timeless pageantry. Almost invariably, bird-of-paradise feathers come into play, weaving and bobbing from the men's headdresses as they dance in the long-held tradition of their ancestors.

Claw-to-Claw Combat

by Kate Douglas

They call it boxing, but lobster brawls have more in common with a well-choreographed wrestling match. The opponents approach head-on and begin whipping each other with their antennae to size up the competition. Then things really get physical. Push leads to shove, and soon the lobsters are locked claw to claw. Sometimes this ritualistic wrestling progresses to all-out fighting. More often, though, one individual submits before any damage is done—but not before both have squirted large quantities of urine squarely into their opponent's face.

"The more aggressive the lobster becomes, the more urine it produces," says Jelle Atema of Boston University in Massa-

Based on their performance in periodic boxing brawls, American lobsters establish within their local population a hierarchical social system.

chusetts. In three decades of studying lobster communication, he and his collaborators have come to realize that a lobster's urine carries crucial messages that shape the social interactions of these animals. And their recent findings go one step further, suggesting that the urine of each lobster contains a unique marker—an individual calling card by which they can identify and remember each other.

KNOW THY PLACE

The American lobster, *Homarus americanus*, lives a fairly solitary life, sheltering in its own small cave or rock crevice. But when one meets another, it soon becomes evident that lobsters have a complex social system. There are hierarchies among both males and females and, for males at least, social status can make the difference between whether they get to reproduce or not.

Urine—released by the lobsters in copious amounts during combat—carries critical information that the creatures can perceive with their antennules.

Boxing is the key to establishing the pecking order. Put a group of unfamiliar animals together in a tank, and their first reaction is to fight. Two by two, they go through the ritualistic boxing bouts. Thereafter, the winners assume a dominant position in the social group, while the losers become submissive, backing away from any aggressive approaches from their superiors. Somehow lobsters know their place, and so live in relative harmony.

KEEPING THE PEACE
But how is the status quo maintained? There are two possible explanations. One could be that lobsters have some way of distinguishing dominant individuals from subordinates. For instance, top lobsters might adopt a certain body language, or subordinates might produce large amounts of stress pheromones during social interactions to demonstrate their relative standing. The alternative is that lobsters have a true pecking order, with each individual able to recognize the other members of the group and to remember how they fared in the previous encounter with that individual. But this is unusual among such animals. "The list of invertebrates proven capable of individual recognition is a very short one," notes

Christa Karavanich of Richland College in Dallas.

To distinguish between these two possibilities, Atema and Karavanich engineered a series of lobster boxing matches. They took pairs of healthy, well-matched males who had never met before, placed them in a tank together, and recorded their interactions. All of the lobsters were extremely aggressive toward any clawed stranger. Even so, most of the fights ended without physical injury after less than 10 minutes when one animal withdrew. "The loser seems to determine the end of the fight," says Atema.

ROUND TWO
Then, a day later, Atema and Karavanich arranged a second round of matches—some between previous opponents, and some between winners and losers that had not previously met. They found that the losers backed away from opponents that had outwrestled them in the first bout, and avoided aggressive displays, whereas former winners went in with claws and pincers flying. But, crucially, when animals met an unfamiliar individual in the second round, even those that had lost the first bout were just as aggressive in the second round as they had been originally. They seemed unable to get the message that their opponent was a dominant individual. "The loser will not engage the previous winner, but will fight unfamiliar individuals," says Atema. "We see that as evidence of individual recognition."

URINARY SIGNALS
Atema suspected that urine was the key to a lobster's expression of individuality. Each animal has two bladders on the sides of its body, and during a fight it releases a large amount of urine into a powerful current that it generates over its gills. This allows a lobster to shoot the liquid at a target that is

up to seven body lengths away. Lobsters are known to use the controlled release of urine to send messages to one another during courtship. So could the liquid also carry information about their identity, so that just a little squirt would allow animals to recognize their previous opponents?

Over the years, Atema and his colleagues have come to understand how lobsters decode urinary signals. In effect, the crustaceans have a very acute nose, with receptor cells arranged inside the bristles of a toothbrush-shaped structure on the antennules—the small antennae. They sniff their environment by flicking these back and forth. The signals they pick up have an important influence on their behavior, as Diane Cowen showed a decade ago when she was a student with Atema. She found that without antennules, lobsters were unable to form stable hierarchies and that there was constant aggression.

And, sure enough, when Karavanich and Atema removed the antennules from some of their lobsters between boxing matches, former losers pulled no punches in a second fight against an opponent that had defeated them just 24 hours earlier. Blocking urine release had the same effect, showing that the critical information is contained in the urine.

REMATCH RUMBLE

To find out how long lobsters can remember one another, the researchers waited a week before letting some of the initial opponents fight a rematch. This time, 3 out of 10 losers from the original round avoided the individual that had beaten them. The figure was the same whether they had been kept in isolation or had gone back to their communal tanks. Some animals remember who defeated them for at least a week, says Karavanich, "even if they had numerous interactions with other lobsters in between the one-on-one bouts."

But after two weeks, all memory of the original encounter seems to have gone, and pairs that had previously met fought with the same ferocity they had shown in their original match. In fact, all the former losers ended up losing again. Fights between pairs of females and mixed-sex pairs follow the same pattern as in males. All lobsters, it seems, are capable of individual recognition.

UNIQUE CALLING CARDS

The next step is to work out exactly what it is in urine that communicates a lobster's identity. Atema's money is on a group of large proteins produced by a cluster of glands that release their products into the urine as it is squirted. "We know that large amounts of protein are released, and we know that the urine is involved in individual recognition," says Atema. "But the connection is still inference."

He is now looking for a way to isolate these large proteins and test their effects directly on lobster behavior. Atema is confi-

Found in southerly waters, Panulirus argus (above), are clawless relatives of American lobsters. The asocial juveniles settle disputes by thrashing one another with their antennae.

dent that this will prove to be the first example of an animal using proteins for individual recognition, but he admits that it will require clever experimental designs to distinguish between this and the many other messages in the urine. "In addition to individuality, lobsters communicate dominance status, sex, and receptivity by chemical signals in their urine," he says.

▶ *Do all insects have compound eyes? Do they see multiple images? Can this confuse the insect? Do insects perceive color?*

Virtually all adult insects have compound eyes, each an intricate mosaic of thousands of hexagon-shaped lenses, says University of Illinois entomologist May Berenbaum, author of *Buzzwords: A Scientist Muses on Sex, Bugs, and Rock 'n' Roll.* But they do not see a confusion of multiple images. According to one widely held theory of insect vision, each facet of the compound eye contributes a tiny piece of what the insect sees, much like how the tiles in a mosaic form a complete picture. Compound eyes tend to be particularly sensitive to colors in the blue-green range and the ultraviolet, but only a few insects can discern red. As many flowers reflect ultraviolet light (invisible to the human eye), two separate blossoms, each of which appears white to us, may look markedly different to a butterfly or bee.

Caterpillars, maggots, and most other larvae, or immature forms of insects, see the world through single-lens eyes called stemmata that do little more than detect light. They enable the larva to discern light from shadow, an important ability for creatures whose survival depends on, say, climbing up plants (toward light) or digging down into the soil (away from light). A few adult insects (such as certain worker ants) remain blind all their lives.

▶ *Why do rosebushes have thorns? Are thorns considered their natural defense mechanisms? Have*

horticulturists made advances in the development of thornless roses?

First, biologists distinguish a rose's "prickles" from true thorns such as those of a cactus or hawthorn, says rose expert John Dickman, whose question-and-answer column appears in *American Rose* magazine. True thorns, which are modified leaf structures, clearly serve as defense mechanisms, explains Dickman. The purpose of a rose's prickles is not so clear-cut. "Some believe that their primary purpose is to trap moisture close to the cane, and in that way help supply water to the plant," says Dickman. No doubt the prickles also discourage hungry animals from eating the leaves and flowers or from trampling the bushes, adds horticulturist Malcolm Manners of Florida Southern College in Lakeland. "But as many rose growers know, rabbits and deer are not so easily discouraged."

As for thornless roses, nature has produced at least one such variety: the white Banksian rose, *Rosa banksiae*, a native of China. Since the 19th century, horticulturists have bred several more varieties with smooth stems. One of the first, and still most popular, is the Old Garden Rose known as 'Zephirine Drouhin.' In recent years, a California rose breeder has produced a series of nearly thornless roses.

▶ *Do most land mammals that live by the sea take an occasional dip in the water? As a rule, are most mammals shy of water?*

Some mammals are more adapted to water than others, but none could be said to be literally "shy" of it, says David Webster, a mammal ecologist with the Center for Marine Science at the University of North Carolina, Wilmington. For instance, aquatic mammals such as dolphins and seals have the ultimate adaptation to spending time in water—flippers. Semiaquatic animals such as beavers and muskrat have webbed feet. But even terrestrial animals such as the horse—with its hooves adapted for running—will not hesitate to swim across an ocean inlet.

More to the point, any mammal entering the water, even for a "dip," probably has some reason for doing so. Since salt water doesn't quench thirst, coastal mammals would be entering the water for other reasons—such as foraging for food, escaping danger, or perhaps cooling off on a hot day. Raccoon and rats often feast on crabs and other shellfish in tidal pools and other shallow coastal waters. The wild horses of the Carolina barrier islands often enter the surf on hot days and are sometimes herded through the water during annual roundups.

▶ *Do scientists understand how electric eels generate electricity? Can an eel shock kill a person? Do any other animals produce electricity?*

In reality. all animals produce electricity. That's how nerve and muscle cells communicate with one another—by sending and receiving tiny ripples of electric current. The electric eel (*Electrophorus electricus*) produces its high-voltage zap with a long chain of special cells adapted from ordinary muscle cells. A single one of these electrocyte cells discharges only 80 millivolts of electricity (not enough to make your skin prickle). But line up 6,000 of these electric cells in the tail end of an 8-foot (2.5-meter)-long electric eel, and you can get a truly stunning 600-volt *ZAP*. That's about five times the voltage that comes out of a standard wall socket, and more than enough to kill a small animal or stun a person.

The real trick, according to ichthyologists (fish scientists), is the electric eel's ability to discharge all of its electricity-generating cells at the same instant, an ability it shares with about 500 other species of electric fish, including electric rays and electric catfish. However, no fish comes close to producing the high-voltage stun of *E. electricus*. Still, despite many stories, experts doubt whether a single eel, even a big one, could kill a person.

By the way, the electric eel is not a true eel at all, but a member of the freshwater-tropical-fish family known as knifefishes.

▶ *How do homing pigeons know where they're going? Do they require training? Are homing pigeons still used today?*

Scientists do not fully understand how homing pigeons can find their way home over great distances. Research suggests that the birds use a combination of inborn navigational abilities. In addition to recognizing various landmarks, the pigeons have an innate sensitivity to geographic differences in sunlight intensity as well as to Earth's magnetic field.

The ancient Greeks were the first to train domesticated pigeons to carry messages from town to town. Today, as in ancient times, homing pigeons are trained by familiarizing them with their "loft," or home cage, and the area around it. The trainer then takes the birds farther and farther away, each time releasing them to return home for food and shelter.

People around the world continue to keep and train homing pigeons for sport and pleasure. Racing-pigeon clubs hold annual contests in which participants arrive several days before the race to familiarize their birds with the territory and the location of their homing cages. On the day of the competition, the pigeons are released simultaneously from a central location, equidistant from their individual cages. Judges record the time that each bird enters its loft, and the bird with the best time wins.

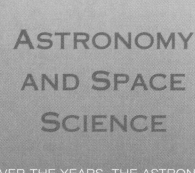

Astronomy and Space Science

■ OVER THE YEARS, THE ASTRONOMY COMMUNITY HAS MORE OR LESS SETTLED UPON A SINGLE THEORY TO EXPLAIN THE FORMATION OF OUR SOLAR SYSTEM. APPARENTLY, GAS AND DUST IN A GIANT DISK SIMILAR TO THE ONE AT LEFT COALESCED, FORMING SOLID ORANGE-GLOWING BODIES CALLED PLANETESIMALS. THESE ENTITIES GRADUALLY GREW LARGER, ULTIMATELY BECOMING THE PLANETS THAT NOW ORBIT THE SUN.

CONTENTS

THE INTERNATIONAL SPACE STATION

by Dennis L. Mammana

A new "star" shines in our sky. It does not glisten as part of a celestial constellation; rather, it circles the Earth every 90 minutes, carrying humans on a wondrous voyage of discovery. This shiny new "star" is the *International Space Station.*

ITS PURPOSE

The *International Space Station* (commonly abbreviated *ISS*) is designed to provide scientists and engineers with a world-class, state-of-the-art research center in the microgravity environment of outer space.

In-orbit research projects will span such diverse fields as biotechnology and medicine, microgravity sciences, combustion sciences, fluid physics, materials science, Earth science, space science, engineering and technology, and product development. In addition, the station will create excitement and wonder in the field of science education, and foster world peace through an extended term of international cooperation in space.

With a price tag of about $100 billion, the *ISS* will be the largest, most expensive, and most complex multinational scientific proj-

ect in history, representing an undertaking of unprecedented scale and a change in direction away from our home planet and into space. Permanently.

SOME ASSEMBLY REQUIRED

The 470-ton station, expected to be fully assembled by the middle of this decade, will house a crew of six or seven astronauts in 46,000 cubic feet (1,300 cubic meters) of pressurized volume (rough equivalent: two Boeing 747 jetliners) in six laboratories, two habitation modules, and two logistics modules. With nearly 1 acre (0.4 hectare) of solar panels providing electric power, the *ISS* will ultimately measure 356 feet (109 meters) across and 290 feet (88 meters) long, more than four times larger than its predecessor, the *Mir* space station, which the Russians decommissioned and dropped into the Pacific Ocean early in 2001.

The station will orbit high above Earth at an average distance of 250 miles (400 kilometers), with its orbit tipped at 51.6 degrees relative to Earth's equator. This orbit will provide researchers with excellent Earth observation (some 85 percent of the globe), and allow for accessibility of launch vehicles from a number of other nations.

The *ISS* represents a new era of hands-on work in space, involving more space walks than ever before and a new generation of space robotics. It will take some 45 missions, employing the U.S. space shuttle and Russian *Soyuz* and Progress spacecraft, to haul into space more than 100 elements for the station's construction. Modules, nodes, truss segments, resupply vessels, solar arrays, thermal radiators, and thousands of other components required to make it work will be linked in Earth orbit by astronauts during more than 850 hours of space walks.

Like a self-contained, modern research building, the *ISS* will house laboratories, living areas, water and power systems—and even have parking spaces for visiting space-

A remarkable assemblage of modules, nodes, truss segments, solar arrays, thermal radiators, and more will comprise the completed International Space Station. While moving in continuous Earth orbit, the state-of-the-art research facility will house astronauts in an area equivalent to that of two Boeing 747 jets.

ISS crews will conduct invaluable experiments, encounter amazing views, and welcome supply-laden shuttles, as the cosmonaut above is doing.

craft. The station's abundance of windows and 11 external payload locations will facilitate Earth-observation experiments.

TAKING FORM

The *ISS* began taking form in the mid-1980s, during the closing years of the Cold War between the United States and the former Soviet Union. In 1984, President Ronald Reagan committed the United States to developing a permanently occupied space station, and, with the National Aeronautics and Space Administration (NASA), Reagan invited other countries to join the project.

In 1993, NASA began streamlining the station's design and costs, and brought Russia on board to help out. When the country that once had been the greatest adversary to the United States became its most supportive partner in space exploration, the orbiting research center was designated as the "*International Space Station*."

The first segment of the space station, the Russian-built control module *Zarya*, was launched into orbit November 20, 1998. A few weeks later, on December 7, the *ISS* began to grow when the space shuttle

Endeavour delivered the U.S. module *Unity*—a six-sided module to which all U.S. modules will attach—and subsequently connected it to *Zarya*. The *Zvezda* module arrived in July 2000; and then, in early 2001, astronauts delivered and promptly connected *Destiny*, the U.S. scientific laboratory, which will be used to store scientific gear and will serve a vital role as the station's command and control center. Further additions slated to become part of the orbiting research facility include two Russian research modules, a European laboratory, and a Japanese laboratory.

The *ISS* project is so complex and expensive that no individual nation could possibly have tackled it alone. Led by the United States (NASA), the *ISS* project draws on the scientific and technological resources of many nations—including Canada, Japan, Russia, those of the European Space Agency (ESA), and Brazil—in the largest nonmilitary joint effort in history.

WHO IS UP THERE?

The first full-time crew, Expedition One, arrived via a Russian *Soyuz* launch vehicle in early November 2000. The primary duties of American astronaut William Shepherd and Russian cosmonauts Yuri Gidzenko and Sergei Krikalev were to perform numerous installations, conduct research, and fix or troubleshoot onboard devices. In early March, following a four-month-plus stay, they were relieved by the Expedition Two crew—Russia's Yury Usachev and U.S. astronauts Susan Helms and James Voss—whose duties included building more of the station and preparing for crews who would follow. Once the U.S. habitation module is completed and hooked to the station's *Unity* module (around 2004 or 2005), a crew of up to seven people will live and work aboard the station.

Their life on board the station, though confining, will be busy with research, maintenance, and exercise. However, there is

Building a world-class research center in space takes time, training, and teamwork, as astronauts Jerry Ross and Jim Newman demonstrate during one of 850 space walks planned for the station's construction.

Atlantis *commander Kenneth Cockrell (rear) and astronaut Thomas Jones conduct a "float through" of the* Destiny *module immediately following its linkage to the ISS. Meanwhile, whether upside down or right side up, Susan Helms and Andy Thomas must tend to the day's chores.*

always scheduled time to relax during each day. A crew can read books, play cards, listen to music or watch movies, send e-mails to friends and family, or simply gaze out a window and watch the world go by below.

NEW TECHNOLOGY

Technology to launch a long-term presence in space did not develop overnight. The first Earth-orbiting space station, the U.S. *Skylab*, launched in 1973, survived only six years before plunging into the Indian Ocean. Not until 1986 did Russia's *Mir*, the first truly enduring space station, take its place in Earth orbit.

During *Mir*'s 15-year mission, astronauts from many countries visited, lived there, and participated in valuable research on long spaceflights. In 1995, the United States and Russia teamed up to occupy *Mir*, enabling scientists to study technology, international cooperation, and the physical, cultural, and psychological effects of long spaceflights. For less than 2 percent of the total cost of the *ISS* program, *Mir*'s mission provided both nations with knowledge and experience that could not be achieved any other way.

HIGH-FLYING TOURIST

U.S. stock-market financier and former NASA engineer Dennis Tito had his chance for a weeklong stay in space in early spring 2001. The 60-year-old millionaire had paid $20 million for a ride to *Mir* on a Russian *Soyuz* spacecraft. But when *Mir*'s operation ended in March 2001, Russian officials told Tito he could instead journey with them to the *International Space Station*.

NASA officials objected to this decision, citing the safety issues involved with including an untrained nonprofessional who, they claimed, could disrupt the busy station crew. But Russian administrators successfully argued the point that they can transport anyone they wish to the station in their own spacecraft. NASA eventually withdrew its objection to Tito's journey, but only after Tito agreed to serious restrictions to his activities on board the *ISS*.

NO PLACE LIKE HOME

Scientists and engineers have learned how important it is for astronauts to have a comfortable environment with familiar amenities, especially during long space missions. The crews' extremely busy schedules make comfort even more vital for maintaining harmony while on board. During a typical workday, astronauts spend 14 hours working and exercising, 1.5 hours preparing and eating meals, and 8.5 hours sleeping. Basic comfort systems are in place. An efficient air-filtration system cleans the air. The linked *Zvezda* and *Unity* habitation modules are surprisingly roomy, bright, and kept at a constant temperature of 70° F (21° C).

Zvezda began its journey by rail to the Baikonur Cosmodrome, in Kazakhstan, where it joined with the Proton rocket booster that would carry it aloft for hookup with Zarya, the first orbiting segment of the ISS.

Mental energy in space is quickly spent. Even a simple task such as brushing one's teeth can be ultrachallenging in a weightless environment. Water does not trickle in a stream—it suspends in a bubble. A "space shower" uses only very little water from a trickling hose; a shampoo consists of dry powder that is combed through the hair and toweled off.

Station astronauts enjoy their meals in a special dining galley equipped with water, microwave ovens, refrigerators, and freezers, allowing them to eat more-"normal" types of food, including fruit, vegetables, and—unlike the earlier freeze-dried version—even refreshingly cold ice cream!

Before any food slated for a space mission takes flight, it receives a battery of tests for nutritional value, packaging, storage, and the like by the Food Systems Engineering Facility (FSEF) at NASA's Johnson Space Center in Houston. Additionally, FSEF personnel give each food item a final stamp of approval aboard the NASA zero-gravity KC-135 airplane, affectionately known as the "Vomit Comet," to see how it will react in microgravity. If the food holds up, astronauts will find it on a long list from which they can plan their mission's menus in advance. Food choices range from frozen waffles to thermostabilized items such as frankfurters or chicken à la king (heat-processed and canned or packaged in plastic cups or stored in flexible pouches); from

fresh Granny Smith apples to tasty bananas; and a wide array of soups, beverages, snacks, yogurts, and instant breakfasts. Most foods headed for the *ISS* are frozen, refrigerated, or thermostabilized, since water (needed to make dehydrated food edible) is such a precious commodity onboard. Nearly all food items are packaged in single servings, eliminating the need for a dishwasher.

Whatever their food choices, astronauts must be extra careful about dropping crumbs or spilling drinks that could float through the cabin and cause untold damage.

For sleeping, there is a private room, or "galley," for each crew member. In space, individuals need to be anchored to their beds with three belts to prevent them from floating away—a remarkably comfortable way to sleep, according to astronauts.

Exercise is a must for the crew. In a microgravity environment, muscles and bones atrophy quickly, causing a condition that can be dangerous to the astronauts when they return to Earth. To ward off osteoporosis and serious muscle atrophy, crew members exercise on bikes, rowing machines, and other equipment nearly two hours each day. Still, in-orbit individuals lose about 1.0 to 1.5 percent of bone density a month.

Similar to home, however, not everything in space is pleasant. The *ISS* is rather noisy inside, with all of its valves, pumps, and fans running. Some have likened their experience on board to living in a machine room.

And, speaking of little annoyances, the crew has the distasteful challenge of keeping the station free of mildew and fungus, both of which tend to grow in a place where humidity levels frequently change. This happens despite the fact that the *ISS* was designed to prevent condensation buildup by using special filters to help clean the air. Regardless, astronauts no doubt do their share of mindless cleaning with plain old soap-and-water bubbles.

For the most part, technology has helped to overcome practical living obstacles in space. For instance, the principles that govern the station's limited water supply are complex yet efficient. No water can be wasted—for the squeamish, a profound and justifiably repellent concept. A regenerative system recycles nearly every drop of water on the station. Because hauling duffle-like bags of water from Earth into space is an expensive undertaking, wastewater from hand washing, oral hygiene, the air's humidity, and, yes, even human and test-animal urine is recycled into ultrapure water through a treatment process that mimics Earth's natural process of distillation. Purification begins with the filtering of particles and debris. Water then passes through multifiltration beds where organic and inorganic impurities are removed. Solid waste collects in bags and is stored in airtight containers that are eventually loaded onto space freighters destined to burn up in Earth's atmosphere. In the final step, a catalytic-oxidation reactor removes volatile organic compounds and kills bacteria and viruses, transforming the worst liquid imaginable into water so perfectly purified it can be the beverage choice of champion astronauts. Opinions have been scanty, however, as most will only bathe with the purified water; very few will drink it!

THE ROAD AHEAD

Once fully functional, the station's eight sets of solar arrays will provide scientists with sufficient electric power by converting sunlight to electricity. When all modules are in place, there will be enough laboratory space available to conduct vital research that will contribute to safe, long-term space exploration by humans. The knowledge gained will also benefit research on Earth.

Fifty-two computers will control the station's onboard systems. There will be more than 400,000 lines of software for 16 computers—which, in turn, will talk to 2,000 sensors, effectors, and embedded "smart" hardware controllers. Twenty-two computers mounted outside the station will control functions such as electrical-power switching, solar-panel alignment, disposal of heat generated from the station's environment and electronic equipment, and a mobile transporter that will travel along a rail running the length of the station.

When fully completed, sometime between 2004 and 2006, the *International Space Station* will be a refined city in space, orbiting gracefully at 17,000 miles (27,000 kilometers) per hour above Earth. And, besides being the most advanced laboratory for research, the station will serve as a launching point to destinations across the solar system. ◢

From Expedition One, Sergei Krikalev, William Shepherd, and Yuri Gidzenko uphold a preflight Russian tradition by visiting the grave of Soviet cosmonaut Yuri Gagarin, the first man ever in space.

LIGHT AND MAGIC

by Eric Adams

In the world of big, powerful telescopes, there is one accomplishment that none have been able to claim. It has no scientific value, really, but it would thrill both astronomers and the general public and ensure a lifetime of bragging rights to the first to do it.

Sitting in his office at the European Southern Observatory's (ESO's) Very Large Telescope (VLT) in northern Chile, overlooking an expanse of brown hills and valleys leading to the Pacific Ocean 5 miles (8 kilometers) away, VLT director Roberto Gilmozzi smiles as he edges toward the revelation. "When this telescope is complete, it will have the angular resolution equivalent to that of a telescope with a mirror 433 feet (132 meters) in diameter," Gilmozzi begins. "That means that we will, if we wanted to, be able to resolve and photograph Apollo debris left on the Moon."

Now, there are many, many other celestial targets that the ESO is much more interested in—distant galaxies, dim nebulae, extrasolar planets—but *that* would be a sensational stunt. Many thought it impossible, given

Sunset envelops the Very Large Telescope (above), an array of four telescopes which, when fully operational, will provide images of unprecedented resolution.

how minuscule even the largest Apollo remnant—something about the size of a delivery van—would be from 250,000 miles (400,000 kilometers) away. But with the giant leap that the ESO is about to take in Chile, this and a lot of other accomplishments are indeed going to be possible. The combination of the VLT's perfect location and its exceptional power should deliver many "impossibilities."

QUESTIONS AND ANSWERS

Built atop a truncated mountain in the Atacama Desert, the VLT is actually four identical 8.2-meter-diameter reflecting telescopes that can be used independently or be linked, through a process called interferometry, to create what is essentially a single ultralarge-aperture telescope. (This process is expected to be totally operational by 2004.) Technologies called active and adaptive optics, plus a prime geographic location—one of the driest places on Earth—will enable the VLT to operate with virtually no atmospheric distortion, and its remote location will also provide the darkest skies possible. All of this will make the VLT capable of seeing farther and in greater detail than anything before it. It will capture images at least 50 times sharper than those obtained by the Hubble Space Telescope (HST). It will answer many questions, and raise many new ones—and it will probably place Europe at astronomy's fore.

NON-AMERICAN ENTERPRISE

"The VLT is already the best-working telescope in the world," says British cosmologist Simon White, director of the Max-Planck Institute for Astrophysics in Munich, Germany. White visited the VLT last year to capture details of the rotation of spiral galaxies. "This is the first time in a century that the foremost optical-astronomy instrument has been a non-U.S. facility. When complete, the VLT interferometer will open an entirely new range of phenomena for study—*if* it works to spec."

The VLT's potential isn't lost on the Americans. Says Robert Gehrz, president of the American Astronomical Society (AAS) and a University of Minnesota physics and astronomy professor: "If they can get that

Every major component of the telescope required a dedicated team of engineers to ensure perfection. The enormous, fragile mirrors received meticulous attention and careful handling (above).

thing to work as an interferometer, that's going to be a breakthrough that will make it the most powerful facility in the world. There's no question about that—and I'll probably be applying for time on it."

The VLT was conceived in 1977; in the years since, the ESO—a consortium made up of Germany, Italy, Denmark, France, Belgium, Sweden, Switzerland, and the Netherlands—has spent $500 million on it. All of its major advances have been tested at the New Technology Telescope in La Silla, Chile. But the VLT is one of the most complicated observatories ever built, and its success won't really be verified until 2006, when its four telescopes focus on the same speck of light, and the VLT begins coming up with answers to questions about galactic evolution, the insides of quasars and black holes, and, the precise nature of the planets orbiting stars other than our Sun.

Far from Nowhere

The VLT may as well be on another planet itself. Getting to Cerro Paranal, the mountain on which the VLT was built, is a multi-leg, often multiday affair. Visitors fly first to Santiago and then 800 miles (1,300 kilometers) north to Antofagasta, an isolated, sprawling port city of 250,000 that exists primarily to support the dozens of mines in the region. Here, families flock to the rocky beaches—better for sunbathing than swimming—that span Antofagasta's shore.

From the ocean, the trip east entails a bone-jarring 75-mile (120-kilometer) drive into the Atacama Desert, a dusty plateau on the edge of the Andes that is virtually devoid of vegetation and animal life. There is little but gently sloping mountains and vast fields of boulders that sit evenly distributed, as if placed there by a machine. The wide dirt road, called the Old Panamerican Highway, is used mostly by the observatory and by a nitrate and iodine mine about 20 miles (32 kilometers) beyond the telescopes. There is nothing along the way, and trouble (breakdown, blown tire, accident) means either a long walk or a very long wait. Visitors who don't take the ESO's shuttle and elect to drive themselves are instructed to call the observatory before leaving. If you don't show up in three hours, they send someone out to find you.

Eventually a large white sign materializes, announcing the presence of the VLT. Behind it, a freshly paved road vanishes into the hills—a 280-square-mile (725-square-kilometer) region that Chile donated to the ESO in exchange for telescope time. A slow first-gear ascent leads to the guard shack and the observatory base camp, which sit 7,750 feet (2,364 meters) above sea level. From there, you can visually follow a 2-mile (3.2-kilometer) road up the mountain's remaining 900 feet (275 meters) to its perfectly flat top, where four giant silvery cubes perch, with rocks dribbling over the sides—debris produced when the builders blew 90 feet (27 meters) off the top of Paranal in 1990.

The base camp below is a clean, orderly village that is made up mostly of bright-white ship cargo containers that have been converted into surprisingly nice offices and dorm rooms. On one side of the camp sit a helicopter pad and a soccer field; on the

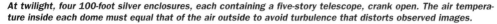

At twilight, four 100-foot silver enclosures, each containing a five-story telescope, crank open. The air temperature inside each dome must equal that of the air outside to avoid turbulence that distorts observed images.

Trucks carrying the glass disks—among the world's largest single-piece telescope mirrors—made an arduous three-day trek along a desert road (above) before ascending the mountain to the observatory (background).

other, a parking lot filled with white four-wheel-drive trucks bearing ESO logos on the doors. Scattered throughout are a two-story telescope service building, a platform with eight 20-foot (6-meter)-tall water tanks that get replenished twice daily by trucks from Antofagasta, a power station, and a dormitory being built for staff and visitors.

Beyond this, there is nothing. As workplaces go, Paranal has little appeal. Although serene and beautiful, it is also hot and dry, and far from any diversions. "Personally, I consider Paranal to be one of the better places on Earth to read books," says VLT staff astronomer Gianni Marconi, a friendly 39-year-old Italian who spends his nights on the mountaintop operating the telescopes for visiting astronomers. "I'm used to walking far from the base camp to where human-produced noise disappears and I am disturbed only by the wind." Visitors aren't encouraged to take such walks, though: Two who wandered off not long ago quickly became disoriented in the featureless hills and ended up lost for two days.

But for astronomers, the lonely desert site has several advantages: the dry air, which makes for clearer skies and a low risk of condensation collecting on telescope mirrors; the distance from any sources of the urban light pollution that plagues much of the world; and the roughly equatorial positioning, which gives it access to objects in both northern and southern skies.

STARING INTO SPACE

When the Sun goes down, any doubts about why someone would travel so far for this are squelched. Scrolling up from the east, the Milky Way shines steadily against the deep-black sky, with dozens of fuzzy nebulae and star clusters visible to the naked eye. Two galaxies, consuming startlingly large swaths of sky, hover in the south: The Large Magellanic Cloud spans the width of about 14 full Moons; the Small Magellanic Cloud, six. On this mountain, you feel as if you are staring *out* into space, rather than merely looking up at the heavens.

At dusk, on the platform of the telescope, the four 100-foot (30-meter)-square silver enclosures, each containing a five-story telescope, await instructions to open their doors and commence their night's work—either observation or, for the unfinished scopes, calibration and testing. All are cast in a shimmery reddish yellow from the sunset. Massimo Tarenghi, the VLT's project manager, stands amid a somewhat treacherous network of half-finished concrete channels and open pits that will soon contain the interferometry hardware. He wonders if the project will end up spoiling his colleagues: "Will we ever be able to work on a telescope that isn't at least as big as this?" he asks.

Although it isn't quite dark yet, the doors to Unit Telescope 1 slowly crank open, and the dome rotates around, assuming a south-facing position. This process helps ensure

that the temperature of the air inside of the dome equals that of the air outside; inequalities would produce turbulence, which would distort images.

A CLOSER LOOK

Tarenghi notes that every major component of the telescope had a team of engineers dedicated to it. One group designed the 8.2-meter primary mirrors. Another focused the active-optics system, which compensates for changes in the thermal conditions around the telescope and for tilt-induced weight changes that would alter the mirror's performance. Still another team mastered the $20 million secondary-mirror system, which collects light focused by the larger primary mirror and directs it into the telescope's instruments. This system consists of a 5-foot (1.5-meter)-long cylinder with a beryllium mirror on the bottom, and within it hundreds of pounds of electronics that constantly adjust the mirror's angle—another part of the telescope's active-optics system. The secondary mirror hovers 40 feet (12 meters) above the primary, and resembles a satellite in structure.

In each of the telescopes (UT1 through UT4), all of this hardware rests on a two-axis altazimuth mount that itself floats in a narrow track on a layer of oil only 0.002 inch (0.05 millimeter) thick. This makes for exceedingly smooth action—the whole 470-ton telescope can be moved with only a nudge of a hand. Of course, the motion of the telescopes is actually controlled by computers, from initial positioning to tracking of celestial objects during prolonged imaging and study. In the control building, a separate cluster of computers operates each telescope and provides continuously updated visibility conditions and tracking information. A fifth cluster of computers at the observatory will call the shots when the interferometric mode becomes functional.

TRIUMPHANT TECHNOLOGY

Although there is much for the VLT's engineers to brag about, several technological triumphs stand out. The first are the mirrors and their control mechanisms. The 8.2-meter Zerodur glass disks are among the largest single-piece telescope mirrors in the world. Manufactured in Europe, they were brought separately to South America on ships and then sent on a painstaking journey from Antofagasta to Paranal. Preceded by grading trucks that smoothed out the dirt road, the trucks bearing the fragile mirrors drove 3 miles (5 kilometers) per hour. The trip took three days.

The 540-square-foot mirrors were aluminized in the ESO's mirror-maintenance facility at Paranal, then inserted into basket-like cells and driven the final 2 miles (3.2 kilometers) up to the enclosures. These cells contain the 150 active-optics actuators, small hydraulic pistons that flex the 7-inch thick mirror in submillimeter increments.

Once light reflects off the actively controlled mirrors, it is further enhanced at an adaptive-optics filter, which also employs a deformable mirror and works to counter errors that can occur, such as high-altitude thermal changes and atmospheric turbulence. These conditions are monitored by focusing on a single guide star; in response, the computer orders changes in the mirror's shape 100 times per second. Although sever-

A *Lot* of Windex

If you think the Very Large Telescope (VLT) is big, just wait. The industrious European Southern Observatory is already several thick reports into its next huge project, the OWL, or OverWhelmingly Large Telescope. If all goes as planned, the OWL (artist's conception, right) will allow astronomers to begin scanning the heavens and beyond with a colossal (100–meter) mirror sometime in the next few decades.

The idea, which is being pursued by other agencies tinkering with so-called extremely large telescopes, is to create a telescope that doesn't rely on interferometry, or groupings of multiple telescopes, to achieve such sizes (compare the capacity of a single big bucket to that of four thimbles). The OWL's mirror will have a surface area of 7,800 square meters—equivalent to 10 times the combined surface area of all observatories ever built. The increased light-gathering ability will enable astronomers to probe even deeper into distant galaxies, and thus farther into the universe's past, compared with what the VLT allows. Indeed, one of the main objectives of the OWL's development team is analyzing the spectra of the remote galaxies of the famous "Deep Field"

The OverWhelmingly Large Telescope's increased light-gathering ability will enable astronomers to probe even deeper into distant galaxies and substantially further into the universe's past.

image that the Hubble Space Telescope (HST) caught in 1995.

The telescope, which will probably consume another big chunk of Chilean real estate, will employ adaptive optics, rest on a two-axis altazimuth mount, measure about half the height of France's Eiffel Tower, and wield a segmented mirror made up of 2,000, 7.5-foot pieces.

ESO scientists have been studying the technologies and costs, and have developed three scenarios: what can be done with $1 billion, $10 billion, or, in a perfect world, an unlimited budget.

al observatories around the world, most notably the Subaru Telescope atop Mauna Kea, Hawaii, are applying or developing active and adaptive optics, the VLT is by far its largest application, and the ESO was one of the first organizations to develop the technology. "When we were developing the active-optics system in the 1980s, nobody was sure that this would work at this scale, and many people actually opposed the idea," Tarenghi recalls.

Another remarkable and innovative achievement taking shape on Paranal is the

VLT interferometer. This setup, common in radio astronomy, capitalizes on the fact that if a telescope has a larger aperture, it can collect more of the light from objects in space. Interferometry enables the four telescopes to focus on the same object and gather its light as if the group of four were actually a single superpowered telescope as big as the combined distances between the individual telescopes—in the VLT's case, a distance of 426 feet (130 meters).

Light beams collected by the four telescopes are deflected by mirrors into under-

Astronomers plan to use the VLT to help them determine the size, age, and composition of the universe, study the formation stages of planets, stars, and galaxies, and search for signs of life elsewhere in the universe.

ground tunnels, where they are gathered at a single sensor. The sensor generates an image that is a cumulative product of the four beams. The trick is getting the light waves to meet at the sensor at the same time: As objects are tracked, the telescopes' relative positions change. Consequently, in the tunnel, the light is bounced off several retroreflectors sitting on small, precisely positioned rail carts that move on 200-foot (60-meter) tracks to compensate for these changes. In addition, three small auxiliary telescopes, also movable, on the surface will fill in the spaces that exist between the four main telescopes to further punch up the VLT's already acute resolution.

Final processing will prove that the VLT is far greater than the sum of its parts, with an angular resolution of 0.001 arc second. (The "celestial sphere" around Earth is 360 degrees; the full Moon has an apparent size of 0.5 degree; a degree has 60 arc minutes; an arc minute has 60 arc seconds.) The Hubble Space Telescope, which sits above the atmosphere but has only a 2.4-meter mirror, can resolve to 0.1 arc second. VLT's resolution is fine enough to capture detailed images of distant galaxies, clues about the chemical and biological composition of extrasolar planets—and snapshots of lunar rovers left behind by the Apollo astronauts.

DUSK TILL DAWN

Putting all this to work means long nights on the mountain. In the evening, the base camp is pitch-dark (no exterior lights are permitted, with the exception of a few dim safety lights) and increasingly silent as the lively chatter and music coming from the dorms of the ESO's 150-plus Chilean and European engineers and administrative and support staff gradually taper off. But atop Paranal, in the control building—already decorated with posters of some of the more spectacular images captured through UT1—a steady buzz of activity lasts until dawn. On average, the observing conditions (the "seeing") are considered excellent 350 days a year, a number envied by most observatories. On those evenings, the telescopes and their attached instruments work feverishly to flush every photon of light-borne information out of the sky.

GETTING TO WORK

The scheduling of science operations at the VLT is controlled at the ESO's headquarters in Garching, Germany. Astronomers compete for observing time, and if their proposal is accepted, they can travel to Chile to supervise the session themselves—as might be necessary for complicated or variable-dependent projects—or request that the

VLT's staff astronomers, such as Marconi, conduct the program on their behalf. Marconi also operates the VLT for visiting astronomers, so that they don't lose time struggling with the technology.

The scientific programs Marconi helps execute are challenging, chosen to push the VLT's capabilities as far as possible. The results are sometimes breathtaking. Marconi recalls a recent observation that remains alive in his mind: "The target was a jet of material ejected from the famous active galaxy 3C273. While looking at the details obtained in the images, I forgot for a moment that I was on the ground."

The VLT will undertake a variety of scientific projects, including measuring the universe, studying galaxy structure and formation, and observing star birth and planetary-system formation. Director Gilmozzi is confident that the VLT will push astronomy even further. "There's a final question that astronomers are asking, and that's whether we are alone in the universe," he says. "We will soon begin to ask how to detect biospheres and ecospheres on extrasolar planets, and the VLT will make those searches possible. I'm also sure that over the next several decades, we will discover an enormous class of objects that is unknown today."

Along the way, ESO hopes to develop new strategies for studying astronomical phenomena. Instrumentation plays a key role in this. The VLT will initially be outfitted with 11 instruments—some as big as a room—capable of wide-range spectroscopy and other types of imaging. Some of these instruments have already paid big dividends for astronomers using UT1. Munich University's Rolf-Peter Kudritzki spent four nights at Paranal recently using the VLT's FORS—FOcal Reducer/low dispersion Spectrograph—to examine a newly discovered population of stars floating in the space between the galaxies of certain clusters. Although Kudritzki's team came well prepared, the members encountered some surprising results, and consequently had to alter their program on the fly. "Many of our objects turned out to be completely different from what we expected," Kudritzki says. "We detected a new class of extreme-emission-line galaxies at very high redshift." High redshifts indicate that the galaxies are moving away from our own very quickly and are at the edge of an expanding universe; because they are so far away, their light took billions of years to reach Earth, so we are seeing them as they were when the universe began.

AN ASTRONOMER'S PARADISE

Peter Barthel, an astronomer at the Kapteyn Astronomical Institute in the Netherlands, spent several days at Paranal in late January. Collaborating with Willem De Vries of Lawrence Livermore National Laboratory in Berkeley, California, and Chris O'Dea of Baltimore's Space Telescope Science Institute, Barthel investigated distant galaxies that appear to be harboring small, young radio sources—potentially other galaxies. "The VLT data will tell if our ideas about these young radio galaxies make sense, and fortunately the data we gathered were excellent," Barthel says. "We got a number of new identifications with very faint galaxies. Though we still have substantial data processing and analysis left, we can, from the raw images, already see the faint host galaxies and study their spectra."

Barthel also devoted eight minutes of observing time to imaging the well-known, and significantly closer, Sombrero Galaxy, M104. He is completing a study on black holes in the center of similar galaxies, and felt the VLT would help. It did—and it made for an impressive picture (one that the ESO made into a poster). "The raw Sombrero data were of sheer beauty," Barthel recalls. "We were making live pictures of a beautiful piece of nature."

Sunrise at Paranal brings a temporary halt to the exploration—and these days a continuation of construction, as there is still much work to be done on the telescopes, the interferometry tunnels, and the new dormitory building below. After coming off the mountain and grabbing a bite to eat in the cafeteria, astronomers usually head for their rooms, which are all clustered in a corner of the container camp and marked with signs reading "Silence: Astronomers Sleeping." For them, this lonely place, bathed in light from suns both near and far, is paradise. ◢

SCOPING OUT THE MONSTER STAR

by Robert Zimmerman

Like a king, the gigantic star Eta Carinae imperiously ordains the life and death of all its neighbors. Some stars it feeds, providing the complex molecular material used by newborn stars to coalesce and form. Others it annihilates, exterminating any life that might dwell within nearby stellar systems.

The star shines so brightly that it would appear as bright as the Sun does in our sky from 185 billion miles (300 billion kilometers) away—some 50 times the distance to Pluto. With about 120 times the mass of the Sun, it comes close to the theoretical limit of how big a star can be. And although it lies 7,500 light-years away, Eta Carinae glittered more brilliantly than any other star in the Galaxy between approximately 1835 and 1855. During this 20-year-long Great Eruption, it blasted two to three Suns' worth of material from its surface.

Considered by many astronomers to be the brightest object in the Milky Way Galaxy and among the heaviest, Eta Carinae is also one of the strangest and rarest of stellar bodies—a gargantuan variable star that has the tendency to fluctuate in an irregular and completely unpredictable manner.

Today, Eta Carinae remains luminous and unstable, surrounded by one of the most beautiful and distinct nebulas in the heavens. Moreover, astronomers were astonished recently when Eta suddenly began to brighten again at all wavelengths. In the past year, its brightness has more than doubled; the star and its surrounding nebula now glow around 5th magnitude, the brightest in more than a century.

Eta Carinae, one of the largest and brightest stars in the Milky Way Galaxy, emits vast amounts of dust and debris to form a surrounding nebula (above).

About 150 years ago, the English amateur astronomer John Herschel asked: "What origin can we ascribe to these sudden flashes and relapses?" His question remains unanswered, no doubt in part because this regal star continues to be cloaked by dusty clouds. In fact, astronomers are not even sure if Eta Carinae is a single star. To paraphrase Winston Churchill, Eta Carinae remains "a riddle wrapped in a mystery inside an enigma."

Yet Eta Carinae's place in stellar evolution is crucial. Its mysterious behavior challenges every theory that tries to explain the life and death of stars—including our own Sun. Its future activity might even tell us why, where, and when other stars go boom.

THE GREAT ERUPTION

Kris Davidson, a professor of astronomy at the University of Minnesota, Minneapolis, has said that Eta Carinae "is to the Southern Hemisphere what the Crab Nebula is to the north." Until the third decade of the 19th century, however, Eta Carinae was considered an unusual but undistinguished variable star, sometimes glowing at 4th magnitude, sometimes at 2nd (1st magnitude being the brightest). Then, in the 1830s, John Herschel noticed that the star's light had risen steeply and, by December 1837, had reached 1st magnitude. Puzzled by this strange jump in brightness, Herschel researched the history of the star, and discovered that it had also reached 1st magnitude in 1827 and again in 1832. After fading in 1838, the star blazed forth in 1843, zooming dramatically to a magnitude of –1 and becoming, for a short period, the second-brightest star in the sky, surpassed only by Sirius.

For the next 20 years, Eta Carinae remained among the sky's most brilliant stars, fading in fits and jerks until it finally dropped below naked-eye visibility in 1868, stabilizing at about 7th magnitude. In 1889,

In the 1830s, Sir John Herschel (above, in a photograph by Julia M. Cameron) became the first astronomer to note Eta Carinae's increasing brightness.

the star brightened for a short while, barely reaching 6th magnitude. Then it settled back down to a relatively quiet, stable glow around 8th magnitude that would last for the next several decades.

In recent years, Eta had been growing slowly brighter, rising almost a full magnitude from 1950 to 1992. During this period, scientists continued to puzzle over the star's nature. Although photographs showed that Eta was surrounded by a rapidly expanding cloud that could be traced back to the Great Eruption of 1843, the resolution of the images wasn't high enough to reveal the cloud's exact structure or how it interacted with the star. Because its shape resembled that of a human, Enrique Gaviola of the Cordoba Observatory in Argentina dubbed this nebula Homunculus, which means "little man."

Then, in 1994, the ailing Hubble Space Telescope received a set of corrective lenses, and Eta Carinae became one of the first high-priority targets for the newly repaired telescope. The stunning image unveiled a star violently erupting. Suddenly, after centuries of unclear vision, scientists and ordinary citizens could view the nebulosity surrounding the star and see its shade and structure.

THE HOMUNCULUS

The most obvious features in the Hubble images are the two large and grayish bipolar lobes, shaped somewhat like an hourglass. With a total mass somewhere around three times that of the Sun, their glow comes mainly from starlight radiated by Eta Carinae that reflects off the ubiquitous dust in the lobes. Ejected from the star during the 1843 eruption, each lobe is expanding outward at the rate of about 1.5 million miles (2.4 million kilometers) per hour. At this great speed—fast enough for a spaceship to travel to the Moon and back three times in an hour—the lobes have expanded in 150 years to span about 4 trillion miles (6 trillion kilometers), or some 0.7 light-year.

In all likelihood, the lobes are mostly hollow, although astronomers have detected evidence of some dust within them. No one knows whether the lobes are shaped like spheres or cones. Either way, they apparently formed when matter was ejected from the star's polar regions. Perhaps this happened because Eta Carinae spins rapidly, possesses a powerful magnetic field, belongs to a binary-star system, or some combination of these factors. Regardless, the ejecta from the 1843 eruption had a harder time escaping from near the equator, and was forced to seek the path of least resistance, traveling outward from the poles.

Less obvious but also seen first in the Hubble images was the strange equatorial disk tilted between 52 degrees and 60 degrees to our line of sight, and about 90 degrees to the two lobes. Faintly resembling a ceiling fan with many blades, the disk consists of many curious objects moving at a wide range of speeds. Three mysterious blobs appear embedded within the disk only a few "light-days" (about 50 billion miles, or 80 billion kilometers) from Eta. Flying outward from the star at about 100,000 miles (160,000 kilometers) per hour, all three seem arranged around the outside edge of the equatorial disk's largest fan (called the Paddle, and visible as the triangular-shaped bright area above and to the right of the Homunculus's center). Astronomers do not yet know what caused these blobs to erupt from the star so asymmetrically, although their speed and distance from the star suggest they were ejected in 1889.

Within the Paddle itself, however, several small regions move at much slower speeds, as low as 30,000 miles (48,000 kilometers) per hour. These relatively sluggish speeds imply that the features were ejected from Eta several hundred years ago, long before the eruptions of the 19th century.

The equatorial disk also contains several mysterious and fast-moving jets—or "bullets," as some scientists have labeled them. The northern jet is shooting away from the star at a tremendous velocity, estimated as high as 3.4 million miles (5.5 million kilometers) per hour. As it rockets outward, the jet appears to be pushing its way through the dense interstellar medium of nitrogen gas that surrounds Eta Carinae, which was ejected in a much earlier, unrecorded eruption. Although some scientists believe that the jet's origin is linked to the 1889 eruption, others contend that it—along with most of the equatorial disk—formed during the Great Eruption of 1843.

In fact, all the data gathered about the equatorial disk so far present scientists with an exceedingly confusing picture of its origin. Depending on when and where they look, different astronomers get different results. Perhaps Ted Gull of the National Aeronautics and Space Administration's (NASA's) Goddard Space Flight Center puts it best when he says, "The disk appears to be the accumulation of many outbursts."

Even more baffling is the disk's odd radial appearance, with its fans, spokes, and jets all pointing toward the star. As Davidson and Roberta Humphreys, also at the University of Minnesota, have written, "We regard the radial streaks as warning arrows pointing inward toward some extraordinary phenomenon near the central star."

SUPER-SIZED LUMINARY

Finding out the nature of that phenomenon, however, has proved difficult. Although astronomers regard Eta Carinae as one of the largest and brightest stars in the Galaxy, it has never been viewed directly, hidden as it is within the gigantic cloud that surrounds it. In fact, the star's dusty lobes prevent scientists from even knowing the exact duration of the Great Eruption, which might have continued long after the star had faded to 7th magnitude in 1868. As the lobes were spewed outward, they drew a curtain on the eruption, making it appear as if the fireworks had ended, when in truth they could have continued for years.

What astronomers do know about Eta Carinae is that it belongs to a rare class of stars called luminous blue variables, or LBVs, objects whose temperature and mass approach the absolute maximum believed possible for a star. Eta Carinae appears to tip

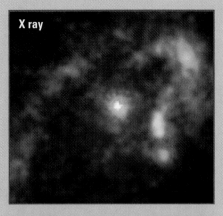

X ray

Optical

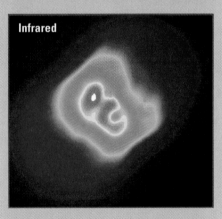

Infrared

Radio

X-ray images reveal Eta's hot inner core (top). The Hubble Telescope captures two giant bursts of gas (center, top). Infrared photography displays the range of Eta's radiated energy (center, bottom). Eta's brightness can also be gauged with radio imaging (bottom).

the scales at a mass 100 to 120 times larger than the Sun, while its surface broils at a temperature that ranges between about 22,000° F and 50,000° F (12,000° C and 28,000° C). Compare this to the surface temperature of the Sun, which comes in around 10,000° F (5,500° C).

At its coolest, Eta Carinae also becomes most compact—although its size would still be large enough to swallow the orbit of Mercury if Eta were to replace the Sun. When the star's temperature rises, its radius swells and would reach the orbit of Mars or beyond. During the Great Eruption, the star probably expanded to a diameter of 2 billion miles (3 billion kilometers), or roughly the size of Saturn's orbit.

Moreover, astronomers think that Eta Carinae has one of the densest solar winds known, blowing off about 0.003 solar mass per year, some 6 trillion trillion tons, or two Earth masses each day. At this rate, the Sun would evaporate in a little more than three centuries. But Eta hardly notices.

Such large, hot objects must periodically shed additional amounts of mass to remain stable. What causes these eruptions remains a mystery, although astronomers suspect that the incredibly high mass and temperature play key roles. The most popular hypothesis says that the star's luminosity is so great that it occasionally overpowers the gravity that holds the star together. The star becomes unstable; its outer layers pulse in and out as if they are unsure whether to remain in place or gush into space. Eventually an eruption occurs, and the outer layers are flung away.

With the loss of this shell of hot gas, the star cools, and its surface temperature drops to a relatively low 13,000° F (7,000° C). At the same time, its electromagnetic output shifts from the high-energy ultraviolet to less-energetic optical radiation, so although the star is now cooler, it radiates more brightly at wavelengths our eyes can see.

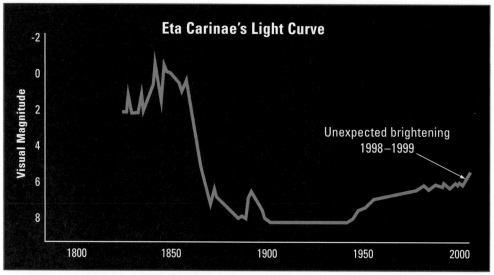

Eta Carinae's visual intensity has varied over time (see graph above). The colossal star hit its peak just prior to 1850, although of late, it seems to be enjoying a gradual—and mysterious—resurgence in brightness.

Luminous blue variables are thought to be short-term transitional stages in the lives of stars, spanning a mere 25,000 years or so. "Most stars above 40 to 50 solar masses will eventually go through an LBV instability phase," explains Humphreys. As a star sheds mass, it evolves from a blue supergiant to a Wolf-Rayet star, thought to be one of the last stages stars reach before they die. Such stars have lost more than half to two-thirds of their original mass. Having exhausted their hydrogen fuel, they are now forced to burn other, more-complex atoms. Their next and final act, astronomers believe, is to explode as supernovas.

MORE MYSTERIES

Ironically, Eta Carinae's recent behavior has punched a few holes in the theories that try to explain luminous blue variables. From 1993 to 1998, the star's light output first dipped and then rose about half a magnitude, an event attributed at the time to Eta Carinae's continuing irregular fluctuations. The star, however, then began to brighten precipitously, rising one full magnitude in less than a year. As of June 1999, the star and the surrounding Homunculus glistened at about 5th magnitude, the brightest it has been since the Great Eruption in 1843. "Without question, the central star has brightened since 1997 by roughly a factor of two," notes astrophysicist Jon Morse of the University of Colorado in Boulder, whose Hubble images in June 1999 confirmed this brightening. And if the brightening trend continues, Morse adds, "In two years, we will not be able to take an image with Hubble without saturating the camera. [Eta Carinae] will be too bright."

While astronomers had expected the star might brighten sometime in the next century, no one had anticipated it happening so abruptly. As Kris Davidson points out, "If you had asked us, we would have told you it probably *wasn't* going to happen."

The brightening is even more puzzling because it is occurring across all wavelengths. If the star were merely ejecting an outer shell in response to radiation pressure, the brightening would happen only at visible wavelengths, with the star's outer layers cooling, and its output shifting from the ultraviolet to the optical. An increase in brightness across the entire electromagnetic spectrum implies that Eta is growing intrinsically brighter, a possibility no theory predicted. Moreover, this brightening implies that the star's luminosity may soon overwhelm its gravity, once again causing the star to become unstable and erupt as it did in the past century. "And Eta Carinae can't brighten very much," notes Humphreys, "or else it will go boom."

Adding to Eta Carinae's baffling story is the recent discovery by Augusto Damineli of the University of São Paulo in Brazil that the star's light fluctuations are not as irregular as once thought. Damineli's analysis of the star's spectrum reveals that every 5.5 years, Eta's ultraviolet and X-ray outputs undergo a short-term change. In X rays, the flux increases steadily, then plunges, followed by a slow recovery. In the ultraviolet, several dark emission lines on the star's spectrum disappear. Damineli was able to trace this cycle back through the past 50 years. He also found that all the major outbursts of the previous century—in 1827, 1832, 1838, and 1843—seemed to line up with it. Finally, he successfully predicted an event in December 1997, at which time the star's X-ray output plummeted and the ultraviolet emission lines faded, as they had in previous cycles.

Based on this cycle, a number of astronomers immediately proposed that Eta Carinae was actually a binary system with both stars hidden by the system's dense surrounding nebula—and that all previous eruptions might have been caused by the orbital interaction of two stars.

Unfortunately, no proposed binary system has yet explained Eta's behavior completely. Furthermore, a bewildering wave of new facts has swamped the theorists and left them scrambling to recover. "We've got so much data from so many wavelengths, it's difficult to get one model to explain everything," notes astrophysicist Michael Corcoran of the Universities Space Research Association (USRA). For example, recent observations have discovered an additional 85-day cycle in X-ray emissions and a 200-day cycle in the ultraviolet, with hints of a 58-day cycle in the optical.

Although there's still much disagreement about the existence of all these cycles, most astronomers now attribute the star's powerful X-ray emission to the collision of two dense stellar winds, emanating either from the two stars of a binary system or from the fast and slow stellar winds of a single star. Astronomers suspect that the 5.5-year cycle occurs when the region where these winds collide is periodically eclipsed, either when one star moves behind the other or when the rotation of a single star moves the region out of our line of sight.

While most scientists today favor the binary hypothesis, others argue that a single star could still produce all the phenomena that have been observed. Some have even considered the possibility that the system is made up of a barely stable three-star system, whereby the Giant Eruption of the past century was caused when two of the three stars switched positions in an orbital dance of grand proportions.

In general, astronomers remain skeptical of all of these theories. No hypothesis is yet able to explain all the known facts, among them the star's inexplicable and stunning jump in brightness since 1998. As Davidson notes, "We really, truly do not understand what is happening, even at a fairly rudimentary level."

THE LIFE AND DEATH OF STARS

Astronomers now firmly believe that the formation of more-commonplace stars is linked to the feverish life and death of massive stars such as Eta Carinae. These kingly objects not only process huge amounts of hydrogen fuel into more-complex atoms such as carbon, oxygen, nitrogen, and iron, they also spray it into the interstellar medium, accounting for a large percentage of the material found in the dense clouds that surround them. When such majestic stars go supernova, the explosion sweeps up this debris, forming a shock wave which eventually flowers the longer-living but less-massive ordinary stars—stars such as our Sun.

Corcoran recently said, "The death of Eta Carinae is likely to be one of the most explosive events ever experienced in the Galaxy." When such massive stars go supernova, the energy released can be so powerful that it equals and possibly exceeds that of the rest of the Galaxy. Such explosions might also be the progenitors of gamma-ray bursts, events so energetic that even from a distance of several thousand light-years, the explosion could seriously damage life on Earth, possibly even wiping it out.

So while the explosion of lordly stars such as Eta Carinae leads to the birth of new stars, it concurrently causes the destruction of life in nearby solar systems. Let us hope that our solar system is at a safe distance: just far enough away so that we can enjoy the show without any tragic consequences. ◪

Space-Shuttle
Impersonator

by Debbie Gary

For a brief moment, at 28,000 feet (8,500 meters), the aircraft floats, as the nose gently arcs downward through the starry night sky. We are in one of the National Aeronautics and Space Administration's (NASA's) Shuttle Training Aircraft (STA), simulating shuttle commander Jim Halsell's next return from space. The main gear is down, the thrust reversers are deployed, and gravity shoves the crew against their seat harnesses. Cold air from the back of the aircraft spills down the aisle and into the cockpit.

Halsell, in the left seat, has no throttle and no engine gauges. On the left side of the cockpit, black window masking narrows his view. Colorful screens and a head-up display tell him he is maneuvering a 230,000-pound (104,000-kilogram) orbiter, which plunges toward the New Mexico desert floor like Wile E. Coyote in a Road Runner cartoon. In fact, the NASA aircraft is a highly modified Grumman Gulfstream II twin-engine business jet.

NOTHING SHORT OF PERFECTION

Halsell's right hand is on a control stick that looks, feels, and reacts like the rotational hand controller he will use to maneuver *Atlantis* back to Florida's Kennedy Space Center, which he did in May 1999. In the right seat, Steve Nagel is ready to kick the STA out of simulation mode if need be. His hands hover above the yoke, which is commanded by computers in the back of the aircraft, and moves back and forth as if it had a mind of its own. From the jump seat, flight-simulation engineer Alyson Hickey calls out speeds, altitudes, and various reminders. The altimeter unwinds almost cartoonishly, and the vertical-speed indicator says we are descending at a rate of 14,000 feet (4,300 meters) per minute.

NASA's Shuttle Training Aircraft (above, graphically superimposed on the space shuttle Columbia) effectively simulates the gravity, turbulence, and wind shear that confront astronauts when landing a shuttle.

Over the next hour, Halsell will shoot 10 two-minute approaches, coaching and critiquing himself on the most-minute details of his performance. He seeks perfection.

When a pilot becomes a space-shuttle commander, he or she faces two of the toughest minutes of his or her flying career: the first shuttle landing. Everyone who takes off in a single-seat airplane for the first time has to land an airplane he or she has never flown before. But add a few complications: The pilot is returning from weightlessness, fighting nausea and possibly vertigo, and feeling every force of gravity as if it were doubled. Balance is shot, and muscle memory, which pilots train so hard to build, has vanished. The pilot is encased in a full pressure suit, helmet, bulky gloves, and boots. The aircraft, a 115-ton glider, is worth $2 billion. There are no go-arounds, in which a pilot can add power and make a second approach if things aren't going well the first time around.

SUPERLATIVE SIMULATION

NASA has other simulators, ground-based ones programmed with thousands of possible situations and emergencies, where commanders and pilots learn to fly a machine that is part rocket, part spacecraft, and part airplane. But in simulating the airplane part, none is as effective as the Shuttle Training Aircraft. STA instructors can throw only a few curves—lower-than-expected visibilities and cloud bases, navigation errors, and onboard-display malfunctions—but this is the only simulator in which astronauts feel the crush of gravity, wind shear, turbulence, and that breathtaking sensation of ground rush, where Earth races toward you like a locomotive. From the instructor's seat, the craft flies like a normal airplane. From the commander's seat, it flies like the shuttle, thanks to a bank of computers housed in blue cabinets in the cabin.

In the early phases of shuttle flight training, Nagel and the other instructors talk the students through an approach, but tonight Nagel is quiet. Halsell is a veteran, with two shuttle flights as pilot and two as commander, and he has flown 1,300 approaches in the STA. Nagel is also a veteran shuttle pilot and commander, having been in the astronaut corps for 17 years before retiring in 1995 to join NASA's Aircraft Operations Division as a pilot and instructor.

Halsell banks and spirals down, flying the Heading Alignment Cone, which leads the orbiter into a descent to intercept the final approach course. On his control stick, Halsell makes tiny, nearly imperceptible pulselike movements that are recorded on a roll of paper, which unwinds from the side panel next to Hickey. The paper graphs the flight path and every pulse of the stick, a record of which goes to the chief of the astronaut corps for postflight scrutinizing. It also shows the angle of the STA's descent—18 degrees for heavier flights and 20 for lighter ones, up to seven times steeper than an airliner's descent angle.

In the cockpit, projected onto a clear panel in front of his windshield, the head-up display tells Halsell if he is on his intended flight path. The flight-director software tells him when to increase or decrease roll and pitch, both of which are "energy-management" commands that ensure the aircraft will intercept the glide slope with the proper airspeed and altitude. When he rolls onto final approach, red and white lights on the ground also guide him. At this dive angle, we are aimed 7,500 feet (2,300 meters) short of the runway. Following head-up display guidance, Halsell pulls the nose up and shallows the glide angle to 1.5 degrees when he passes through 2,000 feet (600 meters). With the change in glide angle, the aircraft is now aimed 2,500 feet (760 meters) beyond the runway threshold. The craft gradually begins to slow toward the shuttle's landing speed of 205 knots.

IT TAKES TWO

Up ahead, the gigantic White Sands runway looms in a pool of light. Since the shuttle has no onboard landing lights, the landing zone is lit by high-intensity lights, which sit on flatbed trailers on either side of the approach end. Twenty feet (6 meters) above the runway, Halsell pulls the nose up as if to land, but then levels off, holding the same eye level he will have when he lands the shuttle—"height of eyes," in astronautspeak.

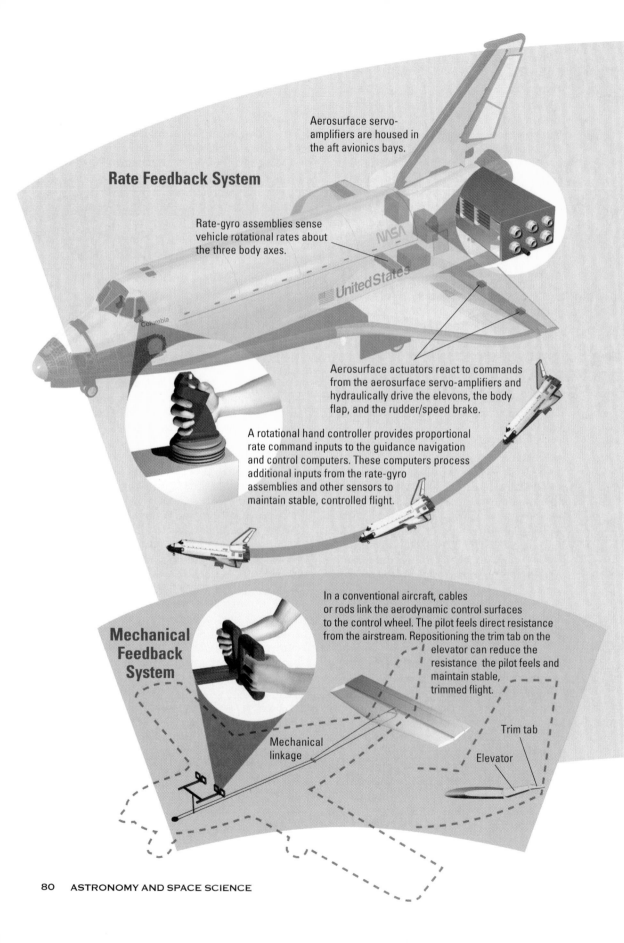

Rate Feedback System

Aerosurface servo-amplifiers are housed in the aft avionics bays.

Rate-gyro assemblies sense vehicle rotational rates about the three body axes.

Aerosurface actuators react to commands from the aerosurface servo-amplifiers and hydraulically drive the elevons, the body flap, and the rudder/speed brake.

A rotational hand controller provides proportional rate command inputs to the guidance navigation and control computers. These computers process additional inputs from the rate-gyro assemblies and other sensors to maintain stable, controlled flight.

Mechanical Feedback System

In a conventional aircraft, cables or rods link the aerodynamic control surfaces to the control wheel. The pilot feels direct resistance from the airstream. Repositioning the trim tab on the elevator can reduce the resistance the pilot feels and maintain stable, trimmed flight.

Mechanical linkage

Trim tab

Elevator

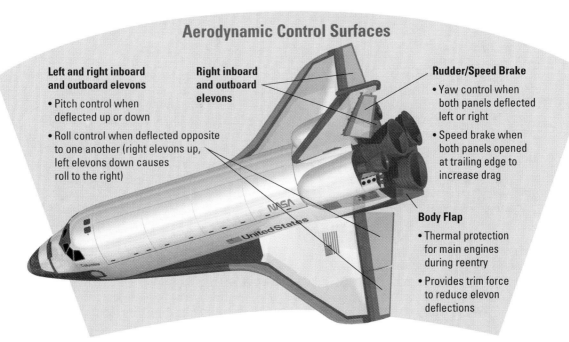

Aerodynamic Control Surfaces

Left and right inboard and outboard elevons

- Pitch control when deflected up or down
- Roll control when deflected opposite to one another (right elevons up, left elevons down causes roll to the right)

Right inboard and outboard elevons

Rudder/Speed Brake

- Yaw control when both panels deflected left or right
- Speed brake when both panels opened at trailing edge to increase drag

Body Flap

- Thermal protection for main engines during reentry
- Provides trim force to reduce elevon deflections

On Nagel's panel, a green square lights up. "Touchdown," he calls, kicking the STA out of computer-simulation mode, and he climbs back up into the inky darkness to begin once again.

Behind us, in another STA, Scott Horowitz flies the same approach with another training crew. Horowitz will be the pilot on Halsell's next mission. Both pilots are trained to fly the space shuttle, in case a commander is incapacitated. The pilot functions somewhat like a copilot on an airliner, bringing perspective the commander may not have. "When you are involved in the actual eye-to-hand coordination, you tend to get fixated on controlling one parameter," says Scott Altman, the pilot on mission STS-90, *Columbia*, which flew in 1998. "But when you are sitting in the right seat, you get a better big picture of what is going on. A lot of commanders use their pilots to back them up, to call altitudes, airspeeds, and to maybe give him your impression."

Pilots generally make two spaceflights before they move up to the commander's position. They will have made at least 1,000 approaches in the STA, but they know that the only one that counts will be the one in which the dust flies as the rubber hits the tar.

In orbit, the shuttle's aerodynamic control surfaces—the rudder and the four elevons, which function as combined ailerons and elevators at the trailing edge of

each wing—are nonfunctional. Maneuvering in orbit is accomplished by the reaction-control system, which consists of 44 thrusters on the nose and tail. Pitch, roll, and yaw are accomplished by firing certain thrusters. Charlie Precourt, chief of the astronaut corps, compares maneuvering in orbit to sliding on ice: There is no resistance. So inputs, made with the rotational hand controller, are extremely small. When the shuttle reenters the atmosphere, the aerodynamic surfaces begin to exert an effect around 300,000 feet (91,400 meters), phasing in completely by 120,000 feet (36,600 meters). There is a brief overlap between thruster control and aerosurface control. Before the first powered flight, no one was sure how this transition would work. John Young, the first shuttle commander, helped find out.

Young had been an astronaut since 1962. On his fourth spaceflight, in 1972, he landed and took off from the Moon as the commander for *Apollo 16*. About piloting the shuttle through its transition from spacecraft to aircraft, he says, "We shot profiles based on what the X-15 was doing, but we were scared of how the elevon and rudder system and yaw jets were going to interact."

TAKING CONTROL

Today, the commander takes control around Mach 1 (the speed of sound, defined as

1,125 feet—or 343 meters—per second), but Young started testing the controls much sooner on that first shuttle flight in April 1981. "I was flying roll control from about Mach 6 on down," he says. At that speed and altitude, the rotational hand controller is governing both the aerosurfaces and the reaction-control system as they phase in and out under commands from the aerojet digital autopilot. "On the second mission, Joe Engle did push over/pull up maneuvers at very high Mach numbers" to test the pitch axis. "We found that you could take over anywhere, but the agreement now is a little past subsonic," says Young. These days, the commander takes over at about four minutes to touchdown. The commander will have had plenty of experience in the simulators (though the STA can provide only a two-minute ride), but he or she still has to be able to quickly evaluate the real machine for its reactions.

When commander Eileen Collins landed the shuttle for the first time in July 1999, she thought, *Is this going to be what I expect?* When she took over manually at 40,000 feet (12,200 meters), her test-pilot instincts kicked in. "I did some control inputs, trying to get a qualitative feel for it," she says. "In the pitch axis, it was sensitive. You need to make very deliberate, small inputs." (Commanders say that in the pitch axis, the shuttle handles like a fighter; in the roll axis, it's more like a big transport.) She noted that it is easy to get into a pilot-induced oscillation, in which the pilot's inputs and the airplane's actions get out of synch, with a disastrous landing a distinct possibility. She told herself, *I'm going to keep an eye out for this when I get down low on the landing.*

A New Attitude

In a conventional aircraft, the pilot pulls or pushes on the control stick until the nose reaches the attitude desired. The rate at which the nose moves is determined by how hard the pilot pulls or pushes. It's a simple one-to-one ratio: The harder the pilot pulls, the more the nose moves.

In such a system, cables or rods are used to link the control stick and the rudder pedals to the elevator, ailerons, and rudder. The forces acting on these aerodynamic control surfaces "feed back" to a pilot through the pressure he or she must exert on the control stick to climb, descend, or maintain a more or less straight-and-level flight. An elevator-trim system—a small tab on the trailing edge of the elevator, connected by cable to the cockpit—is set to maintain a particular nose attitude.

An airplane is aerodynamically stable in the pitch axis—that is, it wants to remain in straight-and-level flight. If you lower the nose to descend, for example, while maintaining a constant airspeed, you will need to exert constant pressure on the control stick to counter the increased airflow over the elevator. By adjusting the trim tab to react against the changing lift force due to the increased airflow, the pilot rebalances, or "trims," the aircraft and no longer needs to exert pressure on the control stick to maintain a nose-down attitude.

This mechanical-feedback system would be unmanageable in a hypersonic aircraft like the shuttle, which must maintain a steady nose-down position while its speed changes thousands of miles per hour in minutes. Instead of cables mechanically linking the control surfaces to the stick, computers transmit control input and response to aerosurface servoamplifiers—the electronic devices connected to each aerodynamic control surface. Deflection is governed by a rate-feedback system.

"Every time the stick is out of detent [the neutral position], it is commanding, for a given deflection of the stick, one degree per second, two degrees per second, and so on," Precourt says. He refers to the rate at which the nose will move toward where the commander wants it. "When you are on final approach, you can let go and the orbiter will stay on that path, because when you let go, you had zero degrees per second of change in attitude at that airspeed. That is the rate that the stick is going to command." The flight-control system compensates for the aerodynamic forces that want to move the nose back to level flight.

"In a conventional aircraft, the pilot pulls the stick back less at higher speeds than at lower speeds to get the same pitch rate—say,

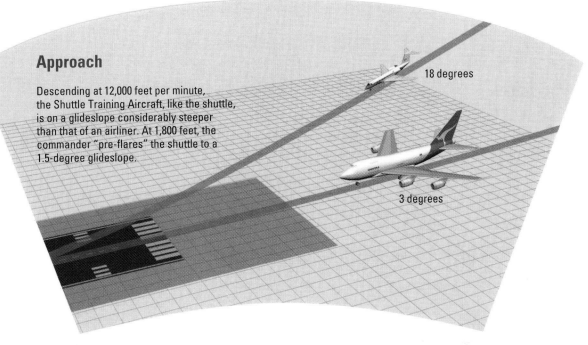

Approach

Descending at 12,000 feet per minute, the Shuttle Training Aircraft, like the shuttle, is on a glideslope considerably steeper than that of an airliner. At 1,800 feet, the commander "pre-flares" the shuttle to a 1.5-degree glideslope.

18 degrees

3 degrees

for a pitch rate in a loop of a constant 10 degrees per second, he or she has to change the amount pulled back on the stick as the speed changes," Precourt says. "In the shuttle, the pitch rate you get is independent of the aircraft speed. The same rate results for the same deflection no matter what your speed. The benefit of this kind of system is that you don't have to be trimming off stick forces." But there is a disadvantage, too.

"When you are down low, closer to the flare, and you make an input, you don't want to hold the stick back because it will overrotate," or pitch up too much. "So," Precourt continues, "you pull the stick back at the rate you want to get a new attitude. When it approaches that attitude, you have to let it go. Instead of continuing to pull, you make a series of pulses. The controls take quite a bit of getting used to. That is why we train so much in the Gulfstream."

Shuttle commander Ken Cockrell describes another complication, an effect of the digital fly-by-wire control system. In this system, when the commander moves the hand controller or rudder pedals, it sends a signal to a computer, which then sends a message to move the control surface. The control surface moves, and, ultimately, the orbiter responds. This all takes time.

The pilot relies on immediate feedback to fly smoothly. With a computer running the show, there's a delay. "It has to figure out quite a few feedback parameters before it allows itself to make the next move, so there is a slight delay—150 milliseconds, around a tenth of a second," says Cockrell. "That is noticeable to humans. If you try to make too many inputs too quickly, you'll get way out of sync with it and it's not so easy to fly.

"So we use the term 'open the loop.' You make an input based on your experience, see if the vehicle responded the way you wanted. If it didn't, make a little more or take out some of that input. You have to build this patience factor into your hand. Once you build it in, it seems like you are flying a pretty reasonable flying vehicle. But at first, people find themselves overreacting. On approach, there is a little time compression. You are a little behind."

THE REAL THING

Pilots don't have much time to process information on an STA flight, but when it's the real thing, the difficulty is part of the excitement. "To land the first time you ever fly a vehicle, to land within three seconds of when you planned, on speed, with millions of people watching you, is hard," former commander Curtis Brown says.

Tonight, over the desert, the air is smooth. Nagel and Halsell agree that on a night like this, it feels like the real thing.

ASK THE SCIENTIST

▶ *Have scientists spent much time investigating the moons of Mars? Could a person standing on the surface of Mars discern the fact that there are two moons? Do they ever eclipse each other?*

Ever since they were discovered in 1877 by the American astronomer Asaph Hall, the Martian moons Phobos and Deimos have been fascinating objects of study. Still, no one knows if these were born as moons of Mars or were once asteroids that somehow became captured by Mars' gravitational field.

These two moons are very tiny. To a hypothetical astronaut on Mars, Phobos would appear about one-third the size of our Moon, and Deimos would appear even smaller—only about half that size. Observers on Earth know that our Moon takes about 28 days to make one complete orbit of Earth—changing its phases from night to night as it goes. A Martian observer would see Phobos whip through its phases in less than eight hours; Deimos takes a comparatively leisurely 30 hours to complete one orbit.

A person standing on Mars would, indeed, see both moons in the sky—sometimes both at once. But only from near the Martian equator would someone ever have a chance of occasionally seeing Phobos pass in front of Deimos.

▶ *When a shuttle crew is assembled, are the personalities of the various members considered? Has there ever been a space mutiny? Are most of the personal interactions*

among astronauts that occur during a space-shuttle mission considered classified information?

For the space-shuttle missions, personalities of the crew members have not ever really been considered. All astronauts are professionals who are highly trained, and all have the same high standards for mission success. But that doesn't mean they don't have their occasional disagreements and conflicts.

During the 1971 *Salyut 1* mission, two cosmonauts had a serious disagreement that almost became a mutiny. On *Salyut 5*, it is said that two cosmonauts even came to fisticuffs, although spokespeople for the Russian space program are disinclined to comment about this incident. Even American astronauts have had their problems in space. In 1985, one shuttle/Spacelab astronaut had to be restrained when he lost his temper over equipment failures and other problems. But never has there been a problem of a magnitude sufficient enough to cause a mutiny.

Personal interactions among astronauts are not classified—unless, of course, they are part of a classified mission. In fact, anyone able to receive NASA TV through their local cable system or satellite dish can watch shuttle missions live, and can see for themselves many of the personal interactions of the crew.

▶ *Why haven't we heard about Neptune lately? Do scientists know everything about this planet? Are astronomers still curious about the other nearby planets?*

Our last close-up images of Neptune came in 1989, when the Voyager 2 spacecraft sped past the mysterious blue planet. Since then, the public hasn't heard much about Neptune, but that doesn't mean that scientists have lost interest totally. Scientists don't know everything there is to know about Neptune—or anything else in the universe, for that matter—and they're still quite fascinated by this distant world. A number of questions remain about Neptune: What makes its clouds move as they do? How did Neptune's thin ring system form? How did its moons become the way they are?

In recent years, understanding the planets has entered the realm of a new group of scientists: the planetary scientists. Technically, these researchers are not astronomers, but are, instead, experts in geology, meteorology, physics, chemistry, and a variety of other sciences. They are constantly looking at other worlds and trying to understand where our planets came from, how they've evolved to their present condition, and how they are similar to or different from planets that are in orbit around other stars. Their observations come from telescopes positioned beyond Earth's atmosphere.

► **Did pulsars get their name because they pulse? If so, do astronomers understand the mechanism that causes this pulsation? Are there many known pulsars in the universe?**

The first pulsar was discovered by British astronomer Jocelyn Bell in 1967. It appeared as a source of faint radio radiation that seemed to be pulsating regularly. Today, we have identified more than 600 such pulsars.

Scientists now believe pulsars to be rapidly spinning neutron stars—tiny, dense remnants of powerful supernova explosions—each between only 6 and 12 miles (10 to 20 kilometers) across. They seem to have jets of particles shooting out at extremely high speeds from their magnetic poles, which produce powerful beams of radiation. As these tiny stars rotate—with complete-rotation periods ranging anywhere from 4 seconds to more than 1,000 times per second—the beams sweep past our telescopes, and we see a rapidly pulsing object. Pulsars have been found to pulse in every wavelength of radiation—not just in radio wavelengths.

Astronomers have taken photographs showing that some even pulsate in the visible-light part of the spectrum. The first of these so-called "optical pulsars" was discovered in 1969; it was the star at the center of the Crab Nebula, and became known as the "Crab Pulsar."

► **Is the telescope that Galileo used weaker than ones that everyday people can now buy at the store?**

Even the least expensive telescopes available in stores today are far better in optical quality and magnifying power than the best that Galileo had.

Many people think that the Italian astronomer Galileo invented this optical device, but he didn't. While on a trip to Venice in July 1609, Galileo heard of the invention and rushed home to Padua to build his own.

His first telescope had a diameter of about 1 inch (2.5 centimeters), and a magnifying power of only about 15 times. It wasn't a particularly good telescope; its glass lenses were filled with little bubbles and had a greenish tinge. Looking through Galileo's telescope allowed one to see only a tiny area of the sky—about one-quarter the size of the full Moon.

Over time, however, Galileo built bigger and better telescopes. He was eventually able to see such things as the mountains and craters on the Moon, the moons of Jupiter, the phases of Venus, and the myriad stars that make up the Milky Way.

Virtually all of the "backyard" telescopes available today can bring these features—and much more—into view.

EARTH
AND THE
ENVIRONMENT

■ A TANGLE OF SUNFLOWERS BEARS
UNEQUIVOCAL TESTIMONY TO THE
RESOURCEFULNESS AND TENACITY OF
PLANTS. EVEN ALONG A DUSTY ROAD-
SIDE, A FEW SEEDS MANAGE TO GER-
MINATE, EXTRACTING FOR THEIR SUR-
VIVAL WHAT LITTLE MOISTURE MIGHT
BE LOCKED IN THE PARCHED SOIL.
BEFORE TOO LONG, LOVELY GREEN
FOLIAGE APPEARS, PROVIDING THE
PLATFORM FROM WHICH GLORIOUS
GOLDEN BLOSSOMS ARISE.

CONTENTS

THE GALÁPAGOS:
Islands on the Edge

by Elaine Pascoe

On January 16, 2001, the fated tanker *Jessica*, carrying 243,000 gallons (920,000 liters) of diesel and bunker fuel oil, ran aground in pounding surf a few hundred yards off the coast of San Cristóbal, in the Galápagos Islands. Within days, oil oozing from the stranded tanker spread toward the vulnerable islands, whose unique plants and animals had inspired Charles Darwin's theory of evolution. One of the world's great wild treasures was suddenly on the brink of disaster.

Government agencies and environmentalists joined forces to contain the spill, and in the end, disaster was averted—thanks as much to a lucky shift in wind direction as to human effort. But the threat served to direct fresh attention on the wildlife of the Galápagos, under pressure from many causes even

before the spill, and on the fragile nature of island ecosystems.

THE ENCHANTED ISLES

The Galápagos Islands lie in the Pacific Ocean roughly 600 miles (1,000 kilometers) from the coast of Ecuador, their governing country. There are 13 main islands and many islets, all formed by undersea volcanoes some 5 million years ago. With their rugged volcanic terrain, rocky shores, and bare hills, the islands present a forbidding appearance. Charles Darwin, who arrived in 1835 on a worldwide research voyage aboard the HMS *Beagle*, recorded his impressions:

"Nothing could be less inviting than the first appearance. A broken field of black basaltic lava, thrown into the most rugged waves, and crossed by great fissures, is every-

The once unspoiled Galápagos Islands today hedge on environmental disaster, their precarious position the result of human intrusion. Near-devastation from oil spills, such as that from the tanker Jessica (left), tourist impositions on indigenous wildlife (right), and pollution (below) pose serious threats to the vulnerable islands' ecosystems.

where covered by stunted, sunburnt brushwood, which shows little signs of life." As uninviting as the alien islands seemed, their strange life-forms ultimately would inspire the English naturalist's greatest work.

By the time of Darwin's visit, the Galápagos Islands had been known to sailors for 300 years. The islands were discovered in 1535 by a Spanish bishop, Tomás de Berlanga, whose ship drifted off course while en route to Peru. He named them *Las Islas Encantadas* ("The Enchanted Isles") for their remoteness. The name Galápagos, which means "tortoises" in Spanish, was bestowed later, in reference to the giant land tortoises that are among the island chain's most notable animals. Because the tortoises can live up to one year without food or water, ships would stop at the islands and stock their holds with these animals to provide a source of fresh meat for their long voyages.

When the Galápagos Islands first formed, however, there were no tortoises or any other life—just the volcanic ash and hardened lava that coated the land. The ancestors of the plants and animals that live there today all arrived from other parts of the world, carried in by Pacific Ocean currents or other means. Seeds, for example, may have been carried by wind or deposited in bird droppings. Storms may have carried small animals from the coast of South America out to sea; a lucky few survived the journey and washed up on the Galápagos.

Because the islands are so far from any other land, only a smattering of life-forms ever reached their jagged shores. And the plants and animals that did arrive faced harsh conditions. Because the Galápagos Islands lie near the equator, they are hot and dry for most of the year, although cold ocean currents bring a cool season each summer. The slopes of some volcanoes trap fog and drizzle, providing enough moisture for trees and grasses to flourish, but the plant life in the drier lowlands remains brown for much of the year.

Nevertheless, some of the plants and animals that reached the Galápagos managed to adapt to the islands' conditions and survive. They reproduced and passed on qualities that helped them endure, and in time, their descendants developed characteristics that increased their chances of survival. In this way, new species of plants and animals evolved—species found nowhere else. The

Galápagos tortoises

are true giants, weighing in at as much as 550 pounds (250 kilograms). They lumber across the land, grazing on cacti and other plants, and live 150 years or longer. At one time, there were about 250,000 tortoises on the islands, but today, only about 15,000 survive. Of the 14 original subspecies, each distinct to a separate island, three are extinct.

Seabirds of many kinds use the islands for nesting. Among them are the waved albatross, pelicans, frigate birds, and three kinds of boobies—blue-footed, red-footed, and masked. The blue-footed boobies, which nest in rocks near the shore on most islands, are among the more flamboyant.

Marine iguanas are the world's only seagoing lizards. Darwin described this animal as "a hideous-looking creature, of a dirty black colour, stupid, and sluggish in its movements." Marine iguanas ocean dive to graze on seaweed, staying submerged for 30 minutes at a time. Back on shore, they stretch out on the rocks and bask in the sunlight. The coasts are home to more than 200,000 of the unusual iguanas.

island's isolation is so complete that in many cases, subspecies developed only on one island, with related but separate subspecies developing on nearby islands.

WEIRD AND WONDERFUL WILDLIFE
Ecuador has set aside 97 percent of the Galápagos Islands as a national park, and thousands of tourists visit the islands each year to marvel at the unique plants and animals there. Of the roughly 600 plant species on the islands, about one-third are found nowhere else, and many have quite unusual characteristics. For example, many of the trees on the islands are members of the Scalesia family, plants that on mainland

Galápagos penguins live farther north than other penguin species. Rare and diminutive, these birds range into equatorial waters and nest in the tropics. They are able to survive in the Galápagos because ocean currents bring cool, nutrient-rich waters bearing fish, their favored prey.

Fur seals and sea lions are rarely seen in the tropics. With their heavy fur coats and thick blubber, they prefer cooler climates. But because of cool ocean currents, some have made their homes in the Galápagos, living in large shore colonies.

Flightless cormorants are unique to the islands. The ancestors of these birds, which feed by diving for fish, probably arrived from the mainland of South America thousands of years ago. They found plenty of fish in the cool ocean waters around the islands, and with no predators to bother them, they had little need to fly. Over many generations, the birds' wings became stunted and useless.

South America are low-growing and void of woody stems. Galápagos Scalesia varieties have woody trunks and grow 30 feet (9 meters) tall. Prickly pear cacti, stunted on the mainland, grow into small trees on the islands. The unique conditions of the Galápagos suit these plants, which also do not have to compete with the thousands of other plant species for moisture and soil nutrients on the mainland.

Fully 80 percent of Galápagos animals are unique to the islands. There are the miniature penguins, flightless cormorants, and marine iguanas—the world's only seagoing lizards. Playful seals and sea lions gather on the coasts. There are only 57 species of land-dwelling mammals, birds, and reptiles that call the Galápagos Islands home. Few land mammals could survive a trip of 600 miles (1,000 kilometers) by sea, so native mammals are rare and amount to only a few species of bats and rice rats. As visitors quickly learn, reptiles, notably iguanas and giant tortoises, dominate on land.

Many birds have adjusted well to life on the islands. Seabirds such as boobies and frigates nest on the islands. But the best-known birds are the 13 species of what are commonly known as Darwin's finches, all members of the genus *Geospiza*. Biologists believe the finches probably descended from a single South American species, carried to the islands by storm winds long ago. Interestingly, in the Galápagos, finches on the closely knit islands developed different beak

A tenacious cactus finch (below) symbolizes Charles Darwin's early recognition of the amazing evolutionary process. Plants, too, such as the curious lava cactus (bottom), have adapted to seemingly impossible conditions, thriving atop aged and ashen lava banks.

structures and feeding habits, each suited to foods available in its peculiar habitat.

Charles Darwin's observations of these birds were a key factor in his development of the theory of evolution. Darwin did not publish his theory until many years following his first observations, but the five weeks he spent in the Galápagos helped to shape his ideas about how new species develop from older species through the processes of adaptation and natural selection.

FRAGILE ISLAND ECOSYSTEMS

Islands contribute far more to global biodiversity than their landmass would suggest, a fact that has made them environmental "hot spots." Island ecosystems are highly vulnerable both to natural disaster and to the effects of human interference. When island habitats are damaged or destroyed, species have nowhere to go; when unique island species are wiped out, there is no reserve population from which to draw. Altogether, about 80 percent of documented animal-species extinctions in the past 400 years have been of island species, according to a study by British ecologist Robert J. Whittaker. People have been responsible for most of these extinctions, through overhunting and overfishing, the spread of diseases, the destruction of habitats, and the introduction of competitive alien species.

For example, the tiny South Atlantic island of St. Helena was once home to dozens of unique plant species. Then, in the 1500s, Portuguese mariners made the island a supply station and brought goats ashore to breed. Thanks mainly to the goats, today many of the island's hills are stripped bare, and its plants are seriously endangered.

Mauritius, in the Indian Ocean, fared even worse. Uninhabited before European colonization in 1638, the island endured waves of settlers from Holland, France, and Britain who cut forests for ebony and cleared lowlands to plant sugarcane. Hunting and habitat destruction decimated native birds, including the flightless dodo. Since independence in 1968, Mauritius has seen industrial and pesticide pollution, while its coral reefs have been damaged by dynamite fishing.

As the tanker *Jessica* lists starboard (right), her fuel oil oozes through San Cristóbal's blue coastal waters. Meanwhile, rescuers rush to set up a barrier to contain the slick from reaching toward unsuspecting wildlife. For at least one pelican (above), the emergency efforts came too late.

Similar to the living things of many remote islands, the plants and animals of the Galápagos were under intense environmental pressures even before the *Jessica* ran aground. In the past, people cleared parts of the islands for farming and hunted tortoises, iguanas, fur seals, and doves and other birds. Equally threatening to the indigenous species were the dogs, cats, pigs, goats, rats, guava plants, and other alien species that escaped into the wild.

Today, the grazing goats and pigs that compete with island tortoises and iguanas make food a competitive commodity and destroy essential vegetation. Dogs and cats prey on native animals. Introduced plants have spread, particularly in the moist highlands, and are pushing out indigenous plants. Offshore, fishing has seriously reduced native populations of lobsters, sea cucumbers, and other ocean species.

AFTER THE OIL SPILL

When oil began to leak from the *Jessica*, wildlife officials and volunteers rushed to the islands, hoping to prevent disaster. They knew that if significant numbers of plants and animals were to die, rare species would be forced closer to extinction. A U.S. Coast Guard team arrived to help pump oil out of the stricken tanker and into barges, but some 160,000 gallons (600,000 liters) of oil had already escaped into the water. Barriers were set up to keep the oil from coming ashore. Workers set up rescue stations to clean the oil from sea lions, birds, and other animals, expecting the worst.

Then, in a great stroke of luck, westward winds and ocean currents broke up the oil slicks and carried them away from San Cristóbal Island, lessening the impact of the spill. A few oil-drenched birds were the only direct casualties. Despite some concern that a residue of spilled bunker oil might still wreak havoc by poisoning the food chain, many wildlife experts expect the Galápagos ecosystem to fully recover within four years.

But overfishing, competition from alien species, and other dangers still threaten the Galápagos. Ecologists say that preserving the unique life-forms of these and other islands will require a concentrated effort involving habitat protection, predator control, rigorous policing of hunting and fishing, and captive-breeding programs.

Meanwhile, the half-submerged wreck of the *Jessica* lies off the coast of San Cristóbal, a vivid reminder of just how close the enchanted Ecuadorian archipelago came to environmental disaster.

The Dark Side of Light

by Joe Bower

Glitzy Las Vegas it's not. But the small city of Kalamazoo, Michigan, still puts on quite a light show. As night falls, thousands of lamps flicker, blink, pulsate, and shine. Incandescent, fluorescent, mercury vapor, metal halide, and halogen. White, red, blue, yellow, orange. They are all there in Kalamazoo. It is a sight, especially during the holidays. But if you are ever admiring the spectacle, you must appreciate the costs involved in staging it.

Leaving the lights on is more expensive than you would think. It not only costs a chunk of change, but it also takes a surprising toll on the environment. The proliferation of artificial lighting threatens wildlife, ruins habitat, fouls the air, squanders resources, and blocks our view of the heavens. No wonder the pervasive problem has come to be called light pollution.

Astronomers were the first to notice this problem. About 30 years ago, they began to grow frustrated as sky glow, the eerie radiance that emanates from settled areas and has spread with urban sprawl, began impairing their ability to see the stars.

Today, as few as 1 in 10 Americans live in areas where they can see the 2,500 or so stars that should be visible under normal nighttime conditions. In most big cities, you are

Artificial lighting—besides consuming energy—can have a great environmental impact. Many animals, for example, are subject to disrupted sleeping, feeding, and migration patterns as a result of light pollution.

Every year, thousands of amateur astronomers visit Breezy Hill, Vermont, one of the best sites in New England for stargazing. But light from a proposed prison could make the annual Stellafane festival a less-than-stellar affair.

lucky to glimpse a few dozen—on a good night. But light pollution isn't just an urban problem. In Springfield, Vermont, a controversy has erupted over the economically depressed town's decision to permit the construction of a prison; the lights from the site, it is feared, would mar the view from Breezy Hill, one of New England's best places for stargazing. Each year since 1926, thousands have flocked to Breezy Hill for a celebration of the stars called Stellafane. David Levy, an astronomer, has led the protest against the proposed prison. "Stellafane is a magical place, a sanctuary to the stars," he wrote in *Sky & Telescope* magazine.

DEATH BY COLLISION

Although light pollution's impact on stargazing is as clear as day, its effects on other environmental elements are just coming into focus. The evidence shows that artificial lighting has dire consequences for animal behavior, particularly on an animal's ability to navigate at night.

The hundreds of species of migrating birds that fly after the Sun sets, including most songbirds and many shorebirds, are prime examples. Normally they rely on constellations to guide them during their twice-yearly migrations. But scientists speculate that when the birds fly near urban areas, the bright lights short-circuit their steering sense. Numerous reports have documented birds flying off course toward lights on buildings, towers, lighthouses, even boats. "Both birds and insects demonstrate positive phototaxis," says Sidney Gauthreaux, a Clemson University, Clemson, South Carolina, biologist. "To put it simply, birds are attracted to light much like moths are to a flame. But the reasons are unclear. They may use it as a reference and home in on it." When birds suddenly reach the light's source, they often seem to become disoriented, confused, or blinded by the glare, which can be disastrous.

Birds may slam into windows, walls, floodlights, or even the ground. On the night of October 7, 1954, for instance, 50,000 birds were killed when they followed the beam of a guide light at Warner Robins Air Force Base in Georgia—straight into the ground. The problem is particularly acute when the weather is bad. On a rainy, foggy Labor Day weekend in 1981, more than 10,000 birds collided with the floodlit smokestacks at Ontario Hydro's Lennox generating station near Kingston. And on January 22, 1998, between 5,000 and 10,000 Lapland longspurs crashed into radio-transmission towers near Syracuse, Kansas.

Birds that are distracted by tower lights also may end up crashing into one another. "Around communication towers with constant lights, birds curve, circle, pause, and hover around the lights," Gauthreaux explains. They are apparently trying to orient their flight to the light, which they mistake for the Moon or a star. "Over time, there's a buildup of migrants [all trying to adjust their course], raising the possibility of hitting guylines or other birds."

Nobody is certain of the total number killed across North America. But Michael Mesure of the Fatal Light Awareness Program (FLAP), a Toronto, Canada, organization working to publicize the problem, estimates that at least 100 million birds are killed annually by human-made structures. "More birds die each year through collisions than died in the *Exxon Valdez* spill," he says. A tall building in the path of a migration can claim hundreds of lives. One example: from 1982 to 1996, no fewer than 1,500 migrating birds smacked headlong into Chicago's McCormick Place Exposition Center.

BIRDS FACE WORST FATE

Although few nocturnal migrants seem immune to light's dark side—for example, dead or injured members of 141 different bird species have been found at McCormick Place—songbirds may be most at risk, Mesure says, because they fly at low altitudes dominated by artificial light.

Passerines are not the only order of birds waylaid by lights. The Newell's shearwater, an endangered Hawaiian seabird, is particularly vulnerable. After their parents abandon their cliffside nests in October and November, fledglings make their first flights by relying on their innate attraction to light to guide them. Normally, because of the light's reflection on water, they fly out to sea, toward the horizon. But when the Moon is neither full nor visible, many of the shearwaters instead glide toward lights in seaside resorts and towns. Disoriented, hundreds crash into structures or drop from the sky. In 1998, volunteers gathered 819 shearwaters on the island of Kauai. Most were exhausted or injured, though, fortunately, only 77 died.

A FATAL ATTRACTION

Other animals are threatened by light pollution, too. Hatchlings of at least five sea-turtle species found in Florida rely on an instinctive attraction to light to guide them to water. But lights on or near the beach can confuse the turtles and cause them to head in the wrong direction. Scientists have seen hatchlings cross parking lots, streets, and yards—transfixed by shining streetlights or porch lights. "Their reliance on light is so strong that they'll continue heading to a light source, even if it's an abandoned fire that burns them alive," says Blair Witherington, scientist at the Florida Marine Research Institute (FMRI), headquartered in St. Petersburg, who studies sea turtles. Disoriented hatchlings usually die from exhaus-

Loggerhead sea turtle hatchlings normally crawl from the sand to the water. These days, city lights are likely to lead them in the wrong direction.

A satellite view of the continental United States suggests that few areas remain entirely free of congestion and urban sprawl—or from the unnatural glow that accompanies the country's ever-expanding metropolitan areas.

tion, dehydration, or predation. Many others are simply squashed by passing cars.

Insects cannot seem to resist this fatal attraction either. Most people know that moths find lights irresistible. But what they may not realize is that the energy moths expend in this way can cost females the chance to attract a mate. What's more, it can interfere with locating prime spots to lay their eggs, thus giving larvae inadequate conditions to develop, according to Michael Collins, a lepidopterist at the Carnegie Museum of Natural History, Pittsburgh. Some entomologists speculate that the proliferation of outdoor lights has contributed to the decline of numerous saturniid-moth species in the northeastern United States.

INTERNAL CLOCKS GO HAYWIRE

Visual orientation is just one sense disrupted by artificial light, though it probably isn't the only one, says Meredith West, a professor at Indiana University, Bloomington, specializing in avian development. Studies of animals raised in controlled settings, such as laboratories and poultry farms, indicate that lighting can affect certain "photoperiodic" behavior, including foraging and reproduction. "Animals are very sensitive to light," West says. "Lighting is a powerful stimulus on behavior. If there's enough of it, it can make them act in ways they wouldn't normally." If enough light is present—say, in a well-lit neighborhood—it's possible that animals living there would be stimulated to act as they do during longer days. Overexposure to light may explain reports from English researchers about robins singing at night if there are streetlights in their territories, or why some birds build nests during the fall instead of spring: their internal clocks have gone haywire.

Adult female sea turtles will not emerge from the water to nest and lay eggs on beaches that are bathed in artificial light. Many behaviors influenced by changing light—from night to day and the seasonal increases of longer days—involve hormones. "Anything that alters the hormonal system will bring enormous changes," West says. "Hormones regulate growth and immune functions. But they're not produced all the time. If they don't shut down, you overload the body. It can't get rid of them. Hormones are toxic in the wrong amounts." Indeed, a 1998 study at the Mary Imogene Bassett Research Institute in Cooperstown, New York, found that cancerous liver cells in lab rats grew rapidly when the rats were constantly exposed to light.

Even if wildlife were able to ignore direct sources of light, lighting's impact on the environment would still be unavoidable. Burning coal and oil, according to the U.S. Environmental Protection Agency (EPA), generates most of the electricity for lights. The process is a dirty one that each year spews out billions of tons of carbon dioxide (CO_2), a greenhouse gas; sulfur dioxide (SO_2), an ingredient of acid rain; and nitrogen oxides (NO_X) which cause smog. Sadly, much of this atmospheric pollution is produced for nothing. "One-third of our lighting is wasted because it shines upward or sideways, illuminating nothing but the bottoms of birds and airplanes," says David L. Crawford of the International Dark-Sky Association (IDA), a 10-year-old anti-light-pollution group based in Tucson, Arizona. Every year, this waste squanders the equivalent of 8.2 million tons of coal or 30 million barrels of oil.

BRIGHTER IS NOT BETTER

How did we reach this point? A big reason is a push toward overlighting. "People think brighter is better," says Crawford. To lure customers, retailers plug in bigger, brighter signs and entrance lights. In commercial buildings, more electricity is now used for lighting than anything else, even computers or air-conditioning. Urban sprawl has increased the number of lights on streets, billboards, and buildings. Meanwhile, homes are getting bigger and using more electricity. The average single-family home currently consumes 1,500 kilowatt-hours a year for lighting—40 percent more than it did in 1970. To produce that much electricity, power plants emit more than a ton of CO_2, 13 pounds (6 kilograms) of SO_2, and 8 pounds (4 kilograms) of NO_X. "Most people are in the dark about lights," Crawford says. "There's a total lack of awareness" of the consequences of lighting.

Of course, using less energy would reduce emissions. In addition, research in Toronto and Washington, D.C., shows that when building lights are dimmed or turned off, the number of fatally attracted birds drops dramatically. "If you have a tower without lights, you'll cause bird collisions, but at least you won't be attracting more birds to it," Gauthreaux says.

ENLIGHTENING THE PUBLIC

The challenge for the government and environmental groups is to, no pun intended, enlighten people. The EPA has created an energy-saving program, Energy Star, to help companies and residents reduce lighting use. Several manufacturers have begun producing energy-efficient lights and appliances. FLAP launched a 12-step bird-friendly program that encourages buildings to turn down lights during migrations; it has been adopted at 100 buildings in downtown Toronto since 1997. FLAP organizers are leading similar efforts to raise awareness in Chicago and New York City. And educational drives to publicize the impact of light on turtle hatchlings and seabird fledglings are now being sponsored by the National Park Service in Hawaii and by county governments in Florida. Some cities, including Tucson and Miami, are replacing inefficient streetlights with ones designed to focus the beam more sharply. In addition, last August, two workshops at the American Ornithologists' Union conference explored light pollution's impact on birds.

Meanwhile, lawmakers in hundreds of communities have passed ordinances that restrict lighting types, power, and use. Recently, Texas and New Mexico became the fourth and fifth states (along with Arizona, Connecticut, and Maine) to implement a statewide light-restriction program. The ordinances vary in scope from banning certain types of streetlights or limiting their wattage to shielding security lights. Similar actions are being considered in other states.

Any dark-sky proponent will admit that the national impact of these programs is minimal. But Crawford of the International Dark-Sky Association believes that they're a good start. "I liken lighting to smoking," he says. "All the evidence shows it's bad. But we have to educate people about the consequences. Smoking bans are coming quickly now. But the education that brought them about took a long time."

LAKE VOSTOK:

PROBING FOR LIFE BENEATH ANTARCTIC ICE

by Richard Stone

Imagine for a moment that you are a strange device called a cryobot. You are a glint on a featureless plain of snow. A feeble summer Sun glazes the drifts, nudging temperatures to the low 40s—below zero. The bone-dry air here at the coldest spot on Earth doesn't bother your steel skin or the companion nestled inside your belly.

Nor does the dazzling glare from the endless white affect you, although a human being without sunglasses would go snow-blind in only a few hours' time.

You plunge into a hole in the ice sheet drilled by boiling water, and sink through the rapidly cooling water nearly 2.5 miles (4 kilometers) to the shaft's bottom, where the pressure is a crushing 366 times that at sea level. In a final rite of purification in the utter darkness, you rinse your body in hydrogen peroxide to kill any surface or ice-dwelling microbes that might have hung on for the ride down. A heater in your nose cone switches on, and you start thawing your way down the homestretch.

The fragile and frigid depths of Lake Vostok in Antarctica might someday be explored by a cryobot, an unmanned probe still in the planning stages. This hostile environment may mirror the icy oceans that astronomers think may exist on Jupiter's moon, Europa.

Images of microbes in core samples of ice taken from Lake Vostok have given scientists reason to expect even more startling discoveries in the water itself.

For the final 600 feet (180 meters) or so, the path is glassy smooth, like November ice on a New England lake. As the shaft above freezes, sealing your icy grave, you at last encounter slush, then, a little farther on, water—you've burrowed all the way through the thick ice blanket covering the Antarctic continent. Your cargo door opens, and your companion eases out. A smaller probe, called a hydrobot, revs up its propeller and disappears into the gloom on a mission to explore one of our planet's last great virgin territories: Lake Vostok.

IMMEASURABLE BURIED SECRETS

Isolated from the rest of the world for longer than humankind has walked Earth, Lake Vostok's dark and gloomy depths have cast a come-hither spell ever since the lake's true proportions—roughly half the area of Lake Ontario—were reported four years ago. The lake does not freeze solid because of heat rising from Earth's interior. For biologists, Vostok beckons with the promise of organisms possessing untold strategies for surviving in a lightless crypt. Paleontologists, meanwhile, would love to get their hands on the thick muck presumed to coat Vostok's bottom, which might encase fossils of undescribed life-forms that roamed a continent once balmy enough for dinosaur life. Climatologists might analyze the lake's sediments for clues to Antarctica's climate before it became

the frigid wasteland it is today, while cosmologists could mine the lake floor for a wealth of extraterrestrial particles that have rained on Antarctica through the eons and have been dumped by the ice sheet into Vostok's basin. Taking a dip in this wintry wonderland, says Chris Rapley, director of the British Antarctic Survey, "is one of the most high-profile and interesting projects of the next decade."

A PROVING GROUND FOR EUROPA?

A voyage to Vostok could also be a big step toward a discovery that, if it were to happen, would surely rank among the greatest of all time: finding life elsewhere in our solar system. Bearing an uncanny resemblance to Vostok is the Jovian moon Europa, which recent spacecraft images suggest is covered by an ocean about 60 miles (100 kilometers) deep (far deeper than any on Earth), and topped by a rind of ice that in spots could be less than 6 miles (10 kilometers) thick. If life arose in Earth's primordial ocean, could it not then have also arisen—or be on the verge of doing so—in Europa's? Lake Vostok could serve as a proving ground for probes designed to explore Europa without spiking the broth with microbial ingredients from our own planet.

Now scientists around the world are joining forces to blaze a trail to the mysterious lake, despite some formidable hurdles. There are, for example, the delicate matters of lining up millions of dollars from several countries and establishing a hierarchy to oversee the project, as well as developing the technology to even get there—technology that also must protect Vostok's pristine waters from contamination.

Yet those captivated by the lake's allure foresee no insurmountable obstacles. And they are especially tantalized by hot new evidence that life does exist in Vostok: images of microbes in refrozen lake water taken from a core sample. According to Richard Hoover, an astrobiologist who leads the search for evidence of microbial life beyond Earth at the National Aeronautics and Space Administration's (NASA's) Marshall Space Flight Center in Huntsville, Alabama, "We're seeing things we've never seen before."

Putting Vostok on the Map

At first, nobody paid attention to hints that a behemoth lay beneath the ice. In 1960, Soviet pilot R.V. Robinson described remarkably flat stretches of the East Antarctic ice sheet, discernible only from the air, near a remote Soviet outpost called Vostok Station. He called these indentions "lakes." A decade later, British airborne radio surveys of the ice sheet's thickness proved the flier right, revealing mirrorlike reflections that were interpreted as pools of water sandwiched between the ice sheet and the bedrock. These and later soundings have pinpointed at least 76 subglacial lakes in Antarctica, the largest by far extending under Vostok Station. After analyzing all the older studies, along with newer satellite sensing data, British and Russian scientists published a report in 1996 describing Lake Vostok as a body of freshwater much longer than it is wide, covering somewhere between 3,900 and 5,400 square miles (10,000 and 14,000 square kilometers) and plunging to a depth of 1,600 feet (500 meters) or more under the research station.

As news broke of the biggest geographic feature discovered on Earth in the 20th century, the Galileo spacecraft was beaming back images of an icy orb fractured in crisscrossing patterns that resemble ice floes in the Arctic Ocean. The tortured surface of Jupiter's moon Europa is shaped by what is presumably an ocean below—but the images and other data do not reveal how much of that ocean is liquid versus ice. Whatever it is must taste salty: the wavelengths of infrared light absorbed by the ice suggest that it is laced with sodium carbonate and magnesium sulfate. "This is the stuff that appears to constitute the brine in the Europan ocean," says Frank Carsey, an Earth scientist with NASA's Jet Propulsion Laboratory (JPL) in Pasadena, California.

On the Road to Europa

A polar oceanographer himself, Carsey was the go-to person for JPL engineer Joan Horvath, who in 1996 sought his advice on how a spacecraft might puncture Europa's icy crust. It didn't take long for the two to focus on Lake Vostok. Carsey seized on the idea of using Vostok as a parallel for a Europa mis-

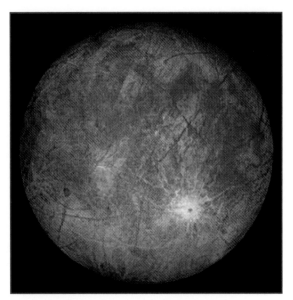

Europa, Jupiter's ice-covered satellite, may have an ocean roiling beneath its rather barren crust. But how much of this ocean is liquid—or frozen solid?

sion. That fall, he made a pitch for a project involving players from three NASA fiefdoms: the space, Earth science, and technology divisions. He did not know that just the day before, NASA administrator Dan Goldin had lambasted Earth-science personnel for not reaching out to their space colleagues. As Carsey said later, "My timing was impeccable."

Given the green light to draft a Vostok strategy, Carsey and Horvath in 1997 opted in favor of a thermal probe, or cryobot. The idea is that upon reaching the water beneath the ice on Lake Vostok, the cryobot would release a hydrobot equipped with miniature sensing instruments.

The NASA scientists are not the only ones drawn to the siren call of Vostok. In recent months, a chorus has risen for a concerted effort to get to know the lake and whatever creatures might lurk there. Not surprisingly, some of the most eager voices are coming from Russia, where scientists view the lake's exploration as a fitting new endeavor for the station.

The Pole of Cold

Vostok has a legendary reputation. Since Soviet scientists established this icy toehold at the south geomagnetic pole in 1957, crews have manned the station year-round, shuttering it for only a few seasons under dire circumstances. Since then, Vostok has earned another title: the pole of cold. Situated in a region that probably hasn't seen the mercury rise above 0° F (–18° C) for several million years, the station set a record low for Earth's surface: –128° F (–88° C) on July 21, 1983. The station (as was a spacecraft that carried Yuri Gagarin, the first man in space) is named after the flagship of Russian explorer Fabian Gottlieb von Bellingshausen, who the Russians proudly claim was the first person ever to glimpse Antarctica, on January 27, 1820.

Flying to Vostok from the American McMurdo Station on the coast is like being whisked by helicopter from Portland, Oregon, to the top of Mount Hood: because the station is perched on a bulge on the ice sheet nearly 11,500 feet (3,500 meters) above sea level, most newcomers experience mild altitude sickness—numbing fatigue and sharp headaches—for their first day or two.

The weather and tales of hardship have given the *Vostochniki*—those who work through the long, dark winter there—a reputation for perseverance. It is a land where it takes phenomenally harrowing experiences to stand out among the everyday risks posed by whiteouts, body-swallowing crevasses, and, of course, constant cold. A fire in April 1982 knocked out power to the station, killing a mechanic and forcing the rest of the station's crew to spend two dark weeks in a small room, barely heated by an oil stove, until emergency generators could be brought on-line. "The team barely survived," says Vladimir Papitashvili at the University of Michigan, who worked at Vostok the following year.

RECORDING AND COLLECTING DATA

The scientific exploits, too, are compelling, and include a masterpiece: a record of Antarctic climate over the past 420,000 years, interpreted from carbon dioxide and other gases trapped in the ice. Drilling into the ice sheet, which piles up at a rate of about 1 inch (3 centimeters) a year at Vostok, is like turning back the clock—the deeper the ice retrieved, the older it is.

At the station, in a cavern hewn from the ice, Russian climatologists maintain an unusual library: pieces of the core itself.

Alexandr Krassilev plucks what at first looks like a rolled newspaper wrapped in plastic from a wall lined with hundreds of cardboard cubbyholes. "This is some of the oldest ice on the planet," says Krassilev, cradling the precious opaque log in a hand heavily mittened against the chamber's constant –67° F (–55° C). Krassilev, a drilling engineer from the St. Petersburg Mining Institute, offers his visitors a chance to hold this valuable key to Earth's past. "Don't drop it," he says lightly, his breath freezing into twinkling diamond dust that drifts slowly to the packed-snow floor.

INSIDE THE DECAYING STATION

A Lake Vostok mission comes at a critical time for the aging, dilapidated station. Its only landmarks are the 32-foot (10-meter)-tall drilling tower clad in peach-colored sheet metal, and a haphazard array of radio antennas and machinery in various states of disarray. The inhabited section of the station, says Papitashvili, is "almost completely covered by snow." The crew has abandoned some buildings that are now buried in the drifts. Station entrances have triple doors to retain heat, but fit loosely in the door frames. Inside, the cramped labs double as living quarters, heated by hazardous-looking electric radiators. An artificial Christmas tree with scraggly trimmings perches on an unplugged microwave oven in the mess hall. The only midafternoon diner is a Russian technician hunched over borscht, black bread, and compote. An exercise bike and a folded Ping-Pong table gather dust in a corner behind him.

TRASH OR TREASURE?

In February 1998, the drilling ceased 2.2 miles (4 kilometers) into the ice, about 400 feet (122 meters) above the lake's surface. At these depths, the freshwater ice forms large, clear crystals—useless to climatologists, but a potential gold mine for biologists, as this ice is lake water that has frozen to the bottom of the ice sheet. Scientists who have laid their hands on this essence of Vostok have watched a new world unfold before their eyes. "We're looking at microorganisms essentially as they're coming out of the ice,"

Vostok's core samples are keys to Earth's past. The deeper the sample's origin, the older its ice—a biological gold mine. "We're looking at microorganisms essentially as they're coming out of the ice," says Richard Hoover (above).

says Richard Hoover. With Sabit Abyzov of the Institute of Microbiology in Moscow, he has used an electron microscope to image white filaments that are hundreds of microns in length, just visible to the human eye. Hoover speculates they may be strands of a microbial mat that was somehow dislodged from the lake floor. "It could have floated upward and come to rest against the ice-covered roof," he says.

Also getting a piece of the action last year was John Priscu of Montana State University in Billings. Working with a section of ice drawn up from near the bottom of the borehole, Priscu's group has found rod-shaped bacteria. DNA analyses point to several kinds of bacteria in the lake ice. If these bacteria are alive in the lake, Priscu says, "there's plenty of food down there." His group has measured about as much dissolved organic carbon in the ice sample as is found in an average North American lake.

How Such a Lake Came to Be

Tied to the question of what might survive in it is the riddle of Lake Vostok's origins. The land around the station has long been thought to be a stable region of crust, called a craton. That suggests the lake bed was scoured out by glaciers, much like Lake Ontario was during the last ice age.

Cratons can develop rifts or depressions, however. Lake Vostok's narrow, crescent shape and great depth are reminiscent of Lake Malawi, which fills a basin in a rift valley in East Africa. Making a stronger case for rifting are the mysterious Gamburtsev Mountains. Geologists have no indisputable theory for the origins of the mountain patch, which juts anomalously from the otherwise flat terrain. Ancient rifting is as good an explanation as any. And if the Gamburtsevs are still growing, as some scientists speculate that they are, it would lend credence to a recent hypothesis by Robin Bell at Columbia University's Lamont-Doherty Earth Observatory. Bell thinks that rifting is still occurring even today. This, she says, could explain three moderate earthquakes in the past century that struck within 100 miles (160 kilometers) of Lake Vostok.

An active rift would provide a vital ingredient for life. The energy thrusting the Gamburtsev Range upward must have melted portions of underlying crust and heated the lake bed, perhaps nurturing unique ecosystems around hot geothermal vents—like those that sustain life independent of sunlight at the bottom of the Pacific.

Comprehending such survival strategies would influence a mission to search for organisms in Europa's ocean, which some

Russia's Vostok Station is almost completely covered with snow. The most conspicuous feature at the site is the 32-foot-tall drilling tower (facing page).

NASA scientists hope will be launched in the next decade. An ocean alone is insufficient for known life—some form of energy must trickle into the system. It's unlikely that sunlight, necessary for plant life on Earth, can penetrate Europa's ice cover. More likely, the energy comes from gravity. Specifically, the solid material of Europa flexes as the moon moves closer to and then farther from Jupiter as it travels in an elliptical orbit. The flexing would generate heat. And Europan microbes will have figured out how to tap such energy sources.

DETECTING LIFE UNDER THE ICE

Whether scientists find clues to Europa's life in the most forlorn lake on Earth will depend on what they search for. Retrieving a sterile sample from under the ice sheet is an expensive and complicated proposition, so the first experiments will be done with remote instruments that transmit data by radio or by cable to the surface. One obvious experiment is to measure the pulse of life—metabolic activity—by tracing the incorporation of radioactive carbon into biological molecules. Other instruments could count cell numbers or measure nucleic acids, the raw stuff of DNA molecules. Any assay must be designed to spot life-forms that would prefer to remain anonymous.

One intriguing possibility is that Lake Vostok became an arena for a contest of survival of the fittest. Before icing over, the lake might have supported a thriving ecosystem with many species of microorganisms, plants, and fish. "Life was very abundant on Earth when Vostok formed, so there is no doubt that things should have been in, on, or around the lake site from its genesis as an ice-covered lake," says Ken Nealson, a biologist at JPL. But as ice piled higher, obscuring the Sun and choking off photosynthesis, the organisms depleted the remaining oxygen—bringing on something akin to a famine in Vostok. The grittiest oxygen-consuming bacterium, the last of its kind, could be clinging to life even today.

PROTECTING THE LAKE'S ECOSYSTEM

Whether Vostok is home to a sole survivor or to many novel microbes, it would be a disaster to upset the lake's delicate balance by introducing surface organisms. True, microbes are blown in from distant lands all the time; much of the dust that has settled on the Antarctic ice sheet originated in Patagonia, the region between the Andes and the Atlantic in southern South America.

Snow that fell on the ice above Vostok half a million years ago, freighted with Patagonian dust perhaps, is just now melting into the lake—where it releases microbial cargo crushed by the accumulations above. Any organism that survives this punishing passage has earned a chance to eke out an existence in Vostok. On the other hand, microbes that sneak aboard a cryobot—either at the surface or on the way down—could irrevocably alter whatever fragile web of life exists down there.

For this reason, a Vostok mission has drawn the attention of groups that are not convinced that the benefits of probing the lake outweigh the risks to a possible ecosystem. "There's little justification for this project," contends Ricardo Roura, a geologist by training who lobbies for environmental protection on behalf of the Antarctic and Southern Ocean Coalition (ASOC). His organization argues that any probe sent down must be completely sterile. "Science does not exist in isolation of environmental protection," he says.

That message is not lost on scientists, says Carsey. "We fully appreciate that contamination is bad science," he says. Thus, a daunting task for JPL engineers is to devise a method of sterilizing a probe after it has passed through much of the ice sheet, but before it penetrates the lake itself. One idea is to equip a probe with a powerful ultraviolet light for frying any lingering life-forms. Another is to have it spritz itself with sterilizing agents such as hydrogen peroxide, which rips into cell membranes, destroying any microbial life it contacts. After the carnage, all that is left is water, oxygen, and the remains of shattered biomolecules.

DRUMMING UP RESEARCH DOLLARS
So far, however, he and his team have struggled to find funding for their project. As they wait for government dollars to materialize, they have held discussions with drug companies—"they would pay millions to get ahold of some lake water," Carsey says—and entertainment companies that might like to film a mission to the lake or glean profits from publicizing the adventure. The latter category of potential bedfellows strikes some people at NASA as strange, Carsey admits.

But Carsey no longer must beat the scientific drum on his own. A meeting in Cambridge, England, last fall whipped up enough interest for an international team to start putting together a game plan for a Vostok mission as early as 2005. "It's an extremely difficult mission for any one country to mount on its own," says Erick Chiang of the National Science Foundation (NSF). That's why some say it might be wise to slip into a smaller subglacial lake first. Carsey, however, argues that a better dress rehearsal would be to send a cryobot through an ice shelf and into the Ross Sea off Antarctica. If the sterilization equipment were to fail there, he says, contamination wouldn't be a big deal. "It's inappropriate for us to put Lake Vostok on some kind of pedestal and declare one of the other subglacial lakes a pointless environment that we can mess up," he says.

BRIDGING THE PAST AND THE FUTURE
As scientists chart a course to the once-undiscovered lake, their next indirect glimpse could come from a project that would bridge the past and the future of Vostok Station. For more than a quarter of a century, Russian scientists have drilled into the ice to sample gas bubbles hinting at what the region's climate was like over the millennia. The drilling stopped about 400 feet (120 meters) above Lake Vostok to prevent the kerosene, which keeps the borehole open, from contaminating the waters below. Some scientists have talked about lowering a laser to the bottom of the borehole, where it would shoot a beam of light through the final stretch of ice. Reflections could unmask any biomolecules floating in Lake Vostok—offering a peek at the secret inhabitants of a lost world.

Creative Destruction

by Calvin Lieberman

A century ago, when the age of the automobile was just beginning, few people worried about what would happen when cars wore out. After all, there were plenty of junkyards, where horse carts and carriages and the rest of premotorized America ended their days. Most people probably figured that old automobiles would be taken apart and sold for scrap, just like their predecessors. The problem, if it was a problem, would have been small in any case, since autos were still a luxury item with limited sales.

But sometime around 1927, when Ford sold its 15 millionth Model T, Americans began to notice that an awful lot of worn-out auto bodies were accumulating on the landscape. Some were dumped in rivers or lakes; others were put in landfills or abandoned mines or quarries; but most were simply piled up in unsightly heaps. More cars were now being sold than ever before, and they tended to be bigger and heavier than the older models. The scrap market absorbed some of the bodies, but far from all. Something had to be done.

Each day, untold millions of automobiles clog America's roads. Also each day, untold thousands of worn-out and abandoned cars become part of the vast U.S. auto-scrap industry—surprisingly to some, one of the most successful recycling efforts in history.

DISMANTLING THE HULK

In scrapyards, auto wreckers were using the same basic disposal process they would follow for most of the 20th century. First, they removed salable parts—engines, transmissions, batteries, wheels, and some nonferrous die-cast components, such as copper radiators. Next, the glass was smashed and sent to a landfill. What was left of the hulk—large amounts of upholstery, wood, and rubber—was burned. Any leftover parts were usually cut up and sold as scrap.

The laborious process left behind dreadful eyesores and polluted the air and water. Moreover, since the car-wrecking business was dispersed and labor-intensive, it could easily turn unprofitable when scrap-metal prices dropped. With each downturn in the market, car bodies piled up higher and higher. Auto wreckers and scrapyards sometimes charged a fee to accept cars, leading frustrated owners to simply abandon their jalopies in the streets.

The first step toward large-scale, systematic recycling of cars came in the 1930s. As before, the most salable components were salvaged. Glass, cushions, and other easily dismantled items were stripped, and what remained was burned. But now, instead of being cut up, the hulk was crushed into a "bundle"—a compact block that might weigh half a ton to a ton or more. Some of these blocks were sold to steelmakers, who mixed them with raw iron in their furnaces. Using the open-hearth process, which was then prevalent, it took six to eight hours to process a batch of steel. During this time, most of the nonmetallic impurities either went up the smokestack or were removed in the form of a by-product called slag.

TAINTED SCRAP

A typical pre–World War II steel mill used 40 to 60 percent scrap, but most of it came from sources other than cars. Many steelmakers refused to accept automotive scrap because of its high levels of copper, which is present in a car's wiring, fuel lines, and instruments. Removing the copper before compacting was too expensive, so automotive bundles had to be sold at the low end of the scrap market.

During this era, the Ford Motor Company went into the car-disposal business. By paying $20 for each old car traded in toward one of its new models, the company also promoted new sales. Dealers shipped the bodies to Detroit, where Ford had engaged the German firm of Logemann to build the world's largest automobile baler. This enormous machine could crush an entire automobile, and the remnant bales were fed into an open-hearth furnace. Unfortunately, the baling plant could not reduce the nonmetallic components to acceptable levels, so the undertaking was abandoned after six months. Ford eventually sold the baler to the Proler Steel Corporation of Houston, Texas, which persuaded Lone Star Steel to modify its furnace to accept the baler's output.

During the 1950s, as post–World War II cars began to be replaced, several factors combined to make bundled cars even less attractive to steelmakers. Design changes increased the nonmetallic components and nonferrous metals in cars. Particularly troublesome were lead, chromium (in vogue then as a decorative element), and tin (used for repairing dents). Even in small amounts, these elements can seriously alter steel's performance. At the same time, the hearth process was mostly phased out and replaced by the oxygen-furnace method. In contrast to the open hearth's slow simmer, a basic oxygen furnace processes a batch of steel in less than an hour.

Now steelmakers had less time to remove more impurities from automotive scrap. The biggest problem involved contaminants that lay buried deep inside a densely compacted scrap bundle. For this and other reasons, most basic oxygen furnaces in the 1950s and 1960s used only 10 to 35 percent scrap. Faced with a rapidly shrinking market, the scrap industry grew desperate for ways to separate the steel from the rest of a car's body, purify it, and break it into small pieces so that it would melt more readily.

WISER SIZERS

Another innovation that lent urgency to the problem was more positive for scrap dealers: the advent of hydraulic "auto sizers" small enough to be mounted on trailers. These units flattened car hulks down to a manageable size for hauling, so that a single trailer could transport as much as 10 tons of scrap. Auto sizers allowed a dealer to cover a circuit of auto wreckers and salvage yards, collecting hulks for recycling at a large, central

Henry Ford's mass-produced Model T (above, left) enabled more people than ever before to own cars. Unfortunately, the Model T's limited life span meant that millions of rusting hulks were soon part of the landscape.

facility. Scrap processors were pleased with these advantages. However, precrushing hulks made it even more difficult to remove contaminants before processing, so it became all the more important to find ways of removing them afterward.

To meet this frustrating challenge, the scrap industry developed new equipment and technology. For example, a 1960s Japanese invention baked a car hulk rotisserie-style at successively higher temperatures to melt out different metals. A similar scheme was invented by Harris Press & Shear of Cordele, Georgia, but neither of these processes was cost-effective.

When regulations banned the open incineration of scrap automobiles, pro-

cessors switched to enclosed furnaces with emission controls that greatly reduced the smoke problem. Even so, incinerating automobile hulks was a risky business. The combination of paint, plastics, aluminum, and other materials that burned or evaporated turned the exhaust into a witch's brew. The need was clear for a solution that did not require incineration.

Industry leaders began to recognize the potential of shredding machines that would cut scrap into pieces and separate out the steel. The first ones had been invented decades earlier as specialty items to serve the copper-production market. When dealing with low-grade ores, the most efficient way to extract the copper is to leach it out with acid and then add iron to the solution. The iron displaces the copper, causing it to precipitate. This method of extraction is also used to draw out small concentrations of copper from water that has been used for washing and for processing ore.

Scrap is the usual source of iron for this process. Clearly, the greater the surface area of the scrap, the more effective it will be. So in the 1920s, a Los Angeles firm, L.A. By-Products, developed machines that would tear chunks of scrap steel—from any source, not just auto bodies—into smaller pieces. Tin-coated steel cans were the most common feedstock.

Besides serving copper processors, L.A. By-Products also sold shredded scrap to steelmakers. Since the open-hearth method still dominated, ease of melting was not a priority, and the shredded pieces were often compressed back into bundles for transport. But thanks to the company's pioneering work in magnetically separating ferrous from nonferrous material, these bundles were purer than those made from untreated car hulks. The market for such scrap was still

In a typical 1920s auto graveyard (above), rusty frames were abandoned after tires, engines, batteries, and other valuable parts were removed. Sprawling eyesores, junkyards were reason enough to develop systematic recycling.

small, and since cars were not the only source of raw material for shredding, there was no reason to build a machine that could process entire cars in one shot. Instead, they still had to be cut up first.

Except for a brief flurry of interest during World War II, shredding remained a minor corner of the scrap industry. As the postwar building boom kept demand for steel high, even small dealers found a ready market for minimally processed scrap through the mid-1950s. But the good times came to an end with the 1957–58 recession. As automobile hulks piled up and the shift to basic oxygen furnaces continued, a few scrap processors began to appreciate the possibilities of shredder technology.

The pioneer was Proler Steel Corporation, the same company that had earlier bought Ford's surplus auto baler. Its chairman, Israel Proler, had learned shredding at L.A. By-Products as part of a wartime government assignment. Building on that experience, he and his brother Sam designed a shredder specifically to serve the steelmaking industry, one that would turn car bodies into scrap suitable for basic oxygen furnaces. In 1958, the company opened its first shredding plant, and the innovative machine remained hidden behind thick steel walls to prevent industrial espionage.

Proler patented the revolutionary shredder. The new machine used a modified hammer mill—the type that crushed rocks

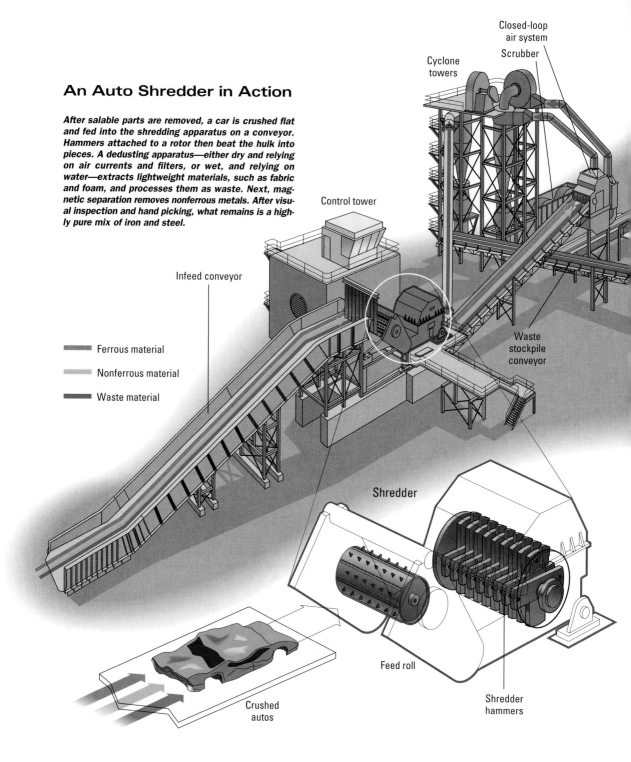

An Auto Shredder in Action

After salable parts are removed, a car is crushed flat and fed into the shredding apparatus on a conveyor. Hammers attached to a rotor then beat the hulk into pieces. A dedusting apparatus—either dry and relying on air currents and filters, or wet, and relying on water—extracts lightweight materials, such as fabric and foam, and processes them as waste. Next, magnetic separation removes nonferrous metals. After visual inspection and hand picking, what remains is a highly pure mix of iron and steel.

Closed-loop air system

Scrubber

Cyclone towers

Control tower

Infeed conveyor

Waste stockpile conveyor

Ferrous material

Nonferrous material

Waste material

Shredder

Feed roll

Shredder hammers

Crushed autos

in quarries—to tear the cars apart, and magnetic and other methods to separate the steel. Proler claimed his scrap would come out of the shredder in convenient, fist-sized, 1-pound (0.45-kilogram) pieces. But it was 90 percent steel, as opposed to regular bundled automobile scrap, which contained only 65 to 80 percent. Proler was already selling "Prolerized" scrap to Armco Steel of Houston for $8 to $10 a ton more than conventional scrap. Other scrap processors with their own technology flocked to the market.

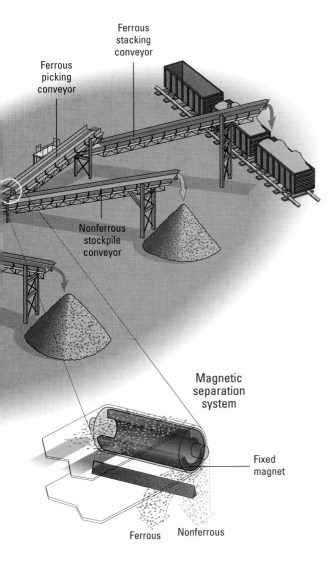

Ferrous stacking conveyor

Ferrous picking conveyor

Nonferrous stockpile conveyor

Magnetic separation system

Fixed magnet

Ferrous Nonferrous

plate as much as 4 inches (10 centimeters) thick. The machinery weighs a total of several hundred tons, and its cost may run into the tens of millions of dollars. Supplemental equipment includes magnetic separators, air knives, cyclones, trommels, cranes, and other accessories. Additional millions must be spent on noise abatement, waste treatment, antivibration, and other environmental-compliance measures.

BEAT TO SHREDS

Before an auto body enters the shredder, salable parts are removed, its fluids are drained, and the interior and trunk are inspected to see if any irregular items (especially tires and lead batteries) have been left there. The hulk is then flattened and fed into the shredding apparatus on a conveyor. Inside, many hammers (several dozen in the larger models) attached to a rotor beat the hulk into pieces against a breaker bar or grates. The rotor, which can weigh 25 tons or more, typically turns at several hundred revolutions per minute. The banging continues until the pieces are small enough to fall through a grating. The parts that perform the shredding are made of especially tough alloy steel, but even so, a shredder will typically lose a total of 0.5 pound (0.23 kilogram) off its hammers with each car that is put through the process.

As a car is being shredded, a dedusting apparatus extracts smoke and small particles of dirt and other nonmetallic components. This apparatus may be either dry (relying on air currents and filters) or wet (spraying in water to precipitate the dust). An operator monitors the entire shredding process to see that it is running smoothly. If the main rotor jams, its direction can be reversed, and if a large, unshreddable piece appears, it can be manually ejected. Operators usually rely on sound to alert them when something goes wrong during the process.

REDUCED TO FLUFF

After the car has been reduced to pieces of manageable size, the next step is to separate the ferrous portion from the nonferrous metals and nonmetallic material. Some of the nonmetallic portion will already have

THE TECH SPECS

Shredding technology can be applied to any kind of scrap, but by far its biggest source today is automobiles. A successful automobile shredder must do three things: reduce a huge hulk of steel—often consisting of high-strength alloys, as in engine blocks and axles—to small pieces; separate the ferrous metal from the nonferrous; and remove the small metallic fragments, known as fines, from the residue. Other fragments include plastics, rubber, foam, fabric, wood, insulation, glass, and dirt. A typical shredding system might be 1,000 feet (305 meters) long and cover 1 acre (0.4 hectare) or more. The shredder's housing and the removable liners in the main shredding area are made of steel come off as dust, and most of the rest can be extracted with blasts of air that leave the metal behind. The steel is magnetically separated from the rest of the scrap and diverted to a conveyor belt, where workers visually inspect it and pick out nonmetallic and nonferrous pieces that have slipped through. Copper, often in the form of wiring entangled with the steel, is of particular concern, since most steel mills require a copper content well under 0.5 percent in their scrap.

The majority of the materials left behind—known collectively as auto-shredder residue (ASR), or "fluff"—is landfilled. A typical composition might be 33 percent fabric and batting; 22 percent plastic; 20 percent sponge and foam; 19 percent glass, sand, and dirt; and 6 percent small-mesh metal fragments (mostly brass and zinc). Over the past three decades, much work has been done in salvaging as many useful components as possible from ASR. These effective methods take advantage of the different properties of the various components, including size, density, melting point, and coefficient of friction.

SHIFTING DIRECTION
A unique approach to separating the wheat from the chaff was first patented in 1975 by Professor Richard D. Stafford of Vanderbilt University in Nashville, Tennessee, and then successfully installed at a scrap-processing facility, also in Nashville. It was a steel tower with a series of curved descending troughs that operated on gravity and friction. The exit conveyor of an on-site shredder fed ASR into the top of the tower, and the troughs separated the metallic components into various grades according to their particular densities. The remaining material fell to the bottom and was removed for disposal at a landfill. The Stafford Slide was a clever solution, but in the end, its friction-based separation method was not complete enough to be reliable.

Then, in 1979, a Dutch firm, Dalmeijers Metalen BV, developed a system to recover aluminum scrap known informally as "sink and float." It used liquids in a centrifuge to separate materials based on their specific gravity. Other firms experimented with

water elutriation (which amounts to mixing ASR with water and skimming off the materials that float to the top, sometimes with the aid of an upward air current) and other density-related methods. By the 1980s, it was possible to remove the metals from ASR so thoroughly that the fluff actually became acceptable in several states for use as daily cover in landfills.

As the industry grew, the development of shredders split into two directions. Newell, Universal, and other firms concentrated on building larger and more powerful machines, with motors up to 6,500 horsepower. These behemoths can take in a complete car, flatten it, and reduce it to "corn flakes" in one minute. Other manufacturers developed smaller units to process cars that first received a rough preliminary chopping from a machine called a ripper.

EFFICIENT MINIMILL MODE
All of these advances in processing scrap have been crucial to the biggest development in steelmaking of recent years: the shift to minimills in the 1930s. As the name implies, minimills are much smaller than the huge integrated works of traditional steelmaking, which take in raw ore and coal and turn them into finished steel products. Minimills rely entirely or almost entirely on scrap as their input, eliminating the need to process these raw materials. The price of scrap is usually higher than that of iron-ore pellets, but minimills more than make up the difference on other costs. Little or no coke is required, and because their furnaces run on electricity, minimills burn no fuel.

After World War II, their number increased slowly but steadily. Most of them concentrated on turning out one or two finished products, unlike integrated works, which make a whole range of goods. The most common minimill product was (and remains) reinforcing bars for concrete, which allow fairly generous tolerances for impurities. In recent years, minimills have diversified into structural-steel shapes, wire rods, sheets, tubes, and other products.

The growth of minimills picked up during the 1960s, and when the American steel crisis hit in the 1970s and 1980s, they proved

Electric furnaces turn out nearly half the steel produced in America today. The great majority of them are located in minimills, cost- and energy-efficient plants that rely entirely on scrap as their input.

scrap from other companies' manufacturing processes, and a third source is postconsumer (or "obsolete") scrap.

Minimill operators use computers to mix and balance the various items in the feedstock, and, depending on a variety of factors, a heat in an electric furnace may take one to two hours. Whatever the source of scrap, uniformity and a low level of impurities (or, in the case of certain alloys, carefully controlled levels of specific impurities) are important. Big, unwieldy chunks of varying composition are not acceptable for these plants. Shredded steel, with its small size, free flow, and warranted specifications, has been a vital factor in the success of the minimills, and car hulks account for 90 percent of it for the industry.

Although nearly all automobile manufacturers today are experimenting with how to make cars even more recyclable, a growing challenge to the scrap industry has been the introduction by the auto industry of new combinations of materials, such as plastic bumpers with steel inserts. As the amount of aluminum in car bodies increases, recyclers are concentrating on improving their techniques for recovering that metal. Design alterations that apply newer materials such as these will require modified shredder techniques or apparatus.

Yet automobile shredding remains one of today's most efficient recycling efforts. In 1997, some 15.4 million new vehicles were sold while 13 million old cars were destroyed in America's more than 200 shredders. Each shredded car yielded about a ton of scrap, or enough steel from old cars to produce almost 13 million new cars. These figures help explain why the automobile, despite its bad reputation among environmentalists, can be considered the most successfully recycled item in history.

much better able to adapt to changing times than old-line plants. Among their advantages, minimills need not be located near supplies of ore and coal, because their raw material, scrap, can be found virtually anywhere. Since minimills can therefore be established wherever there is demand for their products, they reap a great savings in transportation costs. Today, electric furnaces turn out nearly half the steel produced in America, and the great majority of them are located in minimills.

THE PURER, THE BETTER
To be sure, not all the scrap used by minimills comes from automobiles or other postconsumer uses. Part of it—more than half, in some cases—is "home" scrap left over from the mill's own operations. As production methods become more efficient, including a shift to continuous casting, this becomes less plentiful. Another available scrap source is industrial (or "prompt")

ASK THE SCIENTIST

▶ *Lyme disease is a very big problem where I live. Why don't
health officials conduct sprayings to
kill ticks, just as they do to kill mosquitoes that spread West Nile virus?*

Lyme disease is caused by a bacterium
transmitted by the deer tick, *Ixodes scapu-
laris*. According to the Centers for Disease
Control and Prevention (CDC), acaricides
(chemicals that are toxic to ticks) are sometimes applied to control tick populations in
limited areas, but questions remain about
the effectiveness and environmental safety
of this practice.

Deer ticks are difficult to reach with
sprays. Unlike flying mosquitoes, they
spend much of their time hiding in shady,
moist ground litter, although they also cling
to grass, brush, shrubs, and low tree
branches. Ticks are often found at the
edges of woodlands and around old stone
walls—areas frequented by deer and
white-footed mice, their preferred hosts.
Eradicating the ticks entails soaking the
area with dangerous chemicals.

Acaricides are sometimes used in areas,
such as gardens and lawns, where people
are likely to come into contact with ticks.
Application should be supervised by a professional; most of the chemicals that are
effective tick killers are not licensed for
home use. Homeowners may place
Damminix, a product that provides insecti-
cide-laced nesting material for mice, in
these areas; it kills immature ticks while
they are still attached to burrowing mice.

The CDC (http://www.cdc.gov) and the
American Lyme Disease Foundation
(http://www.aldf.com) advocate preventive
steps in high-risk areas.

▶ *Is acid rain still of concern to
environmentalists? I don't read
much about it anymore.*

Acid rain is still very much of a concern.
But in the United States, Canada, and
some European countries, the furor over
this environmental problem has died down
following the passage of laws designed to
reduce the pollutants that cause it.

Acid rain is caused by emissions of sulfur dioxide and nitrogen oxides, primarily
from coal-burning power plants, metal-
smelting plants, and cars, trucks, and
buses. Once in the atmosphere, sulfur dioxide and nitrogen oxides can convert to secondary pollutants such as nitric acid and
sulfuric acid. These secondary pollutants
dissolve easily in water, and return to Earth
as acid rain, snow, or fog. Such forms of
precipitation acidify lakes and streams,
killing fish and other forms of aquatic life.
Acid rain also weakens forests and harms
monuments and buildings.

Mounting concern over acid rain in the
1980s led a number of governments to take
action. Canada, the European Community,
and the United States adopted new limits
on emissions. The U.S. Acid Rain Program,
established in 1990 under the Clean Air
Act, called for sulfur dioxide emissions to
be cut to 10 million tons below 1980 levels.
To achieve these reductions, the law
required a two-phase tightening of the restrictions placed on fossil-fuel-fired power
plants. The law also called for a 2-million-
ton reduction in nitrogen oxide emissions,
to be achieved mainly by new, cleaner
technology for coal-fired power plants.
Progress toward these goals has reduced
the amounts of acid deposited in some
areas, allowing ecosystems to begin to

recover. However, acid rain remains a serious problem. And because rain travels over long distances in clouds, it is a global one.

▶ *I read that weather records go back only 100 or 150 years. If that's true, how do scientists know that global warming is occurring?*

Changes in climate have left marks on Earth throughout the planet's history, and paleoclimatologists—scientists who study ancient climate patterns—are learning to read those marks with increasing accuracy. Tree rings, ice cores drilled from glaciers, soil deposits, fossils, and ocean and freshwater sediments contain clues to past temperatures, rainfall, ice sheets, and other climate conditions.

For example, the presence of tropical plant and animal remains in polar regions reveals that the climate in those regions must have been far warmer when those animals lived than it is today. Glacial scarring marks areas that were ice-covered in colder times. Periodic increases in the strength of sunlight, which tend to warm Earth's surface, can be tracked by measuring concentrations of carbon 14 in tree rings and of beryllium 10 in ice cores. Volcanic activity, which tends to cool Earth by obscuring sunlight, can be gauged from sulfate deposits in ice cores.

Deep sediments on the ocean floor reveal much about climate history. The sediments are formed by the shells of tiny surface-dwelling animals, foraminifera (or forams), that live near the surface. Over millions of years, the shells have piled up in layers hundreds of feet deep. The shells are made of a form of calcium carbonate, and their composition varies slightly depending on the temperature of the water. By analyzing the shells from various sediment levels, scientists can deduce likely water temperatures in past eras. Many factors work together to create climate. Paleoclimatologists use sophisticated computer models of the atmosphere and ocean circulation, correlating the models with the physical data.

While paleoclimatologists cannot measure temperature shifts with the detailed accuracy of modern weather instruments, a number of studies indicate that natural variables such as changes in solar intensity can not fully explain the current global-warming trend.

▶ *On a recent visit to the Virgin Islands, I noticed that some houses have tanks to catch rainwater. Is this a common practice in dry climates? Is the water sterilized?*

The tanks you describe are cisterns, one of the oldest means of supplying water to homes. They are still widely used in dry climates and in rural areas where public-water supplies are not available.

A cistern collects and stores rainwater. These tanks are usually (but not always) placed underground, and are often made of reinforced concrete, steel, and plastic. They are tightly sealed to keep out groundwater or (if above ground) animals, dust, insects, and light. Rainwater is not pure, and the roof, gutters, and other channels the water passes through on the way to the cistern may be contaminated by airborne dust, material from overhanging trees, deposits from chimneys, bird droppings, and other sources. Unless the water is disinfected, it should only be used for watering plants and for washing; it is not considered suitable for drinking.

A sand-and-gravel filter will remove some contaminants and, if the gravel is limestone, help neutralize acidic rainwater. However, filters will not remove bacteria. Cistern water can be made potable by treatment with chlorine. There are pump systems that inject chlorine into the water as it enters the house, disinfecting the water just prior to use. The water can also be treated by adding 1 ounce (30 milliliters) of chlorine bleach per 200 gallons (760 liters) of water to the cistern weekly. These types of purification treatments can make water suitable for drinking.

HUMAN SCIENCES

MEDICAL AND PHARMACEUTICAL RESEARCH DEMANDS A KNOWLEDGE OF PROCEDURES FAR BEYOND THE TYPICAL LABORATORY TECHNIQUES. TODAY, IT IS NOT UNUSUAL FOR SCIENTISTS TO CONDUCT TESTS AND OTHER STUDIES ON VIRUSES AND BACTERIA STRIPPED TO THEIR MOST VIRULENT STATE. SUCH EXPERIMENTS REQUIRE EXTRAORDINARY MEASURES TO PROTECT RESEARCHERS FROM ACCIDENTAL EXPOSURE AND LABORATORIES FROM POSSIBLE CONTAMINATION.

CONTENTS

WEST NILE VIRUS

by James A. Blackman, M.D., M.P.H.

The Nile is a mysterious, exotic river, as old as time itself. Close your eyes and you are likely to see the biblical baby Moses being plucked from the reeds along its bank. Or perhaps you'll get a glimpse of the avuncular Hercule Poirot interrogating suspects aboard a luxury Nile riverboat in an Agatha Christie murder mystery. But how did the Nile, whose origin is Lake Victoria in east-central Africa, become associated with a killer virus?

About 60 years ago, a 37-year-old woman in the West Nile district of northern Uganda came to a clinic where health officials were conducting a sleeping-sickness survey. Her temperature was mildly elevated at 100.6° F (38° C). She denied feeling ill, although she

The West Nile virus usually causes mild symptoms, but it can be deadly to elderly people or those with weakened immune systems. Mosquitoes spread the virus to other animals after feeding on infected birds.

may have done so to avoid hospitalization. Nevertheless, officials drew a sample of her blood, and inoculated serum from it into the brains of 10 mice. Only one mouse survived. Subsequent testing showed the culprit to be a new infectious agent that was dubbed the West Nile virus.

West Nile virus is spread by the bite of an infected mosquito. It usually causes only mild symptoms, but occasionally can cause inflammation of the brain (encephalitis), the brain lining, or the spinal cord (meningitis). However, even in areas where transmission of West Nile virus is occurring, only a small proportion of mosquitoes are likely to be infected (1 in 1,000). Even if bitten by an infected mosquito, the chance of developing illness is approximately 1 in 300. People with weakened immune systems and the elderly are at greatest risk of developing a more severe form of the illness, which occasionally results in death.

The typical symptoms of West Nile virus include fever and muscle aches, swollen lymph glands, and sometimes a skin rash. In the elderly, infection may spread to the nervous system or bloodstream and cause sudden fever, intense headache, stiff neck, and confusion—the signs and symptoms of encephalitis or meningitis. Healthy children and adults may have no symptoms. Symptoms generally appear three to six days after exposure, but time frames can vary.

West Nile virus belongs to the family of flaviviruses and is closely related to the St. Louis encephalitis virus found in the United States. These viruses are termed arboviruses (arthropod-borne) because they are maintained in nature through biological transmission between susceptible vertebrate hosts by blood-feeding arthropods (mosquitoes, sand flies, "no-see-ums," and ticks). Vertebrates can contract the virus when an infected arthropod bites them in order to take a blood meal.

The arboviral encephalitis diseases are zoonotic—that is, they are maintained in complex life cycles involving nonhuman pri-

mary vertebrate hosts (for example, crows) and primary arthropod vectors (such as, mosquitoes). These cycles usually remain undetected until humans enter the cycle (by becoming infected) or the virus escapes the usual cycle via a secondary vector or vertebrate host as the result of some ecological change. Humans and domestic animals can develop clinical illness, but usually are inci-

The West Nile virus had never been identified in the United States until 1999. Now, the apparent frequency of reports has many communities testing mosquitoes to determine if they are carriers.

dental or "dead-end" hosts because they do not produce significant levels of virus in the blood, and do not contribute to the transmission cycle.

Mosquitoes become infected by biting infected birds, which may circulate the virus in their blood for a few days. After an incubation period of 5 to 15 days, infected mosquitoes can transmit West Nile virus to humans and animals while biting them to take blood. The virus is located in the mosquito's salivary glands. During blood feeding, the virus is injected into the animal or human, where it multiplies and may cause illness. West Nile virus is not spread from one person to another or directly from birds to humans. The virus can infect dogs, cats, horses, and other vertebrates; but this seems

A Mosquito-Borne Virus

Humans contract West Nile virus when they are bitten by a mosquito carrying the virus. Mild infections may result in fever, headache, and body aches. Severe infections may cause encephalitis or meningitis, potentially life-threatening conditions marked by high fever, stupor, tremors, and paralysis.

Transmission

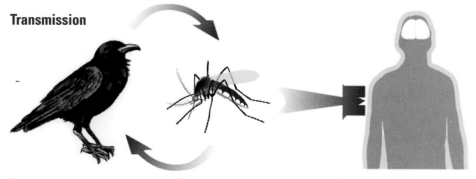

1. A primary host, usually a bird or small mammal, carries the virus in its blood. Some animals die, but many recover from the infection and develop an immunity.

2. Mosquitoes feed on the infected bird and in turn pass the virus back to birds and other creatures.

3. Humans are an accidental, dead-end host for the virus. Only mosquitoes transmit the West Nile virus; transmission does not occur between humans.

to be rare, and these animals do not pass the virus to other animals or to humans.

There is no specific treatment for West Nile virus infection. As with most other viral infections, treatment is supportive. If the symptoms are mild, such as fever or muscle aches, simple over-the-counter medications, such as acetaminophen or ibuprofen, are adequate. In more severe cases, an individual should seek medical attention and may require hospitalization and even intensive care with life-support technology. The risk of death from West Nile virus infection is estimated to be between 5 percent and 15 percent, with elderly people among those in the higher-risk category.

HOW THE VIRUS GOT TO AMERICA

After West Nile virus was discovered in the 1930s, it took decades for experts to determine how it spread. It became recognized as a cause of severe infections of the brain in elderly patients during an outbreak in Israel in 1957. Other more recent outbreaks of West Nile virus encephalitis have occurred in France, Algeria, Romania, Czech Republic, and Congo.

West Nile virus grabbed the attention of the general public when an outbreak occurred in the northeastern United States in 1999. There were

Neighborhoods in suburban New York (left) and elsewhere have hired private pest-control companies to help keep the local mosquito population to a minimum.

Protecting Yourself from Mosquito-Borne Encephalitis

• Stay indoors at dawn, dusk, and in the early evening, when mosquito activity is high.

• Wear long-sleeved shirts and pants outdoors.

• Apply repellents to exposed skin and/or clothing as directed.

• Spray clothing with repellents containing permethrin or DEET, since mosquitoes may bite through thin clothing.

• Apply insect repellent sparingly to exposed skin. An effective repellent will contain 35 percent DEET (diethyltoluamide). DEET in high concentrations (greater than 35 percent) provides no additional protection. Repellents appropriate for use on children should contain no more than 10 percent DEET because the chemical is absorbed through the skin and can cause harm.

• Never use repellents over cuts, wounds, or irritated skin.

• Do not apply to eyes or mouth, and use sparingly around ears. Never spray directly onto face; spray hands first, and then apply to face.

• Do not allow children to handle repellent products. When using on a child, apply to your own hands, and then put it on the child.

• After returning indoors, wash treated skin with soap and water or bathe. This is particularly important when repellents are used repeatedly in a day or on consecutive days. Also, wash treated clothing before wearing it again.

---

62 cases of severe disease, including seven deaths. West Nile virus had never been reported in the United States before 1999. The rapid outbreak of the disease caught public officials off guard, and drove home the need for local, state, and national public-health agencies to be better prepared for any new epidemics that might occur.

While no one knows when or how West Nile virus was introduced into North America, international travel, importation of infected birds or mosquitoes, and migration of infected birds are all possibilities.

Birds in affected areas commonly house antibodies to the virus, indicating previous infection; these birds usually have few if any symptoms. It was very unusual that many birds in New York, mostly crows, were found dead with evidence of acute infection. This suggested that the strain of West Nile virus in the United States might be much more virulent than in previous cases.

The virus has spread up and down the East Coast of the United States, and has been identified in more than 70 species of dead birds. Officials have discovered the virus in

Many organizations study the West Nile virus. The University of Connecticut's avian pathology lab conducts autopsies on birds that may have died from the disease.

What You Can Do to Help Fight Mosquitoes

• Empty standing water in old tires, cemetery urns, buckets, plastic covers, toys, or any other container where "wrigglers" and "tumblers" may live.

• Empty and change the water in birdbaths, fountains, wading pools, rain barrels, and potted-plant trays at least once a week, if not more often.

• Drain or fill temporary pools of water with dirt.

• Keep swimming pools treated and circulating, and rain gutters completely unclogged.

• Use mosquito repellents whenever necessary.

• Wear head nets, long sleeves, and long pants if you must venture into areas with known high mosquito populations.

• If there is a mosquito-borne disease warning in effect, stay inside at night if at all possible.

• Make certain that window and door screens are "bug-tight."

• Replace outdoor lights with yellow "bug" lights.

• Contact your local mosquito-control district or health department. Neighborhoods are occasionally sprayed to repel mosquitoes. If you have any questions about mosquitoes, feel free to call your local authorities. This information is provided by the U.S. Environmental Protection Agency (EPA) in partnership with the American Mosquito Control Association (AMCA).

26 other mammals, including bats, rodents, rabbits, cats, raccoons, skunks, and horses.

One controversial theory explaining the virus' entry into North America concerns global warming. Mosquitoes are sensitive to changing climatic conditions; they thrive in seasons and regions where the temperature stays above a certain level. Winter freezing kills mosquito eggs, larvae, and adults. The mosquitoes tend to proliferate faster and bite more when the air is warmer; internally speaking, viruses multiply and mature more quickly inside mosquitoes that live in warmer climates. The shorter the time it takes for a virus to mature, the greater the likelihood that a mosquito will take a blood meal and infect a new host before it dies. As regions that were previously cool grow steadily warmer, mosquitoes can carry new diseases into those territories.

Some experts contend that floods and droughts induced by global warming could trigger epidemics by creating breeding grounds for insects. When droughts occur, streams become stagnant pools where mosquitoes lay their eggs.

Unusual climate conditions may have contributed to the rapid spread of West Nile virus in the United States. The mild winter of 1998–99 enabled many mosquitoes to survive into the early spring. That summer's drought killed off mosquito predators, such as lacewings and ladybugs, that would otherwise have helped limit mosquito populations. It led birds to congregate in greater numbers, as they shared fewer and smaller watering holes, many of which were frequented, naturally, by mosquitoes.

Infected mosquitoes seeking blood meals were able to rapidly spread the virus to birds. Bird after bird became infected, and the cycle ultimately fanned out to include human beings. Torrential rains toward the end of August provided new breeding grounds for mosquitoes, unleashing even more potential virus carriers.

West Nile virus is transmitted principally by the *Culex* species of mosquito. They are painful and persistent biters, attacking at dusk and after dark, and they readily enter dwellings for blood meals. They prefer domestic and wild birds over humans, cows,

Several states monitor the spread of West Nile virus by using fowl-surveillance equipment placed in areas of high mosquito concentrations. The "sentinel" chickens housed in each unit are observed closely for any sign of infection.

and horses; but if breeding sites are available near people's homes and domestic-animal enclosures, then people and animals are potential targets.

PREVENTION EFFORTS

The U.S. Centers for Disease Control and Prevention (CDC) in Atlanta, along with state and local health departments, are in a constant battle against the West Nile virus. Forty-four states are conducting virus monitoring among mosquitoes and other animals. This effort provides public-health officials with an early warning. A coordinating committee composed of various federal agencies, including the National Institutes of Health (NIH) and the Environ-

The research of epidemiologist Dominic Travis may someday lead to methods by which zoos can guard against mosquitoes passing on the disease from wild birds—the identified carriers of the virus—to the irreplaceable animals in captivity.

mental Protection Agency (EPA), has been formed to deal with this new health threat.

In monitoring the spread of the West Nile virus, surveillance systems are a priority in those states already affected or at high risk because of bird-migration patterns. Health-care providers have been alerted to test for West Nile virus in people who develop viral encephalitis. Veterinarians have been asked to do the same for horses and other animals with neurological symptoms.

At this time, there is no vaccine to prevent the West Nile virus disease. The key to reducing the risk of West Nile virus infections is eliminating breeding sites near homes to interrupt the life cycle of the *Culex* mosquito. In emergency situations, wide aerial spraying and ground applications have been used to quickly reduce the number of adult mosquitoes. Despite worries about community exposure to these pesticides, specifically the organophosphate malathion, the EPA has determined that risks to human bystanders from possible skin contact, inhalation, or incidental ingestion are below levels of concern.

As our society becomes more globalized and mobile, regional health problems can become international crises. Countries must cooperate in fighting disease. Individuals can participate in the West Nile virus prevention effort by eliminating sources of stagnant water on their property and in their community, and people can protect themselves from mosquitoes by applying insect repellent before going outside. ◸

SPEED LIMITS

by Guy C. Brown

Imagine that by some fluke, and despite your protests, you had been entered for the 10,000-meter race instead of your usual 400 meters in the 2000 Summer Olympic Games in Sydney, Australia. Get ready! You resolve to make the best of it. As you enter the stadium, the crowd roars, and adrenaline surges through your veins. Get set! You approach the starting line. The adrenaline prepares you for action, increasing the rate and strength of contractions in your heart, diverting blood to your muscles, stimulating your lungs and sweat glands, and mobilizing energy stores from your liver, fat, and muscles. Go! The starter's gun fires. Nerve impulses from your brain ripple down your motor neurons, releasing a wave of neurotransmitter molecules over your muscles. Channels open across the membranes of your muscle cells, and calcium floods into the cells' cytoplasm, causing the muscle fibers to contract—all within a fraction of a second.

ATP: THE BODY'S ROCKET FUEL
Muscle fibers contract, causing massive consumption of adenosine triphosphate (ATP), the general-purpose immediate energy source for cells of the body. ATP is being burned so quickly that your muscles' supply is depleted in a second. Fortunately for you, ATP can be replenished from a small reser-

Physical conditioning transforms a runner into a high-performance racing machine, with the heart, lungs, muscles, and blood among its fine-tuned components.

voir of phosphate energy known as phosphocreatine, but unfortunately, that second stage of your rocket fuel lasts only another 10 seconds or so. You had better start calling on the carbohydrate known as glycogen, which is stored in your muscles and liver. Glycogen can be broken down into glucose, a sugar that can then be further disassembled to make more ATP.

A few hours ago, you ate a high-carbohydrate breakfast of waffles and bananas, which stuffed your muscles and liver full of glycogen. But breaking down glycogen and glucose via the simplest chemical pathway can supply enough ATP for only another minute or two. The body has a second, more sophisticated way to break down glucose—one that squeezes out more ATP. The reaction takes place in the mitochondria—small brownish-red organelles within the cells that function as power stations, turning food and oxygen into energy. That reaction, though, demands abundant oxygen. Conveniently, the blood vessels in the muscles dilate, and a 20-fold increase in the blood supply provides enough oxygen to kick the mitochondria into life.

As a medium-distance runner in a long-distance race, you are coasting out in front of the pack. You're on a high, as natural, opiumlike drugs called endorphins flood your brain. But suddenly you begin to tire. Your body simply cannot supply energy fast enough to power your muscles for this demanding event. Lactic acid is accumulating in them and making them ache. The other runners, who have trained to build up their endurance, are now passing you. The finish line becomes an impossible dream, a place where the pain and fatigue might finally end. When you finally reach it—dead last—you collapse, and your body begins repairing the damage.

Competition and tests of endurance have always been a part of civilization. The urn below suggests that sports imagery has also enjoyed a long history.

INTRIGUING QUESTIONS

Could diet, training, and desire have taken you farther, faster? Are there limits to the athletic performance of any human being? If so, what are they, and how are they determined by anatomy, physiology, and biochemistry? Will the competitors in the Olympic Games in years to come continue to smash existing world records to achieve new levels of excellence? Or, instead, are the limits of human physical performance fixed, dooming the world's top athletes to battle over ever-diminishing fractions of seconds and centimeters?

What keeps athletes from throwing farther or from swimming faster? Where within the body are the performance limits set? And why does performance decline when the athletes become fatigued? Those puzzling questions have intrigued biologists and medical scientists ever since the secrets of physiology began to be revealed in the 17th century, and they have haunted athletes even longer.

A LOOK INSIDE

To assess the biological limits to athletic performance, one must search inside the body of the human athlete. As the unprepared runner described earlier quickly discovered, the start of a track event initiates a second race: one that takes place inside the runner's body to supply the contracting muscles with energy. Exercise at maximum intensity burns great amounts of energy: the total energy consumption of the body per unit time, the so-called metabolic rate, increases 10-fold in an untrained individual, and 20-fold in an athlete. A resting athlete consumes energy at a rate of about 100 watts, roughly the equivalent to the power of a standard light-bulb; working flat out, the same athlete burns energy at a rate of 2,000 watts.

Virtually all of the extra energy consumption takes place in the muscles, and that requires a massive increase in energy production, also within the muscles. In the short term, the energy-producing machinery can feed on reserves of phosphocreatine or glycogen within the muscle. But as those reserves dwindle, the muscles must import glucose, fatty acids, and oxygen from the blood in order to keep going. A runner, for instance, consumes about a sextillion (10^{21}) molecules of ATP per stride, an amount roughly equal to the existing ATP in the runner's muscles. To keep running for more than about a second, that means more ATP must be made in the muscles at least as fast as it is being consumed, for as long as the exercise continues.

MAKING ATP

Each of the three fundamental methods for manufacturing ATP has benefits and disadvantages for the athlete. The speediest method—to rapidly recharge the ATP supply with phosphocreatine—is the option of choice during intense power events such as a sprint race, pole vault, or javelin throw. Since this method fails after 5 to 10 seconds, however, the athlete in training for lengthy events must attend to the second option—converting the glycogen stored in the muscles into lactic acid.

That second stream of ATP, from a process known as glycolysis, kicks in automatically as the phosphocreatine is depleted. The advantage is that its raw material, glycogen, is much more plentiful than phosphocreatine. The disadvantage is that the end product of glycolysis, lactic acid, is toxic in higher amounts. Lactic acid is responsible for the painful sensation of "burn" or "stitch" that people who are unfit experience when they overexercise, and it is one of the main causes of fatigue. As the body's muscles accumulate lactic acid, they begin to cramp, causing reduced muscle function and eventually slowing down glycolysis itself.

The third method for making ATP in muscles, the reaction within the mitochondria of the muscle cells, is about 30 times more efficient than glycolysis. Another advantage of this method is that it enables the muscles to generate energy from fat as well as from glycogen and the glucose. But because mitochondrial ATP production requires sufficient oxygen, and because the oxygen must travel a long path—from the lungs to the blood to the muscle cells to the mitochondria within those cells—the process is relatively slow.

MAXING-OUT OXYGEN

It is worth mentioning that as long as the athlete's energy needs can be supplied by the mitochondria running on oxygen, the athlete is exercising aerobically, and the exercise can proceed, in highly trained athletes, for hours. If the exercise rate is faster than the rate at which oxygen can be supplied to the muscles, the exercise is anaerobic, which leads to a rapid depletion of phosphocreatine and glycogen and a buildup of lactic acid: the two major causes of fatigue. In other words, when the available oxygen cannot meet the body's demands, peak performance plummets. Consider the experience of high-altitude climbers, superbly conditioned athletes who must function, say, at the summit of Mount Everest, where the oxygen level is only about one-third of what it is at sea level. There, the peak metabolic rate of the climbers also drops to about one-third of normal levels, because the availability of oxygen limits their performance. The climber's cardiovascular system can slowly adapt, however, to supply that limited oxygen to the muscles more efficiently. Accordingly, athletes who seek to improve their aerobic conditioning often spend time training at high altitudes: at the Olympic Training Center in Colorado Springs, Colorado, for instance, which is 6,000 feet (1,830 meters) above sea level.

WHERE IS THE WEAK LINK?

The 18th-century French chemist Antoine-Laurent Lavoisier was the first to prove that people consume ever-greater amounts of oxygen as their physical exertion increases. But oxygen consumption, too, eventually hits a plateau, and that places an upper boundary on the rate at which mitochondrial ATP is manufactured. Once that level is reached, an athlete cannot row any faster, run any harder, or, in general, exercise more intensely without resorting to short-lived, anaerobic sources of energy, which are rapidly depleted.

Where in the human body is that seemingly unfair performance limit imposed? In the biochemical chain of events that begins with the intake of oxygen by the lungs and ends with the consumption of energy by the contracting muscles, there are four possible weak links. It could be within the muscle fibers themselves, which consume the energy during exercise; the lungs, which transfer oxygen to the blood; the heart and the circulating blood, which bring oxygen to the muscles; or the muscle mitochondria, which consume the oxygen and produce energy.

More oxygen is required during strenuous exercise. But there is a limit to the amount of oxygen the body can process, a factor that can restrict performance.

The muscle fibers do not appear to be the limiting factor. Research by the physiologist Bengt Saltin of the Copenhagen Muscle Research Centre in Denmark has shown that when muscles are exercised individually, their maximum oxygen consumption is much greater than when many muscles are exercised together. For example, when a single limb—say, an athlete's leg on a bicycle pedal—is worked to its utmost, the athlete's oxygen consumption increases to about 2 quarts (nearly 2 liters) per minute. If two limbs are worked flat out, the person's oxygen uptake almost doubles, as one would expect. But here's the catch: If all four limbs are worked at the same time, as they are in sports such as rowing and swimming, there is no further increase in oxygen consumption. Some limiting factor comes into play, preventing the arms and legs from doing as much work simultaneously as the sum of what they can do alone. That factor is clearly not the muscles, since each limb is capable of working harder on its own.

The lungs are not usually the problem, either, because even during the most strenuous exercise, when the lungs are inhaling and exhaling 25 times more air than they do when the body is at rest, they are working at only two-thirds their maximum capacity. Furthermore, if oxygen intake by the lungs were a limiting factor during exercise, oxygen levels would drop during strenuous exercise, but they do not: The amount of oxygen and carbon dioxide in the blood is remarkably constant, even at the maximum exercise rate. Exercise training does not increase the capacity of the lungs, however, whereas training does improve the performance of all the cardiovascular and muscle components. So some fraction of highly trained, elite athletes may approach the point at which their lungs begin to limit their performances.

What about the heart? In contrast to the lungs, the heart can be reshaped by exercise. With extensive training—particularly with the kinds of regimens followed by marathon runners and others who take part in endurance events—the four chambers of the heart enlarge. As a result, the heart pumps more blood with each beat, and the rate at which blood circulates increases by as much as 40 percent. That difference makes it possible to judge a person's fitness level simply by taking a pulse. At rest, the heart of a sedentary person beats, on average, about 75 times a minute, whereas an athlete's heart rate is much slower—about 50 beats a minute. Clearly, a heart that pumps a large amount of blood with each beat can maintain a given circulation rate (say, the circulation needed by the resting body) with a relatively low number of beats per minute.

But assume that an athlete achieves optimum cardiovascular conditioning. Does the heart still act as a limiting factor in oxygen consumption, thereby constraining the athlete's performance in some way? The answer is probably yes. In endurance sports such as long-distance running, the heart works at 90 percent of its maximum capacity: close to its limit. If it could push more blood through the body, an athlete could run, swim, row, or ride a bicycle faster than usual. But precisely why is blood flow so important to the athlete? The reason, of course, is that red blood cells contain hemoglobin, a protein that grabs onto oxygen in the lungs and releases it where it is needed in the muscles.

WHAT IS AN ATHLETE TO DO?

Athletes therefore employ a variety of methods—many of them banned by competitive sporting organizations—to increase the amount of oxygen in their blood. Blood doping is one technique: typically, 1 or 2 pints (about 0.5 to 1 liter) or so of blood is removed from the body and stored; the body readily adapts in the next few weeks by making more red blood cells. The stored blood is then reinfused shortly before a competitive event to boost the athlete's level of hemoglobin. Another way for determined athletes to increase the hemoglobin content of their blood is to inject erythropoietin (EPO), a hormone that stimulates the production of red blood cells. EPO caused a scandal in the middle of the 1998 Tour de France: The top-ranked Festina cycling team from Spain was disqualified after a stash of the hormone was discovered in a team trainer's car. Single-minded athletes have gone so far as to submit to elective surgery to widen major arteries. The effectiveness of all those devious procedures demonstrates that performance in endurance sports is at least partially limited by the cardiovascular system.

SUSPICIOUS LIMITERS

What about the fourth possible limiting factor in the race for the gold medal: the mitochondria? They, too, it turns out, are prime suspects. Work by the physiologists Hans Hoppeler and Ewald R. Weibel of the University of Bern in Switzerland has demonstrated that when mitochondria are isolated in the laboratory, they cannot be forced to consume oxygen (and thereby produce ATP) much faster than they already do inside the body of an animal exercising at its peak metabolic rate. Consequently, if the mitochondria are already working as fast as they can, they could be one of the factors that limit aerobic performance. Training can increase the number of mitochondria in the muscle cells in order to crank up the body's ability to manufacture crucial ATP energy. It is known that the concentration of muscle mitochondria in a trained athlete can be more than double the amount present in a sedentary person.

Thus, the biological limits to athletic performance—at least for sports such as cycling, swimming, and long-distance running—lie somewhere along the chain of subsystems of the body that affect the supply or consumption of energy. By contrast, power sports, such as weight lifting or pole vaulting, require a single supreme effort that lasts no more than a second or two. The limiting factors are unrelated to oxygen;

Endurance training—the key to preparing for the Tour de France—enhances aerobic capacity. An athlete's peak metabolic rate can go up by as much as 25 percent during exercise.

instead, performance is limited by the muscles themselves.

Gaining a Real Edge

Even when an athlete has achieved an exceptional rate of metabolism and oxygen consumption, however, the specter of fatigue always looms. Records are often set not so much because the winner has a high peak metabolic rate, but because he or she excels in endurance—that is, the length of time the athlete can sustain the peak rate before that rate begins to drop.

Building endurance is where training gives the real edge. Whereas training can boost the peak metabolic rate by between 5 and 25 percent, it can increase the endurance of an untrained person by as much as 500 percent. Training enhances aerobic capacity by increasing the number of muscle mitochondria and the supply of oxygen to the mitochondria. That decreases the need for the anaerobic processes. Endurance training also leads to another metabolic change: fat begins to replace glycogen and glucose as the fuel of choice. As a result, the athlete's glycogen reserves, which are vital for both brain and muscle function, last longer. That is a key boost to athletic potential, because the depletion of glycogen is a major cause of exhaustion. Marathon runners call it "the wall" because it feels just like running into one. Muscles become weak

and heavy, the legs shake, and the brain becomes confused. The impact of the wall can be softened by beverages that contain glucose, which can partially compensate for the glycogen depletion.

Dehydration can hasten the onset of fatigue even faster than the depletion of glycogen does. The condition reduces the body's capacity to sweat, and the consequent reduction in heat loss leads to an intolerable rise in body temperature. That is why drinking plenty of fluids is so vitally essential for endurance athletes. One recent study showed that well-hydrated athletes performed 30 percent better than athletes who drank less water.

Good and Bad Alternatives

To increase their performance and simultaneously combat fatigue, some endurance athletes have turned to stimulant drugs, such as amphetamines ("speed") and cocaine, which are banned, and caffeine, which is legal at reasonable levels. Such stimulants can mimic the effects of adrenaline, but they also act on the brain, causing it to ignore the warning signs of fatigue. Recent studies suggest that the caffeine equivalent of between two and three cups of coffee enhances endurance as well as performance in the high-intensity power sports.

But the biggest legal breakthrough in preparing endurance athletes for competition has been the practice of so-called carbohydrate loading, which was developed by the biochemist Eric Hultman and his colleagues at the Karolinska Institute in Stockholm, Sweden. The regimen begins a week before a race: The athlete tapers to a light training load and a high-carbohydrate diet (70 percent of calories from carbohydrates). That diet can double the amount of carbo-

World-Record Times for Power and Endurance Events

Category		1901–20	1921–40	1941–60	1961–80	1981–2000	2020 (projected)
100-meter dash	Men	——	10.2	10.1	9.93	9.79	**9.73**
	Women	——	11.6	11.3	10.88	10.49	**9.95**
1,500-meter run	Men	3:54.7	3:47.8	3:35.6	3:31.4	3:26.0	**3:20.2**
	Women	——	4:41.8	4:29.7	3:52.5	3:50.5	**3:26.7**
10,000-meter run	Men	30:58.8	29:52.6	28:18.8	27:22.4	26:22.8	**25:14.5**
	Women	——	——	——	32:52.5	29:31.8	**24:14.7**
100-meter freestyle swim	Men	1:00.4	56.4	54.6	49.4	48.2	**45.3**
	Women	1:13.6	1:04.6	1:00.2	54.8	53.8	**51.7**
1,500-meter freestyle swim	Men	22:00.0	18:58.8	17:11.0	14:58.3	14:41.7	**14:13.0**
	Women	——	21:10.1	19:23.6	16:04.5	15:52.1	**14:17.5**

hydrate stored in the muscle. This increases by about 50 percent the amount of time that an athlete can run at near-maximum speed.

SETTING SENSIBLE GOALS

One important training goal can be formulated from the recognition that there are two main kinds of muscle fiber: fast-twitch fiber, which can contract and relax rapidly (but is also rapidly fatigued), and slow-twitch fiber, which has high endurance. A muscle made up largely of fast-twitch fibers—the breast of a chicken is a good example—is white. Such muscles rely mostly on glycolysis to supply ATP, and therefore do not need much oxygen. They contain few blood vessels or mitochondria, which is why they are light in color. Muscles made up largely of slow-twitch fibers, by contrast, are packed full of blood vessels and mitochondria; they are red, brown, or gray in color (think of the leg of a chicken). Training can change the relative proportions of fast and slow muscle fibers. In a sprinter or a weight lifter, some 80 percent of the fibers are fast and 20 percent are slow, whereas a marathon runner mixes the two kinds of muscle in the opposite proportion.

Training can also help the power-sport competitor by increasing the size or mass of the relevant muscles, which is one of the major determinants of performance in such sports. There are tempting and effective shortcuts to the athletic goal that are potentially harmful. The most familiar examples from the sports pages are the anabolic steroids, drugs that are chemically related to the male sex hormone testosterone. Combined with a diet rich in protein and carbohydrates, steroids increase muscle mass. They are banned in most competitive sports, partly because they confer an unfair advantage, but also because they have damaging side effects, from acne to sexual impotence, and even sterility. The Canadian sprinter Ben Johnson was stripped of his 100-meter gold medal in the 1988 Olympic Games after his urine tested positive for anabolic steroids. Other substances that increase muscle mass, such as human growth hormones, are also banned, but they are more difficult to test for because they occur naturally in the body.

In the 1990s, a controversial substance called creatine became a widely used supplement for sprinters and other power-sport competitors. Creatine is taken up by the muscles and converted into phosphocreatine, the quick-start source of ATP. The utility of creatine was discovered by the physiologist Roger C. Harris of the Animal Health Trust in Newmarket, England. In

1993, Harris determined that feeding people between 20 to 30 grams of creatine a day keeps the resting levels of phosphocreatine in the muscles slightly higher than normal, enabling those levels to be restored more quickly after exercise. The investigators asked trained athletes to run four 300-meter and four 1,000-meter sprints, interspersed with three- or four-minute rest periods. The tests showed that in the last of the four races, the runners who took creatine supplements performed better than the runners who received a placebo.

WHAT IS NEW?

World-record running times have been decreasing ever since records have been kept. If there is a physiological maximum to the running speed of a human being, one would expect that as athletes approached that limit, improvements would become both rarer and smaller. Remarkably, neither of those trends has shown up; world-record running times have declined almost linearly in the past 100 years. The men's record for the 1,500-meter run, for instance, has decreased from 4:06.2 in 1900 to 3:26.0 at the time of this writing (a record set in 1998), at roughly 10-second intervals every quarter century.

Women have generally been unable to match men's records, and their poorer performance has been attributed to inherent physiological differences: less cardiac output, lower hemoglobin levels, less lung capacity, more fat, and shorter Achilles tendons. The women's world records are intriguing, however, because they are improving faster than the men's are. In 1992, the physiologists Brian J. Whipp and Susan A. Ward of the University of California, Los Angeles, studied the rate of improvement of men and women in a variety of running events. They discovered that the world-record running speeds for women in the 200-, 400-, 800-, and 1,500-meter events improved by between 14 and 18 meters per minute per decade between 1925 and 1992. Men's speeds, by contrast, improved only between 6 and 7 meters per minute per decade in that same period. Whipp and Ward predicted that if those rates of improvement continue, women will outrun men in most events by the year 2035, and much sooner in endurance events such as the marathon.

Improvements in equipment and training methods also continue to shave seconds off athletes' records. In the Sydney 2000 Olympics, some swimmers wore a new swimsuit developed by Speedo International, which is based in Nottingham, England. The suit covers the swimmer's arms, legs, and torso with a special, finely ridged fabric designed to mimic the skin of a shark. Speedo asserts that the new bodysuit helped increase swimmers' times by a whopping 3 percent—an extraordinary advance for a sport in which races are often won by hundredths of a second. New technology is also being adopted to aid athletes during training. An electronic device known as e-GO was recently developed by the electronics company FitSense Technology in Wellesley, Massachusetts. When the device is clipped to a runner's shoelace, it measures stride length and rate, distance, calorie-burn rate, and speed—information that can help runners fine-tune their performance.

THE BOTTOM LINE

The steady advance of athletic performance throughout the past century can be attributed not only to better preparation and equipment but also to a vastly increased pool of athletes from more diverse genetic backgrounds. But eventually, the genetic diversity of humanity will be fully tapped. Around that time, advanced surgeries, implants, and genetic engineering might endow athletes with a variety of superhuman abilities: speedier muscle fibers, more elastic tendons, higher phosphocreatine levels, more muscle mitochondria, higher blood-oxygen levels, and faster blood circulation. Therefore, future limits to performance will be determined less by the physiology of the athlete than by technological advances and the evolving judgment of rules committees on where to draw the line between what is "natural" and what is "artificially enhanced." Happily, the human qualities necessary to bring about the next wave of athletic improvements—motivation, creativity, and persistence—will remain.

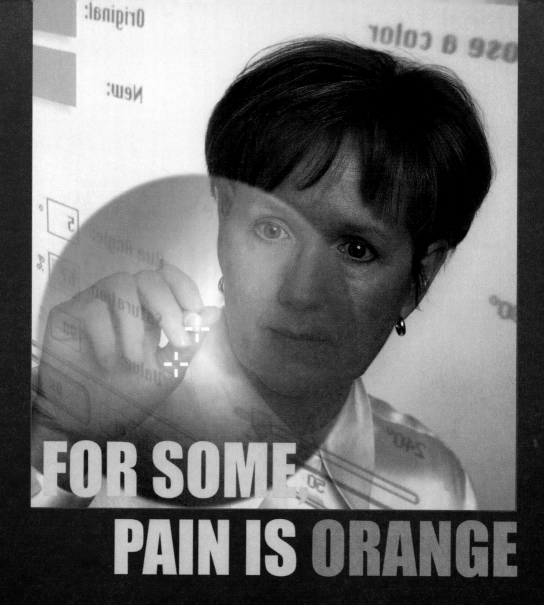

FOR SOME, PAIN IS ORANGE

by Susan Hornik

W hen New York City artist Carol Steen was 7 and learning to read, she exclaimed to a classmate as they walked home from school, "Isn't *A* the prettiest pink you've ever seen?" Her young chum responded by saying, "You're weird."

Shabana Tajwar was a bit older when she discovered that her world was more colorful than most. In 1991, as a 20-year-old intern, she and a group of friends were trying to remember someone's name over lunch. "I knew the name was green. It started with *F*, and *F* is green," says Tajwar, now an environmental engineer. "But when I mentioned that, everyone said, 'What are you talking

about?'" She shrugs. "I was sort of in shock. I didn't know everyone didn't see things the same way."

Commingling Senses
While most of us experience the world through orderly, segregated senses, for some people, two or more sensations are commingled. For Steen and Tajwar, hearing a name or seeing a letter or word in black and white causes an involuntary sensation of color. To Tajwar, the letter *T* is always navy blue. "I don't see the actual letter as colored," she says. "I see the color flash, sort of in my mind's eye." Steen not only delights in pink

In synesthesia, a person's senses commingle in remarkable ways. Carol Crane (facing page), for example, "sees" the numeral 2 as a shade of blue.

A's and gold *Y*'s, she experiences colored taste as well. "I see the most brilliant blue after I eat a salty pretzel," she says.

Others with synesthesia—from the Greek *syn*, meaning together, and *aisthesis*, perception—may feel or taste sounds, or hear or taste shapes. The strumming of a guitar may be a soft brushing sensation at the back of an ankle; a musical note may taste like pickles; a trumpet may sound "pointed"; the taste of chicken may feel "round." A teenager once confessed that her boyfriend's kiss made her see "orange-sherbet foam."

TO EACH, HIS/HER OWN

Even more baffling to outsiders: while synesthetes' perceptions are consistent over time, they are not shared. Letters, for instance, don't evoke the same color for everyone. Steen jokes that her good friend and fellow synesthete Patricia Duffy is "great" but misguided. "She thinks *L* is pale yellow, not black with blue highlights," says Steen with a grin as she pours a mug full of coffee in her downtown Manhattan loft. Separately, over lunch in a sunny bistro, Duffy, a language instructor at the United Nations in New York City, confides, "Some of Carol's colors are so wrong!"

Even relatives who have synesthesia—it seems to run in families—see things differently. The Russian novelist Vladimir Nabokov tells in his memoirs about playing with a set of wooden blocks when he was 7 years old. He complained to his mother that the letters on the blocks weren't the right colors. She was sympathetic. She, too, objected to the shades—though she also disagreed with some of her son's color choices. According to one study, only one letter elicits consensus among a majority of synesthetes; apparently, some 56 per-

cent see *O* as a shade of white. For Nabokov, it radiated the hue of an "ivory-backed hand-mirror."

INTRIGUED AND BAFFLED

People with synesthesia have described their unusual perceptions to baffled researchers for more than 200 years. At times, they were viewed as mentally defective; at other times, idealized as artistically gifted. Often they weren't believed at all. Only in the past decade or so, using controlled studies, in-depth interviews, and computer-aided visual tests, have scientists begun to identify and

Researchers, such as Peter Grossenbacher at Naropa University, Boulder, Colorado, are just beginning to understand the synesthetic experience, and are attempting to map the pathways to such perceptions.

catalog the staggering variety of these automatically induced sensations. "We've gone to great lengths to identify the range of forms," says Peter Grossenbacher, a cognitive neuroscientist and one of the foremost U.S. researchers on synesthesia. "We understand it's a real experience. But we don't yet know how it comes to pass."

But scientists have discovered that synesthetes frequently have more than one form of the trait. Carol Steen's tall-windowed loft (part living space, part art studio) is jammed

Patricia Duffy perceives her week as a path of colored rectangles; edging toward the weekend, she steps from yellowish Wednesday to turquoise Thursday.

with her synesthesia-inspired paintings and sculptural models. Pulling letters painted on business-card-size pieces of paper off a shelf, she struggles to make clear the unique sensations that thoroughly color her life and work. "It's like viewing the world in multimedia," she says. "I want to show other people what I'm seeing."

What Steen is seeing is not only color triggered by certain sounds, smells, and flavors; when listening to music, she also sees shapes, which are reflected in her sculpture.

Steen also feels pain in color. When on vacation in British Columbia two years ago, she jumped down from a rock and tore a ligament. "All I saw was orange," she says. "It was like wearing orange sunglasses." In her paintings, she depicts similar color sensations that she experiences during acupuncture. One shows a green slash arcing through a field of red; in another, a tiny red triangle drifts on a sea of bright blue.

Researcher Peter Grossenbacher and a small cadre of scientists in the United States, the United Kingdom, Canada, Germany, and elsewhere are currently doing research with volunteers to try to figure out why Steen sees orange when the rest of us just ache. So far, they agree that synesthesia is more common in women than in men, and that it is an international phenomenon. Grossenbacher primarily employs sophisticated screening and interviewing methods to identify possible synesthetes. Others, bolstered by dramatic advances in imaging techniques, are observing the neural activity of synesthetes and measuring the unique ways their brains respond to stimuli. In the process, they are shedding light on how we all perceive the world around us.

"It's the only way I know of perceiving," Steen points out. "If someone said they were going to take it away, it would be like saying they were going to cut off my leg."

MISUNDERSTOOD REALITY

Embarrassment used to be the norm for synesthetes. In 1812, Dr. G.T.L. Sachs published the first scientific treatise on synesthesia. In it, he described how he and his sister experienced vivid color sensations when seeing, hearing, or even thinking about various vowels, consonants, names, and numbers. For the next 70 years, the only synesthetes to describe their symptoms publicly were doctors and researchers whose curiosity about their conditions outweighed their fear of being ridiculed.

Despite the obvious intelligence of the physician witnesses, most researchers viewed synesthesia as an illness. In 1864, Ernest Chabalier, a French doctor, described how a friend, who was also a physician, saw colors when he heard vowels, numbers, time periods, and proper names. But Chabalier thought it significant that his friend had suffered hallucinations as a child. A decade later, when Dr. Jean Nussbaumer of Vienna vividly described his own and his brother's colored hearing, another Austrian physician suggested, not too tactfully, that the Nussbaumers were mentally unbalanced. Only in the late 1870s did George Henry Lewes offer a more sympathetic portrayal, comparing the twinned sensations of synesthetes to his own feeling of a chill in his legs when he witnessed an unpleasant sight.

Grossenbacher, who has studied synesthesia for the past seven years, says that for many of the dozens of people he and a team at the National Institutes of Health (NIH) have interviewed or analyzed, "synesthesia doesn't present a problem, but in the back of their minds, some worry that they're mentally ill." In fact, synesthetes appear to be perfectly normal in every other way. Some have even exhibited above-average ability in recalling information, leading Grossenbacher and others to begin researching synesthesia's effect on memory.

Tajwar says synesthesia makes it easier for her to remember things such as a person's name. "When I meet someone, their name is a color, so I'll always associate that color with them," she says. (For example, she associates the name Sue with a bright "white"—primarily because in her mind's eye, the first letter, S, is white.) Michael Torke, a New York composer who associates colors with both letters and musical keys, also admits that synesthesia can frequently serve as a memory aid.

A MIXED BLESSING

In the 1980s, Torke wrote a series of compositions inspired by synesthesia—including "Bright Blue Music," written in D major; "Green," written in E major; and "Ecstatic Orange," "Yellow Page," "Purple," "Rust," and others—all named for the shades Torke found himself "swimming in" when composing pieces in particular keys. The artist David Hockney has used synesthesia in his work as well—to paint the colors of music that he was listening to at the time. When designing sets for the Metropolitan Opera, he would listen to music and, inspired by the colors, paint the sets accordingly. "When it came time to paint the tree for Ravel," he told Richard Cytowic, a Washington, D.C., neurologist, "I put on the tree music for the opera, and it had a certain weight and color. The music would dictate the shape."

But for Torke, synesthesia became a mixed blessing. "The colors became all anyone wanted to talk or write about. I started to resent it." Blame the cultural world's giddy love affair with "colored hearing" (and the notion that synesthetes are more artistically attuned), in part, on the French poet Arthur Rimbaud. In 1871, his sonnet "Voyelles" turned a medical curiosity and a seeming scientific rarity into an international cultural craze. "*A* black, *E* white, *I* red, *U* green, *O* blue . . . ," read Rimbaud's much-debated verse. A melding of the senses fits perfectly with the romantic view of the unity

Synesthete Shabana Tajwar has her own "time landscape": each month on the calendar has a particular color, and the year surrounds her like a clock. Her unique calendar will forever remain her reality.

of man and nature. Overnight, the fusion of color and sound showed up in symbolist poetry, fin de siècle English literature, and French and Russian theater and music.

The American painter, James McNeill Whistler, said art should "appeal to the artistic sense of eye or ear." He titled the famous painting of his mother *Arrangement in Grey and Black No. 1*, as though it were a musical composition. Russian abstract painter Wassily Kandinsky would later proclaim that for synesthetes, colors "call forth a vibration of the soul" like a violin at the touch of a bow.

FAD OR FACT?

In the decades surrounding the turn of the century, synesthetes came out of the closet and pseudo-synesthetes came out of the woodwork. Among the literati, having synesthesia became the yardstick for measuring an artist's genius. One enthusiast raved, "Color hearing marks for us a true progress in the perfection of our senses."

The fad reached its peak with Russian composer Aleksandr Scriabin, a purported synesthete. In his 1910 orchestral work, *Prometheus*, he ambitiously tried to meld music and color through the use of a mute "light organ" with which he intended to paint the concert hall with colored light in the form of beams, clouds, and other shapes. It proved technically impossible at the time. When finally attempted at Carnegie Hall on March 20, 1915, only "a white sheet at the back of the platform . . . was illuminated by streaks and spots of light of various colors," according to a critic who was dismissive of any meaningful connection between the colors and the music.

Regardless, the faddishness of synesthesia had already fostered a flurry of scientific interest. Doctors suddenly had hundreds of self-confessed synesthetes willing to be interviewed. In 1893, some 26 articles were published on the phenomenon. But researchers had no way to differentiate between pretenders and true synesthetes. How could they identify—never mind study—a seemingly subjective experience? Synesthesia increasingly became identified with decadent swooning artists, turbaned spiritualists, and, more recently, with psychedelic drugs like LSD.

Battling those stereotypes, researchers have spent the past decade or so gathering tantalizing clues about the cluster of traits and brain anomalies that make up synesthesia. Thanks to their efforts, few now doubt that the phenomenon exists. "It's gone from complete disbelief to less of a disbelief," says Richard Cytowic, whose research and popular book *The Man Who Tasted Shapes* are credited with helping spark the current renewed interest in synesthesia. "People are aware now of the amazing things happening inside the brain, so this is less strange."

Carol Steen can remember the precise hour—one o'clock on August 31, 1993—when she heard Cytowic talking on National Public Radio about synesthesia as a real condition. "I burst into tears," Steen says. "I was no longer alone." She immediately got in touch with him. "I had so many questions. In a 20-minute phone call, I barely let him get a whole sentence out," says Steen (who has talked with Cytowic many times since). "That day changed my life."

THE "HOWS" AND THE "WHYS"

On a steamy August afternoon at the NIH campus in Bethesda, Maryland, Peter Grossenbacher is drawing a web of circles and lines on a blackboard. There are several tentative theories about why synesthesia happens: one suggests that all infants may have it until about 6 months, but as their brains develop and multisensory linkages die, their responses become segregated.

Grossenbacher offers a slightly different view. In all brains, he says, input goes from single-sense modules (he chalks in little circles representing hearing and sight on a blackboard) along a pathway into a multisensory region (a large circle that he draws with a flourish). There are also pathways leading back again, but for most of us, those backward routes are inhibited. Grossenbacher thinks synesthetes may have an unusually strong feedback mechanism. Hallucinogenic drugs can produce synesthesia artificially, suggesting that we all have the feedback connections that make synesthesia possible. "The connections are normal," he conjectures. "They're just abnormal in the way they're used.

"We know synesthesia does happen," Grossenbacher says, "but scientists can't study the phenomenon without having ways of determining whether a particular person actually experiences it." Using a specially designed computer program with extremely specific color choice, the NIH team can precisely test the consistency of a synesthete's selections over time. Sitting at a computer in a white-walled windowless booth, Grossenbacher's colleague Carol Crane, a psychologist and synesthete, is staring at a color wheel on the screen and painstakingly

Synesthesia runs in families and occurs more often in women; many synesthetes "see" sound or "hear" colors. Artist Carol Steen weaves a pattern of light that reflects what she sees when listening to music.

selecting the precise shade and brightness of blue to match her number 2. "The first time I did this, it was agonizing trying to find the exact color," says Crane. "I was so afraid there wouldn't be a color to match."

This intensity of association of a letter or word with a particular shade is a hallmark of "colored-language" synesthesia. "It's not enough to say it's orange," says Pat Duffy of her tangerine *A*. Her *G* is not just black, but black with glints of gold, and *Z* is a brownish black with bubbles. The initial letter of a word usually gives a cast to the entire word—but there are glints of the other letters as well. "It's like looking at a vase from a distance and thinking it's one color," says Duffy, "but when you're close-up, you see it's really multicolored."

Reading a page of print, explains Carol Steen, can be like looking at a mosaic. "I 'see' the printed letter in black, or whatever color it's printed in," she says. "But I also see an overlay of my colors for those letters." Spoken words have the same colors as the words in print, but for some, the tone of a person's voice can add its own hues to the mix.

Accompanying the high degree of exactness is the consistency of the color choice over time. Dr. Simon Baron-Cohen, a psychologist at the University of Cambridge in England and the leading British researcher in this field, conducted a landmark study in 1993 that convinced many skeptics of synesthesia's existence. He asked a group of col-ored-language synesthetes, and a nonsynesthete control group, to describe the color or shape elicited by a list of 100 spoken words. Even a year and a half later, synesthetes gave the same answers an amazing 92 percent of the time. A week after the initial test, the group of nonsynesthetes had an accuracy rate of only 37 percent.

Sitting in a noisy café in the Chelsea section of New York City, Pat Duffy, a petite and graceful 48-year-old, bristles at the thought of one of her numbers changing color. "It never changes," she insists as she spears a lettuce leaf. "It can't. Can the shape of *V* change?"

Using positron-emission tomography (a PET scan), which shows patterns of cerebral blood flow and thus indicates neural activity, Baron-Cohen and his colleagues scanned the brains of synesthetes who link colors to spoken words. They also tested a control group. When the blindfolded volunteers listened to a tape of recorded words, they all showed activity in the language areas of their brains. But only in synesthetes did blood flow soar in areas of the visual cortex associated with such tasks as sorting images based on color. The implication is that "visual" information was being processed in the brains of synesthetes, even though they had not seen anything. Those results were confirmed using functional magnetic resonance imaging (fMRI), a new technique for detecting changes in cerebral blood flow.

Time, Numbers, and the Alphabet

Many colored-language synesthetes share yet another "visual" aberration—a very concrete perception of time, numbers, and the alphabet. Duffy has what she calls an "internal calendar," or "time landscape." For her, the week ahead is a pathway of colored rectangles. Tuesday is dark blue. Her alphabet is a slightly inclined string of letters. "I glide up the alphabet trail till I get the letter I need," she explains. Torke insists, "Numbers are like mountain peaks and valleys. At 20, there's a sharp turn to the right. At 100, they turn left."

A Canadian study of a synesthete doing arithmetic suggests how innate and spontaneous these traits are. Not just the sight of a number, but the mere concept of a number, can trigger color. When the subject was shown a math problem such as 5 + 2 =, followed by a patch of yellow (the color that corresponds to her number 7), she named the color and number faster than did the control subjects. But when she was shown the "wrong" color as an answer, she took longer than the control group to respond.

Color cues can be an aid or a hindrance. Such a strong association between colors and letters or numbers can easily cause confusion. Once when navigating Prague's subway system, Duffy saw that the A Line was green and the B Line yellow, but found herself getting on the wrong line because they were nearly the reverse of her colors. "If the color coding doesn't match mine, it's a problem," she says. Admits Tajwar: "Because a numeral 2 and letter S are similar whites, I sometimes write 2 instead of S by mistake."

Reality Varies

When Carol Steen stubbed her toe recently and let out a yelp, her husband dashed out of the bedroom to see what was wrong. It took a few moments for her to explain what had happened. "The first word out of my mouth was 'orange!'" she says. "Then I managed to tell him I'd hurt my toe."

At times, all the additional stimuli can be distracting. Carol Steen laughs that she gets sidetracked when looking up a word in the dictionary: "I end up looking at all the colors." Her friend Pat Duffy sometimes feels slightly overloaded. Duffy, who is currently working on a book about synesthesia, says: "I can't listen to music when I'm writing."

Despite the few negatives, synesthesia more often provides unequivocal pleasure. "It makes life more rich," says Michael Torke. An elderly English synesthete, who describes the word "emperor" as gray with silvery shimmers, says, "It enhances my ability to enjoy literature. I enjoy not only the sense of the word but the appearance."

For all the advances in understanding the condition, many fundamental questions remain. Even the number of synesthetes is under debate. Richard Cytowic once suggested that 10 people in a million have synesthesia. According to studies by Britain's Baron-Cohen, it's about 1 person in 2,000. But Grossenbacher suspects that the trait is more common—with maybe 1 person in 300 having had some form of synesthetic experience. On average, studies in England have shown about six females to every male. "That's not inconsistent with our findings," says Grossenbacher, who is continuing his NIH research with Carol Crane, in addition to other projects, as he takes up a new post at Naropa University in Boulder, Colorado.

Because the trait appears to run in families, researchers are now examining synesthetic family members and searching for a genetic factor. Their work may provide a missing piece of the puzzle. As Grossenbacher puts it, "Why does it happen in those brains and not others?"

When Michael Torke was in the second grade, the teacher asked his class to imagine a useful machine and write a short story about it. Excited, Torke described a device that would show how different people experience similar sensations, such as the color yellow. His parents and teacher were unenthusiastic. "They said, 'Why do you need it at all? Everyone experiences sensations the same,'" he remembers. "I really wanted to know how someone else tasted ice cream." As research into synesthesia continues, scientists are optimistic that they can gain more insight into human consciousness and perception. Their discoveries so far are a striking reminder that little Michael was right: reality isn't the same for everyone. ◢

Building from BABY BABBLE

by Bruce Bower

When you tell someone to stop babbling, your meaning is obvious: Quit talking confusing gibberish and speak more clearly.

Give the youngest babblers a break, though. Scientists have now come to suspect that the ingrained babbling of babies ranging in age from 7 to 12 months contains remarkably systematic vocal features that, soon enough, enable the tots to utter such delightful parental favorites as "No," "More," and "Why?" A better understanding of babbling may even allow researchers unprecedented glimpses into the controversy that surrounds the prehistory of human languages.

In fact, the gift of gab appears to grow out of roots that extend much deeper than babbling. One line of research finds that by age 3 months, babies communicate by combining vocalizations with facial expressions. A number of other investigators suggest that young babblers exploit their hand-to-mouth existence (i.e., whatever their hands can grasp gets jammed into their mouths), and they learn how to communicate with precisely timed words and gestures.

"Words are put into play by movements of the human body," says psycholinguist John L. Locke of the University of Cambridge in England. "Physical effects [on learning to speak] may be more pervasive, and languages less arbitrary in structure, than linguists have previously supposed."

The seemingly unintelligible chatter of 7- to 12-month olds may contain the vocal features that lead to coherent speech. Baby jabber may even offer researchers clues to the origins of human language

RESEARCHERS LISTEN VERY CLOSELY

Babbling research has come of age over the past 20 years. Investigators have established that between ages 7 and 10 months, infants begin to alternately lower and raise the jaw while making consonant and vowel sounds. Babbling of repeated sequences of consonant and vowel combinations then takes off.

For instance, opening and closing the lips with the tongue flattened allows a baby to say "baba." Open the lips and thrust the tongue tip off the mouth's roof to get "dada." Bunch the tongue up against the back of the mouth for "gaga."

Little by little, yet with astounding speed, these manipulations of speechlike sounds lead children to talk.

When babbling research got off the ground, several maverick teams of linguists began searching for speech sounds that are applied comparably in all or most of the world's languages. They reported such universal language consistencies as the use of single, distinct consonants and syllables that consist of a consonant followed by a vowel.

Enough of these shared linguistic properties exist to allow for the reconstruction of precursor languages all the way back to a prehistoric "mother tongue," according to some of these renegade researchers.

Mainstream linguists reject such claims. They argue that rampant changes and innovations by speakers of a language erase any of the features it might have shared with languages spoken more than about 5,000 years ago. According to their view, the relentless tweaking people do to their native tongues makes the search for linguistic universals hopelessly impossible.

Support for the mavericks' argument now comes, literally, from the mouths of babes. Peter F. MacNeilage and Barbara L. Davis, both psycholinguists at the University of Texas at Austin, say that a handful of basic sound patterns lurks within babies' babbling, infants' first words, and the reconstructed words of long-dead languages. Moreover, MacNeilage and Davis say that reconstructed words that have similar meanings across different language families usually contain matching arrangements of these fundamental sounds.

"Our findings provide totally independent support for the theory that there was one original language, a mother tongue," MacNeilage says. "It's wrong to assume that related languages cover up their tracks every 5,000 years."

"MAMA," "DADA," AND "GOGO"

MacNeilage and Davis statistically analyzed strings of speech sounds in the babbling of six babies and the first words of 10 slightly older infants. Tiny microphones attached to bibs worn by the diminutive participants, ages 6 to 18 months, recorded their vocalizations as the youngsters played with an English-speaking parent. The researchers also examined extensive lists of words from 10 modern languages, including English, Japanese, and Swahili.

MacNeilage and Davis identified three sequences of sound patterns common to babbling and words in general. Each consists of a consonant-vowel combination: lip consonants leading into vowels generated in the center of the mouth with a flattened tongue (such as "mama"), tongue-front consonants preceding vowels produced at the front of the mouth (such as "dada," the vowel pronounced as in "daddy"), and tongue-back consonants followed by back-of-the-mouth vowels (such as "gogo").

Additional studies directed by MacNeilage and others have identified these three sound sequences in the babbling of infants exposed to native French, Swedish, Japanese, Portuguese, and Quechua, a language spoken in Ecuador.

"FRAMES" LINK ANCESTORS, INFANTS

A fourth, more complex sound sequence appeared in infants' first words and across all 10 languages, but not in babbling. Sounds in this three-part sequence start with a lip consonant, followed by a vowel, and then a tongue-front consonant (as in "mad"). Other researchers have noted that people have an easier time articulating speech sounds from the front to the back of the mouth, such as "pug," than the reverse, such as "gap."

The physical arrangement of the mouth and the vocal tract—which by a baby's third

Some researchers believe that baby babble shares some basic sound patterns; indeed, the first words of early humans may have sounded like gibberish, but they gradually evolved into meaningful discourse.

month lengthens and bends dramatically—encourages certain sequences of oral movements, or frames, to occur during speaking, MacNeilage theorizes. The first words of human ancestors may have been built out of these frames, and thus may have sounded much like the first words of modern infants, he proposes.

Attempts to string together frames in more-complex ways—as in the front-to-back-of-the-mouth articulations of budding talkers—then fueled the evolution of more-complex words, in MacNeilage's scenario. He refers to this two-step process as the frame-content theory of speech evolution. According to the theory, mouth movements essential for simple speech sounds would have laid the groundwork for devising a meaningful vocabulary.

The three consonant-vowel frames found in babies' babbling also frequently appear in lists of words from 27 ancestral languages from different parts of the world, the Texas researchers say. Maverick linguists reconstructed these lists from groups of related

modern languages. In addition, reconstructed ancestral words contain many more instances of the front-to-back sequence of consonant and vowel sounds observed in infants' first words than of the back-to-front sound sequences.

MacNeilage says the new data challenge claims by critics of ancient-language reconstruction that the sound similarities of words with the same meaning in different languages often arise by chance.

SQUEALS, GROWLS, AND RASPBERRIES

Among scientists who study babbling and other types of infant vocalizations, the frame-content theory has attracted considerable interest. When MacNeilage published his position in 1998, he received generally favorable comments in 27 published peer reviews from psycholinguists and developmental psychologists.

"I think the frame-content hypothesis has real merit," remarks psycholinguist D. Kimbrough Oller of the University of Maine in Orono, who did not write a published

Young infants utter a wide variety of sounds, such as squeals and growls, that gain in frequency when a tot gazes at a parent. The gibberish stage usually begins at around 6 months.

review of MacNeilage's paper. "This provides an interesting addition to the debate over the reconstruction of ancient languages," he says.

Beginning around 20 years ago, Oller helped pioneer the study of speechlike sounds infants make while babbling. He has recently published his acute observations of infants' responses to their caregivers.

Before 6 months of age, infants emit a variety of sounds that appear to prepare them for babbling, Oller notes. These include squeals, growls, incomplete speech sounds, and the lip-rattling blasts known as raspberries. Such vocalizations, as well as smiling and other expressions, gain in frequency when infants younger than 6 months gaze at their mothers' face.

Youngsters also begin to coordinate vocalizations with their facial expressions months before they start to babble, presumably to communicate with their caregivers, Oller and his coworkers have reported.

The scientists videotaped 12 infants, each at age 3 months and again at age 6 months, interacting with one of their parents. Each parent was instructed to divide time between playing with the child and staring at a picture on the wall while maintaining a neutral facial expression.

In these situations, both 3-month-old and 6-month-old infants paired specific vocalizations with their facial expressions, Oller reports, although the older kids did so more frequently. For instance, a 3-month-old child who was confronted with a wall-gazing parent blurted out a remarkable harangue of growling noises just after adopting an angry facial expression. The outburst of ominous sounds faded away shortly before the youngster stopped looking upset and annoyed and assumed a happier, more-cheerful countenance.

SYLLABIC SOUND-MAKING

Vocalizing that precedes babbling may even contain rudimentary types of syllables, according to psychologist Kathleen Bloom of the University of Waterloo in Ontario. She argues that from around 3 to 6 months of age, infants make "syllabic" sounds that have more in common with babbling than with growls and most of the other prebabbling sounds cited by Oller. Syllabics consist of sustained vowel-like and consonant-like sounds with acoustic frequencies comparable to those measured for babbling.

In a series of studies from 1988 to 1996, Bloom reported that parents and other adults talk more to infants who make syllabic sounds, view those infants more favorably, and tend to regard infants' syllabic sounds as attempts at communication.

Syllabic sounds increase in length and acoustic complexity from around 2 months to 4 months of age, but then become shorter and less distinct for about a month before regaining momentum toward babbling, according to a long-term study of 13 infants that was directed by psychologist Hui-Chin Hsu of the University of Georgia in Athens.

Vocalization, from prebabbling to speech, requires the coordination of more than 70 muscles and many different body parts, ranging from the diaphragm to the lips, Hsu's team says. The temporary setback in the ability to vocalize probably results from major structural changes in the vocal tract that occur at around 4 months of age, upsetting the vocalization system that infants had been working so hard to master.

Vocalization may thus develop in fits and starts that vary greatly from one child to another, the researchers propose. Other researchers have applied this perspective, known as dynamic-systems theory, to motor development.

GABBING AND GESTICULATING

A contrasting view of speech development posits the existence of progressively unfolding, genetically controlled stages of vocal ability that differ little from one child to the next. This approach draws inspiration from the influential theory that infants have a genetically programmed ability to understand grammatical rules.

Oller sees much value in dynamic-systems theory. However, he and many other psycholinguists remain skeptical about reports of syllabic vocalizing by 3- to 6-month-olds. Syllabic sounds are poorly defined acoustically, Oller contends.

From a dynamic-systems perspective, infants and young children learn to communicate by seamlessly combining two movement systems, one for speech and the other for gestures, according to Jana M. Iverson of the University of Missouri in Columbia and Esther Thelen of Indiana University at Bloomington. It's time to rethink the popular notion of gestures as a decorative sideline to the real business of saying what you mean, the researchers argue. Instead, gabbing and gesticulating go hand in hand.

"In adults, language and movement are very closely related in the brain," Iverson says. "The question then becomes, How did they get that way?"

THE BABIES AREN'T TALKING

Mental activity arises through bodily interactions with the world, a process that forges a deep connection between talk and gestures, Iverson and Thelen have argued. For example, as Iverson and a colleague reported in 1998, even blind speakers gesture while talking to blind listeners. Arm movements apparently play an integral role in a speaker's ability to express ideas, whether or not anyone else sees the motions.

In learning to communicate, infants probably employ some type of general ability to produce rhythmic sequences of both hand movements and speech sounds, Iverson suggests. Rhythmic arm and hand movements emerge at about 6 months of age, at roughly the same time as rhythmic babbling begins to occur.

The tight linkage of mouth and hand movements also explains the emergence of so-called "manual babbling" in both hearing and deaf infants, Iverson says. First reported for deaf babies in 1991, manual babbles consist of cycles of repeated gestures that have no meaning. For instance, a child might rhythmically jab the index finger of the left hand into the palm of the right hand.

Researchers initially explained this as evidence for an innate language-learning facility that works through gestures instead of speech in deaf babies. However, a 1995 study found that hearing infants with no exposure to sign language babble with their hands as well as with their mouths.

Manual babbling represents a rhythmic behavior that appears during a child's transition to achieving fine-motor control over the hands, just as rhythmic vocal babbling heralds a shift to speech-worthy control over the vocal tract, Iverson argues.

By adulthood, people unthinkingly time each of their gestures to coincide precisely with the word or phrase it accompanies, she notes. Investigators have found that when a speaker stutters over a word, an accompanying gesture tends to freeze until the moment that speech resumes.

Still, comprehensive explanations of speech development—and the capacity for understanding grammar in particular—elude scientists. If the babies babbling into microphones and repetitively poking their palms have an opinion on the matter, they're not saying.

Ask the Scientist

▶ *Is it a sign of health trouble when a person has one blue eye and one brown eye? Are such people especially prone to vision problems? Can eye color be changed somehow?*

Eye color is a trait that is based entirely on genetics, meaning that a person's eye color is determined by the eye color of his or her parents and grandparents. Several genes control the trait, although the exact number is not known for certain. While eye color is not absolute, and varies from person to person, it is not possible to permanently change one's eye color. Colored contact lenses come in a variety of shades and can be used to temporarily change eye color.

It is possible for an individual to have two different-colored eyes, probably due to a genetic anomaly. There is no evidence that such people have any higher incidence of vision problems as compared to the rest of the population.

▶ *Do most people who lose their teeth do so from disease or neglect? Are dentures glued directly to the gums? How can that possibly be comfortable?*

Neglect and disease are both leading causes of tooth loss. Disregard for proper tooth care—brushing after meals and snacks, flossing on a regular basis, and eating correctly—can lead to decay of the tooth enamel. When sugars remain in between or on the surface of the teeth, they draw bacteria, which produce acids that break down and erode the tooth enamel, causing the tooth to decay and eventually die. Children, the elderly, and people taking certain medications are particularly vulnerable to tooth decay, and need to be especially diligent about taking care of their teeth.

Neglect, as well as other causes, can also lead to periodontal diseases, which can lead to tooth decay. The most common periodontal disease is gingivitis, which causes the gums to become inflamed and to recede. This condition leads to exceedingly painful infections of the bone and tissue surrounding the tooth, which may ultimately cause tooth loss.

Dentists often replace teeth with full or partial dentures. Partial dentures are essentially false teeth that are attached to a wire-and-plastic apparatus much like an orthodontic retainer. This apparatus fits into the mouth and adheres to teeth. Full dentures are whole sets of teeth that are secured to the gums with adhesive glue. If inserted properly, dentures should not be uncomfortable. Newer techniques utilize permanent tooth implants.

▶ *Is it still considered as necessary as it once was for doctors and nurses to scrub their hands all the time? Do medical personnel wear face masks to protect themselves or the patients from germs?*

Even though standards of sterility vary from place to place, it is extremely necessary for health-care workers to pay attention to cleanliness in order to prevent the spread of disease. Doctors and nurses often work in sterile environments, such as the operating room, where proper sterile technique is essential to protect them as well as the patients. These procedures include scrubbing hands carefully; wearing germ-free gowns, gloves, and masks; and never touching any object that has not been sterilized.

Hand washing remains a vital way to prevent the spread of disease. Doctors and nurses must wash their hands many times throughout the day, generally after every patient they see, and advocate that the general public does the same.

Is weight training considered a wise form of exercise? Are the physique-enhancing results achieved by lifting weights to build muscle mass more or less permanent?

Weight training is considered an important part of an exercise routine, as it improves strength and flexibility, and aids in weight loss when performed properly. It is advised that prospective weight lifters seek the advice of a doctor or personal trainer to avoid injury and to gain maximum benefits. An effective exercise program consists of both weight training and cardiovascular exercise to promote the health of the heart and lungs. However beneficial these exercises are, the results persist only if the individual is able to continue the program.

What is the function of the knee's ACL? Is it easily ruptured? If ruptured, what treatment options are usually recommended?

The ACL (anterior cruciate ligament) connects the bone of the thigh (the femur) to one of the bones of the calf (the tibia). It controls the forward-extension movement of the leg at the knee, and works in conjunction with other ligaments. The ACL is the most commonly injured ligament of the knee, although ACL tears often occur

along with tears of the medial collateral ligament (MCL). With the rising popularity of many sports, ACL tears have also risen, but there has been a concurrent increase in the number of treatment options available. In recent years, ligamentous injuries have dramatically increased among young women who are now participating in more sports than did earlier generations.

Patients often sustain an ACL injury by hyperextending their leg or twisting it in an awkward angle; frequently, a sensation of tearing or an audible "pop" as the ligament ruptures is reported. Swelling and bleeding often occur directly after the injury, which may subside; sometimes it is necessary to remove fluid and blood from the knee through a needle. The extent of the tear is then generally assessed with a combination of X rays and magnetic resonance imaging (MRI).

The course of treatment for an ACL injury depends on its severity. If the ligament is not completely severed, a physician may recommend physical therapy and the use of a specially fitted brace. If a total rupture has occurred and the joint is unstable, surgery may be the best course of action. During this surgery, an arthroscope is used to graft, or substitute, the existing torn tendon with other tissue from the patient. Arthroscopic surgery leaves few scars and is highly successful in repairing this kind of ligament damage.

Following surgery, the patient must undergo physical therapy to strengthen other areas of the leg to prevent further injury and to attain a complete recovery. It normally takes nine months for the reconstructed ligament to heal. But successful rehabilitation is a lengthy process, particularly for a person who suffers a complete tear, and it can take a full year or more to recuperate. Athletes who participate in high-impact sports—like football—are often victims of this type of injury. But with the latest advances in therapy and treatment, most players are able to find their way back onto the field.

C. Andrew Salzberg, M.D.

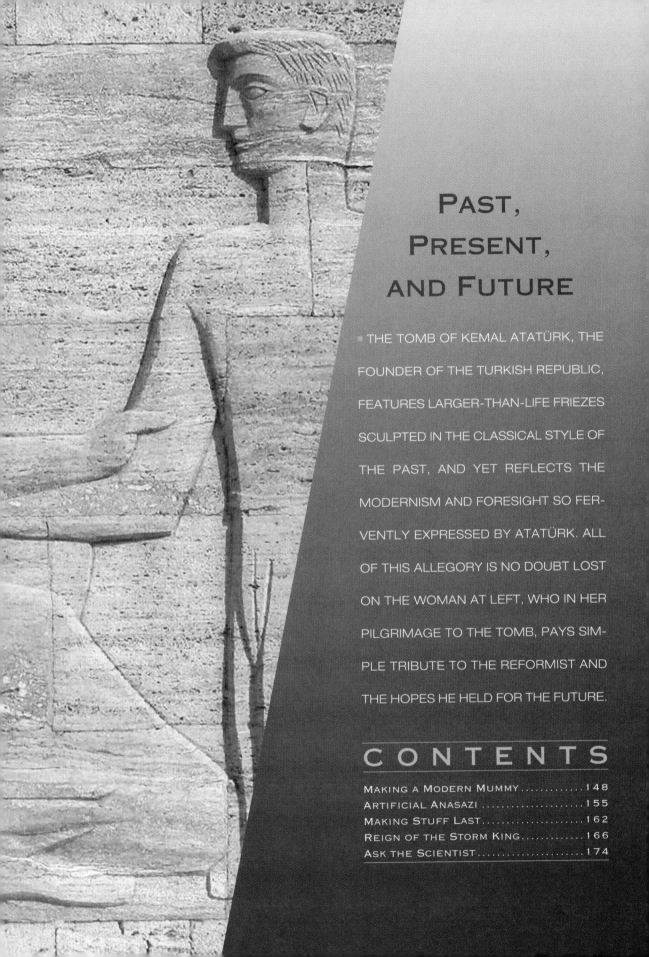

PAST, PRESENT, AND FUTURE

● THE TOMB OF KEMAL ATATÜRK, THE FOUNDER OF THE TURKISH REPUBLIC, FEATURES LARGER-THAN-LIFE FRIEZES SCULPTED IN THE CLASSICAL STYLE OF THE PAST, AND YET REFLECTS THE MODERNISM AND FORESIGHT SO FERVENTLY EXPRESSED BY ATATÜRK. ALL OF THIS ALLEGORY IS NO DOUBT LOST ON THE WOMAN AT LEFT, WHO IN HER PILGRIMAGE TO THE TOMB, PAYS SIMPLE TRIBUTE TO THE REFORMIST AND THE HOPES HE HELD FOR THE FUTURE.

CONTENTS

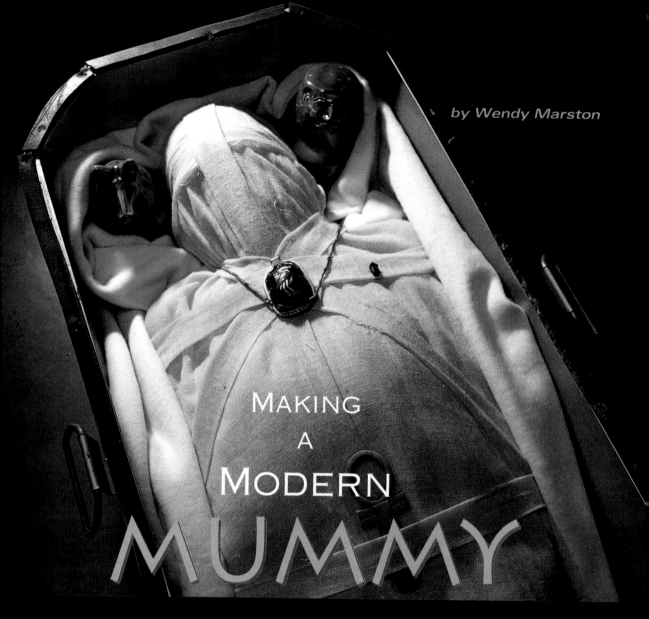

by Wendy Marston

MAKING
A
MODERN
MUMMY

Using ancient techniques, scientists successfully
re-created a genuine mummy—and in the process, gained new
insight into the dynamics of tissue preservation.

The first mummy, it is said, was the Egyptian god Osiris—brother and husband of Isis—who was slain and dismembered by his brother Seth. The pieces of Osiris's body were then distributed throughout Egypt. But Isis retrieved them, pieced them back together, and wrapped them in linen. Thus revived, Osiris resumed his life, but, because of his death and subsequent rebirth, he reigned as

sovereign of the dead, one of the most revered and powerful deities.

And the last mummy, it may someday be said, is a man who died in Baltimore in 1994 of a heart attack. His body was donated for scientific use and his identity remains anonymous. He left this life when he was in his 70s. By now, his mummifiers imagine, this man has already approached Osiris and been deemed worthy.

One of his mummifiers is Ronn Wade, director of the Maryland State Anatomy Board and director of the Anatomical Service Division of the University of Maryland in College Park. He is in charge of finding and allotting to medical schools the cadavers of those who have donated their bodies to science. Offices at the University of Maryland have been Wade's primary domain for 27 years, and he hurries through underground corridors, past a covered body on a gurney—with only a pale toe peeking out—without a glance. More than five years ago, these quarters opened a small window onto the funerary practices of the ancient Egyptians.

Scientists speculate that ancient mourners believed preserving a human body through elaborate mummification rituals would help protect the spirit during its transit to the afterlife.

STOPPING TIME

Inside Wade's dim, windowless office stands a large Styrofoam replica of an Egyptian sarcophagus (aboveground coffin), and, but for a few replicas of human organs, the room looks as if it belonged to an Egyptologist at the British Museum. In 1994, Wade was contacted by the classical scholar Bob Brier, a professor of philosophy and Egyptology at the C.W. Post campus of Long Island University in New York. After years of studying hieroglyphs and investigating tombs, Brier had decided that his research would not be complete until he mummified—properly— a human body. The problem: where to get the body. A colleague put him in touch with Wade, who agreed to help. They became partners in a plot to re-create ancient Egyptian techniques of body preservation.

Once certain of their mission, Wade and Brier waited months for the perfect subject—someone who had been relatively healthy and whose body was physically intact. Finally, the ideal candidate arrived: a 187-pound (85-kilogram) man in his 70s, dead after a massive heart attack. By carefully following the 2,000-year-old descriptions of mummifying techniques and using only replicas of ancient tools, Wade and Brier painstakingly transformed the body into an Egyptian-style mummy. Now, five years later, the duo's mummy by and large retains the physiological condition it had immediately after mummification. There is no sign of bacterial decay. The skin remains remarkably intact. Like ancient Egyptian practitioners, Brier and Wade stopped time for a corpse, and their work is likely to remain intact for thousands of years.

Although critics say the team's project was frivolous, both men insist their purpose was to understand—in real time—how and why certain procedures were accomplished. "The goal was not a mummy," Brier says sternly. "The goal was knowledge."

RESURRECTING TRADITION

The Paraca Indians of Peru mummified their dead, as did the Guanches in the Canary Islands. But Egyptian mummies have always commanded the most attention, perhaps because such meticulous care was given to maintaining the body and the accoutrements of the deceased. Surviving accounts of Egyptian funerals come from the Greek historians Diodorus Siculus, who traveled in Egypt between 65 and 57 B.C., and Herodotus, who visited Egypt in the 5th century B.C. From those reports, we know that not all mummies were created equal. A poor man would be dispatched to the afterlife after a perfunctory mummification, either rubbed in oils or briefly covered with natron—a naturally occurring baking-soda and-salt compound—or tree resin from conifers. Both

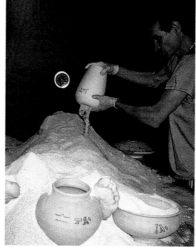

The preservation ritual began by extracting the brain. Vital organs—except for the heart, which was considered sacred—were removed and stored in jars (top). Next, the cadaver underwent treatment with natron, a compound that absorbs water and foul odors (bottom).

Funerals for rich Egyptians were far more public and elaborate than they were for commoners, and none more so than the pharaoh's. The death of the pharaoh was said to inaugurate a 70-day period during which normal life ceased. No sacrifices were made; everyone wept and rent their garments. Throngs sang dirges in the street, mud caked upon their heads. For 70 days, no one bathed, drank wine, made love, or ate meat. Meanwhile, the pharaoh's body was prepared and mummified.

The accounts of Herodotus and Diodorus are the only texts that describe how mummies were created. Although the Book of the Dead sounds as if it would be crammed with grisly secrets, it reads more like a papyrus chain letter filled with rituals, magic spells, and incantations to help the dead more easily make their way into the afterlife. Mummification, like modern undertaking, was probably a family trade, with techniques passed down from generation to generation. Wade is no stranger to this sort of artisan tradition. His father was an undertaker, as was Wade before his appointment to the Anatomy Board.

compounds drew water, essential for decay-causing bacteria, out of the body. Wrapped in a single sheath of linen, the body would be laid in a hole, a cave, or even in desert sands, with sandals, a staff, a few possessions, and some amulets. Archaeologists suspect the early practice of burying the dead in the dry sand produced naturally preserved corpses and may have inspired the art of mummification. The preserved state of such bodies, scientists speculate, might have convinced the living that keeping the body intact would also protect the spirit.

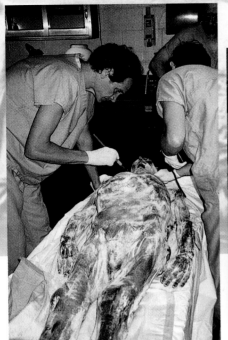

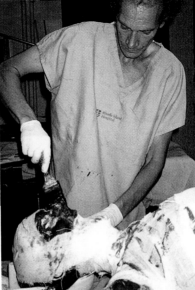

PROBING FOR ANSWERS

Brier and Wade were determined to answer some nagging questions about Egyptian mummification. Why did it take 70 days? How did they remove the organs and minimize injury to the body's exterior? How was the brain removed?

Removing the brain, Brier emphasizes, was the critical step—and it proved a challenge. Herodotus had described taking brain tissue out by hooking it on the end of a metal tool and lifting it out one chunk at a time. But Wade and Brier found that brain tissue was not dense enough to hold together for that kind of removal. "The tissue just doesn't adhere to the tool," Brier says. "It's too liquid, too moist; it won't come out. We had to put the hook in and rotate it like a whisk."

To get their technique down—and to be especially careful not to injure the mummy's face at the same time—Brier and Wade first experimented on at least two other severed heads. "We tried a few things, like forcing water into the head cavity, but that put pressure on the eyes," Brier says. Wade recalls that they removed the top of one of the heads before they inserted

an instrument called the brain whisk—a comparatively long hooked bronze tool half as thick as a pencil—and were able to observe the path the liquefied tissue took as it churned inside the skull. From that experiment, they learned that they needed to thread the whisk up the nostril and through the olfactory tract to get it into the skull.

To cleanse the skull, they wound linen strips on the end of the hook and swabbed out excess tissue and moisture. Then they packed the skull with linen rubbed with

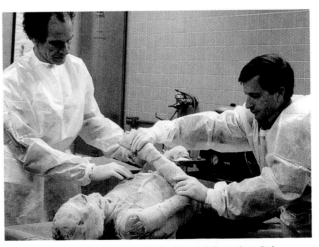

With the ritual nearly complete, the body was fully enshrouded, and special prayers were inscribed on the cloth. Positioning the mummy with arms crossed over the chest helped to re-create the look of preserved Egyptian bodies.

Looks That Last

A cloth-wrapped figure skulking around in inky darkness is the typical depiction of a Hollywood mummy, but mummies are hardly walking predators to be feared. Real mummies are actually deceased humans or animals whose bodies have been preserved, or mummified, to stop natural decomposition. Often associated with ancient rituals,

Unlike ancient Egyptians, whose dead were mummified in preparation for the afterlife, most modern-day "mummifiers" have concentrated on such larger-than-life personalities as Eva Perón (above) and Vladimir Lenin (right), whose preserved bodies helped to some extent to sustain in their followers a certain cultish devotion.

mummification has also been used to immortalize prominent people in more recent times as well.

Eva Perón, "Evita," the second wife of Argentine President Juan Perón, is remembered as a willful, compassionate voice for the lower economic classes. When Eva died in 1952, her body

was preserved with paraffin in a painstaking process that took nearly two years.

When he was exiled from Argentina, Juan Perón had to leave Eva's body behind. Fearing reaction from Perón loyalists, military leaders secretly buried the body in a cemetery in Milan, Italy, under a false name. Eva remained there for 14 years until 1971 when the Argentine government finally returned her body to her husband.

When Eva Perón's body was exhumed nearly 20 years after her death, it was remarkably intact and appeared incredibly lifelike. In 1976, Eva Perón was put to final rest in a family crypt at a Buenos Aires cemetery.

Perhaps the best-known "modern" mummy is that of Vladimir Lenin, mastermind of the Russian Revolution and founder of the Soviet State. Lenin's body has spent the past 77 years in a mummified state—on display in a mausoleum in Red Square, Moscow, Russia. When he was mummified by a still-secret process shortly after his death, Soviet scientists had to work at a furious pace to halt natural decay. They also attempted to conceal the signs of their leader's mortality: dark spots on Lenin's skin were bleached, his hair was darkened, and pink lights give his skin a rosy hue.

Despite semiregular treatments with preservatives, the Lenin mummy has begun to show the ravages of time: only Lenin's face and hands are still made visible to the public; the rest of his body is now covered with a black cloth.

frankincense—one of the seven sacred substances the ancient mummifiers used. The other sacred substances known are myrrh, cedar, lotus, and palm wine.

BY THE BOOK

The next step was to extract and preserve the internal organs. (The brain, considered unimportant, was discarded.) Because ancient Egyptians believed that the dead would use their bodies in the next life, minimizing damage to the exterior was crucial. The organs had to be removed through a small 3-inch (8-centimeter) cut in the abdomen. "Imagine sticking your hand inside a dark, crowded closet and untangling the clothes," marvels Wade. "You can't see anything. You have to feel your way through."

According to Herodotus, the first incision was made with a sharp "Ethiopian stone." Brier took the term to mean obsidian—a glassy black volcanic rock that can be flaked to a razor's edge. "Obsidian is sharper and thinner than any surgeon's scalpel," says Brier. "Inside the body, we used bronze and copper knives, but obsidian was definitely meant for making the first slit."

Wade, the designated surgeon, then reached into the slit with a small copper knife firmly wedged between his first and second fingers so that only a few centimeters of blade peeked out. The first organs removed, Wade recalls, were the upper intestinal tract and the pancreas. Next were the spleen, kidneys, bladder, and more of the digestive tract. The intestines, he says, were tricky. "The intestine doesn't just run like a worm; it has a lot of connections to other organs. But it came out collectively, with the rest of the colon, in two sections." The stomach was next, then the liver. "That's a large, dome-shaped organ, and it's like delivering a small child through a tiny opening." Wade was forced to extend the 3-inch slit by 2 inches (5 centimeters).

After the liver came the lungs. "Lungs are like a wet sponge. You can compress them, so it wasn't hard to get them out," Wade

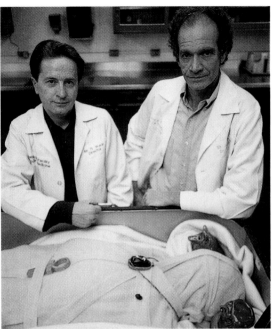

The modern mummy rests, accompanied by jars containing the body's dried organs and adorned with symbols of rebirth.

says. "They're connected to the heart, so I had to cut a lot of vessels off them." For this, Wade used a bronze knife, much sharper than the copper blade.

The heart—considered the nexus of thought and soul by ancient Egyptians— was left in the rib cage. When the deceased approached Osiris in the afterlife, his heart would be weighed. If it was as light as the feather of Maat, the goddess of truth, the person was a step closer to being accepted by the gods.

FINAL TOUCH

As a final touch, 29 linen-wrapped packets of natron were tucked inside the body. In addition to collecting water, hastening desiccation, and absorbing any foul odors that might be produced, the packets helped preserve the natural contours of the body for its resurrection in the afterlife.

Now Wade and Brier placed the body on a wooden platform covered with natron and heaped more natron upon it. The spleen, liver, kidneys, lungs, and other organs were placed on ceramic platters nearby. They, too, were covered with natron. Just as salts will preserve and dry meats, the natron—580 pounds (263 kilograms) of it—would draw out the body's moisture and render the dried flesh impervious to bacteria. The platform holding the body and the other organs was put into an embalming preparation room in the basement of Wade's department and kept at 90° to 107° F (32° to 42° C). Two dehumidifiers working around the clock for 35 days would re-create the dry desert conditions of Egypt.

At midday of the 35th day, Wade and Brier opened the room containing the body. "The natron was wet," Wade remembers. "It smelled like wet sand." The white, sandy compound had clumped on top of the body and become stiff from the fluids it had absorbed. Originally 156 pounds (71 kilograms) with its organs removed, the body "now weighed 79 pounds (36 kilograms)," says Wade. "It had lost 77 pounds (35 kilograms) of water."

Now it was time to remove the natron packets through the initial cut. "The incision had been drawn tight by the body's shrinking," says Wade. "I could barely get my hand in it." Brier and Wade managed to get out all but a few.

WRAPPING IT UP

At this stage, the body had become what most people would consider a mummy. No longer was it a normal corpse. The body was stiff and shrunken and blackened—it resembled an object, not a person. Wade and Brier began the beautification process. First they rubbed the skin with linen strips that had been soaked in oil containing frankincense, myrrh, cedar, lotus, and palm wine. Then they wrapped the body with linen strips, securing it with dabs of lacquer made of cedar resin. "My hands smelled of it for months," Wade recalls.

According to ancient Egyptian texts, the body was supposed to be kept under natron for 35 days, and then kept around, exposed, for another 35—perhaps for a period of mourning or other religious rituals. At this stage, Brier and Wade departed from Egyptian tradition and waited 140 days to make the final preparations.

The body had lost more moisture. It now weighed about 70 pounds (32 kilograms). This was the day to complete its linen shroud and inscribe the cloth with appropriate prayers. Each finger, toe, and limb was wrapped individually, and as each was done, Brier recited a prayer. For example, one prayer, translated by Gaston Maspero in 1875, was to be said as the head was being bandaged. It included this plea: "O doubly powerful, eternally young, and very mighty lady of the west and mistress of the east, may breathing take place in the head of the deceased in the netherworld!" Brier, an expert in hieroglyphs, says he is not certain he pronounced the prayers correctly. Hieroglyphs contain no vowels, so Brier's pronunciation was mostly guesswork.

The last step, says Brier, was to cross the mummy's arms over its chest to re-create the pose of many Egyptian mummies. The arms, however, would not stay in position. Most of the body's pliability had evaporated along with the last few pounds of water. Wade and Brier were surprised. Their mummy, like the mummies from the Old Kingdom, now lies with its arms at its sides. "We should have positioned it when we first got it out at day 35," Wade says. "But we never even thought of it."

HISTORY REBORN

Now the mummy rests three doors down from Wade's office. It has been admired by museumgoers and coveted by Egyptologists as a control for analyzing the physical conditions of ancient mummies. Forensic archaeologists can already determine if the person mummified had parasites, arthritis, or, sometimes, bacterial disease. Now that they know what mummification does to the body's tissues, they can extrapolate with more accuracy the health conditions of ancients who were mummified.

At each shoulder and foot of the mummy stands a blue-green canopic jar, each containing dried-out organs. On the breastbone sits a black stone scarab with an ibis upon it. Both are symbols of rebirth. If Brier uttered the proper prayers as the final wrappings were applied, the Egypt of the afterlife may have a new, unexpected citizen.

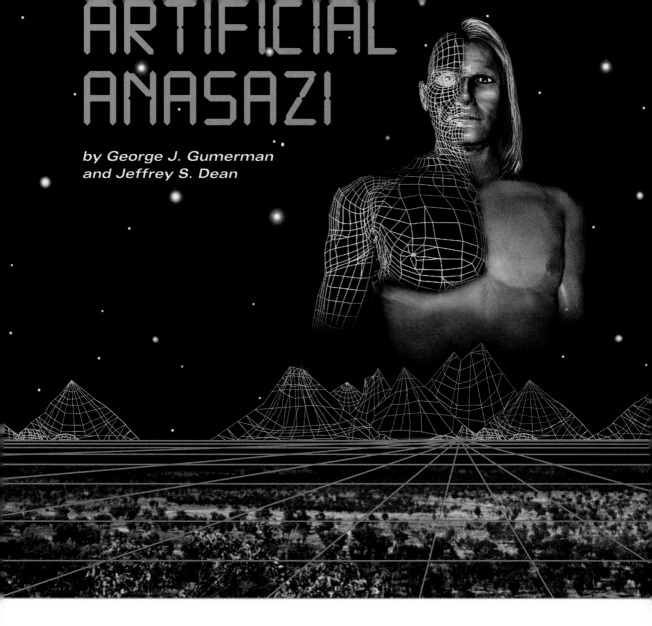

ARTIFICIAL ANASAZI

by George J. Gumerman and Jeffrey S. Dean

The problem with studying the past is that it is past. The people who prospered in times of peace and plenty and struggled through conflict and drought are long dead. The forces that drove them to settle here or move there, that brought them together as families and clans, villages and

Researchers have created a computer simulation to digitally resurrect the Anasazi, the intriguing prehistoric people of the American Southwest. Such models may help to shed new light on ancient civilizations.

cities, have faded from memory. Archaeology provides hints and clues of what was, but we cannot test our hypotheses with experiments on cultures living or dead. We cannot, as paleontologist Stephen Jay Gould has noted, rewind the tape and watch a replay of the past.

Then again, perhaps we can.

The Santa Fe Institute in New Mexico is a multidisciplinary research and education center that explores how physical, biological, and cultural systems become more complex.

Long House Valley in northern Arizona (inset) was home to Anasazi tribes from about 1800 B.C. until A.D. 1300. Nestled between mountain ranges and self-contained, the valley was almost completely isolated (above), and an ideal spot for a settlement to flourish. It was also the perfect setting for the electronic simulation it inspired.

An eclectic group of researchers there (archaeologists, a dendroclimatologist, several computer theorists, a programmer, and a physical anthropologist) have applied new computer-simulation techniques to the well-studied Anasazi people of the prehistoric American Southwest in order to compare the behavior of computer-created "artificial Anasazi" with the real thing.

Computer modeling allows researchers to re-create prehistoric landscapes and environments, and to populate them with virtual people—digital creations with some of the needs, independence, and capabilities of real-world humans. We can establish rules of conduct and replicate social units. Then we can turn down the rainfall—or turn up the population—and watch how this cyber-culture and its artificial people react.

DIGITAL PEOPLE

We call these digital people "agents," and agent-based modeling offers intriguing possibilities for archaeological experiments. A major test on a long-occupied and well-studied valley in northeastern Arizona near

Monument Valley demonstrates the potential power of the computer model to examine the natural and cultural forces that act upon individuals and societies.

With agent-based modeling, we can create a landscape which is largely imaginary or that includes important aspects of a real-world environment. We then introduce onto the landscapes our agents, each endowed with such attributes as life span, vision, nutritional requirements, and the ability to move about and consume or store available resources. Our artificial agents play out their lives on this landscape, adapting to changes in their physical and social environments. They move about, bring new sites under cultivation, form new households, follow certain kinship rules, and die out. The goal is to mimic in important ways individuals or social units, such as households, lineages, clans, and villages.

A set of anthropologically plausible rules defines the ways the agents can interact with each other and with their environment. Altering the rules, the agents' attributes, or features of the landscape allows us to exam-

Archaeologists acquired a wealth of knowledge about the Anasazi by studying the artifacts and ruins they left behind. This data was essential in developing the Artificial Anasazi Project.

ine behavioral responses to changing environmental and social conditions.

To test the validity of agent modeling, we applied it extensively to a landscape where we know a great deal about the people who inhabited it from roughly 1800 B.C. to A.D. 1300, the environmental changes they faced, and how they reacted to them. Long House Valley, on the Navajo Indian Reservation in northeastern Arizona, was home to the Kayenta Anasazi, the prehistoric ancestors of the modern Pueblo cultures of the Southwest.

The Artificial Anasazi Project evaluated our agent-modeling program against the real-world experience of the Kayenta Anasazi in their discrete, 36-square-mile (93-square-kilometer) valley.

LONG HOUSE VALLEY

Long House Valley is an ideal test bed. Topographically bounded and self-contained, the landscape can be conveniently reproduced on a computer. A heavily studied paleoenvironmental record allows us to accurately reconstruct annual fluctuations in potential maize production. Detailed ethnographic research in the region provides a basis for generating the agents' behavioral rules.

Finally, we know much about what the Kayenta Anasazi did during their long stay in Long House Valley. Intensive archaeological research throughout the valley offers a remarkably complete database on human behavior, which is the real-world target for the simulation.

Maize, or corn, was probably introduced around 1800 B.C. It sparked a transition to a food-producing economy, which led to the Anasazi cultural tradition that persisted until the valley was completely—and mysteriously—abandoned about A.D. 1300.

In our model, artificial agents representing individual households—the smallest social unit consistently definable in the archaeological record—populate the changing environment of Long House Valley. These household agents have independent characteristics such as age, location, and grain stocks, and shared characteristics such as death age and nutritional need. Agent demographics, nutritional requirements, and marriage characteristics were derived by anthropologist Alan Swedlund from studies of historic Pueblo groups and other subsistence agriculturists throughout the world.

HARVESTING CYBERGRAIN

In the Artificial Anasazi model, the size of households is always fixed at five individuals. Each household is both matrilineal and matrilocal (meaning kinship and residence are established through the wife's family), so household formation and movement center on females.

Every year, household agents harvest the grain that is available where they have chosen to farm. They choose their farmland on the basis of environmental data, plus random factors that are intended to reflect site-specific variations in soil quality, moisture, height of water table, erosion and deposition, and annual fluctuations caused by weather, blight, and other things not available in the data.

Each agent consumes its own nutritional requirement, bringing the total maize needed per household to 1,763 pounds (800 kilo-

Surviving in Sugarscape

Sugarscape is an unforgiving world of sugar and spice. Its inhabitants wisely settle the rich sugar mountains, or they struggle, and often starve, on the sugar-poor badlands. Generations pass as families form, children are born, and parents die. Wars are fought and alliances forged. Trade sends sugar and spice across the landscape. Sugar barons and spice kings emerge. Evolution rewards the fittest, while the weakest—except the heirs of wealthy parents—are mercilessly weeded out. And life goes on at Sugarscape.

The "people" of Sugarscape are digital dots of red or blue, each with its own abilities and needs, that scamper across a virtual world. They compete for the coins of the realm, arbitrarily designated "sugar" and "spice." They repeatedly play out their lives in a computer at the Brookings Institution in Washington, D.C. This is the genesis of "agent-based modeling," a potent tool that grows artificial societies to create an unprecedented laboratory for social scientists.

The Sugarscape model, on which the Artificial Anasazi Project is based, was developed at Brookings by computer scientist Robert Axtell and social scientist Joshua Epstein. It follows early efforts by a handful of researchers, notably Thomas Schelling's model of racial segregation by neighborhoods in the 1970s. Only in the past decade have computers made large-scale, agent-based models possible.

The broad aim of Sugarscape is to develop a computerized approach to studying diverse spheres of human activity. Axtell and Epstein have said the disciplines of social science—economics, political science, demographics, and so forth—tend to analyze their subjects in relative isolation from one another. Yet these divisions are clearly artificial; the processes play out in a complex mosaic of cause and effect.

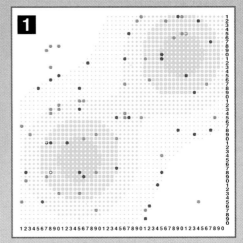

Virtual "tribes" evolve gradually in the Sugarscape model. At the outset, red and blue "agents" wander the digital environment (panel 1). Over time, two separate groups form, each with its own steady supply of sugar (panel 2). Population pressures eventually force interaction between the two colonies (panel 3).

Agent-based models examine a broad range of human phenomena: trade, migration, group formation, combat, environmental interactions, transmission of culture, the spread of disease, and population dynamics. Artificial societies are laboratories in which we can seek fundamental mechanisms that produce the social structures and collective behaviors we see in the real world.

Sugarscape evolves as more rules are added to increase the complexity of its foundation. The people of Sugarscape, the agents, have one rule: find as much food (sugar) as you can, go to it, and eat it. Each agent is born with "genetic" properties that are fixed for life: gender, metabolic rate (how fast the body burns sugar), and vision (how far the agent can see in searching for sugar). These are passed on to their children as a mix of attributes from both parents. Other traits—wealth, cultural identity, health—change as the agents move and interact with the landscape and each other.

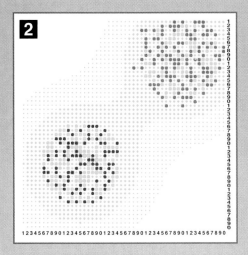

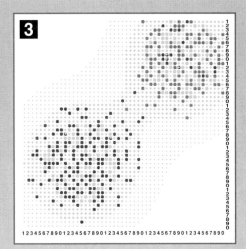

Their virtual world is a two-dimensional landscape: some areas are rich in sugar, others have none at all; most fall somewhere in between. Every time an agent moves, it burns sugar. If an agent burns up all its sugar, it dies.

If seasonal variations in local sugar production are introduced, populations quickly outgrow the available resources. Migrations occur and competition begins. Researchers can provide changeable cultural attributes (denoted by red or blue coloring) and rules for transmitting them across generations to explore the development of culture, intertribal warfare, assimilation, and other cultural activities.

When the simplest hunter-gatherer scenario is expanded to allow agents to store excess sugar, some become wealthy, while most end up with very little—a highly skewed distribution of wealth seen in actual human societies. Introducing a second resource (spice)—and rules for the trade of sugar and spice—brings commerce to Sugarscape. But supply and demand do not often achieve the balance predicted by laissez-faire economics. Allowing credit to finance the birth of children results in very elaborate borrower-lender networks.

As generations pass, you can actually watch evolution at work. For example, selection pressures lower the average metabolic rate and improve average vision. The model can even turn loose infectious disease, which increases a victim's sugar-burning metabolism, and can endow each agent with its own adaptive immune system to combat the disease.

Sugarscape gives agents attributes and rules of behavior, then spins the system forward in time to see what social structures emerge. This approach contrasts sharply with much social-science research, in which social aggregations are studied as a constant or are deconstructed from the top down.

The agents are individuals, and yet their collective structures or institutions created by these individuals produce feedback that affects behavior. Agent-based modeling allows social scientists to study the interactions between individuals and institutions.

Artificial societies demonstrate that certain sets of "microspecifications" can generate "macrophenomena" similar to those of the human world. The ability to grow social structures holds the prospect of a new kind of social science.

grams) per year. Surplus grain is lost if not eaten within two years of harvest.

At this point, households may cease to exist, either because they do not have enough grain to satisfy their nutritional needs or because they have aged beyond a certain maximum (30 years in the current model). A household's "death" means it no longer exists as a single unit—not necessarily that all household members have died: for example, some might die, or they might be absorbed by other households or simply leave the valley.

Next, household agents estimate how much grain they will have the following year, based on current harvest and grain stores. If this is not enough to meet minimum requirements, the household moves. Determining how and where a household moves is critical in creating a meaningful relationship to the historical record. First, the agent finds a new location to farm by searching for the most productive, available land within 5,250 feet (1,600 meters) of a water source. To be considered usable, the land must be unsettled.

The agents look for a settlement location near their farmland with a water source. Agents choose their own homesites according to the rules of the model.

Finally, household agents may "fission." If a household is older than 16 years, it has a defined probability (one chance in eight) of triggering a new household through the "marriage" of a female child. The minimum fission age combined with fission probability enables us to approximate the odds that a household would have daughters, and the time it would take a daughter to reach maturity, find a mate, conceive a child, and form a new household.

EXPLANATION, MINUS ILLUSION

We have no illusions about our ability to explain all of local Anasazi history. At present, our agents respond largely to environmental stimuli, some kinship rules, and basic biological conditions—the simplest plausible rules we could devise. The simulations are basically "cartoon" interpretations of reality that will hopefully provoke and refine questions and point inquiries in new directions.

Our simulation runs from A.D. 800 to 1350. It begins with the historically known number of agents, but not necessarily their historical settlement locations. Each household executes its full behavioral repertoire each year, as the program tracks household fissions, deaths, grain stocks, and internal demographics. If the correct decisions are made, the household produces enough food to get through another year; if not, it runs out of food and is removed from the simulation through death or emigration.

While a single simulation run may produce plausible and interesting outcomes, numerous runs with altered initial conditions, parameters, and random-number generators are performed to assess the robustness of the model.

Our simulated population generally tracks the real-world population trajectory; that is, the curve of the simulated graph closely resembles the archaeological curve. Each shows a population increase up to about A.D. 900, then a leveling off, followed by major growth from 1000 to 1050. Population levels off again from 1050 to 1150, drops in the mid-1100s, recovers in the late 1100s to a peak in the 13th century, and crashes in the late 1200s.

But the simulated and archaeological curves also exhibit important differences. The simulations often show greater population decline in the 12th century and a smaller post-1150 recovery. Significantly, the simulation does not drop to zero at A.D. 1300, when the Anasazi completely abandoned Long House Valley.

Also, both total population and individual settlement sizes are much larger in the typical simulation than seems to have been the actual case. The simulation packs more households into residential sites than did the real Anasazi, who tended to distribute members of a residential unit into discrete but clustered habitation sites.

This is an example of how the simulation makes us challenge our assumptions. We initially believed the simulation would have difficulty duplicating the observed packing of population into larger villages. The reverse was true: the virtual Anasazi congregated into much larger settlements than

The Long House ruins remain in the valley that bears their name. The Anasazi built other structures throughout the U.S. Southwest, but the culture ultimately—and inexplicably—disappeared more than 700 years ago.

their real counterparts. This discrepancy was caused partly by our rule that when a daughter "fissioned" to form her new family, she moved to the closest good land near her mother. Apparently, the real Anasazi were much more like our own society: they wanted to live close to their relatives—but not too close. Some buffering mechanism probably tended to provide a small distance between relatives.

But on a larger scale, the simulation replicates with uncanny accuracy important aspects of the settlement history of the valley and its surrounding region. Patterns of aggregation into large- and medium-size settlements (from 900 to 1000, 1150 to 1200, and 1260 to 1300) and dispersion into smaller sites (from 1000 to 1150 and 1200 to 1260) virtually duplicate the settlement history of the eastern Kayenta Anasazi area.

CHASING WATER

The eastern Kayenta Anasazi settlement changes are related to low- and high-frequency fluctuations in environmental conditions. Population tended to gather in a few favorable locations when water was tight, then disperse when water tables rose. The Artificial Anasazi Project captured this dynamic relationship between settlement patterns and environmental variability.

Yet the simulation does not abandon the valley after 1300—and this failure to repli-

cate reality provides important new data. Since the model clearly shows the valley could have supported at least a remnant population, the exodus cannot be explained by a deteriorating environment alone; something else—ideological or sociological factors, or external forces, such as an aggressive new enemy—must have sent the last of the Anasazi on their way. The simulation tells us what humans could have done—but did not do—in the real Long House Valley. Explaining why not suggests a potentially productive line of research.

This test run demonstrates that agent-based modeling can test hypotheses for which we have only indirect evidence. It can explain much of the behavior we find in history, and can encourage us to consider factors of cultural change. For the Artificial Anasazi model, we could introduce new elements—such as mobile raiders, environmental catastrophes, or epidemics—and let them run their course.

Our future research is aimed at extending and improving the model to more accurately reflect the world as it was. Agent-based simulations may never fully explain real history—these, after all, are rather simple instruments—but they enable us to scientifically explore questions that often cannot be addressed in other ways. The concept promises powerful insights into other ancient peoples and cultures. ◿

Making Stuff Last

by Jessica Gorman

A round the world, archives, museums, and their storage facilities brim with society's most prized objects. Some have been stashed on dusty back shelves for decades, while others bask under spotlights and curious gazes.

If you are a patron of museums and archives, how can you be sure that on those shelves or under that glass, the treasures you value aren't slowly withering away? Are they really being preserved for future generations?

Truth is, behind the scenes, chemists and materials scientists are still struggling to understand how objects deteriorate. That is the first step to learning how to increase the life spans of the full menagerie of ancient and modern treasures, be they Rembrandts, retro medical devices, Barbie dolls, or beetles long extinct.

Sometimes deterioration sneaks up so subtly that, for at least awhile, it's noticeable only on the molecular level. Once deterioration becomes visible, however, age may have altered the basic chemical foundation of a museum specimen. Then it is often difficult or even impossible for conservators to successfully clean or repair the aging piece.

That is why fundamental chemistry and materials science have become so central to museums' and archives' preservation efforts. With new understanding about how long-term-storage environments can affect the condition of paper, wood, rubber,

Science continues to seek antidotes for the damage that time inflicts on historical objects. The conservators above are chemically treating the flag that inspired the writing of the "Star-Spangled Banner" in 1814.

and cloth, for example, researchers hope that the need for difficult, risky conservation interventions will become less frequent.

Meanwhile, ongoing research is revealing which materials in historic objects have stood the test of time, and those insights offer guidance about what materials to use for making new objects that will last.

"What we're trying to do is put our conservator friends out of business," jokes Charles S. Tumosa of the Smithsonian Center for Materials Research and Education in Suitland, Maryland.

CLEANING ART: TRICKY BUSINESS

Some of the best-known museum preservation efforts are those that focus on art. This is a tricky business, Tumosa says. Scientists can't go around experimenting on centuries-old masterpieces.

Instead, researchers try to study the effects of different environments and cleaning procedures by testing new materials that are similar to the old ones. For this to be relevant, however, the researchers have to find ways to quickly age the young materials so that they better reflect the mechanical and chemical changes that the old materials have suffered. Then the younger samples can be used to test conservation techniques.

The more researchers discover about materials, the more often they learn that even their testing methods can be misleading. For example, Tumosa recently reported that a heating protocol commonly used for artificially aging materials doesn't work well for oil paints. He and his colleagues found that thermal treatments above 122° F (50° C) did not age fresh oil paintings to look like genuine 200-year-old paintings. Their chemical composition didn't match that of the older artworks, the team reported.

That mismatch suggests that testing new cleaning treatments on such heat-aged samples can be dangerously misleading.

More recently, Tumosa studied white zinc oxide pigments in modern artists' oil paints. He and his colleagues found that these pigments produce a surprisingly brittle film.

The White House National Millennium Time Capsule holds items that represent late-20th-century life in the United States. The memorabilia in the capsule—including a pair of Ray Charles' sunglasses, a plastic model of DNA, and various compact discs—should remain intact for at least 100 years.

Following common preservation treatments, such as the application of a varnish overcoat, the zinc oxide–containing underlayer gets even more brittle, says Tumosa.

He has reported his results to three major producers of the zinc oxide paints, and they are now considering replacing the pigment to make modern oil paintings more stable.

"The people who are going to be doing conservation in the 21st century and 22nd century are going to be facing these problems," Tumosa says.

PICKLED FROGS AND MONKEY PARTS

Artwork gets a lot of attention when it comes to preservation, but there's more to museums than art. Consider the category David W. von Endt, also of the Smithsonian Center, calls "pickled frogs and things that go bump in the night."

In the world's natural-history museums, some 2 billion biological specimens are

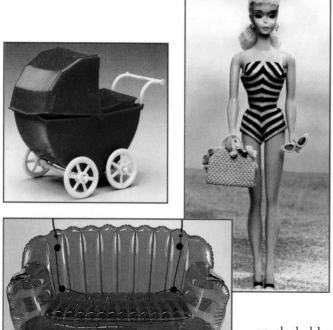

"Vintage" plastic items—including the toy baby carriage, early Barbie doll, and inflatable sofa grouped at left—can feel sticky to the touch, the result of phthalate additives that migrate to the surface over time.

By heating samples, von Endt has found that keratins (proteins in feathers and hair) and collagen (a protein in bones and skin) have different relative stabilities in the different fluids. Feather keratin, for example, is only half as stable in alcohol-based storage fluids as hair keratin is.

Adding formaldehyde to an alcohol-based storage fluid made collagen—but not keratin—more stable.

As von Endt learns which fluids better protect particular materials, the long-term stability of the biological molecules in new specimens is likely to improve. Old samples could also be placed in new fluids to make them last longer, he says.

Most current genetic and molecular-biology analyses did not exist when the typical natural-history-museum biological sample was collected, notes von Endt. "These specimens never were preserved with [modern research tests] in mind," he says. What's more, he adds, "we have no idea of the kinds of questions that are going to be asked of these specimens in the future."

Newer Materials Fare Poorly

It is no shock that museum professionals find deterioration in objects that have outlived many generations of people. Conservators, for example, have worked hard to restore the flag that inspired the writing of the "Star-Spangled Banner" by Francis Scott Key during the War of 1812. Surprisingly, however, scientists are finding that many modern materials deteriorate even faster than those of older objects.

Some of the most vulnerable new materials are plastics. Museums display them as toys, medical equipment, footwear, inflatable furniture, and more, says Yvonne

stored in fluids such as formaldehyde, says von Endt. The specimens represent a planetwide library of biological samples. Some animals on shelves today were prepared as far back as the mid-19th century and have become extinct, he says. And some have proved valuable for biomedical research, including monkey specimens that yielded clues to the history of AIDS.

Von Endt investigates causes of deterioration in preserved biological artifacts, and then looks for better ways of treating specimens for future scientists' use. Although many bottled animals appear well preserved, important biological molecules such as lipids, proteins, and amino acids have leaked into the fluid, he says. The tissues may no longer contain all the biochemicals that molecular biologists might need to study them.

Currently, von Endt is examining the preservation of proteins such as those in skin, hair, bone, and feathers. Rather than focusing on an individual animal, he searches for molecular constituents common to many species. For example, by studying a molecule in a preserved field mouse, he is also likely to learn about a chemical process in, perhaps, a preserved squid.

Shashoua of the National Museum of Denmark. "They're found in every museum in the world," she says.

Yet many plastics exhibited in museums can change so much chemically that within a decade, they start to feel tacky. Many such objects must be taken out of a collection after just 20 years, says Shashoua. These plastics—including those in Barbie dolls—are made of polyvinyl chloride, or PVC. Dolls from the 1950s and 1960s usually contain potentially toxic chemicals called phthalates, which were added during manufacture to soften the material.

In recent experiments using microscopy and spectroscopy, Shashoua identified phthalates as the cause of the plastics' tacky surface. This discovery was unexpected, she says, because previously published literature had indicated that phthalates remain combined with the PVC.

To preserve plastic objects in museum collections for longer periods, Shashoua is now trying to figure out how to keep the phthalates within the plastic. First, she is measuring how fast phthalates evaporate from newly manufactured PVC, and why phthalates migrate out of the plastic.

SPACE SUITS ARE NOT IMMUNE

Recently, Shashoua also finished analyzing the PVC deterioration in one of the high-tech marvels of the 20th century: Apollo-era space suits, 12 of which made it to the Moon. Just 30 years ago, these materials protected astronauts from the deadly void of space, but now they need protection themselves. An 18-month project funded by the Save America's Treasures program is under way to determine the best method for handling and storing the deteriorating suits.

Lisa Young of the National Air and Space Museum's Paul E. Garber Facility in Suitland, Maryland, works with the museum's Space History Department coordinating the Apollo space-suit project. The members of the museum team are analyzing all 12 suits and devising methods to preserve them.

Her team does a variety of tests, including visual inspection of each suit and CT (computerized-tomography) scans to see inside the suits' 20 layers of synthetic polymers and

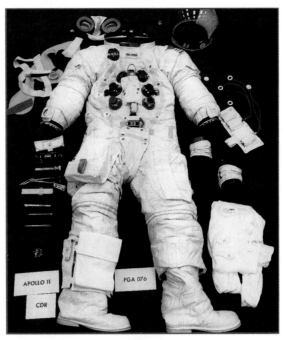

Some cleaning and restoration efforts may do more harm than good—something preservation scientists must bear in mind with deteriorating space suits.

natural rubber. The investigators are also interviewing the original designers.

Young is now tracing the origins of the natural-rubber components and investigating the changes that producers made over the years in the composition of rubber used in the suits. In 1971, for example, rubber makers added an antioxidant, and the suits created since then have held up better than the earlier ones. Young also aims to identify a gas that the aging rubber emits.

Young is also examining aluminum space-suit pieces to determine the alloys used, as well as the type of corrosion occurring. That information could indicate whether the aluminum parts need to be stored under different conditions than the other material, or if conservation treatments are needed.

Young emphasizes that preventive measures usually work best. Trying to clean or restore museum artifacts can often do more harm than good.

Take, for example, the case of lunar dust. In the 1970s, most of the Apollo space suits were cleaned of the Moon dirt that soiled their white surfaces. Today, just one suit remains in pristine condition, says Young: the one Harrison Schmitt wore on *Apollo 17*, and it was never treated or cleaned. ◪

The Reign of the
SIERRA STORM KING

by Mark McLaughlin

The vision most Americans have of California's weather is of an endless summer paradise of golden sunshine, gentle breezes, and year-round moderate temperatures. From the "perfect" climate of San Diego to the balmy beaches of Los Angeles and the romantic fog of San Francisco, our view of California is that of a meteorologic utopia.

But away from the coast, there is another side to California's weather. In the Sierra Nevada—a mountain range in the eastern part of the state—winter brings intense storms that produce tremendous amounts of snow. In these mountains, snowstorms of several feet or more are commonplace, registering totals that would even stagger residents of the eastern snow havens of Rochester or Syracuse, New York. Many annual snowfall totals in the Sierra range from 400 to 450 inches (1,016 to 1,143 centimeters)—that's an astounding 33 to 37 feet (10 to 11 meters) of snow per winter!

For more than 150 years, overwhelming snowstorms in these rugged mountains have

The extraordinary summer landscape of the Sierra Nevada mountain range in eastern California belies the region's winter reality: bitter cold and blizzards that produce more than 35 feet of snowfall each year.

etched their impact into the history of the West. Early pioneers, railroad men, and modern motorists have all dealt with the awesome power of what I call the Sierra Storm King. When he asserts his meteorologic power over this captivating domain, travelers beware.

Born under Mesozoic seas 220 million years ago, the highest peaks of the majestic Sierra Nevada now scrape the sky at more than 14,000 feet (4,267 meters), and encompass an area nearly as large as the French, Swiss, and Italian Alps combined. In 1776, Padre Pedro Font

of Spain gave the name "Sierra Nevada" to the mountain range on the eastern fringe of Spanish California. In Spanish, *Sierra* means "mountains," and *Nevada* means "snow covered." John Muir, a prominent 19th-century naturalist, loved these mountains, as did famed photographer Ansel Adams, who called them the "Range of Light." The vistas have inspired generations of visitors.

During the dry summers of the Sierra, crystal-clear alpine lakes dot the forested landscape while stubborn snowfields cling to northeast slopes below ridgeline. In winter, as the jet stream moves south in concert with cold air, storms move over the Sierra Nevada. As these systems approach, moist air from the Pacific is drawn inland. As the air travels up the western slope of the mountains, the uplift produces heavy snow in the upper elevations.

A NOTORIOUS CROSSING

Although there are nearly a dozen trans-Sierra routes, Donner Pass (elevation: 7,239 feet; 2,206 meters) is the most notorious of all the crossings. For more than 150 years, severe weather and difficult topography have combined to challenge those determined to take this route. For early American settlers struggling with ox-drawn farm wagons, crossing the range ranked as the most difficult obstacle in their 2,000-mile (3,220-kilometer) trek to the Pacific. Fantastic tales of the perpetual summer paradise of coastal California were tempered by the fear of mind-boggling snowfall totals in the mountains. The average annual snowfall in the Donner Pass region, for example, is about 34 feet (10 meters).

In 1844, a Paiute Indian chief named Truckee came upon a wagon train of pioneers searching for an overland route to California. Truckee found them stalled at the Humboldt Sink in present-day Nevada, so the friendly native pointed them toward an unnamed pass—soon to be known as Donner Pass—off to the west. The Stephens-Murphy-Townsend Party, a group of 50 men, women, and young children, had to dismantle the wagons and hoist sections by rope to ascend the sheer granite escarpment, but they succeeded in getting 5 of their 11 wagons over the pass.

Exhaustion and late-November snowstorms forced them into a winter-survival camp along the south fork of the Yuba River while some of the men pushed on to Sutter's Fort for help. Bred for endurance and blessed with luck, all 50 settlers survived the ordeal. Two babies were born during their journey, including Mary "Yuba" Murphy, who was born at the survival camp on the river. The Stephens Party was the first group

Tales of California's perpetual summerlike bliss helped inspire the westward movement. The unsuspecting pioneers were then shocked to encounter brutal winters and difficult terrain on the way—conditions that forced them to haul wagons and supplies over mountain ridges. Some parties were compelled to set up winter-survival camps.

of American emigrants to haul wagons over the mountains, and they are credited with opening the long-sought California Trail.

Today, the town of Truckee, California, is nestled along the Truckee River, a few miles east of Donner Pass, and is named after the helpful Paiute chief. Truckee, where logging and ice-harvesting industries have been replaced with snow sports and tourism, often ranks as one of the nation's coldest locations in the spring and summer. Despite being located on the protected lee side of Donner Summit, the town of Truckee gets its fair share of snowfall. The Truckee Ranger Station (elevation: 5,995 feet; 1,827 meters) averages more than 17 feet (5.2 meters) of snow. (The modern snowfall record in Truckee is 37 feet—11.2 meters—recorded during the winter of 1951–52.)

THE DOOMED DONNER PARTY

In 1846, Truckee's pass gained perpetual notoriety as well as its infamous moniker when the Donner Party was caught east of the summit by early-winter storms. The snow was already 3 to 5 feet (1 to 1.5 meters) deep in the pass when the California-bound

emigrants arrived on October 31. (October snows are not unusual in the Sierra, but two storms heavy enough to impede traffic this early in the season are rare.)

More storms in November closed the pass for good and forced the travelers to wait for rescuers from the Sacramento Valley. Trapped for months with diminishing food supplies, the starving pioneers were reduced to cannibalism. There were 10 major storm events that winter, beginning October 16, 1846, and ending April 3, 1847, with intervening fair weather. Hard as the successive storms were to take physically and mentally, the sunshine and thaws in between gave rise to false hopes that winter was breaking.

In mid-December, a lull in storm activity encouraged 15 members of the party to attempt a crossing on improvised snowshoes. Provisioned with only enough food for one week, they took 33 days to reach the closest settlement on the Sierra west slope; only seven survived their ordeal of fatigue and starvation, including all five women who set out.

Settler Patrick Breen kept a diary recording the weather at Donner Lake from

November 20, 1846, until he and his family were rescued around March 1, 1847. On November 29, 1846, Breen wrote, "Still snowing now about 3 feet [1 meter] deep, wind West. Killed my last oxen today. Will skin them tomorrow. Gave another yoke to Fosters. Hard to get wood." The following day, his entry read, "Snowing fast. Wind W. About 4 or 5 feet [1.2 or 1.5 meters] deep, no drifts. Looks as likely to continue as when it commenced. No living thing without wings can get about."

For the hapless pioneers, the winter only got worse. Several major storms occurred during December, January, and February. On January 23, 1847, Breen wrote, "Blew hard and snowed all night; the most severe storm we have experienced this winter; wind west." On February 4, Breen penciled in, "Snowed hard until twelve o'clock last night; many uneasy for fear we shall all perish with hunger." The Storm King was literally burying them alive.

On February 5, Breen observed, "It snowed faster last night and today than it has done this winter before; still continues without intermission; wind south-west." The emigrants spent three months at Donner Lake, their crude cabins buried under the snow. The first of several rescue efforts did not reach them until February 18, 1847. After spring melt, stumps of trees cut by the stranded pioneers ranged from 15 to 18 feet (4.5 to 5 meters) high, indicative of the exceptional snowpack. Nearly half of the 81 settlers stranded at the camps died before reaching sunny California.

In 1849, the region was invaded by history's greatest gold rush. Hordes of miners, merchants, prostitutes, and desperadoes flocked to the rich diggings on the Sierran west slope. Just one year later, California joined the Union as the Golden State.

During the 1850s, Californians lobbied for a transcontinental railroad to stitch the nation together, but Congress and investors doubted that iron rails could be linked over the Sierra Nevada. Theodore Dehone Judah, a brilliant New York–trained engineer who believed that he could snake the tracks through the snowbound mountains, persuaded Congress to pass the Pacific Railway Act.

Judah had seriously considered the problem of snow in his exhaustive study of the best route over the Sierra. As a comparison, Judah examined the snow conditions back East on some of the higher rail crossings of the Appalachians. He observed the eastern railroad crews successfully operating in heavy snowfall zones, and felt confident that Sierra snowstorms would not be a problem.

In reality, Judah had little information regarding the prodigious Sierra snowpack, and the Central Pacific Railroad was later forced to construct 37 miles (60 kilometers) of expensive wooden snowsheds in order to protect track and trains from snowdrifts and avalanches. The visionary Judah never saw his railroad to completion. He died of yellow fever in 1863 at the age of 37.

The Donner Pass is named for the Donner Party, who were trapped for months by storms. The party gained enduring notoriety by resorting to desperate measures—including cannibalism.

Although the transcontinental railroad made travel easier through the Donner Pass, the hazards remained. Rotary snowplows (left) churned through deep snow to rescue marooned trains caught in ruthless blizzards.

AN EPIC UNDERTAKING

Conquering the Sierra by rail was an epic undertaking. Much of the initial construction material had to be shipped from New York around South America's stormy Cape Horn to San Francisco, an exhausting voyage of some 19,000 miles (30,000 kilometers). William Tecumseh Sherman, who later became a Union general in the Civil War, was an experienced engineer and surveyor familiar with the Sierra Range. When he heard of Judah's plans, he wrote to his brother of the project, "If it is ever built, it will be the work of giants." Those giants turned out to be Chinese laborers who diligently shoveled, picked, and blasted their way through the Sierra's granite spine.

James Harvey Strobridge, superintendent of construction, initially did not want to use the foreign labor force, but California's white laborers were mostly undisciplined gold miners and incapable of such work. Strobridge later said that "labor sufficient for the rapid construction of the Central Pacific was then not on the coast and the labor as it existed could not be depended upon, if the first mining excitement meant a complete stampede of every man and a consequent abandonment of all work."

Thousands of Chinese laborers endured blinding blizzards and lethal avalanches to construct the railroad over the storm-swept Donner Pass. Where a roadbed could not be built, a tunnel was chipped and blasted out.

In the heavy snowbelt that lies between 6,000 and 7,000 feet (1,830 and 2,135 meters), nine train tunnels were excavated through the solid granite, totaling 5,158 feet (1,570 meters) in overall length.

The 44 storms during the winter of 1866–67 pounded the summit with 44 feet (13 meters) of snow. The biggest dropped 10 feet (3 meters) in 13 days. One avalanche wiped out an entire work camp; when the bodies were discovered the following spring, tools were still clutched in the corpses' frozen hands. The following week, another slide mercilessly swept 20 Chinese workers to their deaths. The next winter was little better. Subtropical storms deluged the region with more than 40 inches (100 centimeters) of rain in December 1867, causing extensive flood damage. The South Yuba Canal Company, near 3,000 feet (900 meters) in elevation, recorded more than 115 inches (290 centimeters) of rain during that season.

The weather was eerily calm for much of January and February 1868, but in early March, a fierce blizzard deposited 10 feet (3 meters) of snow in five days. The *Virginia City Territorial Enterprise* newspaper stated, "This winter has been pretty rough on the Chinese along the line of the railroad, and a great number of them have been killed and crippled by similar accidents at various points on the road."

Despite every obstacle the Storm King threw, the Chinese crews pushed the track through the mountains, reaching Donner Summit on November 30, 1868. Winter had taken its toll on the laborers, but the transcontinental railroad was finally completed in Utah in May 1869.

During the Great Sierra Snow Blockade, snowplow crews and 5,000 shovelers had to be hired to clear the buried tracks. Even so, the deep snow nearly prevented journalist Nellie Bly (right) from achieving her goal of circling the globe in less time than it took voyagers in the fantasy Around the World in 80 Days.

THE GREAT SIERRA SNOW BLOCKADE

The railroad made the Sierra crossing much more comfortable, but danger still lurked. In January 1890, a relentless barrage of blizzards and a string of marooned passenger trains shut down Donner Pass for 15 days. Nevadans remember the brutal winter of 1889–90 as the "Great White Ruin" when deep snow on the range decimated their cattle and sheep herds.

But in the mountains, avalanches and drifting snow caused the "Great Sierra Snow Blockade." As the snow piled up on the desert floor, cutting livestock off from forage, desperate Nevada ranchers began shipping their starving cattle by boxcar into California. On January 15, 1890, one of the westbound trains derailed, shutting down northern Nevada's only lifeline through the snowbound Sierra.

The wild and woolly railroad crews organized an incredible show of strength against this massive assault by the Storm King. In addition to an armada of snowplows and railroad crews, Central Pacific had recently acquired two new rotary snowplows, which could churn through deep snow and throw it off the track. The heavy machinery was supplemented by nearly 5,000 snow shovelers hired to assist in clearing the tracks. Even with such an extensive counterattack, the 66 feet (20 meters) of snow that fell during the winter of 1889–90 generated so many avalanches, it overwhelmed these valiant efforts.

For journalist Nellie Bly, the blockade nearly stymied her attempt to circumnavigate the globe in less time than novelist Jules Verne's fictional voyage *Around the World in 80 Days.*

Bly, a 23-year-old reporter for the *New York World* newspaper, was circling the globe in an effort to beat the French novelist's fantasy journey. Bly shipped out eastbound from New York City to London on November 14, 1889. At the train station in Amiens, France, Jules Verne met the young woman who was bringing his story to life. She traveled by mail train to Brindisi, Italy, and then sailed through the Mediterranean, continuing on to India.

By the time Bly reached San Francisco, she had burned 68 days. Unfortunately for Bly, the news she received in California was not good. Donner Pass, blocked by blizzards, avalanches, and several train derailments, would not be open for days. Her second problem was the "Nellie Bly Escort Corps," which consisted of her two New York editors along with other professional associates traveling from the East. While Bly was stuck in California, the members of this elaborate delegation were trapped with 700 other stranded westbound passengers on the eastern side of the Sierra in Reno, Nevada. It seemed that after circling most of the globe, a California snowstorm was going to foil her success as a real-life Phileas Fogg.

However, all was not lost. Bly's editor, John J. Jennings, had somehow managed to reach Donner Summit before railroad officials held down all westbound traffic in Reno. Jennings caught a ride on a snowplow until it was hit by an avalanche. He survived, but the machine was disabled. Despite sober advice for Jennings to remain with the plow, the resourceful editor found himself a pair of 8-foot (2.4-meter)-long wooden skis, the first he had ever seen. He skied all night until he broke past the blockade site where he could get a train to Sacramento. Jennings remarked, "I have seen snow and blizzards in New York, but the people back there don't know what snow is."

A Southern Pacific Railroad telegrapher and his family bear vivid testimony to the vast amount of snow that still blankets the Donner Pass region each winter.

For the millions of Americans reading about the drama in their hometown newspapers, the tension was electrifying. Embarrassed Central Pacific officials rerouted Bly and Jennings on a special express train south into the California desert and then east to Chicago. Nellie Bly arrived back in New York City on January 25, 1890, having traveled 72 days, 6 hours, and 11 minutes on her epic world-circling journey.

ALWAYS READY FOR BATTLE

Although the Storm King causes havoc with transportation at some point nearly every winter, the army of men, women, and machinery stationed in the Sierra is always ready to battle for control of the highways and railroad. But no matter how prepared, sometimes nothing can withstand the Storm King's meteorologic assault.

Another prolonged trans-Sierra blockade occurred in January 1952, after an onslaught of powerful Pacific-bred storms inundated the mountains. When blizzard conditions stranded the luxury streamliner train *City of San Francisco* high in the mountains, the event made national news.

On Sunday morning, January 13, 1952, Truckee–Lake Tahoe residents were three days into a weeklong blizzard. An intense storm had stalled off the California coast in a position favorable for heavy amounts of snow. Despite the best efforts of California road crews on this fateful Sunday, all northern Sierra highway passes were closed due to deep snow and avalanches. Only Southern Pacific (SP) trains were still able to cross the rugged Sierra.

That changed when one of SP's luxury streamliners, the *City of San Francisco*, rammed into a snowslide near Yuba Pass, west of the Sierra crest. Despite three 2,250-horsepower diesel-electric engines, the crew could not back up the train, and quickly realized they were stuck. There were 226 passengers and crew members on board the 15-car westbound train, but everyone assumed the powerful express train would not be there long.

Their laissez-faire attitude, however, turned to anger when they were still snowbound 24 hours later. The wind was fierce,

The Sierra Storm King's wrath inevitably causes transportation havoc along Interstate 80, the only major trans-Sierra freeway. An arsenal of snow-removal weapons helps keep the busy route open during the winter season.

howling at speeds in excess of 90 miles (145 kilometers) per hour, and drifts towered 20 to 30 feet (6 to 9 meters). Many feared it would be just a matter of time before another avalanche shoved the entire train into the dark ravine below. On Monday night, 36 hours into their ordeal and with no rescue in sight, the supply of diesel fuel ran out, cloaking the train in a cold, eerie darkness.

Unbeknownst to the frightened passengers and crew, SP rescue trains were inching their way closer from both east and west toward the stranded streamliner. On the morning of the 16th, the skies suddenly cleared, giving relief operations a chance to reach the train. The critical mission had taken four days and cost the lives of two rescuers, but all 226 passengers and crew were eventually saved.

From January 10 to 17, nearly 13 feet (4 meters) of snow fell. The winter of 1951–52 dumped 65 feet (20 meters) of snow on Donner Summit, and the snowpack reached 26 feet (8 meters) deep, the greatest depth ever recorded there. Trans-Sierra Highway 40 was blocked by snow for one month.

LONG LIVE THE KING

Although cars, trucks, and SUVs have replaced trains, horses, and oxen as the primary mode of travel across the Sierra, the Storm King continues to instill fear for those daring enough to cross Donner Pass during a winter storm. Interstate 80, completed in the early 1960s, is today the only major trans-Sierra freeway. California's Department of Transportation (Caltrans) strives to control snow and ice on I-80 and other Sierra highways to provide safe travel for motorists, while keeping traffic delays to a minimum. But it is not an easy task.

On I-80, heavy traffic (both recreational and commercial) makes it difficult for Caltrans to keep this busy freeway open during winter storms. The number of cars using Donner Pass increases yearly; westbound motorists must share the road with 2,000 commercial trucks that enter the Golden State every day via I-80.

From state-of-the-art snowplows to the latest technology in weather prediction, Caltrans is doing its part to combat the power of the Storm King—along with the inexperience and hubris of many California drivers unprepared for the challenge and danger of driving in heavy snow.

This challenge will continue to be a part of the wintertime legacy of these "snow covered mountains," so aptly named more than two centuries ago. Ever since those first settlers struggled to overcome the awesome power of the Storm King, winter travelers braving Donner Pass have been warned, "Stay smart—or stay home."

ASK THE SCIENTIST

◣ **Did primitive tribes ever really practice head-shrinking? Do scientists currently have any authentic "shrunken heads" in their possession?**

Head-hunting—removing and preserving human heads—was practiced in various cultures on every continent, beginning as far back as the Paleolithic era and continuing in some cultures until the mid-20th century. In virtually every case, these cultures believed that a person's soul resided in the head, and that the preserved head would grant magical powers, fertility, or agricultural good fortune.

Among the best-known of these head-hunting cultures are the Jívaro, a fierce native people living in the Andes Mountains in what are now Ecuador and Peru; their notoriety derives from their practice of shrinking the heads of those captured during tribal warfare. To create the shrunken heads, or *tsantas*, the Jívaro decapitated their victims and cut a slit up the back of the head, allowing the skin and hair to be peeled from the skull, which was later discarded. The skin was then boiled, excess flesh removed, and the slit sewn up. The cavity was filled with hot stones and sand to complete the lengthy shrinking process. The final product—a head that retains its original features but has been reduced to about the size of an orange—was hung over a fire to harden and blacken. The *tsanta* was kept as a trophy or worn around the neck of tribal warriors.

Authentic shrunken heads have been sought after and obtained by museums and curio collectors, but their great popularity created a thriving market for fakes as well; new *tsantas* have become progressively more difficult to procure because of the near disappearance of the practice of head-hunting.

◣ **Is the practice of keeping pets a comparatively recent phenomenon? Which were domesticated earlier: dogs or cats?**

The world's two most popular pets—dogs and cats—have a long history as human companions. Archaeological records suggest that dogs were among the very first domesticated animals, serving as protectors and hunters in societies as far back as 12,000 years ago (some researchers say DNA evidence indicates that the canine-human relationship is much older, perhaps beginning 100,000 years ago!). Ancient peoples probably recognized that the speed and senses of their hunting dogs were superior to their own, and they began breeding dogs to improve these characteristics. As a result, at least five distinct breeds existed by about 4500 B.C. By the Middle Ages or earlier, some dogs were bred specifically as pets. There are currently more than 400 distinct breeds of dogs.

Cats were domesticated later than dogs, because they were highly valued by the agricultural societies that came later in human development. The relationship probably began when humans noticed that cats could protect grain stores from rodents, and private homes from snakes. Cats were proclaimed sacred in ancient Egypt by 2500 B.C. By 1500 B.C., records indicate that the cat was fully domesticated, and likely being bred in much the same manner as dogs.

▶ *Do videophones exist? If so, do scientists foresee a time when videophones will be widely available like cellular phones are now?*

The videophones once imagined by science-fiction writers currently exist in several configurations. Among these are expensive videoconferencing devices used by large corporations. As was once conceived, these devices allow the parties on either end of the line to view one another while speaking via telephone.

Handheld mobile videophones, using cellular technology, are already on the market, and telecommunications companies consider them a potentially popular and lucrative device. To date, however, mobile videophones are costly and capable of transmitting only choppy images. But improvements in video software have led marketers to promise smoother images for lower prices in the near future.

However, the opportunity to see the person on the other end of the line is currently available to any of the millions of personal-computer (PC) users who own a Web camera. Streaming video can travel over a phone line and turn any PC into an audio-video communication device.

▶ *Why are silent movies rarely shown on television? Have most been preserved? Are they currently available on videotape?*

Silent movies are occasionally shown on public-television stations. There are many Internet sites maintained by silent-film enthusiasts that include upcoming listings for these films. Many repertory movie theaters hold silent-film festivals.

Most of the silent movies made in the first decades of the film industry have been lost or are badly damaged (some experts estimate that only about 10 percent of movies produced in the United States before 1929 have survived). Early films were printed on fragile, highly flammable stock; few prints of each film were produced; and there was not a serious commitment to preservation among early film companies. Recently, the Library of Congress in Washington, D.C., and other organizations throughout the United States have set about preserving and archiving surviving films, including silent films, from the early period of film history.

▶ *In ancient times, were the Greeks and Romans aware of the civilizations in the Far East? Did the empires in the Far East and those in the Mediterranean region exchange ambassadors or otherwise conduct some sort of relationship?*

It is difficult to say for sure whether the ancient Greeks were aware of the cultures in the Far East; but the Greeks were in contact with Middle Eastern cultures, who may have provided at least some rudimentary knowledge of the world beyond.

In the 1st and 2nd centuries A.D., however, there was at least partial contact established between the Roman Empire and the empire of China. Chinese records indicate that an embassy from the Roman emperor Marcus Aurelius, possibly traveling by sea, presented itself to the Chinese emperor Huan-ti around the year 161. This time period saw the beginning of what would come to be known as the "Silk Road," an artery of exchange stretching thousands of miles from Xi'an, in China, through Central Asia, India, and the Middle East, and finally to the Mediterranean Sea.

The Silk Road was not really a road, but rather, a series of caravan routes by which goods such as silk traveled westward, and wool, gold, and silver went east. No trader traveled the entire way; hence, middlemen mediated the contact between the two great empires at either end of the road.

Ideas were exchanged along the road, as well; Buddhism reached China from India in this way, and, later, Christian missionaries and explorers such as Marco Polo headed east along these ancient routes.

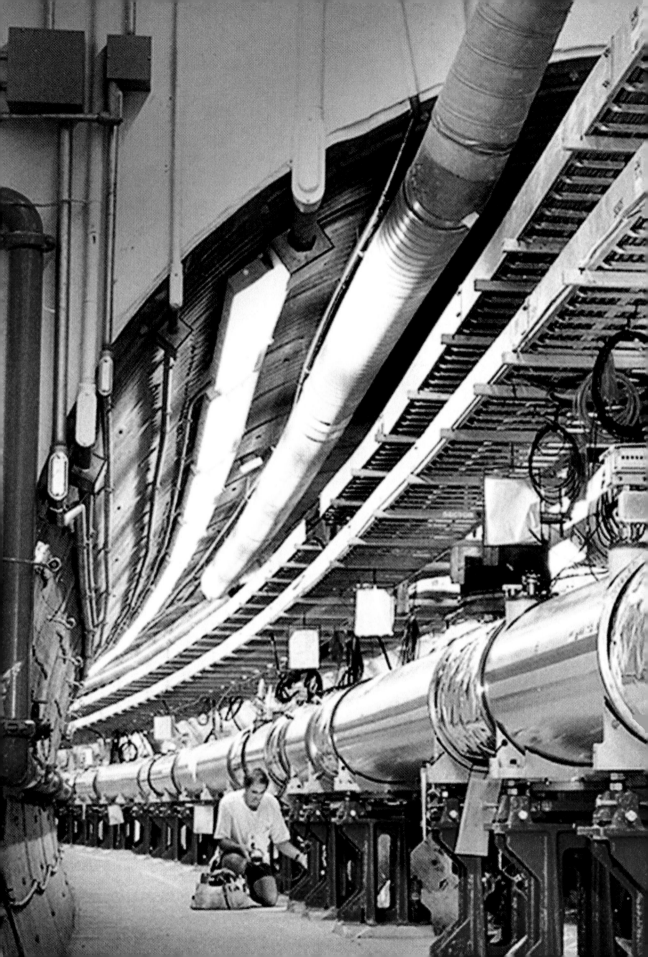

PHYSICAL SCIENCES

THE RELATIVISTIC HEAVY ION COLLID-
ER AT BROOKHAVEN NATIONAL LABO-
RATORY HURTLES THE HEAVY NUCLEI
OF CERTAIN ELEMENTS (SUCH AS
GOLD) INTO EACH OTHER AT NEARLY
THE SPEED OF LIGHT. THROUGH THESE
VIOLENT COLLISIONS, SCIENTISTS HOPE
TO KNOCK LOOSE QUARKS AND OTHER
SUBATOMIC PARTICLES AND, MOMEN-
TARILY AT LEAST, AVAIL THEMSELVES
OF THE OPPORTUNITY TO EXAMINE
THESE ELUSIVE ENTITIES.

CONTENTS

REFINING THE ART OF
MEASUREMENT

by Malcolm W. Browne

The National Institute of Standards and Technology is hardly a household name, especially compared with those of the famous federal agencies that deal with space travel, taxes, nuclear weapons, environmental problems, crime prevention, and medicine.

Famous or not, the institute, or NIST for short, has immeasurably deepened our understanding of things as diverse as electricity, gravity waves, drugs, whale blubber, and Chesapeake Bay sludge.

The scientists, technicians, and other staff members of NIST (which is a branch of the U.S. Department of Commerce) observed the agency's 100th anniversary in 2001. The 3,200 employees at the institute's campus in Gaithersburg, Maryland, and its time-measurement division in Boulder, Colorado, used the centenary as an occasion to publish new accounts of some of the agency's achievements. The object was to show taxpayers anew that NIST earns its keep—currently about $720 million a year.

Working closely with kindred agencies around the world, especially the International Bureau of Weights and Measures in Sèvres, France, NIST has revolutionized the definition of global standards and the art of measurement. And there is more to do.

But despite NIST's achievements, public unfamiliarity with its functions has made the agency vulnerable to drastic cost-cutting measures. In the mid-1990s, for example, members of the U.S. Congress, eager to reduce federal spending, campaigned to close down the Department of Commerce and to parcel out NIST's laboratories to private research organizations.

Legions of scientists were horrified. In an open letter in 1995, 25 American winners of Nobel Prizes and the presidents of 18 scientific societies protested the proposed change, urging Congress to "make every effort to preserve this national treasure." Both the Commerce Department and NIST survived the assault, but agency officials are still wary of possible new initiatives to pare down the institute.

The nation's need for standardization was strongly demonstrated in 1904, when a conflagration swept across Baltimore, destroying more than 1,500 buildings. Fire departments from cities as distant as New York were called in, but because it was discovered too late that Baltimore's fire-hose connectors were incompatible with those of other cities, outsiders were unable to provide much help.

The standards institute, at the time a branch of the Treasury Department called the National Bureau of Standards, led a successful effort to standardize fire hoses across the nation. It continued to standardize thousands of other things, and today it sells about 35,000 "standard reference material" samples a year, with which manufacturers, laboratories, and other institutions can compare their own products. Samples available from NIST include standard spinach (which contains a

defined amount of nutrients), standard blubber from dead beached whales (as an index of environmental pollution), and standard Chesapeake Bay sludge—another measure of marine pollutants.

WIN SOME, LOSE SOME

A campaign mounted by the agency in the late 1970s to wean the United States away from the traditional English system of measurement to the standard metric system was less successful. Many American manufacturers have adjusted to the nuisance of using the English system for products sold domestically and the metric system for products sold abroad. But although the United States stands almost alone as a nonmetric country,

NIST's custodial work reaches far and wide—from setting global standards for measurement, such as the "national prototype kilogram" (facing page), to sanctioning their applications, as in gauging ocean pollution by testing frozen marine mammal tissue retrieved from its biomonitoring specimen bank (right).

NIST's newest cesium fountain atomic clock (left), developed by Steve Jefferts and Dawn Meekhof, will neither gain nor lose a second in 20 million years. Its 1949 forerunner (below), not as precise, worked by measuring vibrations of ammonia molecules.

that the thrust had been specified in the metric-system unit of newtons.

A RICH HISTORY

Efforts to improve systems of measurement have a heritage as old as recorded history. Early units of length included the English foot and the similar French *pied de roi*, both based on the assumption that all kings have feet roughly the same length. (Even today, people sometimes pace off a floor's dimensions with their feet; a man's size-11 shoe is conveniently close to 1 foot (0.3 meter) in length.

But in 1670, Gabriel Mouton, a French clergyman, proposed the creation of a new unit of length—the meter—equal to one 10-millionth of the distance from one of Earth's poles to the equator. This distance was calculated from a meridian drawn between Dunkirk, France, and Barcelona, Spain.

and despite the consequent disadvantages, even the National Aeronautics and Space Administration (NASA) continues to apply some nonmetric specifications to its spacecraft. A costly accident in 1999 was one of the results.

On September 23, 1999, NASA fired rockets intended to nudge its Mars Climate Orbiter into a stable low-altitude orbit. But after the rockets fired, NASA never heard from its expensive spacecraft again. Scientists later concluded that it had either crashed on the Martian surface or had bounded away, escaping the planet completely.

The reason for the debacle, scientists determined months later, was that the manufacturer, the Lockheed Martin Corporation, had specified the rocket thrust in pounds, while NASA assumed

William Meggers (right) checks the mercury lamp he developed in 1942. NIST endorsed it as an industry standard for measuring length in 1951.

That led to two other units of measurement: the liter, defined as a volume enclosed by a cube with all edges 0.1 meter long, and the kilogram, a mass equal to that of 1 liter of water. These units, together with the second, the basic unit of time, became the key concept of the early version of the metric system.

For nearly two centuries, this self-consistent measurement system sufficed for most uses. The standard meter was represented as the distance between two scratches inscribed on a metal bar housed in France, which was used to calibrate duplicate standard bars maintained in other countries. But this system, based on a manufactured "artifact"—the scratched metal bar—was inherently inaccurate. Each time a bar was subjected to a small change in temperature or other disturbance, its length changed enough to introduce errors into extremely precise measurements.

The idea evolved that measurement should be made more reliable by dispensing with standard artifacts, such as metal bars, and replacing them with values derived directly from nature. This is a quest that has been at the heart of NIST's work for the past century, and it continues to pose challenges even today.

New Standards for Metrics

With the standards institute in the vanguard, international research laboratories have devised entirely new standards for nearly all units of the metric system. The fundamental unit is no longer the meter; rather, it is now the second.

Since the 1949 invention of NIST's first atom-based clock, scientists have devised ever-more-accurate "atomic" clocks, which count the extremely regular vibrations of certain atoms. The agency's latest "atomic fountain" clock, the NIST F-1 is free from timing errors created in traditional timekeeping by Earth's irregular movements in orbit. As the most reliable clock ever made, the atomic fountain clock is used to calibrate the timing of the Global Positioning System (GPS)—the most accurate navigation system ever created.

In fact, NIST's marvelous atomic fountain clock will neither gain nor lose more than one second every 20 million years; if the clock had been running since the last dinosaurs died out, its error today would be no more than about three seconds. The matchless precision of the latest atomic clocks has allowed scientists to redefine the second with unprecedented accuracy. Since 1967, the world's official timekeepers have clocked the second as that period of time that elapses when a cesium atom of a certain type vibrates 9,192,631,770 times.

This has led to a new definition of the meter itself; no longer defined in terms of Earth's physical dimensions, the meter has been redefined in terms of time: it is the distance a beam of laser light of a certain frequency will travel through a vacuum in one 299,792,458th of a second.

The new definition of the meter automatically defines the new definition of the

Marking Time, Naturally

The tireless efforts of archaeologists to accurately date organic artifacts and to trace climate changes through centuries is akin to the unheralded work of NIST researchers. But it was not until the middle of the past century that advances in physics finally provided a means for scientists to ascertain the age of organic material. The process, known as radiocarbon dating, considers that part of the carbon in all living things is a radioactive isotope designated as carbon 14 (C-14).

After a living thing dies, it stops taking in carbon (as carbon dioxide), and the radioactive C-14 in it degrades at a steady rate. By looking at the amount of C-14 remaining in such an organic specimen, and comparing it to the amount of common, nonradioactive carbon 12 (C-12) found in it, scientists can pinpoint when the organism died. If the material being studied is a piece of wood from an Egyptian ship, an archaeologist can determine the age of the ship—and, in turn, the age of the civilization that produced it.

Dr. Henry Michael, a world-renowned pioneer in dendrochronology, examines the rings of a California bristlecone pine to determine the tree's age.

---

liter. But the world's custodians of measurement are still frustrated by their failure to create a new kilogram measure that is independent of all artifacts, including the weight of a liter of water. Scientists at NIST hope that a new definition of the kilogram based on the mass of a single atom will someday be possible.

PRECISION PRECLUDES DISCOVERY

Improvements in measurement techniques often lead to major advances in science. By inventing clocks of inconceivable precision, for example, NIST scientists made possible a great discovery of 20th-century physics: the probable existence of gravity waves.

In the 1980s, two Princeton scientists, Joseph H. Taylor, Ph.D., and his graduate student at the time, Russell A. Hulse, Ph.D., discovered a great rarity while working at the big telescope in Arecibo, Puerto Rico: two ultramassive neutron stars orbiting each other. They precisely timed radio pulsations emitted by this binary-star system with every rotation, using an atomic clock like those developed at NIST.

The speedy rotation of the two stars produced a radio pulse every six one-hundredths of a second, the two scientists found. They periodically repeated their measurements of the binary star year after year, and they learned that the pulses were coming faster as time passed. Dr. Taylor and Dr. Hulse calculated from this that the stars were spiraling in toward each other at exactly the rate that would be expected from Ein-

Radiocarbon dating was a boon to archaeology, but soon discrepancies between some radiocarbon dates and the dates in reliable written records became evident. The hypothesis behind the inconsistencies was that the amount of C-14 in the atmosphere fluctuates over time; as a result, remains from different time periods decay with different levels of the isotope present in their chemical makeup. Unless researchers knew the amounts of C-14 in the atmosphere during the different periods, the ratios of C-12 to C-14 would be meaningless, and radiocarbon data would be of little use.

Specialists realized that there was a basic science that could help them determine the history of C-14 levels—dendrochronology, the study of and dating by tree rings.

Dendrochronologists take core samples from living trees or from dead wood. They use an increment borer—a pencil-thin metal tube inserted into the wood and then drawn out carefully. The scientists then record the sequencing of rings and compare it to other samples from the same area. Dendrochronologists can match the rings from different samples and from their deductions construct a master map of climate changes of an area. If a wooden artifact is found, it can be compared with the map, and dated properly.

Early radiocarbon experts failed to account for fluctuations in Earth's magnetic field that alter the atmosphere's C-14 content. Dendrochronology was the tool that could reliably establish how much the biosphere's C-14 had changed over thousands of years. Best of all, applying its principles toward "reading" history proved to be a relatively simple step in systematically tracing climatic activity. Applying principles of nature, a piece of wood can be dated using the dendrochronological record; then, when a sample of the dated wood is burned and its vapors measured, how much C-14 was in Earth's atmosphere in a given year can be determined and inaccuracies corrected.

stein's general theory of relativity for stars losing energy in the form of gravity waves.

Gravity waves are so faint that no instrument yet built is sensitive enough to verify their existence. (This may change with the completion of several huge gravity-wave detectors under construction in the United States and abroad.)

But the indirect evidence collected by Dr. Taylor and Dr. Hulse by measuring the pulsation rate of a binary-star system convinced most scientists that gigantic gravitational events (such as the explosion of supernova stars and the fast rotation of supermassive binary stars) do produce the gravity waves that Einstein envisioned. Dr. Taylor and Dr. Hulse were awarded the 1993 Nobel Prize in Physics for their discovery.

The very word "measure" can glaze the eyes of people who feel uncomfortable with numbers. But scientists everywhere, including those at the standards institute, regard measurement as the keystone of discovery.

Lord Kelvin, the 19th-century English physicist who discovered the vital pillar of science known as the second law of thermodynamics, put it this way:

"When you can measure what you are speaking about and express it in numbers, you know something about it; but when you cannot measure it, when you cannot express it in numbers, your knowledge is of a meager and unsatisfactory kind."

A statement to which those at the National Institute of Standards and Technology wholeheartedly agree. ◪

Underhanded Achievement

by Curtis Rist

As a boy in Elizabeth, New Jersey, in the 1950s, retired basketball legend Rick Barry got some painful coaching lessons from his father, a semi-pro. While the youngster's friends liked to shoot their foul shots, or "free throws," in the respectable overhand style, the old man wanted Barry to toss them just as he did—underhand. "That's the way little kids shoot, and it didn't help that everybody calls it the 'granny shot,'" Barry says. "I didn't want any part of it, but my father drove me nuts until I tried it. And amazingly, it worked." Barry's average from the free-throw line bounced from 70 to 80 percent—and kept on climbing when he became a pro and lead scorer in both the American Basketball Association (ABA) and the National Basketball Association (NBA). "Nobody ever teased me, but then it's hard to tease somebody when the ball keeps going in."

Rick Barry enjoyed remarkable success shooting underhand. Nevertheless, many players feel silly using the "granny shot."

and Optimum Performance. "It's like bowling. You do exactly the same thing over and over and over again." Yet while Barry can easily sink 9 out of 10 shots, most others fall far short. Basketball legend Wilt Chamberlain, for instance, could shoot a basket from just about anywhere on the court—except when he toed up to that line 15 feet (4.5 meters) from the hoop.

No one has suffered more public humiliation at the free-throw line than the New York Knicks' Chris Dudley. One year, he made only 3 out of every 10 shots, and last season, when Dudley managed to sink two free throws in a row during postseason playoffs, he made headlines ("Chris No Dud at Foul Line!" screamed the *New York Daily News*). "I'm convinced that from a physics standpoint, if everyone was to learn how to throw underhand, you'd see these statistics rise dramatically," says Brancazio.

STANDING TALL, FALLING SHORT

Judging by mechanics alone, this should be the case with just about every foul shot. "There's nothing simpler in basketball, because you can take all the time you want to make it, and there's nobody waving their arms in front of you trying to block you," says Peter Brancazio, a physics professor emeritus from Brooklyn College in New York City and author of *SportScience: Physical Laws*

ADJUSTING THE MARGIN

The key to a successful foul shot lies in the arc of the throw—in general, the higher the better. While an official-sized basket is 18 inches (45.7 centimeters) in diameter, the basketball itself is only about 9.5 inches (24 centimeters), which gives a margin of 8.5 inches (21.6 centimeters). But when the ball is thrown nearly straight at the basket—in the style of Los Angeles Lakers star Shaquille O'Neal—the margin disappears because the rim of the basket, from the perspective of the ball, resembles a tight ellipse. "That's why these guys miss so much," says Brancazio. "Because of the sharp angle of the typical overhand throw, there ends up being a much smaller window for the ball to go in." If the ball comes down at the basket from a steeper angle—the way it does if tossed up in the high arc typical of an underhand throw—the margin reappears. "That means a far greater chance of making the basket," he says.

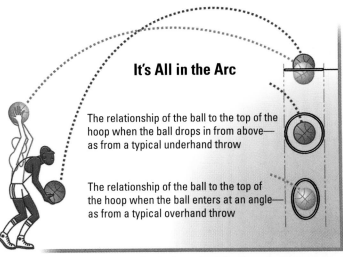

It's All in the Arc

The relationship of the ball to the top of the hoop when the ball drops in from above— as from a typical underhand throw

The relationship of the ball to the top of the hoop when the ball enters at an angle— as from a typical overhand throw

The secret to a winning foul shot lies in the angle of the throw. Instead of shooting the ball straight at the basket, the single upward movement of the granny shot may offer better odds of producing that glorious swish.

ALL ABOUT MATH
Using lots of trigonometry, Brancazio calculated the optimal angle of the arc from the free-throw line. If tossed at 32 degrees or less, the ball will likely hit the back of the rim. "That doesn't mean it won't go in, but it will certainly bounce off the metal and reduce the chance of success," he says. At angles greater than that, the ball has a chance of making a nice *swish*. The optimum angle, he calculated, is 45 degrees— plus half the angle from the top of the player's hand to the rim. "The shorter you are, the steeper that angle has to get to give you the best chance of making the shot," Brancazio says. Of course, lobbing a ball very high so that it comes down nearly straight into the basket would be the most efficient technique, but a shot like that "is almost impossible to aim," says Brancazio.

TIPS AND DIPS
Another factor of the granny shot also helps a free throw win cheers rather than jeers: a backward spin added to the ball. If a ball with backspin happens to hit the metal rim of the basket, the friction of contact reduces its forward velocity. "It's like a drop shot in tennis—the ball bounces, but it doesn't have a forward motion on it," says Brancazio. This effect tends to freeze the ball at the rim, and greatly increases the chance that it will tip into the basket.

The underhand throw can also minimize the drift of the ball. "A little sideward movement at the start of the throw will translate into a big movement toward the end," says Tom Steiger, an assistant professor at the University of Washington in Seattle who teaches basketball physics in a sports-science class. The trick to keeping the ball moving along a single plane toward the basket lies in "minimizing the *x*-axis motion," he says. "In other words, you have to keep your elbows tucked in." If they're sticking out, that can easily add an unwanted nudge to the ball, which results in a missed shot. The underhand throw provides stability "because you're holding the ball with both hands." The movement of the underhand throw is a simple, easy-to-control upward pendulum motion, while the overhand shot involves separate movements of the wrist, elbow, and shoulder that can add errors.

GOOD AND SILLY
No NBA player has used the granny shot since Barry retired in 1980. "That baffles me," Barry says. Over the years, he has tried to convert everyone—from four of his sons who have played professionally to O'Neal to Dudley—but nobody paid any attention. "A lot of guys who are lousy at the free throw would be prime candidates for this, but they just won't do it," says Barry. "I mean, how can guys call themselves professionals when they can't even make 60 percent of their free throws? Where's their sense of pride?"

Good point. "As good as it is," Steiger says, "it does look kind of stupid."

How Squirrels Fly

by Michael Kernan

Frankly, it never would have occurred to me to test flying squirrels in a wind tunnel. I could just see it: little furry things buffeted by the artificial gale, their tiny eyes squeezed shut as they banked and dipped and climbed all in the name of a scientific investigation.

But it's not that way at all. The cute little creatures couldn't withstand the force. Besides, they don't really fly—they glide. And it's this long, graceful gliding that has prompted a study by some scientists at the Smithsonian's National Museum of Natural History in Washington, D.C.

"I was always interested in functional morphology, in the origin of primates, in how animals work," says Brian Stafford, a re-search associate at the museum who did his thesis on gliding mammals. "I got into flying lemurs, and that led me into research on all gliding mammals."

MAKING A CONNECTION

The purpose of using a wind tunnel to study flying squirrels—the test subjects, by the way, are models that Stafford constructs of steel and fiberglass—is to find out exactly how, in terms of physics, this gliding is done, and how the squirrels' bodies work to achieve it. How are the critters able to glide

Flying squirrels technically don't fly—they glide. They accomplish this form of flight by spreading their wings, or patagia, to produce the necessary lift.

approximately 10 to 30 miles (16 to 48 kilometers) per hour?

Stafford has been working with Dick Thorington, curator of mammals at Natural History, whose interest in flying squirrels goes back at least 20 years. The main purpose of the project is to learn more about the animals, Thorington says. "But wouldn't it be fun if we discovered something useful about how to control flight or reduce drag on small objects, such as small flying robots that could be used in aerial photography?"

Studying this animal's wing was a natural place to start. The wing, or patagium, produces lift, enabling the squirrels to glide. When I visited Stafford at the Glenn L. Martin Wind Tunnel at the University of Maryland in College Park, he drew a series of rhombuses (parallelograms with slanted sides) to show me how squirrel wings look when spread out. It's the square shape that's of particular interest to him and Thorington. Our modern aircraft design tends to be long and narrow, so the researchers wondered how the square wings worked.

"Square wings for aircraft were investigated in the early days, but didn't progress," Thorington says. "They were not as efficient as narrow designs in terms of drag."

Squirrels also have a little flap on their patagium, a sort of winglet. The scientists noticed that the winglets curl upward, like the tips on many aircraft wings. One theory is that the slant reduces drag around the end of the wing. Another is that it acts to stabilize or control the glide. Or again, as in commercial planes, it may both increase flight efficiency and help control and stabilize the glide. This theory is quite likely, since the winglet is so far from the center of gravity that it has an exaggerated effect.

MODELS OF STEEL

In 1999, Stafford spent two months in Japan doing research with Takeo Kawamichi, a professor who has studied the Japanese giant flying squirrel for decades. Observing the squirrels in the wild, the scientists stayed up night after night making videos and measuring the animals' speed and flight distances. Once, Stafford saw a giant squirrel at 2:00

To study the physics of nature's perfect glider, life-sized models of the flying squirrel are tested at the University of Maryland. Smoke blows over the model, allowing scientists to see how wing design affects wind flow.

A.M., or rather, he saw the creature's eyes glowing in the dark. Suddenly the eyes disappeared. "Did he just close his eyes, or did he move? They're so quick and quiet, you can't tell."

Coasting low and slow, the Japanese giant flying squirrel was recorded gliding for nearly 160 feet (50 meters). There have even been some reports of 500-foot (150-meter) glides, "but that was on a downhill slope," Stafford explains.

Flying squirrels vary anatomically, he reveals with enthusiasm. "All have a small membrane between the neck and forelimbs, and this seems related to how they glide. Larger ones have a membrane between the hind legs. The smaller animals don't have this, but they do have featherlike tails. What is the function of that?"

Looking for Answers

These questions brought Stafford and Thorington to the wind tunnel and into collaboration with its director, Jewel Barlow, and research manager, Robert Ranzenbach. I got a tour of this remarkable device with Barlow. We entered a vast room with tilting walls. With no parallel sides or right angles, the facility makes for odd optical illusions. On one side, tucked at the end of a 40-foot (12-meter)-long pollywog-shaped structure, is the fan itself, which is 19 feet (6 meters) in diameter and has a 2,000-horsepower electric motor. It spins seven propeller blades modified from a B-29 bomber and can generate winds of up to 230 miles (370 kilometers) per hour. Opposite the fan in a section of an enclosed tunnel circuit is the test area with an observation window.

To test wind impact, the powerful fan blasts a stream of air on objects such as aircraft, boats, cars—"anything that the wind blows on or anything that moves through water or air," Barlow told me. At this particular wind tunnel, a lot of the experiments are conducted to evaluate how various design concepts affect the aerodynamics of new cars. Using three-eighths-scale models that are about 6 feet (2 meters) long, automobile manufacturers try to find out what the level of drag is for a particular design, or the degree of wind noise or debris distribution, even windshield-wiper efficiency on a gusty day.

"We also conduct experiments on wind flow around buildings," Barlow adds. "We measure pressure distribution on models, which helps the structural engineers design windows and glass walls."

Not long ago on television, I saw a weatherman standing in a test chamber, chained to the steel floor, while he stridently tried to describe what it is like to stand in a hurricane. At 100 miles (160 kilometers) per hour, his cheeks rippled, his ears flapped, and he stopped talking.

Stafford has built life-sized model squirrels of clay, fiberglass, and steel rods, reproducing the exact wing shape and several levels of camber, or wing curvature.

"We're now testing steady midflight patterns. We don't have the data yet to study turns. The wing needs to be totally stable for this kind of testing, which is why we build the models out of steel."

Stafford is creating several variations of models that will mimic the different characteristics of flying squirrels. "There are many differences. For example, we will test one model with the winglets bent upward, and another with the winglets held flat. By comparing the results of these tests, we will be able to determine the function of the winglets. We will know what they do. We are building 26 different models, designed to test our hypotheses about the function of different wing structures."

Why Glide at All?

As I listen to all of this, a question occurs to me: Why glide at all? "Gliding may save energy getting from tree to tree," Stafford says. "Predator avoidance may also be a factor. Gliding may be the fastest way for these animals to get from one place to another, or get to widely scattered food sources."

Looking for answers, Stafford has been videotaping several local gray squirrels—the nongliders—in the wild to compare their behavior with that of gliders.

Being nocturnal, flying squirrels must have good eyesight, he says. "Even so, they often triangulate distance. You can see how their heads bob just before they take off."

The flying squirrel's eyes are on the sides of the head so it can spot attackers coming from any direction. But this fact, plus the small size of the head, makes for poor depth perception. That's why the intended flight path has to be checked out from several angles to establish a workable parallax.

Sometimes a squirrel will drop like a stone after takeoff to gain speed. It lowers one arm to turn, just like a kid playing pilot.

I thought it must be exciting to watch a creature seemingly in the middle of an evolutionary change, and I wanted to know where all this was leading: Would squirrels someday fill the sky like birds?

Stafford smiled. "Evolution is not necessarily directional. There are all kinds of gliding animals—mammals, lizards, fish—but their development isn't necessarily going anywhere. Gliding may be an end in itself."

Joining Hands: The Mathematics of
APPLAUSE

by Josie Glausiusz

Trumpeting cherubs, gold-leafed and puff-cheeked, peer down from the walls of the opulent academy in Budapest, Hungary. As pianist Dezsö Ránki pounds and weaves at the keys, his breathing is at times so loud and labored one could swear that someone in the audience is snoring. But there are no spectators nodding off here. When the final chords of Beethoven's Piano Concerto in C Major crash out, the crowd bursts into applause—at first tumultuously, but then, suddenly, in perfect unison. There is no signal, no leader; the synchrony is spontaneous. The pianist bows and then disappears backstage. He returns to applause that grows stronger. Yet as the clapping gathers strength, its synchrony dis-

An explosion of exuberant applause invariably falls into a rhythmic, unified beat—offering physicists a classic example of synchronization phenomena.

solves. Ránki retreats and reappears repeatedly, and so does the rhythm of the applause—one moment chaotic, the next a perfect beat. Then, the entire audience stops, as one, on a single clap.

Tamás Vicsek, a physicist at Budapest's Eötvös University, twists around from his second-row seat and explains. "This synchronized clapping is called 'iron' applause in Hungarian," he says. "There was a time when an iron curtain would descend after a performance between the stage and the audience, which would clap rhythmically to induce the conductor or actors to appear in front of the curtains."

A Matter of Math
The iron curtain is gone from this country—in more ways than one—but the rhythmic applause remains. In fact, it's hardly unique to the theaters of Budapest:

When hockey player Wayne Gretzky retired from the New York Rangers, for instance, the crowd at Madison Square Garden burst into rhythmic applause, and the same response met Cecilia Bartoli when she sang an aria at the Teatro Olimpico in Vicenza, Italy. The reason, Vicsek and his colleagues in the United States and Romania believe, has as much to do with mathematics as it does with aesthetics and psychology.

According to Steven Strogatz, a mathematician at Cornell University, Ithaca, New York, who has studied synchronization for 20 years, the same set of mathematical prin-

A universal principle of synchronicity—mutual interaction—occurs frequently among a group of runners in which the slowest ones speed up and the fastest ones slow down.

ciples governs the phenomenon wherever it occurs—be it among applauding people, flashing fireflies, or roomfuls of grandfather clocks. Strogatz has always been fascinated by synchronization and seems to see it wherever he looks. Asian fireflies flash together each night in the mangrove trees along a riverbank. Crickets chirp in unison, and cicadas emerge from the ground at the same moment every 17 years. The Moon rotates around its own axis at exactly the same rate as it orbits around Earth, which is why one side of the Moon is never seen. Pacemaker cells in the heart oscillate in harmony. There is even the curious case of menstrual synchrony among women who live together.

MUTUAL INTERACTION

To more fully understand the mechanics of synchrony, Strogatz suggests, imagine several athletes running around a circular track. "Suppose these runners are friends, and they would prefer to run together so that they can talk," he says. "If their speeds are not too different—that is, if the slowest one can keep up with the fastest one, then you can get a group of runners all going in sync. But first, they have to be sensitive to each other. They have to be willing to adjust their speeds from what they would prefer. The fastest ones have to slow down, and the slowest ones have to speed up, to find some compromise. And that same principle—that slow oscillators have to speed up and fast ones have to slow down, and that this happens because of mutual interactions—is a pretty universal principle for synchrony."

The interactions, Strogatz adds, can be obvious: The runners see each other; the clappers hear other claps. They can also be subtle. Two grandfather clocks can synchronize their pendulum swings through imperceptible vibrations traveling through the wall against which they both lean. But the story can also be more complicated than that. Picture, for example, crickets living alone in soundproof chambers, as they did in Strogatz's lab. They can listen to their neighbors' sounds only when controlled levels of chirping are piped in. "If we make the sounds loud enough—if we let enough of the chirping sound through—at some point, there will suddenly be enough mutual influence that they can synchronize. Below that point, they can't. This is what physicists call a phase transition," Strogatz says. "There's a critical amount of interaction when synchrony will burst out. It doesn't just build up gradually."

MYSTERIOUS PHENOMENON

A similar phase transition lies behind an audience's sudden switch to synchronized clapping. "Say the people are clapping in a disorganized way, but they all know that

The perfectly timed choreography of New York City's high-kicking Rockettes exemplifies the dynamics of synchronization. The dancers begin as individuals whose movements at a certain point fall into a harmonious pattern.

they're trying to synchronize," Strogatz explains. "However, they don't hear a beat. But then—and this is rather mysterious—suppose a beat just happens to emerge a little bit, maybe because a few clappers get lucky. That beat will then be audible above the din of the disorganized rest of the audience. And since everyone knows that they're trying to clap in unison, the cooperative clappers will try to join in with that beat. The pulse becomes stronger, and then it takes off."

Tamás Vicsek, together with physicists Albert-László Barabási of the University of Notre Dame in Indiana and Zoltan Néda of Romania's Babeş-Bolyai University in Cluj-Napoca, set out to probe the dynamics of clapping more closely. Néda began the project by suspending microphones from the ceilings of concert halls in Romania and recording applause. He and the other researchers then analyzed the recordings and found a fairly consistent pattern: several rounds—up to six or seven—of synchronized clapping, interspersed with incoherent cacophony. Moreover, the periods between claps doubled during synchronization.

Néda and his graduate student Erzsébet Ravasz also asked 73 high-school students to stand alone in a room and clap quickly, as they would after an outstanding performance. Then they asked the students to clap as if they were synchronizing with others. Néda and Ravasz found that the students' clapping rates varied widely when they were asked to clap quickly, but when asked to simulate synchrony, most clapped slowly.

CROWD PSYCHOLOGY

When synchrony sets in, the overall noise level of the applause decreases; when it disappears, the noise level rises. Synchronization, Barabási and Vicsek conclude, triggers a feeling of togetherness among audience members, whereas faster clapping feels more enthusiastic. Conflicting desires swing the clappers between the two modes.

There was a time, Barabási adds, when comradeship reigned supreme in countries such as Hungary and Romania, and exuberance had no place, when swings between synchrony and chaos couldn't be heard. At the giant rallies common to Barabási's childhood in Communist Romania—a childhood marked by the tyrannical regime of Nicolae Ceauşescu—audiences applauding the "great leader" would clap monotonously and dutifully in synchrony in response to party speeches. But there was no enthusiasm to accelerate their clapping to the point of disorder. Then, one day in late December 1989, the synchronized applause ended—quite abruptly.

"When Ceauşescu was overthrown, he organized a huge rally of 250,000 people in Bucharest to show support for him," Barabási remembers well. "People were supposed to clap synchronously, and at the beginning they did. But then the clapping stopped. Some people threw their banners down, and then the shooting started and the revolution began." Just four days later, on Christmas day, Ceauşescu and his wife were shot dead. ◢

What Edward Teller Did

by T.A. Heppenheimer

The world's first hydrogen bomb, designated "Mike," exploded on November 1, 1952. The test took place on a Pacific island named Elugelab, which ceased to exist within a second after detonation. Mike's fireball spread fast enough to terrify people 30 miles (48 kilometers) away who had seen previous nuclear tests. One scientist later described it as "so huge, so brutal—as if things had gone too far. When the heat reached the observers, it stayed and stayed, not for seconds but for minutes." The fire-

ball, initially a blinding white, expanded in seconds to more than 3 miles (5 kilometers) across. Then, glowing purple, it began to rise. At its base, a curtain of water fell slowly back into the sea.

Two-and-a-half minutes later, a shock wave reached the observers, who heard a sharp report. The mushroom cloud rose

Nuclear physicist Edward Teller's "offspring"—the hydrogen bomb—created an awesome and terrifying mushroom cloud over the Pacific Ocean.

until it reached the top of the stratosphere, then spread to form a threatening canopy 100 miles (160 kilometers) wide. Down below, there was a deep crater in the ocean floor. Two hours later, a jet pilot flew his plane into the mushroom's stem and saw it glowing like a furnace. A survey team found fish whose skin was burned on one side, as if they had been dropped into a frying pan.

Edward Teller, the gifted physicist whose work had led to this explosion, was at the University of California in Berkeley. When the appointed hour of detonation drew near, he went to the basement of the geology building and watched a point of light on a seismograph. "At exactly the scheduled time I saw the light point move," he later wrote. He sent a telegram to colleagues at the Los Alamos nuclear laboratory in New Mexico who had designed and built the bomb. The message read: "It's a boy."

A HATRED OF TOTALITARIANISM

Teller's road to this strange paternity began in Budapest, Hungary, where he was born in 1908. Eleven years later, in the aftermath of World War I, his country fell under the Communist dictatorship of the strongman Béla Kun. The new regime billeted two soldiers in the Tellers' home, where they terrified the family by searching for forbidden hoards of currency.

After a few months, this revolution set off a counterrevolution, led by the fascist Miklós Horthy. Kun and many of his commissars had been Jewish, and the Tellers were Jewish, too. Horthy's regime, which would last well into World War II, drove tens of thousands of Jews into exile while building torture chambers and executing at least 5,000 people. The Tellers managed to stay in Budapest, but the Kun and Horthy dictatorships left a lasting mark on young Edward. For the rest of his life, he would have a passionate hatred of totalitarianism and a fierce determination to build defenses against it.

Throughout his long and controversial career, Teller was a leading advocate for powerful defense systems.

Teller showed a great talent for physics. After his studies in Karlsruhe and Munich, Germany, he went to the University of Leipzig. There, he worked with Werner Heisenberg, one of the founders of quantum mechanics. He was awarded his Ph.D. in 1930 and won a position at the University of Göttingen, then one of the world's most prominent centers for research.

Then, in 1933, Hitler came to power. Teller had no doubt about what was coming. He decamped to Denmark in early 1934 and joined Niels Bohr (who had won a Nobel Prize in 1922 and whose work complemented Heisenberg's) at the Copenhagen Institute for Theoretical Physics, which Bohr had founded in 1919. In the fall of 1934, Teller went to the University of London as a lecturer in chemistry, and, in August 1935, he left for the United States, where he took a full professorship at George Washington University, Washington, D.C.

He had seen totalitarianism firsthand in both Hungary and Germany. He escaped by developing an interest in the nuclear reactions that power the Sun and stars. Similar reactions would eventually provide the energy of a hydrogen bomb, but thoughts of such weapons still lay well in the future.

THE MANHATTAN PROJECT

For a long time, the profession of physics had been a rarefied one, but after the discovery of atomic fission in Germany in 1938, its practitioners began to deal with politicians and generals. The threat of war lent particular urgency to fission research. Albert Einstein's famous 1939 letter to President Franklin D. Roosevelt brought a small appropriation, which was followed by a research program that later became known as the Manhattan Project.

Teller accepted a personal call to arms in 1940, as Nazi tanks brutally unleashed their blitzkrieg on the Low Countries. On May 10, Roosevelt addressed a meeting of scientists in Washington, and Teller listened earnestly to the president's words: "If the scientists in the free countries will not make weapons to defend the freedom of their countries, then freedom will be lost." Teller heard this speech as a call to duty: "I had the strange impression that he was talking to me. My mind was made up, and it has not changed since."

GETTING TO WORK

He and his colleagues knew of the work of the physicist Hans Bethe, who in 1938 had described the fusion reactions that power the Sun. Nuclear fusion, like nuclear fission, involves the conversion of mass to energy. But while fission works by splitting an atomic nucleus in two (with the products having less mass than the initial nucleus), fusion works by merging two nuclei together (with

Teller congratulates J. Robert Oppenheimer (left) on his Fermi Award in 1963. The former colleagues disagreed over the ethics of stronger atomic weapons.

the product, again, having less mass than the individual nuclei). Under the intense heat and pressure of the deep solar interior, the reactions described by Bethe convert hydrogen into helium at a rate of more than 600 million tons per second. Scientists also knew that deuterium, a heavy isotope of hydrogen,

readily underwent fusion and could be extracted from ordinary water.

Italy's Enrico Fermi, a leading experimentalist, was part of the emerging weapons community. In September 1941, as he and Teller walked across the campus of Columbia University, New York, (where both had recently joined the faculty), Fermi suggested that current developments could make it possible to duplicate the fusion in the Sun's interior. An atomic bomb (which existed only in theory) might heat a mass of deuterium, Fermi said, and cause it to undergo reactions like those inside the Sun. Teller found the idea fascinating, and explored it with further calculations. As he later recalled, "I decided that deuterium could not be ignited by atomic bombs. I reported my results to Fermi and forgot about it."

During the summer of 1942, J. Robert Oppenheimer, the head of the Manhattan Project, hosted a gathering of physicists at Berkeley. Teller fell in with a young colleague, Emil Konopinski, who was eager to study a fusion bomb. Konopinski suggested using not only deuterium but also tritium, an even heavier isotope of hydrogen. Tritium does not exist naturally on Earth, but Konopinski thought it might be created within the bomb itself by nuclear reactions that involved lithium. Teller tried to show him that this would not work. They made new calculations, and, as Teller describes it, they learned that "the roadblocks I had erected for Fermi's idea were not so high after all. We hurdled them one by one and concluded that heavy hydrogen actually could be ignited by an atomic bomb."

The idea drew full attention from Oppenheimer's summer study group. The physicists concluded that a bomb of this type might yield the energy of 100 million tons of dynamite. Such a weapon would be thousands of times more powerful than the projected atomic bomb. Even so, there was no practical way of bypassing the A-bomb, since it would have to serve as an igniter for the H-bomb (or Super, as it was called). Attention therefore focused anew on the A-bomb, with the H-bomb relegated to the back burner—a topic reserved for sometime in the distant future.

id • What Edward Teller
hat Edward Teller

The target chamber of Livermore's National Ignition Facility was the site of several "hits and misses" during the H-bomb experiments of the 1950s and early 1960s.

SECRET RESEARCH

In 1943, Oppenheimer led a number of his colleagues to a secret new research center at Los Alamos, New Mexico. Teller was one of them. He had assisted Oppenheimer in organizing the work at Los Alamos and recruiting its staff members. The plans called for a theoretical division, which Teller hoped to direct. Instead, he found himself passed over in favor of Bethe. Teller was particularly unhappy because he was now far removed from day-to-day contact with Oppenheimer, a physicist whom he admired. He responded by taking on the design of an H-bomb as a personal challenge. He contributed to mainstream A-bomb studies, but he spent as much time as he could on the H-bomb, even after the war ended with the atomic bombings of Hiroshima and Nagasaki in Japan.

The design Teller favored amounted to a stick of nuclear dynamite. An A-bomb would serve as its detonator, providing a burst of energetic neutrons for ultrarapid heating. This would ignite thermonuclear reactions in a long pipe filled with liquid deuterium. A small quantity of tritium, produced separately in a nuclear reactor, would react with the deuterium, and a wave of nuclear fusion would sweep down the pipe, producing the indiscriminating blast of the H-bomb.

This arrangement became known as the "classical Super." Initial calculations made with the University of Pennsylvania's ENIAC computer in 1945 and 1946 suggested that it might work—if one ignored the possible difficulties. The pertinent computations were very demanding, and computers were still in their infancy, so many assumptions and approximations had to be made. This gave Teller leeway to tailor the calculations in a way that promoted his approach.

AFTER THE WAR

With the war over, Bethe went back to Cornell; Oppenheimer went to Caltech in California for a year, followed by a year at Berkeley, and then to a position at the Insti-

tute for Advanced Study in Princeton, New Jersey. A new lab director, Norris Bradbury, offered Teller the directorship of the theoretical division. Teller wanted it, but only if he could lead a major push toward building an H-bomb. This proved impossible because of postwar cutbacks, so he joined the general exodus, taking a position at the University of Chicago alongside his old friend Fermi.

At first, Teller was still militant and ready to oppose tyranny with arms. Bethe recalls that a few months after the war, "Teller said we had to continue research on nuclear weapons. . . . The war was not over and Russia was just as dangerous an enemy as Germany had been."

But in Chicago, Teller's restless soul found peace for a while with his wife, Mici, and their two children. With America holding a nuclear monopoly, he shared the widespread hope of lasting peace.

TOTALITARIANISM MARCHES ON

Then reality set in. In 1948, the Soviets took control of Czechoslovakia, consolidated a takeover of Hungary, and tried to seize West Berlin by blockading that city. Totalitarianism was on the march again, and again Teller felt it personally. His parents and other family members had survived the Nazis and were still in Budapest, but now they were cut off from him. He responded by leaving Chicago and returning to Los Alamos in July 1949 to build weapons.

In August 1949, the Soviets set off their first atomic bomb. A month later, in Beijing, Mao Zedong proclaimed the People's Republic of China. With the Soviets already in control of Eastern Europe, these events raised the specter of a nuclear-armed Communist bloc commanding the almost-limitless manpower of the Chinese. The Cold War had reached the fever pitch at which it would remain through the 1950s and 1960s.

WASHINGTON PUTS ON THE SKIDS
In Washington, President Harry S. Truman prepared to respond with a stepped-up nuclear program. Oppenheimer chaired the General Advisory Committee of the Atomic Energy Commission (AEC), which was a key source of advice. The committee met in late October 1949 and endorsed plans for expanded production of plutonium and fissionable uranium, for development of nuclear weapons, and for research on fission bombs of novel design. However, the group's members strongly opposed development of the H-bomb. They were convinced that the existing stockpile of fission weapons, which would soon be greatly increased, would be enough to protect the nation. They argued that this would still be true even if the Soviets built H-bombs of their own. Moreover, they raised ethical concerns.

The committee's majority asserted that the H-bomb "would involve a decision to slaughter a vast number of civilians. . . . a super bomb might become a weapon of genocide. . . . We believe a super bomb should never be produced." A minority report, signed by Fermi and Isidor I. Rabi, went further: "The fact that no limit exists to the destructiveness of this weapon makes its very existence . . . a danger to humanity as a whole. It is necessarily an evil thing considered in any light." But Teller knew his way around Washington, and had support where it counted—from influential men who viewed the Super as the answer to the Soviet atomic bomb.

TRUMAN GIVES THE GREEN LIGHT
In January 1950, Truman announced a greatly enlarged nuclear program. He publicly directed the AEC "to continue its work on all forms of atomic weapons, including the so-called hydrogen or superbomb." Although Teller had received the green light he wanted, no one actually knew how to build a hydrogen bomb, for studies had failed to prove that the classical Super was feasible. During 1950, new and more-accurate computations showed that the classical Super would not work. The deuterium simply would not get hot enough.

Help came from a technique employed in atomic bombs that worked by implosion. The bombs used a sphere of plutonium within a thick shell of high explosives; detonation of the chemical explosives produced a shock wave that traveled inward, compressing the plutonium and touching off the nuclear blast. Teller had considered a similar scheme for hydrogen bombs, using implosion to compress deuterium, but chemical explosives would be too weak, and he could not figure out how to use the much greater energy of an atomic bomb for this purpose.

Early in 1951, mathematician Stanislaw Ulam weighed in with a suggestion. Ulam had made some of the recent calculations that had killed the classical Super, and now he was back working on atomic bombs. He proposed a two-step design in which the neutrons produced by exploding one A-bomb could be made to implode a plutonium shell, setting off a second, much larger A-bomb with extraordinary yield.

Ulam pursued this approach and saw that it could achieve very high compression of liquefied deuterium in a hydrogen bomb. This would have a much better chance of initiating fusion than Teller's scheme, which essentially relied on ordinary heat transfer. Ulam took the idea to Teller, who was skeptical. But Teller took up the idea and improved upon it. He was aware that in addition to neutrons, atomic bombs also release X rays—radiation that would be more useful for imploding the deuterium.

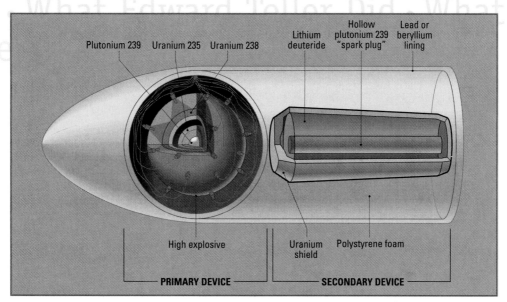

Plutonium 239   Uranium 235   Uranium 238

Lithium deuteride

Hollow plutonium 239 "spark plug"

Lead or beryllium lining

High explosive

Uranium shield

Polystyrene foam

PRIMARY DEVICE   **SECONDARY DEVICE**

In the Teller-Ulam design diagrammed above, an exploding fission "primary device" compresses a uranium shield around a lithium deuteride "secondary device," causing the plutonium within it to explode.

THE H-BOMB'S FINAL DESIGN

In the final design, a large cylinder of liquid deuterium was to be surrounded with a thick layer of uranium. At detonation, X rays from the atomic trigger, or "primary," would be directed onto the surface of the uranium. This would blow off its outer layers with explosive force, which in turn would place the rest of the uranium layer under extreme pressure, compressing it along with the liquid deuterium that lay within. At the center of the cylinder of deuterium was a rod of plutonium, which would be compressed beyond the critical point by the deuterium and undergo an explosion of its own, boosting the yield greatly. This approach to H-bomb design became known as the Teller-Ulam principle.

The Mike test showed the value of this principle on the first try. Mike delivered 10.4 megatons of explosive yield, nearly 1,000 times as much as the atomic bomb detonated at Hiroshima. It did not demonstrate a militarily useful weapon; it weighed 82 tons and relied on liquid deuterium, which was hard to handle. But Teller's colleagues quickly crafted new bomb designs that replaced this deuterium with lithium deuteride, a powder that resembled table salt. This led to true hydrogen bombs that were not only very powerful but also very light.

Teller had long since put aside his musings on world government. When seeking a crash program for the Super, he had predicted that unless the project went forward quickly, the Russians would invade the United States and take him prisoner. He came to see any opposition to him or his hydrogen bomb as a threat to the national interest. Oppenheimer had been the leader of the H-bomb's opponents, and after Teller had gotten his Super program approved, Teller began working to orchestrate Oppenheimer's downfall, on grounds that he was a security risk. Oppenheimer had held high-level security clearance in spite of his family's ties to the Communist Party. Eventually his loyalty became dubious at best, and, following a formal investigation (at which Teller testified against him), Oppenheimer lost that clearance. But Oppenheimer remained esteemed by the physics community. In the end, it was Teller who was ostracized by his colleagues.

TELLER STAYS CONNECTED

Teller ultimately turned to a circle of right-wing conservatives, military leaders, and personal protégés. He had already won air force support for establishment of a second AEC weapons laboratory, separate from Los Alamos. The new center, Lawrence Livermore National Laboratory, opened in 1952, competing with Los Alamos and challenging its monopoly in nuclear-weapons design. Although Teller was not the laboratory's director, he ran the show. He handpicked his acolytes for the top positions and managed the laboratory as his personal fief.

Los Alamos, with Harold Agnew at the helm, and Livermore became fierce rivals. Several of Livermore's first weapons designs turned out to be duds; hence the center's warhead proposals were rejected in initial design competitions to select warheads for the nation's early ballistic missiles. "We wiped 'em," Agnew succinctly recalled. "Every one—Thor, Jupiter, Atlas, Titan— every warhead was from Los Alamos."

But Teller's Livermore scored a coup with the warhead for the submarine-based Polaris missile. To make it light in weight, Teller used weapons-grade uranium (which, though heavy itself, allowed each pound of the bomb to explode with far more energy). This approach took advantage of a burgeoning supply of uranium.

HOW SMALL COULD AN H-BOMB BE?

At Livermore, the Teller-Ulam principle was a specialty of the house. This principle, again, called for enclosing a charge of lithium deuteride within a thick shell, or pusher, which would then be compressed inward. In warheads, the energy burst needed for compression came from an A-bomb, but other applications might use a different energy source, possibly even one that could fit within a laboratory. This raised the question: On how small a scale could the Teller-Ulam principle work? To put it another way, how small could an H-bomb be?

As early as 1957, Livermore physicist John Nuckolls began making calculations. He saw that this topic offered a possible approach to laboratory-scale H-bomb detonations, which could give new insight into weapons physics. It also offered a potential route to controlled fusion, perhaps through the rapid-fire detonation of small pellets of deuterium and tritium. Just like atomic fission, the process behind the atomic bomb which could be harnessed and used to generate electricity, so, too, might the much greater power of nuclear fusion be applied to civilian use.

Nuckolls left open the issue of what energy source might detonate the pellets. He

didn't even think to use lasers, because they hadn't been invented yet. Even so, by 1960, he had designs that promised to shrink the H-bomb to a device the size of a child's marble for use in generating energy. Lasers eventually emerged as the energy source of choice, but it took time for them to become powerful enough for this demanding task. Around 1970, it seemed the technology was finally available. Construction began on the world's largest laser, named Shiva. Shiva filled a room the size of a basketball court, but it flopped, barely delivering one-fourth of its planned power. Livermore responded by building a new laser, Nova, but its pellets also failed to ignite. In 1976, Teller recommended against "uncontrolled expenditures on controlled fusion" by the government.

HITS, MISSES, AND NEW INTERESTS

With his Teller-Ulam principle, Teller now had a hit and a miss. He had scored a home run with the hydrogen bomb, but Livermore's work in laser fusion fell considerably short of success. The laboratory's overall record was similarly mixed. Its greatest success came at the triple point where physics, weapons design, and defense policy converge. Three Livermore directors—Herbert York, Harold Brown, and John Foster— served within the Pentagon in the highly demanding post of director of defense research and engineering. Brown also became president of Caltech and President Jimmy Carter's secretary of defense.

These men cherished their ties to Teller, who maintained his influence in Washington through eight administrations. During the 1980s, having retired to a position as a fellow of the Hoover Institution at Stanford University in Palo Alto, California, Teller blazed forth anew as he pursued a long-standing interest in defense against missile attack. His hopes took shape as the Strategic Defense Initiative (SDI), which was soon derisively nicknamed Star Wars.

The Pentagon had pursued missile defense since the 1950s, calling for quick-firing rockets that would use atomic bombs to knock out incoming warheads. However, such weapons would produce an "electromagnetic pulse," a powerful surge of voltage that would fry the electronics of missile-guidance systems, as well as telephones, power transmission, and other civilian technology. No one ever found a way around this. This roadblock encouraged the superpowers to negotiate the Anti-Ballistic Missile Treaty of 1972, which placed extremely severe limits on missile defenses.

This treaty did permit research on new methods of strategic defense, and, by 1980, Teller had his eye on the X-ray laser. It would use an array of carefully designed rods, each one capable of being aimed and able to fire a missile-killing burst of X rays. A small nuclear bomb would provide the laser rods with the necessary energy. Livermore was the center for work on this concept, and an initial test, called Dauphin, took place in November 1980. In this test, an instrumented nuclear bomb was detonated deep underground. It seemed to show that an X-ray laser would work.

REAGAN MOVES IN THE ARMS RACE

By then, Ronald Reagan had been elected president. Reagan had met Teller in late 1966, and they shared a concern for missile defense. Teller quickly showed his influence as Reagan chose another of his protégés, George Keyworth, as the White House science adviser.

Reagan was under strong political pressure to take an initiative in the arms race. Some of his Democratic critics favored a nuclear freeze, which the president viewed as tantamount to unilateral disarmament. In a nationwide address in March 1983, he announced his alternative, SDI. At the center of this new program was the X-ray laser.

Other types of missile defense were under consideration, including conventional lasers to be placed in orbit, particle beams, and "smart rocks": weapons resembling precisely guided cannonballs that would home in on enemy warheads. But these existed only on paper or as small-scale laboratory experi-

Edward Teller (left, with President Ronald Reagan in the early 1980s) exerted a powerful influence over eight administrations, and helped spearhead Reagan's Strategic Defense Initiative (SDI)—or "Star Wars" program.

ments, whereas the Dauphin test seemed to suggest that X-ray lasers could soon be operational weapons. Moreover, they promised far more power than rival methods of missile defense. By launching laser-bearing missiles from submarines, SDI avoided the possible need for orbiting laser platforms.

THE FINAL FIZZLE

A second underground nuclear test, codenamed Romano, took place in December 1983. It seemed to give further evidence that the X-ray laser would work. The Cottage test in March 1985 even suggested that the X rays could be focused for greater intensity. However, these promising results came under attack. Physicists at Los Alamos showed that the purported X-ray measurements actually represented radiation from impurities in a component of the instruments used for observation. In December 1985, the Goldstone test confirmed this finding. The X-ray laser proved to be only one-tenth as bright as expected, thus useless in missile defense. Further work proved focusing to be an illusion as well.

That did it. It was now clear that an X-ray laser would demand many more tests and far more time, if it could be built at all. The Star Wars program went downhill, along with Teller's influence. In 1993, with Communism having imploded and with a Democrat back in the White House, Teller was out of the picture completely. Today, he remains a fellow of the Hoover Institution. ◿

ASK THE SCIENTIST

▶ At the store, I see AA, AAA, C, and D batteries, but I never see B batteries. Why not? And what do the letters signify, anyway?

In the 1920s, battery manufacturers got together to select a standard for naming different sizes of batteries. After considering several different systems, they decided to use the letters of the alphabet. At that time, consumers could buy batteries labeled from A to G. The AA, AAA, and AAAA designations were chosen in later years when manufacturers decided to simply add additional A's rather than continue moving through the alphabet.

As time passed, some batteries fell out of general usage because the devices they powered became obsolete. The B battery, for example, used to run the large console radios popular in the 1930s and 1940s, was no longer needed when advances in circuit design enabled engineers to build smaller radios that used less energy.

After nearly a century, this letter-naming system is considered outdated. The American National Standards Institute (ANSI) is currently working with the International Electrotechnical Commission (IEC) in Geneva, Switzerland, to make American battery designations conform to existing international standards.

▶ I coach Little League baseball, and the bats my players use are made from aluminum. But I see on television that the professionals use wooden bats. How do aluminum bats differ from wooden ones? Which is better for Little-League practice?

In baseball's early days, bats were made from hickory wood. Today, wood bats are made of white ash, prized for its strength, resiliency, and relatively light weight. Aluminum bats are made from various aluminum alloys, usually about 85 percent aluminum with varying amounts of other metals such as titanium, magnesium, nickel, iron, and copper. For bats of the same length, aluminum bats are lighter than wood, making it easier for players to control the swing—though a heavier bat provides more momentum to drive the ball farther. Aluminum bats are also stronger and less likely to break.

A bat's "sweet spot"—about two-thirds of the way up from the bat's handle—is the position where the most power can be transferred to the ball during the swing. Aluminum bats have slightly larger sweet spots than do wood bats.

▶ Is lipstick the same as lip balm, except that lipstick has a dye or pigment added to it? What are the ingredients they share? Do all these products automatically protect the lips from sunburn?

Lipstick and lip balm are very similar, and very ancient, cosmetics. At their most basic, both are made from blends of waxes—often candelilla wax and beeswax—as well as oils and alcohol. Lip balm tends to be thicker and slightly greasier than lipstick, and usually contains some flavoring to make it more pleasant to use. Because it is thicker than lipstick, lip balm is better at sealing in moisture, and thus often applied to chapped lips.

Lipstick is firmer than lip balm, designed to soften at skin temperature and form a thin, smooth layer over the lips. It contains one or more pigments to alter lip color, as well as additional chemicals to keep it from smearing or rubbing off. Lipsticks also frequently contain preservatives to keep them from breaking down or supporting bacterial growth.

By themselves, basic lip balm and lipstick do little to protect skin from sunburn. However, many brands now contain sun-blocking chemicals.

◣ Do fluorescent lights use fluorine? Are they considered halogen lamps? Why do fluorescent lights make a humming sound when they're on?

A fluorescent lamp is a sealed glass tube typically filled with a mix of argon and mercury vapor. The ends of the tube are capped with electrodes that allow a current to pass through the gas. The current ionizes the gas, creating excited electrons that release their excess energy in the form of ultraviolet (UV) radiation.

The inside of a fluorescent tube is coated with a phosphorescent substance, usually zinc silicate or magnesium tungstate, which absorbs the UV radiation released from the excited electrons and reradiates it as visible light. This release of energy is called "fluorescing," hence the name "fluorescent" lamp. The hum often associated with fluorescent lights is actually the sound of millions of ionized molecules striking the inner wall of the glass tube.

Halogen lamps, on the other hand, are a very efficient type of incandescent lamp using a tungsten filament surrounded by a mix of halogen gases. The gas combines with tungsten evaporated off the hot filament, forming a charged molecule that is then attracted back to the filament instead of being deposited on the interior of the glass bulb. This process makes for a longer-lasting incandescent lamp.

◣ Is the unit "knot," as in the speed of a boat, a metric unit? Why are knots used only when describing nautical phenomena?

The knot, or 1 nautical mile per hour, is a unit of nautical speed equivalent to approximately 1.15 miles (1.85 kilometers) per hour. The term knot is understood to include an unspoken "per hour"; thus, a vessel moves at 10 knots, not 10 knots per hour. A boat sailing at 10 knots moves as fast as a car driving down the street at 11.5 miles (18.5 kilometers) per hour.

The knot does not belong to the metric system. The term probably comes from sailors using knotted ropes, called log lines, to measure the speed of a ship. Knots were tied at intervals of about 47 feet (14.3 meters) along the log line, that would then trail behind a sailing ship. The speed of the ship was roughly the number of knots that ran out in about 28 seconds.

◣ How does a lightning rod work? Can it transform a bolt of lightning into some form of usable energy? Do any devices use lightning as a primary energy source?

Lightning rods are made of conductive metal, usually copper, and mounted in high positions to take advantage of lightning's tendency to strike the tallest thing around. A wire with low electrical resistance is attached to the rod to conduct the lightning bolt's current harmlessly to the ground. Wires made of materials with low electrical resistance are used to prevent the material from heating up and causing fires or other damage.

The average lightning strike can contain 100 million volts—or more—of static electricity, with a peak current on the order of 10,000 amperes. With a duration of 0.001 second or less, it would be nearly impossible to capture and store such energy. Also, static energy is incompatible with the alternating current in general use.

Technology

FOR THE TYPICAL BUILDING PROJECT, ENGINEERS FOLLOW MORE OR LESS STANDARD PROCEDURES WHEN PLANNING FOR ITS CONSTRUCTION. WHEN THE PROJECT IS A GEODESIC DOME, LIKE THE ONE BEING BUILT AT LEFT, IN CORNWALL, ENGLAND, ALL THE RULES CHANGE. EVERYTHING FROM THE ERECTION OF SCAFFOLDING TO THE SAFETY OF WORKERS ON THE HEMISPHERIC ROOF INTRODUCES A UNIQUE SET OF ENGINEERING CHALLENGES.

CONTENTS

DOUBLE DECKER

by Bill Sweetman

Broad wing
Despite the A380's extraordinary body size, engineers were able to design a wing that would meet airport gate restrictions.

Quiet engines
An extra-large set of fan blades to send air into and around the combustion chamber. Cool air mixing with hot air at the back of the engine acts like a muffler, reducing noise.

Combustion chamber

Fan blades

Hot and cool air mix upon exit

When the Airbus A380 takes to the air late in 2004, it will be the biggest passenger airplane ever put into production. The A380 will weigh 200 tons more than today's biggest commercial jet, the Boeing 747-400. Its wing will span 262 feet (80 meters) and cover an area of 9,000 square feet (830 square meters)—two-thirds bigger than the 747's. The A380 will carry 555 to 800 passengers, at least one-fourth more than the largest 747. And a high-gross-weight version of the A380 will be able to fly more than 10,000 miles (16,000 kilometers) without refueling—the equivalent of a nonstop trip from New York City to Hong Kong.

UNIQUE AND ACCOMMODATING

Understandably, an aircraft as enormous as the A380 comes with its own unique set of jumbo design and manufacturing challenges. For starters, the A380 has to fit into airport gates made for much smaller planes. It can't produce a huge wake that will tip over lighter planes flying behind it. Its

The Airbus A380, with a wingspan of 262 feet and dual decks, will comfortably accommodate up to 800 passengers. When launched in late 2004, it will be the largest passenger aircraft in production, weighing 200 tons more than today's biggest commercial jet.

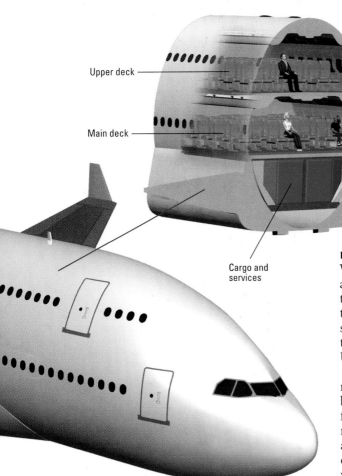

Upper deck

Main deck

Cargo and services

Wide cabin
The A380's oval body (cross-section at left) provides for two full passenger decks. A windowless below-deck area may be used for cargo or passenger services, such as a restaurant, fitness room, or sleeper cabins.

compact, since Airbus builds airplanes from large, fully equipped subassemblies flown in from all over Europe. In a few years, this plant will be building almost as many planes as Boeing.

DOUBLE-DUTY DEMANDS

When Airbus started talking to airlines about a big airplane almost eight years ago, the customers responded with nonnegotiable demands. They not only wanted more seats, but greater range as well, because most traffic growth is on routes from Asia to the United States and Europe.

At the same time, nobody wanted to rebuild airports to suit such an airplane. Airbus concluded that the A380 would have to fit into a 262-foot (80-meter) "box"—the maximum wingspan and length that today's airports could accommodate. With this limit on length, the A380 would either have a very wide cabin or two passenger decks. Dual decks proved more practical, neatly filling up an oval body measuring 20 feet (6 meters) wide.

The main deck seats 10 economy-class passengers abreast, like a 747, but allows more hip room and elbowroom. The upper deck is as wide as Airbus' current A330/A340. To load and unload the A380 in 90 minutes—another demand—the designers have provided extra-wide doors, a spacious "lobby" in front of the cabin, and a double-width staircase between the decks.

Robert Lafontan, vice president for engineering on the A380, explains that several design considerations have caused the new airplane to end up with a lot of square meters in the wing. First, airlines want an aircraft that climbs quickly after takeoff, rather than being stuck among the thunderheads and puddle jumpers until it burns off some fuel. The A380's goal is an initial cruise altitude of 35,000 feet (10,700 meters), with

doors and stairways have to be large enough to quickly load and unload hundreds of passengers. And it has to be economical enough that Airbus (a consortium of French, German, British, and Spanish aerospace companies) can convince airlines to buy at least 240 of the planes—enough for Airbus to turn a profit on its $10 billion–plus investment in the A380.

Airbus does not look like an industry giant. Its headquarters is in Toulouse, France, a historic city almost 400 miles (650 kilometers) from Paris—in French terms, somewhere beyond the orbit of Neptune. The official language is English, but at any Airbus gathering, you will hear most of the languages of Europe.

The assembly plant, in a techno-modern hangar, does not smell of hot metal or rattle to the sound of rivet guns. It is quiet and

Aboard the A380, first-class ticket holders will enjoy numerous amenities (above), including spacious accommodations, seats that recline into beds, Internet access, and individual monitors for movie selections. A double-width staircase between decks (below) leads to a roomy lounge and dining area (bottom). The stairway, along with extra-wide doors and a "lobby" in front of the cabin, allows for faster boarding. Economy-class travelers, while not experiencing this level of luxury, will still be comfortable thanks to ample hip, leg, and elbowroom.

a maximum cruise altitude of 41,000 feet (12,500 meters), or 4,000 feet (1,220 meters) better than current aircraft.

Second, Airbus wants its new aircraft to cruise at Mach 0.85, or 85 percent of the speed of sound. Most Airbus jets cruise at 0.83, a little slower than Boeing rivals—the difference may not seem huge, but it means an extra 20 to 30 minutes on a long flight, and earlier arriving flights show up first on airline reservation systems.

A third requirement is that the wing must hold enough fuel for any future A380 variant. It's possible to add extra tanks in the lower fuselage, but that would displace moneymaking freight.

And finally, wake effects are a key issue. Airports are not going to welcome a giant airplane if it trails invisible vortices that can tip smaller aircraft out of control: such a plane would force air-traffic controllers to leave long intervals between landings, which limits airport capacity. "We considered high-speed performance and drag," says Lafontan. "We considered low-speed performance, and we needed a wing that would carry enough fuel for all versions."

What About Boeing?

Boeing is not building a direct competitor to the A380. The company has spent the past four or five years pooh-poohing the need for an airliner much bigger than its own 747-400. Boeing's argument is that the long-distance air-travel market out of Asia is eventually going to "fragment." Instead of buying bigger airplanes, airlines will use smaller aircraft to provide nonstop service between more city pairs. The most important airplanes in the next 20 years, Boeing predicts, will be long-range 300-passenger twinjets—that is, aircraft like Boeing's own 777.

Boeing had planned to offer a superjumbo 747X with engines similar to the A380's and room for 505 passengers, but has decided instead to focus on a futuristic twin-engine jet called the Sonic Cruiser or the 20XX. The plane will seat 175 to 250 passengers and fly at higher altitudes than conventional jets. For now, the A380's size and range will remain unrivaled by any aircraft in Boeing's fleet.

Airbus A380-100
Length 239 ft. 6 in. Height 79 ft. 1 in.

Boeing 747-400
Length 231 ft. 10 in. Height 63 ft. 8 in.

	Airbus A380-100	Boeing 747-400
Price (in millions)	$218 to $240	$175 to $195
Seats	555	416
Range	9,378 miles	8,430 miles
Fuel capacity	85,900 gallons	57,285 gallons
Max. takeoff weight	1,235,000 pounds	875,000 pounds

LIGHTENING UP

The solution Airbus came up with is a big, lightly loaded wing: each square foot lifts 130 to 140 pounds (59 to 64 kilograms) of weight, compared with 160 pounds (73 kilograms) on a 747. The wing has a long chord, meaning it is broad at its base, and its cross section changes continuously from the root to the tip to distribute the lift most efficiently (although Airbus won't say exactly how the airfoil is shaped; that information is considered "commercially confidential").

The engine nacelles and pylons are designed and located to reduce drag and to tailor the airplane's wake so that the vortices are weak and unstable. Airbus has found that the vortex problem is not just a matter of weight, says Lafontan. "The issue is how to minimize the separation between each aircraft, which means looking at how the vortex decays. We have done theoretical and empirical work [including tests with free-flight models launched by a catapult] to find combinations of flaps, controls, and engine locations that work."

While a Boeing 747 has three flap sections on its wing, with slots between them, the A380's big wing requires only one simple flap. This particular feature saves weight and cost, helps reduce the wake-vortex problem, and also diminishes noise. With today's quiet aircraft engines, half of a jetliner's noise on landing is produced by air rapidly rushing over the airframe.

Airbus will offer a choice of two new engines for the A380: the Alliance GP7200, developed by General Electric and Pratt & Whitney; and the Rolls-Royce Trent 900. Noise is a tough issue for these engine makers. Today's noise rules were written around the 747, and do not permit the A380 to be louder than the smaller Boeing. To reduce noise, both engine options have 110-inch (280-centimeter)-diameter fans, bigger than contemporary engines of the same power.

Airbus is also saving weight by using advanced materials. For the first time on an airliner, the keystone of the airframe—the structural box that links the wing to the body—will be made from carbon-fiber composite material, saving almost 1,800 pounds (816 kilograms). The inboard wing sections will be metal, because the structure has to absorb point loads from the engine mounts, flaps, and landing gear; but the outer wings will be either carbon fiber or rivetless, bonded metal.

A new laminate material—made from thin, alternating layers of fiberglass and aluminum—will be used for the upper-fuselage skin panels. These "Glare" (*glass-re*inforced) panels are 25 percent lighter than aluminum, resist fatigue and cracking, and cost much less than composites.

Airbus will use continuous-laser welding, another technique that is new to the aerospace industry, to fasten stiffeners to the lower-body skin panels. This procedure serves to eliminate thousands of fasteners, and seals the stiffeners to the skin, preventing water intrusion.

And of course, the A380 will include some of the "fly-by-wire" systems for which Airbus is famous. Most jetliners have three or four independent hydraulic systems that move the flight controls and landing gear. The A380 will have two hydraulic systems—running at an unprecedentedly high 5,000 pounds per square inch (psi) to save weight. The hydraulics will be backed up by self-contained, electrically powered hydraulic actuators at each control surface. This is the first system to replace some hydraulics with electric power; the next generation of aircraft will likely do away with all of the big hydraulics altogether.

SAFETY BELLS AND WHISTLES

No airline wants to deal with 555 stranded passengers, so Airbus is aiming for a new standard in reliability. The A380 is designed to be "fault-tolerant," with backup systems that allow the aircraft to depart even after a failure has been detected.

Airbus is working on technology for "prognostic" maintenance. Airplanes are full of sensors that warn the crew if, for example, the pressure in part of the hydraulic system is higher than normal. On the A380, all sensor data will be recorded and downloaded to an information center, and analyzed for trends—in this case, the pressure may be steadily increasing on each flight. The trend is compared with a database covering the entire A380 fleet, which indicates that the pressure will exceed an acceptable limit in another 5 to 10 flight cycles. An automatic e-mail then advises the airline to check the system within the next three flights.

LAUNCHING THE GIANT

With all the pieces in place, Airbus officially offered the A380 to the world's airlines in June 2000. Airbus sees a market for 1,200 A380-sized passenger aircraft in the next 20 years, valued at a quarter of a trillion dollars. Airbus has already secured 66 firm orders for the A380 from nine customers. Buyers include Air France, which has planned to order 10 jets; Qatar Airways, which has decided to acquire two; and Emirates Airline (of the United Arab Emirates) with a firm order for seven.

Building the giant jet will be a unique challenge. Airbus' specially built Beluga transport airplanes fly wing and body sections from factories all over Europe to the final assembly lines, but even the Beluga cannot carry the A380's gigantic body and wing. One option for Airbus is to manufacture a slightly modified Beluga aircraft with an even larger cargo hold.

A more radical shipping solution is to use an enormous airship, the German-developed CargoLifter, which should be in service by the time the A380 enters production. The technology that first made air transport possible could play a crucial role in building the future queen of the 21st-century skies.

Something's Fishy About This Robot

by Douglas Whynott

Before beginning the day's work, RoboTuna II must go through a set of calisthenics. It's a brief session, to be sure, with just a slight turn of the tuna's head, a nearly imperceptible flex of the mid-section, and a mere suggestion of a tail sweep. But that's enough to move the joints, test the cables, and calibrate the sensors. With just this kind of little wriggle, RoboTuna II, a 4-foot (1-meter)-long "biomimetic"

Robotic fish shed light on how real fish are able to swim so efficiently. Comprised of bendable fiberglass spirals, MIT's RoboPike propels itself by flexing its body.

Atlantic bluefin tuna, is ready to make a series of 60-foot (18-meter) runs at the Department of Ocean Engineering Testing Tank Facility at the Massachusetts Institute of Technology (MIT) in Cambridge.

David Beal, a researcher in the RoboTuna Project and one of the two builders of Robo-Tuna II, hurries off to the computer room. He keys in an electronic command, and RoboTuna II backs up to the far end of the tank, like a runner getting into the blocks. The fish doesn't swim on its own—it is suspended from a control carriage that moves on roller-skate wheels and contains motors

RoboPike takes a dip with MIT graduate student John Kumph. Fish use the vortices they generate with their bodies to quickly change direction, an ability humans lack.

and various sensors, plus a video camera pointed toward the water. For this run, cobuilder Michael Sachinis walks alongside, observing the fish and the stability of the camera mount. He keeps an eye on a 6-inch (15-centimeter) cylinder at the front of the carriage that stirs up the water in front of the swimming fish and creates vortices, or eddies. Those vortices are an important focus of the research going on here.

FISH SCHOOL

"We are trying to make this fish learn how to read the vortices in order to unlock the secrets of how fish swim," Beal says. The ability to "read" will come through pressure sensors running along the fish's side; the sensors approximate, biomimetically (imitating nature), a real fish's lateral line. This marvelous sensing mechanism in real fish can detect minute pressure fluctuations that may signal the presence of vortices caused by nearby predators or obstacles. The synthetic lateral line that Sachinis has installed in RoboTuna II is so sensitive that it can detect the pressure difference of less than 0.5 inch (1 centimeter) in depth.

"We're giving the robofish a little bit of intelligence so it can adapt to its surroundings," Beal says. With a synthetic lateral line, he explains, a robotic fish might one day maneuver adeptly in a current. Better yet, an autonomous underwater vehicle equipped with such intelligence might maneuver more precisely in the ocean, more like a fish. This ability to read and react to its environment—which the biological fish has, but the biomimetic robot as yet does not—is something Beal and Sachinis call "vorticity control."

"Ready?" Beal calls out from the computer room.

"Ready!" Sachinis answers from the far end of the tank.

The control carriage begins to move, a small wake forms, and RoboTuna II swims down the towing tank at 27 inches (69 centimeters) per second. A stream of dye trails from the cylinder into the water and swirls by the fish. Sachinis paces along with the anxiousness of an animal trainer; the quality of his research will depend on the performance of this creature. The run takes about 30 seconds. Sachinis rushes off for a look at the imagery captured from this robotic event.

The picture shows the fish's head, seen from above, turbulence in the water, and a whorl of tea-colored fluid. It's a promising image, but the whorl is not yet distinct enough for transfer to a computer for analysis. On the next run, the researchers will put a bit more dye in the water and turn on ultraviolet lights. RoboTuna II backs up, pauses, and surges ahead again.

A FAMILY HISTORY

In this long and narrow basement room, with its 6-foot (1.8-meter)-wide by 100-foot (30-meter)-long tank, are some artifacts of RoboTuna II's lineage. Workbenches run along the wall, and on one of them, poised in a clamp, is Charlie, the first RoboTuna. This father of MIT's robotic fish is about to travel to London for a visit to the Science Museum. RoboTuna I looks as if it has been filleted. One side is laid open so that the ribs, joints, gears, and cables are visible. The

That's not blood in the water. Red dye makes RoboTuna's trail of clockwise and counterclockwise vortices visible. The manipulation of vortices that fish either produce or encounter is what makes them such exceptional swimmers.

other side is intact, still wearing its foam covering and the striking striped Lycra skin that doesn't look fishlike at all, but seems artistic and perfectly appropriate for this startling creation.

The RoboTuna Project began in the summer of 1989, when Michael Triantafyllou, a professor of ocean engineering at MIT, met with Mark Grosenbaugh and other researchers at the Woods Hole Oceanographic Institution on Cape Cod, Massachusetts. Why, they wondered, hadn't any useful technologies been developed from studies of how fish swim? The ocean-engineering industry had come to a point where it needed to develop research vessels that were safer and more economical. Standard designs had limitations. The shapes of a submarine and its propeller were about as efficient as they were going to get. Autonomous underwater vehicles were being powered by batteries that not only took up a great deal of space, but carried power for just a few hours.

Improvements could follow different pathways. One might be to improve battery power, such as the development of radical fuel cells that might convert kelp or shrimp into energy. Or the effort could go into making fundamentally different and efficient propulsion systems such as those used by fish. Although fish move in a medium 800 times denser than air, they are capable of swimming in powerful bursts at more than 40 miles (64 kilometers) per hour and of making 180-degree turns in a distance equal to the length of their bodies. Ships need about 10 times their length to reverse direc-

tion, and have to cut their speed in half. With that in mind, Triantafyllou and his collaborators—Grosenbaugh from Woods Hole, Dick Yue from MIT, and George Triantafyllou (Michael's brother, who is also an ocean engineer) from the City College of New York—decided to study the principles of fish propulsion for the purpose of adapting them to human-made designs. Building a fish was beyond the grasp of contemporary robotics technology, but they thought it was an endeavor worth trying for the discoveries it might make possible.

Addressing Gray's Paradox

One motivating factor in Triantafyllou's research and in the development of the RoboTuna Project was a long-standing scientific problem called Gray's paradox. The paradox had tantalized scientists since 1936, when zoologist James Gray showed that a dolphin has only one-seventh the muscle power it needs to swim as fast as it does. The mystery that Gray's paradox created was: Where did the efficiency come from? What mechanisms do fish possess that allow them to move so effortlessly and travel so far on so little power?

Any object in flowing water will cause a trail of eddies. The team wondered if fish might be using the vortices to move more efficiently. First, they constructed some "foils" similar to fish tails, and studied how they interacted with vortices. Then, in 1995, construction began on a robotic fish. For their model, the team chose the Atlantic bluefin tuna, *Thunnus thynnus*, a highly

migratory species that can easily traverse the entire Atlantic and can reach estimated speeds of 40 miles (64 kilometers) per hour. The tuna also has a somewhat rigid body, and swims by oscillating its tail in the "thunniform mode," a style that would be conducive to replication in the lab.

David Barrett, then a Ph.D. candidate studying both ocean engineering and robotics at MIT, designed and built RoboTuna I. "At a fish market in Cambridge, we bought a tuna, did autopsies, and studied how the creature worked. We tried to rebuild a tuna, following the master designer, which is Nature." Barrett describes the overall process as "reverse engineering."

Barrett constructed a robot with a stainless-steel spine of eight vertebrae, each connected with low-friction ball-bearing joints. The spine was flexed by means of pulleys and cables driven by small electric motors mounted outside the fish on a control carriage. The cables were equivalent to tendons, and the motors to muscles. Steel spines mounted with plastic ribs were attached to the vertebrae. This "flexible hull" was covered with a thin layer of foam rubber—the fish's flesh—and over that went a Lycra sock for the skin. The fish was suspended from the control carriage by a hollow streamlined mast through which ran the cables and sensor wires. There was a controller for the movement of the carriage, and another for the fish, with a single data-collection system. Construction costs were about $30,000.

The next task was more difficult: RoboTuna had to be taught how to swim. The possibilities of the wavelike movement of an eight-jointed spine were nearly infinite. As David Barrett puts it, "There are 287 trillion possibilities of different ways a fish can swim. It would take too long to work them all out, so we asked, 'How does Mother Nature do this?'" The obvious answer is through evolution, which, in the fish's case, took several hundred million years.

Barrett got his answer using a mathematical theory called genetic algorithm, which simulates evolution. He loaded each swimming possibility into a "chromosome." The fish swam down the tank dozens of times, each time programmed with a different set of chromosomes. In 20 runs, the 10 best swimming possibilities were moved on to the next cycle. "Just as in nature, the fish that swam well could survive and produce offspring. The poor performers were retired. If the fish's tail could push, in the next generation, all tails pushed." Barrett estimates, "We compressed 2,057 years of research into a single summer. It was amazing. We were watching evolution."

Once RoboTuna was swimming in peak form, Triantafyllou and his group began to analyze the play of water about the fish. What they saw was a creature capable of vorticity control.

When a boat is moving, the water it encounters rolls and spins along the hull, forming vortices that spin clockwise on one side of the hull, counterclockwise on the other, dragging along each side of the boat, and slowing it down. That drag is compensated for by the boat's propellers, which create opposing vortices strong enough to move the boat. It's an inefficient mechanism, but it's the best we have. When a fish swims, it also creates vortices that spin along its body. Unlike a ship, a fish flexes its body, and in doing so, manipulates those vortices so that they are no longer a drag. Through the lateral motion of its body, "the fish rolls the vortices down its sides," Michael Triantafyllou says, "and pushes them sideways and down with its tail. The tail kicks the vortices." In this way, the fish moves the vortices to its opposite side, and a potentially wasted energy is turned into a propulsive force—the fish can turn drag vortices into propulsive vortices.

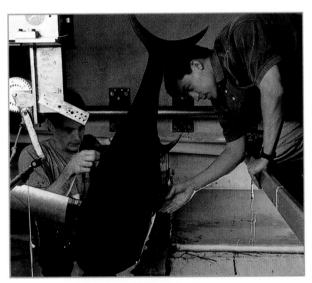

Attempting to re-create evolution through robotics, scientists have taken the first step in understanding the complex hydrodynamics that fish employ to swim.

Sudden, propulsive bursts by a fish at rest are achieved when it sweeps its tail to generate first a rotating and then a counterrotating vortex. Pushing the vortices together creates a strong jet of water, and the fish springs off it. This takes about a millisecond, Triantafyllou says. As he poetically describes it, "The fish flexes its way through the vortical stream. It took them a few hundred million years to evolve this ability."

Although RoboTuna falls far short of the real biological creature, the robotic fish did reveal some of the basic mechanisms of how fish swim. As David Barrett sums it up, "RoboTuna proved that a nonbiological,

flexible-hulled vehicle can be made to reduce massive drag and turn it into propulsion. This addressed the phenomenon in Gray's paradox."

Did the work with RoboTuna solve this frustrating riddle that has puzzled scientists for six decades? Emphatically no, Michael Triantafyllou says. "That's a very controversial subject. We are not biologists, and there are many biological uncertainties that we cannot claim to have solved. But we now have a pretty good understanding of the hydrodynamics of how fish swim. Because of RoboTuna, there's now an accepted understanding of this."

COUSIN ROBOPIKE

The RoboTuna Project spawned other biomimetic-fish programs. A direct offspring of RoboTuna at MIT is a free-swimming fish built by graduate student John Kumph called "RoboPike," 32 inches (81 centimeters) long and modeled on a chain pickerel. Unlike RoboTuna, which swims by tail oscillations, RoboPike swims by flexing its body back and forth, the "carangiform mode." The body is made of fiberglass spirals, and is flexed by means of model-airplane motors.

Studies of RoboPike brought discoveries of how a fish turns so quickly. Flexing its body into a *C* shape, the fish creates a pair of counterrotating vortices on the inner part of the curve. The vortices move toward the rear, and the fish, using its tail, pushes off them, essentially creating a springboard from which it leaps. "It does a dance," Michael Triantafyllou says.

MILLION-DOLLAR DESCENDANT

The most ambitious direct descendant of RoboTuna is a full-sized, free-swimming robotic tuna developed by Jamie Anderson at Draper Laboratory in Cambridge. In the early 1990s, Anderson was a graduate student in ocean engineering in a joint program at MIT and Woods Hole. She examined propulsion and vorticity control with real fish while participating in some RoboTuna experiments.

"We very much stood on the shoulders of RoboTuna," Anderson says. "We tried to take what Michael Triantafyllou has learned and build on it. RoboTuna is basic science. What we did was implementation, how to make a stable fish and how to make it perform. There are a number of different ways to swim, and we built this instrument to study them." The Draper tuna is called VCUUV, for Vorticity Control Unmanned Undersea Vehicle. It cost nearly $1 million to build, and utilizes the most advanced, state-of-the-art robot technology.

VCUUV is "biologically inspired," modeled on a yellowfin tuna caught by a fisherman off Long Island. Anderson and the Draper team constructed a 40-inch (102-centimeter) urethane mold and then scaled it up to 8 feet (2.4 meters) in length. It contains 65 pounds (29 kilograms) of lead-acid batteries, electric motors for moving the pectoral fins, and a hydraulic power system for operating the four links making up the tail, each of which is powered independently. There is a computer inside VCUUV that can be programmed with an "umbilical" cord, and also a compass, depth sensor, leak detector, and inertial instrumentation. The fish has a half-dollar-sized window through which an operator can look to read the indicator lights, "so we can know what the fish is thinking," explains Anderson. There is also an emergency shutoff switch, a big red button on the shore station, which is operated by utilizing sound waves.

VCUUV doesn't have sonar capabilities, cameras, or other orientation devices (a pair of snorkelers usually followed along behind during experiments). So far, it has participated in about 100 experiments. In a testing tank at the University of New Hampshire and at a reservoir in Massachusetts, VCUUV has swum in circles, squares, and various types of zigzag patterns.

The zigzag experiment was Jamie Anderson's favorite. The robot swims at a maximum speed of 2.4 knots—a good clip for an average swimmer wearing flippers. "Every 10 seconds, the fish made a 90-degree turn. The person swimming with it was left in its wake. The guys were lifting their heads and saying, 'Where did it go?'"

During the zigzag experiment, the possibilities of fishlike propulsion systems were evident and, for Anderson, thrilling. "A 90-degree turn every 10 seconds is very fast maneuvering. The fish had a 30-degree-per-second turning rate. A typical rigid-hull vehicle would achieve only about 7 degrees per second."

People who have seen VCUUV have loved it, Anderson says. "It reinforces feelings that fish are doing something right, that it's Mother Nature finding optimum solutions. We knew we would be successful if we were true to the fish."

The goal was to transfer fish maneuverability and propulsion to a vehicle, Anderson says. "The ultimate product would be a fishlike vehicle that can do the same missions as a rigid underwater vehicle—10 years from now, 20 years from now—something that might not resemble the fish as much, but that will use the hydrodynamics of a fish."

HONING IN ON VORTICITY CONTROL

Meanwhile, back at the MIT towing tank, David Beal and Michael Sachinis hone their work with "pressure visualizations." Putting their skills in mechanical engineering to use, they have improved the control of the fish's joints, and its flexibility, partly by installing 500 plastic scales, cut with a laser. RoboTuna II's computers are newer and faster. Its movement is more precise. Sachinis continues to develop the lateral line, adding more pressure sensors.

"Eventually, we should be able to predict the vorticity field with the sensors," Beal says. The goal, of course, is vorticity control, that which the fish developed over hundreds of millions of years.

Ultimately, David Barrett says, "the ocean-engineering industry wants an autonomous vehicle they can put in at the dock and say, 'Fly out to the North Atlantic, do these missions, and come back safely.'" If that vehicle effectively employs the mechanics of fish propulsion, converting forces that hinder into forces that propel, it would be, Barrett says, "like traveling across the United States on a tank of gas." At Michael Triantafyllou's lab, they're refining that process by fitting the fish with sensors. If they succeed, it might create an entire industry of robotic fish.

MICROSPIES

by Peter Garrison

In his cluttered office in the Los Angeles suburb of Simi Valley, Matt Keennon tosses a delicate creature into the air. Tremulous but purposeful, it flaps its way across the room, where waiting hands catch it. Cradled in them, it flutters a moment longer, then subsides when its captor's fingers—huge, clumsy things beside the ethereal flier—click off its master switch.

The little creature is called the Microbat, and was built at the California Institute of Technology's (Caltech's) Micromachining Laboratory by a team of graduate students overseen by Yu-Chong Tai. The effort also

A mock-up of the Black Widow—AeroVironment's most successful micro air vehicle, and the future look of aerial surveillance and reconnaissance—displays its ultra-compact guidance system (above).

involved AeroVironment, which is headed by Paul MacCready, a multidisciplinary engineer famous for, among other things, the Gossamer series of human-powered aircraft. Keennon is AeroVironment's project manager for micro air vehicles (MAVs), a new class of aircraft funded by the Defense Advanced Research Projects Agency (DARPA), the U.S. Department of Defense's research arm. The toys in this game are small, but the players are big.

SPYING MEMS
The Microbat's thorax and wing-flapping mechanism consist of tiny sticks of carbon fiber. Its wings are gossamer plastic webs supported by a network of stiffeners that were not built up of separate components

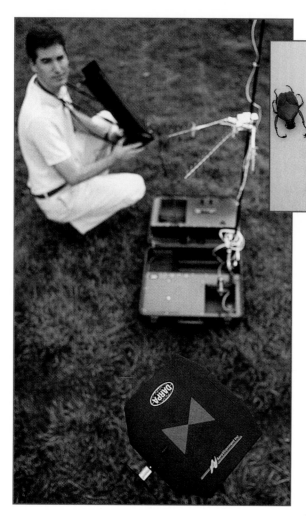

Matt Keennon remote-pilots the Black Widow, using equipment that includes the compact control unit (left). This strange, mechanical insect is baffling to a curious (and real) beetle, as the belly-up MAV reveals what makes it tick (above).

SIX-INCH AIRCRAFT

DARPA became interested in toy-sized airplanes in 1992. The idea that an airplane that would fit in the palm of your hand might be a useful reconnaissance device began to take hold. In 1995, the agency put out a specification for a small camera-carrying aircraft. Six inches (15 centimeters)—an arbitrary value, but one that has turned out to make practical sense—was the basic constraint: The entire aircraft had to fit within a 6-inch sphere.

DARPA also specified a typical mission. The midget spy plane would fly just over 0.5 mile (0.8 kilometer) to a target; loiter there for half an hour in winds of up to 25 miles (40 kilometers) per hour, perhaps negotiating obstacles such as buildings while repeatedly climbing to 350 feet (107 meters) and descending again; then return to its base. Quiet and inconspicuous, its launching and control system had to be mobile and easy to operate, and the whole system had to be both robust and cheap.

In 1997, DARPA issued grants totaling several million dollars to numerous organizations to develop MAVs; AeroVironment, which had already begun attacking the problem on its own, was one of them. The company's Simi Valley facility has produced a number of flying models, including the Black Widow. Most of the models consist of a roughly circular planform, 6 inches in diameter, and are powered by a single trac-

but etched from single sheets of titanium alloy by the same photolithography techniques that are used for the mass production of computer microcircuits. The Microbat carries no payload, and it serves no purpose other than to demonstrate the feasibility of a small electric ornithopter that can operate only at low speeds and indoors, where a drop of rain or a puff of wind will not immediately destroy it. More important, it demonstrates the possibility of building parts of flight-vehicle structures by chemical micromachining. Both demonstrations are telling events.

Slow-moving, mothlike airplanes (as well as crawling robotic cockroaches and other sci-fi stuff) are where reconnaissance seems to be headed now. So-called MEMS (microelectromechanical systems) manufacturing techniques, derived from the tools of computer-chip manufacture, will get it there.

tor propeller spinning at 20,000 revolutions per minute.

BLACK WIDOW

The most successful of AeroVironment's models, nicknamed Black Widow, has remained aloft for more than 20 minutes while flying at 35 miles (56 kilometers) per hour. The ground operator launches it with compressed air from a telescoping rail, then controls it in flight by radio, like a model airplane—which, after all, it is. Unlike the typical radio-controlled flier, however, the Black Widow's operator watches not the airplane itself, which is a mere speck darting in the sky, but the video picture sent back by its tiny television camera. The whole apparatus—airplane plus launch and control mechanisms—fits in a briefcase.

Luckily, Keennon says, various pieces of commercial off-the-shelf hardware are available in just the right size to fit on a 6-inch flying disk. Flight controls, for example, are operated by tiny Swiss-made electric motors 0.125 inch (3.175 millimeters) in diameter and 0.01 ounce (0.3 gram) in weight. The airplane's "eye," also an inexpensive item, is a 510- by 492-pixel color array like the ones used in home video cameras, but stripped down to the size of a bean and the weight of 0.05 ounce (1 gram).

WHAT IS NEXT?

AeroVironment's current MAVs are skittish creatures, with high roll rates and low natural stability. They require skilled radio-control operators. The next step in the program, which the company will fund itself, is to add electronic gyroscopes and autopilots that will keep the airplanes stable and upright. The operator would then need no special skill to fly one, and would be free to concentrate on the mission rather than on controlling the aircraft.

After adding stability, the next improvement will be Global Position-

ing System (GPS) navigation, which would permit the MAV to fly a programmed mission without assistance from a human operator. The icing on the cake would be some kind of system using acoustic or optical sensing that would let the MAV maneuver in an urban environment, avoiding obstacles on its own, just like a bird. That level of autonomy, however, is still far off.

The requirement that it send back usable video images puts an important lower limit on the size of an MAV, because each pixel in the imaging array must be considerably larger than the longest wavelength of visible light. This means that a video camera capable of sending back valuable detail can't be much smaller than the one Keennon's team is currently using. Another nonscalable item is the radio antenna. An antenna that fits within a 6-inch space will work efficiently only with short-wavelength, high-frequency radio waves. Unfortunately, high-frequency radio signals travel by line of sight—both antennas have to be able to "see" each other—and do not readily penetrate walls or travel around hills. A longer retractable trailing wire, however fine, would impose a severe drag penalty. Antenna size will also pose a problem for GPS reception, especially if future MAVs become significantly smaller than the current ones.

THE BEST DESIGN

The peculiar configuration of AeroVironment's MAVs is the logical outcome of the 6-

Robert Michelson of Georgia Tech's Aerospace Laboratory demonstrates an MAV with a unique power plant: the reciprocating chemical muscle (RCM); the wings flap as fuel is consumed.

inch size restraint. If you merely scaled a conventionally proportioned airplane down to a 6-inch wingspan, its wings would have an area of only about 0.04 square foot (0.004 square meter). Flying at 30 miles (48 kilometers) per hour—a higher speed would require too much power—such a wing could support only about 0.75 ounce (21 grams) at most, with no margin for maneuvering or gust response. But the weight of the entire aircraft, including power plant and all the electronic and sensing equipment it is supposed to carry, would in reality be around 2 or 3 ounces (57 or 85 grams).

It turns out that the best solution is simply to make the wing area as large as possible—essentially, to fill the entire 6-inch DARPA circle with wing. This approach has other advantages as well: it provides a simple, stiff, voluminous structure with ample interior space for systems and payload. True, the circular planform lacks the characteristic usually associated with efficient airplanes: a fairly high aspect ratio. The most efficient airplanes have wings with a span from tip to tip that is much greater than their chord— the distance from leading to trailing edges—

and you don't see a lot of airliners with circular wings.

But for an airplane of this size or smaller, a low aspect ratio may not be a hindrance. The very wingtip vortices that produce drag on conventional airplanes help produce lift on small, short-span wings operating at low Reynolds numbers. (The Reynolds number is a mathematical shorthand that describes the relationship between the size of an object and the effect, or feel, of a fluid medium—gas or liquid—upon it.) In fact, recent research on insect flight suggests that the judicious use of tip and leading-edge vortices keeps those notoriously small-winged bumblebees—the ones that, according to legend, myopic scientists have pronounced flightless—aloft. This is only one of the differences, fundamental to the creation of miniaturized aircraft, between full-scale and microscale aerodynamics. The behavior of air on microscale wings is only beginning to be understood.

POWER-PACK PROBLEM

Although most of the systems of an MAV are electronic, and AeroVironment has concentrated on electrically powered airplanes, not everyone agrees that an electric motor is the best choice for a power plant. Batteries have a low "power density"—that is, they pack little punch for their weight. (This is a problem for electric cars as well.) For some tasks, such as peering into upper-story windows or loitering inconspicuously, an aircraft that can hover is essential; at present, battery-powered electric motors don't have the power to hover for long.

Those traveling the all-electric route look to future improvements in batteries, motors, propellers, and miniaturization for increases in power-to-weight ratio and efficiency— the fraction of the available power that goes into useful work—of tiny power plants. But gram for gram, chemical fuels such as gasoline are much more energetic than batteries, and even though extremely tiny internal-combustion engines, unlike tiny electric

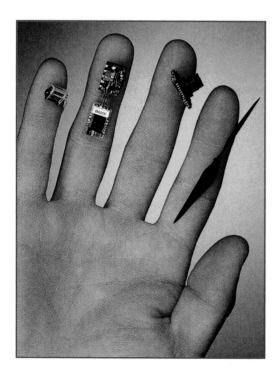

Like the inner gears of a wristwatch, tiny components small enough to fit on a fingertip are part of what makes micro air vehicles operate successfully.

motors, are not readily available, several programs are taking the internal-combustion route instead.

MLB Company of Palo Alto, California, has flown several designs powered by small Cox model-airplane engines. One of them takes off vertically. Stephen Moore of MLB says that at this scale, the power requirement for vertical takeoff and hovering is not terribly different from that for agile maneuvering. Given the tremendous energy content of chemical fuel, a multimode tail-sitter craft that can both fly and hover becomes an attractive possibility.

A BUTTON-SIZED JET ENGINE

A startling solution to the power problem is in the offing at the Massachusetts Institute of Technology (MIT) in Cambridge: a jet engine the size of a shirt button. Components of such engines have actually run in test beds. The baseline design involves a single centrifugal-flow compressor spinning at 2.5 million revolutions per minute on gas bearings. Combustion takes place in a doughnut-shaped chamber surrounding the engine, and the exhaust gas flows back inward toward the center through a turbine. A starter-generator is built into the case; if needed, the engine could serve as a tiny electrical generator, putting out 10 to 20 watts, or perhaps as much as 100 watts, or it can be used as a jet engine with a thrust of up to a third of a pound.

The key to making such a device cheaply and in large numbers is the photolithographic manufacturing technique Caltech used to make the wings of the Microbat. Engine parts would be etched in sheets of silicon, like microchips. (By the early 1990s, electric motors smaller than the point of a pin, invisible to the naked eye, had already been made by this technique.) Just one microengine would be sufficient to supply both the thrust and the electrical requirements of a present-day MAV.

FLYING, CRAWLING ENTOMOPTER

At the Georgia Institute of Technology Aerospace Laboratory, Robert Michelson leads a project to develop and refine an entomopter, a machine that will not only fly like a bug,

Stanford's "mesicopter" is a tiny flying microchip (above). Swarms of them could explore storm systems on Earth—or even the atmosphere of Mars.

but, if need be, crawl like one, too. The entomopter has a "chemical nose" and other features to permit it to home in on certain kinds of targets. Its builders expect to provide the entomopter with navigation and obstacle-avoidance skills as well. But the present centerpiece of the project is its power plant, a device called a reciprocating chemical muscle (RCM).

The RCM is something like the piston and cylinder of a steam engine, except that the gas that drives it comes not from combustion but from a chemical reaction. The energy available from the chemical fuel is much greater than that available from current batteries. And the chemical reaction also has the advantage of versatility: its waste heat can be converted into electricity to operate onboard sensors and transmitters, and spent gas can be vented over the wings to provide differential lift and, therefore, flight control.

By calling their prime mover a "muscle," the Georgia researchers underscore their reliance on the guidance of Mother Nature. "Nothing in nature achieves sustained flight with fixed wings or with propellers," observes Michelson. "All tiny creatures flap their wings continuously. Flies don't glide."

MICROMECHANICAL FLYING INSECT

A similar project, called the Micromechanical Flying Insect, is under way at the University of California at Berkeley, where a team headed by biologist Michael Dickinson has shed light on how insects use their wings. To simulate the Reynolds number of insect flight, Dickinson and coworkers built a pair of 10-inch (25-centimeter) wings driven by six separate actuators, and have observed them flapping in a tank of mineral oil. In addition to a new understanding of low-Reynolds-number aerodynamics, such work has spawned a new vocabulary for talking about flight phenomena, with terms such as "delayed stall," "rotational circulation," and "wake capture."

Wing flapping works in several ways to provide insects with a flying ability that would be the envy of any fighter pilot. To start with, the flapping of wings plays the same role as the spin of a helicopter's rotor: it creates a relative wind over the lifting surface even while the vehicle—or bug—is standing still. But flapping also sets up tiny vortices that take the place of the cambered flying surfaces, high-lift devices, and movable flight controls of fixed airplane wings. The eddies set up by their wings not only keep bugs aloft but also allow them to hover, fly backward or sideways, and turn on a dime (or the corresponding currency of the bug world).

PINPOINTING PRACTICALITY

Putting the new understanding to practical use is the next step, and not an easy one. The Berkeley team, with some sponsorship from DARPA, proposes to duplicate, in a mechanism about the size of a quarter, at least some of the abilities of a large, repulsive, carrion-eating fly called *Calliphora*. "You can't build [robot insects] now based on known principles," Dickinson has said. "You have to fundamentally rethink the problem."

Most of the proposed uses for MAVs are military; the funding, after all, is coming from the U.S. Department of Defense. But some workers in the field propose broader applications for tiny flying robots. Georgia Tech's Michelson has suggested sending robot "terminators" after real-life insect pests, but suspects that the largest potential outlet for small aerial robots might be the toy market. Stanford's Ilan Kroo leads a team developing a "mesicopter," a multirotor electric helicopter. Currently of centimeter size but potentially much smaller, the mesicopter is shaped like a thin, square wafer with a little rotor at each corner.

Essentially a flying microchip, a mesicopter's motors, sensors, guidance, and telemetry systems would be etched in place in a single completely automatic manufacturing operation. Kroo's team envisions swarms of mesicopters investigating the interiors of storms or the atmosphere of Mars.

IMITATING NATURE

The word "swarm" is particularly significant. Of course, it suggests insects, and much of the more startling MAV research is headed in the direction of emulating those successful products of natural selection. But it also alludes to nature's profligacy. Many creatures that live in hazardous environments reproduce in huge numbers so that just a few may survive to maturity. MEMS manufacturing techniques imply a similar approach to machines. Rather than launch a single costly, sophisticated, man-carrying device to do a job, you would launch hundreds of simple, cheap robots. If most of them fail, no matter—they are expendable. Only one needs to complete the task.

A case in point, reminiscent of the wholesale egg-laying habits of marine creatures, is what Kris Pister of the Berkeley program calls "smart dust." Consisting of various kinds of motion or chemical sensors, a power supply, a microprocessor, and a system of communication, all packed into the volume of a grain of coarse sand, these "motes" would be sprinkled from an MAV over a wide area and report back to the MAV what they find.

IS IT A FLY OR AN MEM?

The use of MEMs in the construction of miniature aircraft is likely to bring about, in the next decade, innovations that seem incredible today. The button turbojet could revolutionize propulsion, even if only for model-aircraft builders. Soldiers fighting in blasted cities in Central Asia will be grateful for the ability to look around corners with tiny airborne cameras. Children will shriek with delight as their robot wasps attack a neighbor's action figure.

But will we have to wonder, even in civilian life, whether every persistent fly we encounter is carrying a listening device?

The Amazing World of
ENGINEERING

by Daniel Pendick

Imagine the sense of accomplishment that Washington Augustus Roebling must have felt in 1883 upon first walking the length of the world's longest suspension bridge. As he strode the 1,595-foot (486-meter) span of the Brooklyn Bridge—some 14,680 tons of steel and iron suspend-

Every material used, every specification defined, and, indeed, every stage involved in the rise of a skyscraper involves engineers and their expertise.

ed between two massive masonry towers—he must have been so proud, and thinking, *I made this.* His father and mentor, John Augustus Roebling, did not share in this triumph. He had died in 1869 of a tetanus infection soon after work commenced on the project.

The Brooklyn Bridge was a milestone not only for its physical dimensions, but also for the ingenuity of its construction. Suspended on four 16-inch (41-centimeter)-thick steel

Washington Augustus Roebling supervised construction of the Brooklyn Bridge, which was completed in 1883. Roebling devised the necessary technology and building procedures as he went along—an impressive feat in any era.

cables strung in place by a traveling mechanical spinner, the foundations for the bridge's towers were laid from within huge pneumatic caissons—submersible compartments into which compressed air was pumped to hold back the East River. At the start of construction, the technology to build such a bridge simply did not exist. No matter, Washington Augustus Roebling decided; he would invent it himself.

WHAT IS ENGINEERING?

There are many ways to define engineers and their science, but the ingenuity shown by the Roeblings is a good place to start. The American Society for Engineering Education (ASEE) offers their definition of engineering as "the art of applying scientific and mathematical principles, experience, judgment, and common sense to make things that benefit people." However, this definition is appropriate only for *modern* engineers, who rely on proven scientific principles to get the job done. The verb "to engineer" did not even appear in written English until 1843, yet quite a bit of engineering had occurred by then.

For a broader understanding of engineers and their science, one could start with the origins of the word itself. The first recorded use of the word in the English language dates to the 14th century, in a ballad written about England's much-romanticized King Richard the Lion-Hearted:

> *A tour full strong,*
> *That queyntyly*
> *engynours made.*

Richard I, who ruled from 1189 to 1199, distinguished himself in battle, particularly during the Third Crusade. As suggested by the ballad, Richard must have frequently availed himself of the expertise provided by "engynours," the men who built military apparatuses for attack or defense, such as catapults and portable bridges. And indeed, the Latin root of "engynour"—a spelling derived from Old French—connotes inborn knowledge, skill, or genius.

So, in general, engineers are people who tap their ingenuity, skills, and experience to build useful things. Those useful things can be anything from monumental temples of worship to simple devices for lifting water from wells. It was not until the rise of modern, theory-based science in the West that engineers became known as a class of educated professionals who draw on experimentally tested principles and fundamental understanding of matter and energy to conduct their work.

ENGINEERING IN THE PAST

"The first engineer," wrote Ronald W. Clark in *Works of Man,* "was the man who looked at two upright stones before his cave, believed they would support the weight of a horizontal lintel, and contrived to raise into position a third stone which made the structure safe and sound." We do not know if a cave engineer actually invented the first door frame, but we do have plenty of evidence of the earliest acts of engineering in the ancient world. These feats of ingenuity occurred in Mesopotamia, the celebrated "cradle of civilization" along the Tigris and Euphrates Rivers in the Middle East. These ancient societies built cities and grew crops to feed their people. To do that, they needed water.

The Irrigators. The Egyptians were early innovators and built extensive irrigation systems. By 3000 B.C., they had raised at least two masonry dams south of Cairo, an engi-

The origins of engineering can be seen in the vestiges of ancient cultures. Egypt's pyramids exemplify extraordinary engineering, ingenuity, and determination (below). The Romans built ornate three-tiered aqueducts, such as the one at right, which brought in drinking water from faraway sources.

neering feat that required considerable working knowledge of the force exerted by water and how to build a structure strong enough to contain it.

In the 7th century B.C., Assyrian King Sennacherib constructed a canal approximately 50 miles (80 kilometers) long to carry water from Bavia to Nineveh. Lined with more than 2 million blocks of stone, the canal at one point was elevated on an aqueduct so that it could cross a river. A key feature of the canal was the grade of its bed, which was constructed to drop 1 foot (30 centimeters) vertically per 80 feet (24 meters) of its length. This type of design suggests a sophisticated understanding of gravity-fed water-distribution systems.

Dams, including the one under construction in Montana (above), would never have been possible without civil engineers, who specialize in the creation of buildings, roads, dams, bridges, and canals.

The masters of water distribution in the ancient world were the Romans. Beginning in 312 B.C., they built magnificent aqueducts to supply the seat of their empire with water. At one point, 14 different aqueducts channeled to Rome an estimated 300 million gallons (1 billion liters) of water per day. The water supplied a network of fountains, reservoirs, public baths, and sewers. Calibrated bronze nozzles regulated the flow of water into homes. Masters of the keystone-arch bridge, Roman engineers spanned rivers with such monuments to their skill as the Pont du Gard, whose three tiers of stone arches carry water 160 feet (49 meters) above the River Gard in France.

The Monument Builders. No account of engineering in the ancient world would be complete without mention of the spectacular Egyptian pyramids. The dominion of the pharaohs spanned some 31 dynasties, but most of the pyramids were raised during the Old Kingdom, 2815 B.C. to 2294 B.C.

The most celebrated of their works is the Great Pyramid at Giza, constructed about 4,600 years ago as a funeral monument for King Khufu. Built to a height of 481 feet (147 meters), its 751-foot (229-meter) base diverges only 42 inches (107 centimeters) from true north, an error of only 0.06 percent. The pyramid is constructed of some 2.3 million limestone blocks, with granite slabs lining the three internal burial chambers. The Egyptians—with the support of slave labor, of course—showed impressive ingenuity and determination in the various methods they developed to transport and lay the stone blocks in their pyramids.

Although the pyramids loom large in the history of engineering, they were by no means the only notable feats of construction in the ancient world. In the kingdom of Aksum, which flourished in northern Ethiopia from the 1st to the 6th century, engineers displayed their skills in building grand residences and at least 140 stone obelisks. The largest known obelisk, in Aksum, was cut in one piece from a hillside and transported several miles to the city. It may have been the largest single block of stone quarried in the ancient world. However, the massive stone spire appears to have collapsed under its own weight as it was raised, leaving behind five large fragments.

Scientific Engineering. The modern engineer arose in the West from seeds planted during the Scientific Revolution in 17th-century Europe. Engineering's transition

Careers in Engineering

According to the American Society for Engineering Education (ASEE), the kid who built the neighborhood tree house, loved games and puzzles, and was the only member of the family who knew how to put together those items that promised "no assembly required" probably possesses some of the key qualities of a successful engineer.

Not all engineers design new technologies and products. Some work in sales, helping consumers figure out the most useful products and services for them. Other engineers are technologists and technicians who transform the design on the drawing board into the finished product. A construction engineer might design a new type of bridge, while engineering technologists go to the site to see that the design is implemented properly.

As of 1999, there were 1.2 million engineers employed in the United States. According to a 1996–97 survey by the ASEE and the National Science Foundation (NSF), 96 percent of 4,500 engineers polled were employed. Engineering graduates command good entry-level wages, the actual amounts dependent on the area of engineering chosen and the candidate's degree of academic achievement. Engineers report high job satisfaction, in large part because of the numerous intellectual challenges and opportunities that keep their work fresh and consistently interesting.

Most engineering careers require at least a bachelor's degree from an accredited engineering program. From there, a student may decide to continue on to graduate school to complete a master's or doctoral degree (Ph.D.).

Careers in college-level engineering education and research require a Ph.D.

It is possible to obtain training in engineering by various routes. Universities and four-year colleges offer engineering programs. Another option is enrollment at specialized institutes of technology and "polytechnic institutes," such as the Massachusetts Institute of Technology (MIT) in Cambridge.

The military also trains engineers. And prospective technicians and technologists receive their schooling at two-year colleges and community colleges.

Many universities offer engineering programs, although perhaps none so prestigious as those offered by the renowned Massachusetts Institute of Technology (MIT), in Cambridge.

Acceptance to a top-notch engineering program requires solid math and science skills. Writing and communication are also valuable, since engineers often work in teams or supervise others.

One of the best ways to find out about engineering careers is by requesting information in writing or via the Internet from national engineering societies. The ASEE is one such source. Another way is to attend "open houses" at local engineering schools, where a prospective engineer can meet with instructors and current students.

from art to science accelerated in the 19th century, when the first engineering schools were founded. The field soon branched into its basic specialties, and engineers banded together to form technical societies in an effort to foster a professional identity.

Craft, experience, and intuition have their role in engineering today, of course. But ultimately, new technologies are held to standards of evidence rather than the test of time. "The early builders were hardly engineers in the dictionary definition of those who practiced 'the application of scientific principles for the control and use of power,'" as author Ronald W. Clark notes. "But they paved the way for the [modern] engineer."

ENGINEERING TODAY

Traditionally, the disciplines of engineering have been divided into five large categories: civil, mechanical, electrical, chemical, and industrial. Electrical (and electronic) engineers create electrical appliances, automation equipment, computers, power-generating machinery, and the many other devices and systems that use electrical power. Civil and construction engineers design and erect buildings, roads, bridges, canals, and other essential facilities. Mechanical engineers design power plants, heating and air-conditioning equipment, automobiles, and other machinery. Chemical engineers develop the processes and equipment that produce plastics, medicines, foods, and synthetic materials. And industrial engineers design systems that utilize the workers, energy, raw materials, and equipment involved in the manufacture of a product, as well as maximize quality and safety, while minimizing the impact on the environment.

As the needs of society have grown, many new fields of engineering have branched off of the original five main disciplines. Once engineers receive their basic education, they often seek further schooling to specialize in any of the various subfields.

Aerospace engineers, for example, design the technology for commercial, military,

Construction on an extension of the Massachusetts Turnpike near Boston is a gargantuan undertaking. As the field of engineering has evolved, it has taken the ancient Roman invention of the road to new heights.

Manufacturing engineers create the robotic machinery that now dominates automobile assembly lines (above). Car interiors are designed electronically, thanks to the software developed by the computer engineer (right). Biomedical engineers help people with disabilities by devising high-tech prosthetic limbs (below).

and space flight. This includes jumbo jets, fighter planes, rockets, and the equipment required to build and operate them.

Agricultural engineers devise farm machinery, food-storage and processing equipment, facilities for livestock, and all the other technology needed to grow food and transform it into a consumable form.

Architectural engineers work with architects to determine the safest, least-expensive, and most practical design for a building. This includes such considerations as the "load," or weight, a floor can carry and the type of foundations required.

Biomedical engineers design specialized medical devices such as surgical prostheses, three-dimensional imaging systems such as MRI and CAT scanners, and other technology for the health-care industry.

Ceramic engineers transform materials such as clay, minerals, and silicates (sand) into ceramic components for automobiles, engines, and other products. Ceramic engineers designed the U.S. space shuttle's heat-resistant skin, for example.

Computer engineers design, build, and operate computer systems. This includes tasks such as assembling networks of computers, designing digital automation equip-

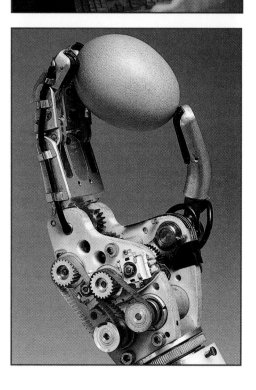

ment, and writing computer software to test designs prior to construction.

Environmental engineers develop systems to reduce the impact of modern technology on air, water, and soil. This includes pollution-control devices in smokestacks and sewage-treatment processes.

Fire-protection engineers design the technology to minimize fire hazards and extinguish fires once they get started.

Genetic engineers use the genes of living organisms as a palette to create altered or even entirely new forms of life. Recently they have created crops with inborn pest resistance, and are at work devising "gene therapies" to correct inherited illnesses such as cystic fibrosis. Despite the use of the word "engineer" to describe this field, genetic engineers are really biologists, and therefore do not study in engineering schools.

Manufacturing engineers design the tools and machinery required to manufacture products, including automation systems to control the process.

Metallurgists and *materials engineers* produce the metals and materials required to build machines and other pieces of technology. For instance, materials engineers created the exotic materials in radar-evading "stealth" bombers.

Mining engineers locate ores, gemstones, and other valuable mineral resources and extract them from the ground. They also devise ways to mine safely and cheaply, transport mined materials, and restore lands damaged by mining.

Naval engineers design, build, operate, and maintain ships as diverse as aircraft carriers and submarines, Coast Guard cutters, and civilian passenger and cargo vessels.

Nuclear engineers design and operate nuclear-power plants and the equipment used to produce radioactive isotopes for brain imaging and other medical uses. Nuclear engineers also develop nuclear-power packs for deep-space probes, such as the Voyager craft that explored the outer planets of our solar system.

Ocean engineers explore and exploit resources of the oceans. For example, they engineer underwater drilling platforms and pipelines, and help design harbor facilities.

Transportation engineers plan the construction of roads, mass-transit systems, and public facilities so that traffic, people, and products move quickly and efficiently.

ENGINEERING IN THE FUTURE

As design techniques and materials continue to improve, engineers will be involved in some of the most ambitious and challenging feats of ingenuity since the pyramids.

One such project is the *International Space Station* (*ISS*), touted as the most complex piece of engineering in history. The *ISS* is a cooperative project among nations that include the United States, Russia, Canada, Japan, Brazil, and the European Union. The completed station, an ungainly amalgam of individual modules and components, will measure 361 feet (110 meters) along its long axis—the length of a football field, including both end zones. The pressurized living and working volume of the station is equivalent to the cabin space of two 747 jetliners.

In civil engineering, few undertakings have matched Boston's Central Artery/Tunnel Project, unofficially known to Bostonians as the "Big Dig." Construction began in 1991 on the $11 billion project. It includes a massive underground expressway and a 10-lane suspension bridge over the Charles River of a design never used before in the United States. The elevated highway that now cuts through the heart of Boston is scheduled for demolition in 2004, and will be replaced by 27 acres (11 hectares) of open ground earmarked chiefly for public parks.

Engineers will also be involved in exotic new technologies of nearly invisible dimensions. Already, research engineers have developed working electric motors that could balance on the head of a pin. In the more distant future, some experts predict the coming of "nanotechnology"—the manufacture of materials and structures with dimensions less then 100 nanometers (100 billionths of a meter). The technology is still in the visionary stage, but proponents of nanotechnology promise exotic advances, such as cell-sized "nanobots" that will navigate through the bloodstream repairing the effects of aging and disease. Engineers will be at the forefront of these fields. ◢

THE WEB
WITHOUT WIRES

by Glenn Fleishman

I't's coming to an espresso bar near you. And to the rival coffee shop across the street—not to mention the bustling coin-operated laundry on the corner, the grand hotel on the next block, and the old railroad station across town. The local airport may already have it.

A TECHNOPHILE'S DREAM COME TRUE
Wireless high-speed Internet access, a long-time dream of the technophile, business traveler, and impatient home user, is arriving at hundreds of access points in unlikely public and private places across the United States. With a laptop computer equipped with a wireless card, anyone within a few hundred feet or so of an access point, or hot spot, can tap into a wireless network that is, in turn, connected to the Internet via a

Thanks to the growing availability of wireless high-speed Internet access, it simply takes a laptop and a click for most commuters to keep in touch (above).

broadband connection. The user can then send e-mail or surf the Web at speeds in the megabit range, usually for a monthly or single-use fee.

By late 2001, industry experts say, the number of hot spots will be counted in the thousands as service providers and entrepreneurs install the necessary equipment—generally a small transceiver and a broadband connection—in all major airport terminals, sports arenas, and other business and consumer sites. By sometime next year, one company expects to have access points in 5,000 Starbucks stores.

"Roaming mobile access is becoming a hot item," says Tim Bajarin, president of Creative Strategies, an industry consulting firm. Bajarin adds that the services are particularly attractive to corporations who want their traveling staff to stay in touch with the home office more frequently.

Some companies and colleges already have wireless local area networks (LANs) using the same modern technology, so Internet and intranet access is available from anywhere within an office or around a campus. But the services for mobile professionals tend to be single access points covering one or more stores, for instance, or several conference rooms in a hotel.

HOT SPOTS AND "INFO FUELING"

Some of these services may be free, run by volunteers intrigued by the community-building prospects of wireless networking. Volunteer efforts are under way in several cities, including Seattle, Boston, and San Francisco. Most access points are and will be commercial, however, run by companies that will charge for the services—the price ranging anywhere from a few dollars for a single session to $50 or more per month for unlimited use of the system.

This new wireless access is about "giving you the ability to roam from one network to another and be 'blissfully ignorant' of the technical intricacies," says Stephen Saltzman, general manager of Intel's wireless-local-area-network division. "It's the kind of thing that's such a fundamental capability that it starts feeding on itself." It is a vision of a seamless world of wireless access, where the business traveler or café habitué can keep in touch via the Internet just by walking into the right place, turning on the laptop, and opening a browser.

Other novel services are envisioned as well. The wireless technology has been shown to work well even if the laptop is moving, so drive-by access from a car may be possible—or gas stations could have hot spots and offer "info fueling."

THE VISION BLURS

"At the same moment you're filling up your gas tank, why wouldn't you fill up your in box?" says Mark Goode, chief executive of MobileStar, a leader in the field. Well, there are a few potential stumbling blocks to such a vision. One is the prospect of competing standards. Right now, a wireless-network protocol with the decidedly unsexy name IEEE 802.11b appears to be the leader, in part because a slower version has been widely used in corporations since the early 1990s,

and Apple Computer used it when the company began giving its models wireless capability in mid-1999. And there are other standards, notably Bluetooth and HomeRF, that could catch on as well. The field could become balkanized, creating compatibility and interference problems for users.

Jeff Groudan, the director for Compaq Computer's business-portables group, says that a single user might need two or three wireless standards to stay connected while traveling from place to place. Regardless, even if only one standard prevails, competition among providers may create headaches for consumers. There are only a few truly national providers, with several regional ones that hope to expand, so some consolidation or other shaking out of the industry seems inevitable. And the user who pays a monthly fee for access through one provider may find that the provider's service is available at some airport lounges but not at others, where another company's network is staked. Ultimately, roaming agreements like those between cell-phone providers will ease this problem.

"We've got to create an industry and stop spending money trying to kill each other," says Richard Garnick, chief executive of Global Digital Media, a service provider focusing on airport terminals, "because we've got to save some money to gather customers." One effort to provide wireless access throughout airport terminals (rather than just in a lounge or two) has already foundered. SoftNet Systems, the parent company of Aerzone, which had contracts to establish access points in San Francisco's and Denver's busy airports, halted Aerzone's operations in December 2000, citing cost concerns. One estimate put the cost of installing wireless access throughout a large airport at up to $2 million.

THE BIG GUYS MOVE IN

For now, the leading companies using 802.11b—including MobileStar, based in Richardson, Texas, and Wayport, of Austin, Texas—are concentrating on single-access-point service. Both companies have access points in hotel meeting rooms and common areas and in premium-membership-based

Now, anyone—nearly anywhere—can tap into the Internet. An idle hour in a hotel, coffee shop, or even a laundromat (right) can be doubly productive with a laptop.

airport lounges. MobileStar, for example, boasts approximately 150 locations, including lounges at all three New York City–area airports. But the company has big plans, including an agreement with Starbucks to create access points in thousands of Starbucks shops within two years.

Wayport has made inroads into hotel chains, signing agreements with Wyndham and Four Seasons hotels, as well as with the MeriStar Hotels & Resorts group, which includes some Hilton and Hyatt hotels. In hotels, Wayport runs Ethernet access to each room and provides wireless access in the lobby and meeting rooms. Phil Belanger, vice president for marketing at Wayport, says that his company has installations at about 150 hotels and at the Austin, Dallas–Fort Worth, and Seattle-Tacoma airports, and that Wayport expects to have 1,200 installations by the end of 2001.

Two other companies, AirWave and Surf and Sip, operate only in California; both companies plan to expand into other states. Surf and Sip turns some of its locations into instant Internet cafés by providing a few wireless-enabled laptops and a printer that can be rented by the hour.

Rick Ehrenspiel, president of Surf and Sip, says that he had looked for nexus points, such as the intersection of Vallejo and Polk Streets in San Francisco. Within a few hundred feet are four coffee shops: Starbucks, Tully's, Peet's, and Royal Grounds. Ehrenspiel placed his access point in a nearby bar to reach all four shops.

HOOKING UP

This illustrates another aspect of mobile-wireless access. Because the technology is based on radio transmissions (802.11b equipment operates in the 2.4-gigahertz range, the same as some cordless phones), it works through walls. So a Starbucks may be "lit up" by MobileStar, but if a competing company has an access point nearby, that company may reach customers at the Starbucks as well. And at some airports, travel-ers who cannot gain admission to an airline lounge may nevertheless be able to get wireless access by just lingering nearby.

And access may not be limited to the ground. Tenzing Communications, a firm in competition with Boeing and others to provide in-flight Internet access, announced a test of 802.11b networking in conjunction with Telia, a Swedish telecommunications company, and the SAS airline. The tests are intended to certify the protocol as safe for use, according to Tenzing's marketing director, Laura Alikpala. "As you're waiting for your flight, you can either work in the lounge or any of the public places in the airport," Alikpala says, "and then use the same link when you get on the plane to access e-mail or our Web cache."

The equipment to hook up a laptop or handheld organizer into a wireless system recently has become inexpensive and ubiquitous, says Allan Scott, business developer at Agere Systems, a Lucent Technologies division that manufactures ORiNOCO wireless-LAN cards. Most laptop manufacturers have added or will add built-in support for wireless networking, and some laptops already come equipped with wireless-LAN cards. Cards can also be purchased for $100 to $150. And some handheld organizers will soon be able to use the same networks. Xircom, Inc., an Intel company headquartered in California, is producing the Handspring Visor module, which was scheduled to be available in spring 2001.

ASK THE SCIENTIST

▲ *Is vinyl siding better than aluminum siding on a house? Is the principal advantage of vinyl or aluminum over wood the fact that wood needs to be painted?*

Vinyl has taken the lion's share of the siding market in recent years. But while both products resist rot and corrosion and keep their good looks for years without painting, neither one is problem free. Aluminum siding is finished with a long-lasting baked-enamel paint. If the finish is scratched, it can be touched up; but in some cases, after many years, the paint fades. The siding can then be painted, but once that is done, it will have to be repainted as often as wood. Aluminum siding can also be dented by ladders, flying baseballs, rocks kicked up by the lawn mower, and the like. To get rid of the dent, an entire section must be replaced, and matching the original color may prove difficult.

Unlike aluminum, vinyl siding doesn't dent; it also costs less than aluminum siding. The color is an integral part of the material, so scratches don't show. But vinyl can be discolored by stains, and it is more difficult to touch up or repaint than aluminum. (Manufacturers generally don't recommend painting vinyl siding.) Temperature fluctuations cause vinyl to expand and contract more than aluminum does. So if the siding isn't properly installed, it can become wavy. Vinyl also tends to become brittle in very cold weather, and under such conditions, a hard blow could crack it.

Low maintenance is the primary reason to install vinyl or aluminum siding. These materials provide neither insulation nor fire protection. And while they are not subject to rot or insect damage, they can mask these problems in the structure they cover. If too tightly applied, siding can seal in moisture and actually encourage rotting. Siding can also protect such pests as carpenter ants and termites from their natural enemies and from insecticides.

▲ *When a food is freeze-dried, what does that mean? What foods are commonly freeze-dried?*

How about mandarin-orange chicken, beef teriyaki, chicken fajitas, beef Stroganoff, zucchini lasagna, bean tostada, or Thai shrimp? Those are just some of the many dishes available in freeze-dried form. Freeze-dried foods are used by backpackers, survivalists, military units, and astronauts, among others, because they are lightweight and compact, have a shelf life of up to 10 years, and are more flavorful and nutritious than traditional dried foods.

In the freeze-drying process, fresh or precooked foods are flash-frozen and then placed in a vacuum chamber. In the vacuum, the frozen moisture sublimates (it evaporates without melting). The moisture is pumped out of the chamber as fast as it forms. Then the dried food is sealed in moisture- and oxygen-proof packaging. Without moisture or oxygen—two "musts" for most bacteria—it can be safely stored at room temperature; and because the moisture has been drawn out, it weighs only a fraction of its fresh form. To prepare freeze-dried food, water is added, and the food regains most of its original taste, aroma, and appearance.

► *Do ceramics have any modern-day applications beyond dishes and decorative objects? What are ceramic items made of nowadays?*

Most people think of ceramics in terms of teacups, tiles, and toilets. But today's ceramics are used in everything from automobile engines to computers, even for heat-shielding tiles on the space shuttle. They are harder and stiffer than steel, resist heat and corrosion, and are lighter than most metals. Ceramics are brittle, but engineers are overcoming that drawback by mixing in other materials.

Ceramics include a wide range of materials that are inorganic, nonmetallic, and typically crystalline in nature. Cement and brick are ceramics. Glass is usually considered a type of ceramic, although it doesn't have the ordered crystalline structure common to most ceramics.

Traditional ceramics are produced using clays and other minerals. According to the American Ceramic Society, advanced ceramics have developed mostly within the past 50 years, with the growing use of chemically prepared powders as raw materials. The powders provide more control over the composition and microstructure of these new ceramics, and they have given rise to products with many uses. Electronic ceramics include insulators, integrated circuits, piezoelectric materials, magnets, and superconductors. Silicon, a semiconductor but also a ceramic, is the primary material used in computer chips. Ceramic coatings and components are used in cutting tools, engine parts, and industrial equipment that faces heavy wear. Bioceramics are used in artificial bones and teeth. Ceramics are also used in filters, fuel cells, catalytic converters, and scores of other devices.

► *What are holograms? Can a nonscientist purchase a machine that will produce a hologram at home?*

Holography, in which three-dimensional (3-D) images are created by means of laser light, has dozens of new applications. Embossed holograms are placed on credit cards and similar items to prevent forgery. Holographic lenses are used in specialized optical devices, such as modern "smart" windshields that display the panel instruments of a car. In medicine, holography can be combined with ultrasound or CT scans to produce 3-D images of the inside of the body that can assist in making diagnoses or performing surgery. Holographic microscopy and holographic radar are other applications. Holography is also used in the entertainment industry.

Until recently, creating holograms required a 2,500-volt helium-neon laser, not something most people are prepared to plug in and operate. However, it's possible to create simple holograms by using common laser pointers and special photographic plates. One useful guide to this process is a book titled *Shoebox Holography: A Step-By-Step Guide to Making Holograms Using Inexpensive Semiconductor Diode Lasers*, by Frank DeFreitas, Alan Rhody, and Steve Michael, published by Ross Books, Berkeley, California.

► *In a book about Mount Everest, I read that helicopters cannot fly high enough to rescue people trapped near the summit. Why is that?*

Helicopters (like all aircraft) rely on lift, the upward pressure of air on the helicopter's rotor blades. At low altitudes, air is densest, and thus provides the most lift. The higher the altitude, the thinner the air and the less the lift.

Every aircraft has a maximum operating altitude, depending on its weight, power, wing area, and other aerodynamic properties. Helicopters generally can't operate at more than 10,000 feet (3,000 meters) above sea level. Mount Everest rises to more than 29,000 feet (8,850 meters) above sea level. Up there, the air is far too thin to provide the lift a helicopter needs to successfully remain aloft.

REVIEWS

2002

AGRICULTURE

IN SEARCH OF PALER PASTURES

With research proving that excessive exposure to the Sun contributes to certain types of skin cancer, people worldwide have taken steps to protect themselves from solar radiation. In Australia, young students are required to wear hats to school, and beachgoers everywhere are less likely to spend a day near the ocean without applying sunscreen to their bodies.

Human beings are not the only living organisms vulnerable to Sun damage. Not surprisingly, the skin of fruit—just like that of a human—can be burned by the Sun's infrared waves and ultraviolet light, encouraging the growth of rot organisms and infestation of insects. This is an ongoing problem that recently has attracted the attention of some interested researchers.

Michael Glenn, a soil scientist and plant physiologist, has been searching for ways to repel "rot" organisms without resorting to synthetic chemicals. In the course of his research, he has conducted experiments that involve the spraying of fruit trees with a white reflective film of kaolin clay.

The clay (commercially sold under the trade name Surround WP Crop Protectant) effectively reflects sunlight, helping fruit to withstand heat. Insects truly dislike the white covering, as it alters the texture of plants and sticks to the insects' bodies. Apples treated with kaolin have been found to be larger in size, pear crops bigger in quantity, and lemons brighter in color and higher in sugar content. Researchers believe the clay can further reduce the damage from frosts by inhibiting fungus growth. The spray is being used in the United States, South Africa, South America, Australia, and New Zealand.

Economically speaking, fruit growers using kaolin clay could have an advantage over those who do not because fruit buyers will pay more for better-looking, sweeter fruit that has been subjected to less pesticide. An additional bonus for both growers and consumers is that the Surround product is less expensive than most pesticides.

THE ORIGIN OF STINK

It is no surprise to anyone that animal manure smells bad. But why? Scientists are working to determine what exactly makes manure such an unpleasant olfactory experience. Pursuing the microbes responsible for the stench could help the livestock industry improve production, while minimizing protests from those rural and urban neighbors offended by the aroma.

According to scientists, certain bacteria common to both waste-handling facilities and the lower digestive tract of swine produce similar smells from partially digested feed. Ammonia, organic acids, alcohols, and certain sulfides are the compounds that give swine manure its offensive stench, which in some cases can pose a threat to the respiratory systems of humans and other animals.

Historically, it has been difficult for scientists to isolate specific odor-producing microorganisms because they thrive in storage pits and treatment lagoons, but recently, DNA-sequence analysis and diagnostic probes have eased this daunting task.

Researchers are comparing samples of manure slurry from various waste-management facilities and farms to pinpoint the most offensive micro-culprits. Discovering which species of bacteria emit the worst odors, and how, will lead to the engineering of new feeds and more-efficient methods of handling waste—two advances that could potentially provide enormous benefits to the farming community.

APPLE FOOLS

Apple maggot flies have long been a thorn in the side of apple growers. The flies lay their eggs beneath the apples' skin, the eggs eventually hatch, and a legion of apple-maggot offspring burrow through the fruit—not very appetite-inspiring! Scientists from the Agricultural Research Service (ARS) of the U.S. Department of Agriculture (USDA) were challenged to create a device that would serve a double purpose: deter apple maggots and decrease the use of traditional pesticides. Joined by university and industry sources, the ARS scientists planned to trick the little troublemakers with a decoy—*fake apples*. Wooden apples covered with pesti-

Decoy apples filled with sugar and coated with insecticide, an antimolding agent, enamel paint, and cayenne pepper lure unsuspecting bugs to their death.

within the model would automatically leak out to recoat the "apple."

The final decoy worked wonders in Michigan and Massachusetts, and thousands were ordered for more-extensive testing. If proved successful, this technique could eventually eliminate pesticide spraying for the apple maggot, blueberry maggot, California walnut husk fly, and Washington/Oregon cherry fruit fly. Widespread use will require final approval by the U.S. Environmental Protection Agency (EPA).

FLYING THE COUPE DEVILLE

Farmers around the country are offering a hot new crop: chicken feathers. That's right: chicken feathers and quills have the ability to be recycled into, among other things, car parts—and a company called Featherfiber Corporation is leading the way. Its president, David R. Emery, made a deal with a Michigan firm to test samples of fibers made directly from recycled chicken feathers— fibers that can be used to make diapers, filters, paper, clothing, absorbent pads, insulation, and upholstery padding. If the industry takes off, truckloads of raw feathers will be needed, and this could be the start of a second industry for poultry-processing plants around the country.

Emery is preparing a Missouri-based manufacturing plant to produce 200 pounds (90 kilograms) of Featherfiber per hour; plans to build more plants throughout the United States are in place. Tyson Foods and Maxim Industries also share rights to a USDA method of mixing feathers with both synthetic and natural fibers to form new fiber products and improve existing ones.

The process is not complex. Once the fibers are sanitized, they are removed from the feather quills; because commercial chickens are bred white, the feather fiber requires no bleach. The fiber's proteins are as strong as nylon, and stronger and finer than wood pulp. Goods made from the feathers will purportedly exhibit excellent filtration, absorbency, and durability. Moreover, the quills themselves can be processed into protein for hair products and dietary supplements, among other things.

Karen Liljedahl

cide and sugar were tailor-made to attract maggots, the idea being that fruit trees laced with the decoys would have no need for dangerous pesticides.

The first decoy model, designed by entomologist Ronald J. Prokopy, was covered in a mixture of sticky sugar and pesticide. During tests, the fakers were swarmed by unsuspecting insects and required frequent, costly, and laborious rinsing and recoating. A second model featured a mixture of sugar, red latex paint, and traces of pesticide that required reapplication only following heavy rains. But even this method required a good deal of extra labor from apple farmers every time it rained. A more efficient solution for repelling insects was needed.

That is why the Biotechnology Research and Development Corporation, along with chemist Baruch S. Shasha, entered the picture. In conjunction with the ARS and the University of Massachusetts, Amherst, their combined efforts resulted in a patent for a much-improved decoy featuring an antimolding agent, latex enamel paint, insecticide, and even some cayenne pepper (to deter wildlife). This model offered a critical enhancement: following rain, which the new insecticide successfully repelled, sugar from

ANTHROPOLOGY

OUT OF AFRICA

According to all evidence available, humans evolved in Africa. From 5 million until 2 million years ago, all fossil bones found of early forms of humans and stone tools are from Africa. Some of the most intriguing questions about early human history being pondered are when and how ancestral humans first moved out of Africa to populate the other continents.

The first form of early human identified outside of Africa is *Homo erectus*, and its fossil bones have been identified in Europe, the Near East, Asia, and as far away as Java, in Indonesia. Much discussion has revolved around the variability among the different *H. erectus* populations in different parts of the Old World. What may be the earliest known fossil evidence for humans outside of Africa has been identified at Dmanisi in the Caucasus Mountains in the Republic of Georgia. Two skulls found in 1999, dated at about 1.7 million years old, provide scientists with new information about some of the first ancestral humans who lived in Asia.

These recently discovered fossils appear to be similar to skulls found in Africa, and different from other skulls known to be from Asia. Furthermore, stone tools found with them are very similar in shape and technology of manufacture to implements from Africa, such as some excavated in layers dating to 1.8 million years ago at Olduvai Gorge in Tanzania. This new evidence suggests that some *H. erectus* individuals migrated out of Africa relatively soon after this form of early human developed, sometime around 1.8 million years ago.

One explanation for this exodus suggests that in the course of evolution, early humans began adding increasing amounts of meat to their standing vegetable-based diet. As the human body size increased, its nutritional needs called for meat, an efficient source of protein. In order to pursue a more meat-based diet, our ancestors had to become more mobile, following herds of animals as they migrated. Such behavior may have compelled early humans to leave their African homeland and, over tens of thousands of years, establish settlements on other continents.

TRACKING DESCENDANTS WITH DNA

A new type of evidence has been weighed against questions regarding migrations of modern humans—*Homo sapiens*—out of Africa and other parts of the world, to complement that of fossil bones and archaeology. Through the study of DNA patterns in modern human populations, scientists attempt to understand which groups are most closely related, and work to reconstruct their early migrations to different parts of the world. Researchers can investigate lines of ancestry by tracing patterns of mitochondrial DNA through women and of the Y chromosome through men. Based on the diversity of DNA patterns in modern populations, scientists believe that all humans are descendants of a group of only about 2,000 early humans who lived in Africa more than 150,000 years ago.

Although some earlier forms of humans, such as *H. erectus*, moved out from Africa to the Near East, Europe, and Asia, most scientists think that modern humans—who also evolved in Africa—began to migrate out of that continent only around 50,000 years ago. A study of both mitochondrial DNA and the Y chromosome among modern populations reveals some unexpected patterns. For example, one configuration that occurs in Europe also appears among some groups native to north-central North America, suggesting the possibility of an early migration from the Old World to the New about which we have no other evidence as yet. Estimates of when *H. sapiens* first arrived in the New World are anywhere from 15,000 to 30,000 years ago.

WHO ATE THE BEEF?

Scientists studying human evolution focus on diet to understand changes in skeletal morphology and in culture. Until recently, many anthropologists believed that premodern humans relied more on scavenging the carcasses of animals killed by other predators, such as lions, for their meat than on the systematic hunting of big game.

Now, new discoveries made in different parts of the Old World are changing their views. Animal bones are usually the best-preserved food remains found on archaeological sites. Nonetheless, it has long been assumed that ancient peoples relied heavily upon vegetable foods that are underrepresented in archaeological deposits. But new evidence suggests that the diet of Neanderthals, who inhabited Europe, the Near East, and Central Asia between about 150,000 and 28,000 years ago, consisted largely of meat. Analyses of nitrogen isotopes extracted from two Neanderthal bones from Croatia dating to about 28,000 years ago further support this assumption.

EARLY SKULL FROM SOUTH AFRICA

Paleontologists in South Africa unveiled details in April 2000 of an unusually complete fossil skull of a relative of early humans, a form known as *Paranthropus robustus*. The fossil—that of a female—was recovered at the site of Drimolen, near Johannesburg in South Africa. One of some 80 bones found at the site since 1992, this skull is from 1.5 million to 2 million years old. It was found next to the mandible (jaw) of a male of the same kind of creature, providing anthropologists an ideal opportunity to compare the skeletal morphology of these early human females and males. Anthropologists have learned that males were larger than females, and that they had a prominent ridge that ran lengthwise along the top of the skull, a feature conspicuously absent in females. Scientists also believe that *P. robustus* subsisted on plant matter and was forced to compete with creatures that were the direct ancestors of modern human beings. *P. robustus* is thought to have become extinct around 1 million years ago, perhaps because human ancestors were the stronger competitors for available resources.

NEANDERTHAL–MODERN HUMAN RELATIONSHIPS

Since the earliest systematic studies of the fossil bones of ancient humans, scientists have inquired into the relationship between modern humans and the Neanderthals. Did Neanderthals play a part in the evolution of modern humans, or were they an evolutionary dead end, dying out without contributing to modern populations? The debate continues, and new studies offer evidence that could support either stand.

Two analyses of DNA from Neanderthal bones suggest that modern humans are not descended from Neanderthals. Several years ago, scientists extracted and analyzed DNA from a specimen that was part of the original discovery from the Neander Valley in Germany. Now a new analysis of DNA from a Neanderthal fossil from Mezmaiskaya Cave in the Caucasus Mountains has yielded a similar result. These studies, interpreted in light of information about the rate of change in DNA patterns, suggest that modern humans do not share an ancestor with Neanderthals any more recently than 600,000 years ago. If that result is confirmed by future research, it would indicate that Neanderthals and early modern humans are probably separate species. On the other hand, some anthropologists interpret the skeletal remains of a boy found recently in Portugal as indicating that modern humans and Neanderthals were indeed interbreeding as recently as 28,000 years ago. That skeleton shows some features that scientists strongly believe are characteristic of Neanderthals, but also other attributes that appear to be those of modern *H. sapiens*.

Peter S. Wells

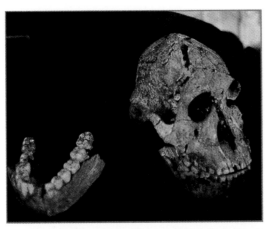

The 1.5 million- to 2-million-year-old fossil of a female *Paranthropus robustus* from South Africa is among the most complete early human skulls ever found.

ARCHAEOLOGY

ROOTS OF SUBURBIA

The great centers of Maya civilization in Mesoamerica have fascinated scholars and the public since they were first brought to the world's attention in the middle of the 19th century. Intensive investigation of the Maya centers during the 20th century focused on the Maya central complexes—the enormous pyramids, temples, and palaces that embellish urban sites, such as those at Copán, Palenque, and Tikal. But attention has shifted to the outlying precincts that surround these core cities—the "urban sprawl" of an ancient civilization.

In present-day Belize, recent investigations at Caracol, a city that flourished between A.D. 500 and 700, reveal an urban and suburban landscape that reminds many archaeologists of the settlement patterns around modern North American cities. In the lavish palaces and ornate temples that surround the centers, archaeologists are finding evidence of simple habitation where workshops produced pottery, stone tools, and other goods. A bit farther away from the centers, but connected to them by roads up to 5 miles (8 kilometers) long, stood outlying residential areas, "suburbs," often with fine-quality housing and clues to the existence of luxury items that only wealthy Maya could afford, such as fine pottery and jade ornaments. Future research will help scientists to understand how the outer precincts of ancient cities were linked to the social, political, and economic functions of the centers.

MAYA PALACE UNCOVERED

The remote jungle region of the Maya lowlands, where Maya civilization flourished between A.D. 250 and 900, is a part of the world where new discoveries are made regularly. At Cancuén in Guatemala in early 2000, archaeologists Arthur Demarest of Vanderbilt University, Nashville, Tennessee, and Tomás Barrientos of the Universidad del Valle, Guatemala City, Guatemala, identified and began investigating an enormous limestone palace that was constructed nearly 1,300 years ago. The lavish palace has three stories, nearly 200 rooms, and at least 11 courtyards, and it covers as much space as two football fields. It is a telling representation of the wealth of a king who once ruled over a thriving commercial city. Inscriptions carved in stone suggest that he was Tah ak Chaan, Cancuén's king during the 8th century A.D.

Unlike most Maya centers, Cancuén apparently did not have the stone pyramids that generally dominated the urban landscape, and shows no indications that the city's ruler engaged in any major warfare. Instead, the archaeologists found abundant evidence for craft production and commercial activity on the site.

Cancuén is an ideal trading port. The city is situated at the end of the navigable portion of the Pasión River and at the edge of highlands that are rich in obsidian (a volcanic glass suitable for toolmaking) and jade (a highly valued ornamental stone). Workshops that have been excavated at the elaborate palace have yielded evidence of intensive production of these and other materials suited for export trade. In one such workshop, archaeologists found a huge piece of jade, weighing 35 pounds (16 kilograms), that craft workers were using to make beads and other ornaments. In another, they discovered pyrite cut to make mirrors. Jade ornaments and pyrite mirrors were prized by wealthy Maya, and were important trade items throughout Mesoamerica.

Archaeologists examined the site of Cancuén in 1905, but they did not think it was an important center. Surveys in the 1960s revealed the palace, but not its extraordinary complexity. Nor did the earlier expeditions realize the size of this urban site. Further research at Cancuén, which is expected to continue for at least 10 more years, will no doubt necessitate a complete reevaluation of the theories regarding the origins and development of Maya civilization.

PERSPECTIVES UPTURNED

Since the intensive research in the first half of the 20th century at major centers of Sumerian civilization in southern Mesopotamia (now Iraq), archaeologists have be-

The excavation at Tell Hamoukar (left) in northeastern Syria uncovered a sophisticated ancient civilization. Someone may have used the goat-shaped stamp above to mark his or her belongings or personal property.

lieved that civilization first flourished there, in cities such as Uruk and Ur, and that it later spread northward to other regions. But recent research in Syria suggests that complex urban centers and civilization developed in both northern and southern Mesopotamia at the same time.

Excavations at Tell Hamoukar in northeastern Syria have unearthed abundant new evidence for a social-ranking system, labor specialization, and monumental architecture—all telltale signs of civilization—by 3500 B.C., as early as have been documented in the south. Evidence of seals—stamps used to mark ownership—suggests the existence of an ancient, large, and complex community in which individuals and groups designated property. A 13-foot (4-meter)-wide and 10-foot (3-meter)-tall wall around the settlement attests to both a need for defense and the community's identification with a clearly defined space. Nonetheless, the earliest evidence of a writing system remains near the point where the Tigris and Euphrates Rivers join to form the Shatt al-Arab, which empties into the Persian Gulf.

THE HUMAN-SETTLEMENT DEBATE
Exactly when humans first arrived in the New World is one of the most debated issues of modern archaeology. Some archaeologists argue in favor of around 15,000 years ago;

others say it was closer to 30,000 years ago. Until recently, the earliest well-dated and generally accepted human-habitation site in the Americas was believed to be Monte Verde, Chile, where evidence of human occupation includes dwellings, food remains, and tools from 10,500 B.C. But by the end of 2000, some archaeologists had shifted their focus northward, to a site at Cactus Hill, Virginia, that may date earlier—to around 13,000 B.C.

Archaeologists found two layers of cultural remains at the Virginia site, which is situated southeast of Richmond. In the upper layer were stone spear points of a form called Clovis, named after a site in New Mexico where that type of tool was first identified. Below the first level, a dig team found another layer with different types of stone tools and charcoal that initially were dated by the radiocarbon technique at about 13,000 B.C., or possibly even earlier.

PERU CENTER DATES EARLY
In South America, archaeologists are investigating a large and complex settlement at Caral, 14 miles (22.5 kilometers) inland from the Pacific coast in Peru. Recent radiocarbon determinations indicate that the site was inhabited around 2000 B.C., much earlier than archaeologists had expected. Especially striking at the site are large mounds and platforms, together with numerous smaller mounds, paved plazas, and houses, indicating a substantial investment of labor devoted to constructing major public mon-

uments. The farmers that supplied this early urban center grew squash and beans, and trade with coastal fishing communities provided a major component of the protein in the diet. Unlike many communities elsewhere at that time, the residents of Caral apparently did not use much pottery, but made containers of woven plant fiber. Ongoing research at this important site will help archaeologists to better understand the development of complex societies and civilizations in South America.

THE ICEMAN'S TATTOOS

The corpse of an unidentified man—aptly dubbed the Iceman—who was discovered in a melting glacier in the Alps in 1991 continues to yield surprises for archaeologists and physical anthropologists analyzing the find. Recent investigations have focused on tattoos on the Iceman's legs and back. Fifty-seven distinct marks have been identified, including lines and crosses made by charcoal that may have been pushed into the skin with a sharp, pointed object. Different hypotheses suggest that the lines and crosses were markers of group identity, religious signs, or counts of some kind. However, since the Iceman is the only known intact individual from Europe of the Neolithic period (dating to about 3300 B.C.), there is no basis for comparison. Many of the marks are in places where modern Asian practitioners generally apply acupuncture, and some researchers suggest that the tattoos are indications of such treatment.

The Iceman was approximately 45 years old when he died, and, as is the case with other early individuals who have been discovered and studied, he suffered from a variety of ailments, including intestinal parasites and hardened arteries.

EGYPTIAN BOATS LAID TO REST

Dugout boats, made by hollowing out logs, are well documented as far back as 8000 B.C. But recently, the earliest known plank-built boats have been found buried in a cemetery at Abydos in Egypt, south of Cairo. Fourteen boats up to 75 feet (23 meters) long have been identified so far. They had been buried and packed around their edges with bricks,

in long pits arranged in parallel lines, and then covered with a layer of mud or clay. All 14 seem to have been buried at the same time, probably during a funerary celebration for one of the early pharaohs. Objects buried with the boats, including ceramic vessels, can be dated to around 3000 B.C., when Egypt's first pharaohs were buried in a royal cemetery at Abydos.

Ancient Egyptian civilizations fed off the Nile River. We know from tomb paintings and sculptures of wood and pottery found in graves that boats played an important role in Egyptian culture. The pharaohs traveled the Nile in ornate craft. At that time, metal was little used in Egypt; the planks for these newly discovered boats were shaped with stone axes and chisels, and bound with ropes. To ensure that the craft would stay afloat, spaces between the planks were caulked with reeds.

RICH TOMB IN SYRIA

An elaborate burial complex at the site of Umm el-Marra, near Aleppo, provides evidence of a wealthy and stratified society that existed about 2300 B.C. in a region when such civilization had never before been documented. Inside a tomb enclosed with mud-brick walls, archaeologists discovered wooden coffins and three layers of skeletal remains. At the base of the tomb was the skeleton of a man about 60 years old, buried with silver pins and a silver vessel. Above him were skeletons of two men—one buried with a bronze dagger, and the other with a silver ornament. Within the top layer of the chamber were the skeletal remains of two women, each buried with lavish ornaments of lapis lazuli, silver, and gold. Next to each woman lay the skeleton of an infant.

The relationships among these five entombed adults are not clear, but future skeletal analyses may help to clarify them. The positions of the skeletons and the different icons and objects of wealth with each individual surely hold social significance. Archaeologists hope to better understand through analysis how this new find fits into our developing picture of the Bronze Age society in this part of the Near East.

Peter S. Wells

ASTRONOMY

OUR PLANETARY SYSTEM

Dramatic new images of Mars show that this planet once had an environment that created sediment-like layers within craters and canyons across much of the planet's midsection. Scientists have counted hundreds of individual beds in some locations, with sediments in some cases extending for hundreds of miles. Some believe the beds indicate that Mars once had huge areas of liquid water that laid down the sediments. Many astronomers think that the Martian atmosphere and the ferocious dust storms on the surface may be responsible for these formations.

The Galileo spacecraft orbiting the giant planet Jupiter has documented that the planet appears to have clear, dry "holes" in the clouds near its equator—some possibly as high as 60 miles (97 kilometers). The planet's moon Io seems to contain many more volcanoes than scientists had thought, many of which seem to have changed dramatically since earlier observations were taken. And the Jovian moon Europa now shows the best evidence yet of a salty liquid ocean deep beneath its thick, icy crust.

The ringed planet Saturn has taken over the lead as the planet having the most orbiting moons. On September 23 and November 9, 2000, scientists in Arizona and Hawaii found the 29th and 30th members of Saturn's family.

A rare meteorite that was seen to fall into a frozen lake in Canada's Yukon Territory in January 2000 was recovered and analyzed. It contains material that appears to be unchanged since the birth of the solar system. This discovery has been hailed as one of the most important in the history of meteorite studies. In addition, scientists have recorded the 14th and 15th meteorites believed to have originated in an ancient asteroid impact on Mars.

Scientists have used the solar-observation satellite TRACE (Transition Region and Coronal Explorer) to photograph coronal loops so immense that they would engulf 30 Earths. And solar astronomers have developed a technique to "see" the far side of the Sun, enabling early detection of dangerous electromagnetic storms that can affect Earth-based satellites and power systems.

ASTROTECHNOLOGY

Giant telescopes continued to spring up around the globe during the past year.

On September 6, 2000, the newly built University of Arizona/Smithsonian's 6.5-meter Multiple Mirror Telescope Observatory (MMTO) telescope on Mount Hopkins, Arizona, photographed the immense spiral galaxy NGC 7479. In May 2000, the new $4

The MMTO telescope, one of several such giants recently built, achieved "first light" when it photographed NGC 7479, a galaxy similar to the Milky Way.

million Australian-Japanese telescope Cangaroo II—designed to seek out and understand black holes—began operation under the clear, dark skies of Australia.

And in September, construction began near Sutherland, South Africa, on the European Southern Observatory's (ESO's) $15 million Southern African Large Telescope (SALT). This new telescope's main mirror is composed of an array of hexagonal 1-meter-diameter mirrors, making it the equivalent of a single 10-meter telescope.

EXTRASOLAR PLANETARY SYSTEMS

Astronomers have found a second multiple-planet system that contains two Saturn-sized planets, one orbiting its parent star every 2.98 days, and the other every 29.8 days.

Another interesting planet orbits a nearby star named Epsilon Eridani—only 10.5 light-years from Earth. A light-year is equivalent to the distance that light travels in a mean solar year. At the rate of approximately 186,000 miles (300,000 kilometers) per second, a light-year is equal to 5.88 trillion miles (9.46 trillion kilometers).

Another multiple-body system orbits the Sun-like star HD 168443, and contains two bodies that seem to weigh in with masses at least 7.7 and 17.2 times that of Jupiter. At present, about 50 stars seem to have at least one planetary companion.

The star Iota Horologii, orbited every 320 days by a planet three times more massive than Jupiter, appears to be surrounded by a disk of dust. Future observations may help scientists determine the temperature, sizes, and composition of the dust grains.

Eighteen planetlike objects have turned up, drifting through the constellation of Orion. Since they seem to exist without a "parent" star, these "free floaters" may challenge scientists' traditional theories about how planets are born.

IN THE MILKY WAY

The Hubble Telescope has found the closest neutron star to Earth, only 200 light-years away. This remnant of a giant supernova explosion (known as RXJ 185635-3754) is racing through the constellation Corona Australis at more than 60 miles (100 kilometers) per second, and may have originated 1 million years ago as a companion to the star Zeta Ophiuchi.

Astronomers suspect that a high-velocity blast of X rays from a nearby binary-star system in January 2000 originated from the closest black hole ever discovered—only 1,600 light-years away. And gamma-ray findings have unveiled a potentially new class of object, one that emits gamma rays continuously rather than in bright flashes or sudden bursts.

Astronomers using the giant Keck Telescope on Mauna Kea, Hawaii, have found an immense black hole at the core of the Milky Way. With the mass of over 2 million Suns, this black hole causes nearby stars to speed up as they revolve around the galactic core.

THE UNIVERSE BEYOND

Deep within the core of the distant galaxy NGC 4395, astronomers have found what may be a new type of mid-mass black hole weighing perhaps as much as 10,000 to 100,000 Suns.

In January 2001, astronomers announced their discovery of a remote group of quasars and galaxies in the constellation Leo. The group spans more than 500 million light-years in length, width, and depth, and may be the largest structure in the universe. The great assemblage seems to be about 6.5 billion light-years from Earth, meaning that we see the group of celestial bodies as it was when the universe was about one-third of its present age. No one yet knows how gravity could have constructed such a huge structure in so little time.

Astronomers using the 10-meter-diameter Keck Telescope found the most distant object ever. The quasar is believed to lie so far away that the light now arriving here began its journey when the universe was less than a billion years old.

SETI UPDATE

The Search for Extraterrestrial Intelligence (SETI) took a few steps forward during the year as well. Microsoft's cofounder Paul Allen invested $11.5 million to help build what will be the world's most powerful instrument designed to seek signals from extraterrestrial intelligence.

On the 40th anniversary of Dr. Frank Drake's Project Ozma, the first scientific search for extraterrestrial life, astronomers revealed a prototype for a seven-dish radio-telescope array that will dramatically expand the search for extraterrestrial intelligence.

And in May 2000, after only one year of operation, the SETI@home project reached 2 million users. In its first year of operation, the project—in which home computers can scour radio-astronomy data for evidence of intelligent signals—has amassed more than 280,000 years of computing time, making it the largest network-computing effort in human history.

No intelligent extraterrestrial signals have been found to date, however.

Dennis L. Mammana

AUTOMOTIVE TECHNOLOGY

TIRES RECALLED

Early in August 2000, Bridgestone/Firestone Inc. inaugurated a partial recall of tires marked as unsafe by the National Highway Traffic Safety Administration (NHTSA). The company voluntarily recalled 6.5 million 15-inch (38-centimeter) tires designed for light trucks and sport-utility vehicles (SUVs). The recall followed a government investigation that linked defects in the tires to numerous injuries and 46 traffic deaths in the United States.

According to the NHTSA, blowouts, tread separations, and other problems occurred in Firestone's radial ATX, ATX II, and Wilderness AT tires. Soon after the recall, an NHTSA consumer advisory warned that an additional 1.4 million tires not marked for recall also had high failure rates. The manufacturer followed up by agreeing to replace all tires noted by the NHTSA as unsafe.

The NHTSA had received nearly 300 complaints, most of which involved the treads peeling off their casings, sometimes during high-speed travel. The majority of the tires were on the world's top-selling SUV, the Ford Explorer. Indeed, approximately 3.6 million of these SUVs were equipped with the tires.

During several congressional hearings on this issue, Bridgestone/Firestone and Ford exchanged heated arguments about which company was more at fault. Ford claimed Bridgestone/Firestone withheld information, which delayed the recall, while the tire company claimed that the faults in the design of the Explorer played a key role in the accidents.

By December, an internal investigation by Bridgestone/Firestone Inc. blamed the problems on flaws in the tire's design and on the rubber-manufacturing process at one of its plants. The report also said that Ford Motor Company had recommended a lower tire pressure and a heavier-than-normal load level for the Explorer. Among the flaws the report cited was the tire's shoulder design, which makes cracking and belt detachment more likely. According to the report, in rare circumstances, this can cause the beginning of tread separation. In addition, tires manufactured in the company's Decatur, Illinois, plant had different belt-adhesion characteristics than tires from other plants. Finally, in response to the fact that the majority of complaints came from warmer Southern states, the report stated that low inflation pressure would make the tires excessively hot during travel, which could also contribute to belt detachment.

In its own investigation, the Ford Motor Company drew similar conclusions. However, the company said that its SUV was not the cause of the trouble, and that it would continue its internal investigation.

DWD

Driving while distracted by a range of high-tech devices is becoming a major safety issue on U.S. roads, according to NHTSA reports. The agency has found that one-quarter of the 6.3 million vehicle crashes that occur in the United States each year are the result of driver distraction or inattention. Among the devices that the agency cites as causing safety problems: cell phones, navigation systems, fax machines, e-mail systems, and complicated sound systems.

According to the Network of Employers for Traffic Safety (NETS), an employer coalition focused on highway safety, the risk level is even higher. The organization estimates that driver inattention accounts for 25 to 50 percent of collisions. That translates to anywhere from 4,000 to 8,000 crashes per day. High-tech devices are not the only problem, according to NETS: other common distractions include eating, reading, picking up dropped objects, adjusting the radio or inserting a tape or CD, or programming a navigation system.

The NHTSA's survey found that 44 percent of drivers either have car phones or carry a phone in their car, 7 percent have e-mail, and 3 percent have fax machines. Although the agency has been studying the link between cell-phone use and driving safety since 1973, it has not offered evidence that conclusively links phone use to accidents. Most likely, this is because states do not report phone use when recording accident data. Nevertheless, a 1997 study published in the *New England Journal of Medicine* found that using a cell phone while driving is akin to driving drunk.

Although most U.S. states have laws against reckless driving, only about half of them have laws that address inattentive driving. The NHTSA has called on states to include information about phone use in all of their crash investigations. The agency has also asked manufacturers of high-tech devices to design products so that they will be easier for drivers to use, and therefore cause fewer distractions.

CLOUD CARS

Many science-fiction writers of the 20th century imagined an Earth teeming with human life, occupying glorious, futuristic cities. If people had not yet learned to fly, their cars certainly had, coursing along pristine, sunlit skyways. Flying cars have long been considered the ultimate step in automobile technology, and they are finally here—sort of. The M400 Skycar is the brainchild of 63-year-old Paul Moller of Moller International and the latest development for tantalizing the public. The Skycar is designed to vertically lift off the ground like a helicopter, but with less noise and chaos. Unlike a helicopter, though, it promises to move at speeds of up to 350 miles (560 kilometers) per hour, and will feature a layman's control panel.

To clarify, the car actually flies. Its predecessor, the M200X, has successfully performed more than 150 test flights, some with Moller at the controls. When asked about his obsession with flight, Moller referenced a fascination with hummingbirds during his youth, and talked about wanting to "fly out to a place nobody had flown before, and then set down."

Growing up in Canada, he built his own helicopter at age 14, but barely graduated from high school. A professor at McGill University, Quebec, helped him enroll in college, a show of support Moller turned into a Ph.D. and a professorship at the University of California at Davis in 1963. In his spare time, he built a working model for a flying saucer. Soon after, his obsession with the flying automobile bloomed, and he began work on predecessors to the M400, coming closer than anybody else has come to "driving" across the sky. The technology is basically there, but obvious stumbling blocks remain.

Developing a car that can successfully achieve vertical lift, as a helicopter does, is actually the least of Moller's many concerns. Significantly more daunting obstacles lie in providing the high-volume engine and airframe production necessary to keep costs down; locating or adapting affordable factories to build them; and developing a control system the average person could understand. Most critical of all will be the regulations for these cars. One can only imagine the abundance of red tape involved: a fender bender along Main Street is one thing; a Skycar spiraling downward into Town Hall is quite another. The obstacles are frustrating, and detractors continue to chime away. But while it will be some time before cars ride among the clouds, Moller and his team have not given up on the dream just yet.

Devera Pine

For now, Paul Moller's M400 Skycar remains in the hangar. But could cars actually fly someday? The possibilities—and complications—are almost endless.

AVIATION

FAA Favors Defibrillators

In a move intended to bolster airline passenger safety, the Federal Aviation Administration (FAA) has mandated that commercial airliners carry heart defibrillators. The ruling, to take effect in spring 2001, materialized following a yearlong FAA survey of in-flight illnesses affecting the passengers and crews of 15 airlines.

The estimated cost to the industry to equip planes with external defibrillators is $138 million, and airlines would have three years to install them and train crews in their proper use. Even before the FAA proposal was announced, however, most major U.S. carriers were already equipped with the devices; the rest reported that they would comply with the proposed rule by the end of 2000. The new FAA mandate will apply to airliners carrying more than 30 passengers and one flight attendant.

Automated external defibrillators work by delivering an electric shock to the heart to either restart it or restore its normal rhythm during a heart attack. The sooner that normal heart rhythm and blood flow are restored during a heart attack, the greater a victim's chance of survival.

The FAA estimates that, on average, one person dies aboard a commercial U.S. aircraft each week. The agency found that the 15 airlines involved in its yearlong study filed 188 medical-event reports, that 177 of these events had occurred on board, that 119 of the affected passengers (whose average age was 62) were thought to have experienced heart problems, and that 64 of the 119 passengers had died.

Airline Consolidations

Two major U.S. airlines, American and United, each took giant steps in 2000, positioning themselves as global rivals and the leaders of 50 percent of all air travel in the United States. With United's purchase of US Airways, and American's acquisition of TWA, Delta Air Lines will land in the shaky number-three spot with an 18 percent share of U.S. air travel.

When both multibillion-dollar deals are sealed, the two majors will benefit in expanding their U.S. routes and their booming presence in the air-travel industry. United, mainly an east-west carrier, will get a grip on important north-south routes with its purchase of US Airways, a north-south carrier. In a more complicated pact, Dallas-based American will acquire the financially troubled Trans World Airlines (TWA) and parts of US Airways, allowing American to expand in the Midwest and along the East Coast and to increase its intercontinental presence. American is already dominant in Dallas/Ft. Worth and Miami.

Reportedly, United's offer to US Airways was $4.3 billion, plus the assumption of $7.3 billion in debt and long-term aircraft leases. American's deal with TWA included an offer of $500 million in cash and the assumption of $3 billion in aircraft leases. American would also pay United $1.2 billion for about 20 percent of assets of US Airways. By unloading some assets to American, United would clear the way for antitrust approval for its merger. Antitrust laws protect trade and commerce from unlawful restraints and monopolies or unfair business practices.

Supersonic Troubles

An Air France Concorde crashed just outside of Paris on July 25, 2000, slamming into a hotel just two minutes after takeoff from Charles de Gaulle Airport. All 109 passengers and crew on board were killed, as were four people on the ground.

While the Air France Concorde disaster was the only crash that involved a supersonic aircraft, several other devastating accidents occurred in 2000 that resulted in the loss of lives. They include an Alaska Airlines flight and a Kenya Airways flight, both in January; an Air Philippines flight in April; a Gulf Air flight in August; and a Singapore Airlines flight in October.

The Air France crash was particularly notable for being the first of any of the world's 12 supersonic transports (SSTs) to go down. (Supersonic means above the speed of sound, or Mach 1, defined as 1,125 feet—343 meters—per second.) At present, all Concordes are operated either by British

Airways or Air France. Both airlines grounded their Concorde fleets after the Paris crash, as investigators sought to determine the cause. One theory is that a metal strip on the runway cut one of the plane's tires, and that rubber debris then hit the fuel tank, causing a leak and subsequent fire. A photo taken of the plane just before it crashed showed that a 197-foot (60-meter)-long flame appeared to be coming from one of its engines and its nearby fuel tank.

By December 2000, French officials were saying that the Concordes might be ready to fly again soon—perhaps in 2001. Air France officials were testing the plane at a military air base in France. British officials said that they were almost ready to begin testing changes to the fuel tanks, which were modified to include a liner designed to reduce the

The British and French Concorde fleets were grounded following the fiery crash (above) of an Air France Concorde on July 25, 2000, that claimed 113 lives. It was the first crash of a Concorde.

chance of a fire. The Concorde must pass tests that ensure that the chain of events that led to last July's crash could not be repeated.

Meanwhile, development of a next-generation SST came to a halt. The ambitious High Speed Civil Transport (HSCT) program at the National Aeronautics and Space Administration's (NASA's) research center, vigorously supported by the U.S. government and the aerospace industry, had been developing the technology for an SST with

greater capabilities than the Concorde. The proposed aircraft would travel 5,000 nautical miles (8,045 kilometers) at Mach 2.4, and carry 300 passengers at only a 20 percent ticket-price increase compared to the cost of subsonic airplane flight. But Boeing, the only U.S. airline manufacturer participating in the program, withdrew from the project, saying that development and use costs would prohibit the setting of reasonable ticket fares. Currently, a transatlantic ticket on the Concorde costs approximately $10,000, and the aircraft carries 100 passengers at a speed of Mach 2.

MAKE THAT A LARGE
Airbus Industrie, a European aircraft maker, has announced that it plans to develop a supersized jumbo jet that can carry up to 940 passengers. Tentatively called the A380, the jet will hold 550 to 940 passengers and cost $12 billion. The world's largest jet is currently the Boeing 747-400, which holds a maximum of 520 passengers.

Large planes are not totally new: In the 1940s, the wood-frame *Spruce Goose*, built by millionaire Howard Hughes, was designed to transport up to 700 soldiers in full battle gear. That plane weighed 200 tons and stood eight stories high. Being a seaplane, and therefore unrestricted by airfield limitations, Hughes' creation could have a 320-foot (98-meter) wingspan to compensate for its size.

The A380, however, will have to be small enough to maneuver around modern runways and airport terminals: It will be less than 240 feet (73 meters) long, and will have two double-aisled decks inside to seat passengers. The Boeing 747-400 is 232 feet (71 meters) long, and also has a double deck. The A380's wings will span nearly 262 feet (80 meters); at that size, special techniques and materials will be required to make the wings lighter than those manufactured before it. The wheels will be mounted under the fuselage instead of the wing, further eliminating any extra weight.

Devera Pine

BEHAVIORAL SCIENCES

EMOTIONS AND MEMORY

Psychologists have long known that different people adopt different strategies for controlling their emotions. Now a growing body of research suggests that there are costs associated with such strategies. One recent study directed by psychologists Jane Richards of the University of Washington, Seattle, and James Gross of Stanford University, Palo Alto, California, shows that suppressing emotions can often interfere with memories of upsetting or traumatic situations. The same study demonstrates that people who reinterpret disconcerting events in a less emotional way are less likely to have difficulty in remembering them.

Participants in the first phase of the study watched a disturbing scene from the movie *Fatal Attraction*. Some were instructed to conceal their feelings, while others (the control group) were told only to watch and listen to the film. Participants in both groups reported negative reactions to the film clip, although those who had been told to suppress their emotions had a more difficult time recalling certain details from the film.

Richards and Gross suspect that suppressing emotions requires people to continually remind themselves to keep their emotions in check. That kind of internal dialogue, the researchers hypothesize, may interfere with how people process emotional events for recall later. To test this premise, the psychologists conducted a second experiment to measure both verbal memory (memory for words and verbal information) and nonverbal memory (memory for spatial relationships, faces, designs, and other factors that are difficult to encode verbally). They also examined whether "reappraisal," or interpreting emotional situations less negatively—for example, thinking of a test as a challenge rather than a threat—would obstruct memory in the same way as suppressing emotions.

In the second experiment, participants viewed slides of people who had suffered traumatic injuries, while they heard recordings that provided the person's name, occupation, and cause of injury. Participants in the first group were told to suppress their emotional reactions to the images, while others were to view the slides with the detached attitude of a medical professional, interpreting the images as objectively as they could. Participants in a control group were asked to watch the slides carefully, with no instructions to stifle their reactions.

As in the first experiment, the participants who had been instructed to suppress their emotional responses experienced more difficulty remembering the slides than did members of the control group. However, that finding applied only to verbal memory; the participants' nonverbal memory (their ability to pick out the slides they had been shown from an array of slightly different versions) was unaffected by their efforts to suppress their feelings.

Unlike the results of emotional suppression in the first experiment, reappraisal did not impair verbal memory in the second group, and the participants' nonverbal memory was actually better than that of people in the control group. The researchers speculate that reappraisal requires less effort than suppressing emotions, and that adopting a detached perspective allows people to be more attuned to visual details than they would otherwise be.

In addition to shedding light on the trade-offs associated with controlling emotions, the study has practical implications. For example, the effort that jurors expend to remain impassive while unpleasant evidence is presented may impede their ability to recall the evidence when it comes time to decide the case.

EARLY ALZHEIMER'S LINKS

Although the causes of Alzheimer's disease remain a mystery, two recent studies—one concerning head injuries and brain trauma among American servicemen and the second regarding the intellect of Scottish schoolchildren—support the growing suspicion by many in the scientific community that the disease develops over the course of several decades. Evidence appears to also suggest that Alzheimer's may, in part, be rooted in one's early life experiences.

In the first study, a team led by Brenda Plassman of Duke University, Durham, North Carolina, and Richard Havlik of the National Institute on Aging (NIA), Bethesda, Maryland, compared World War II military hospital records with present-day psychiatric data for 1,776 veterans. The researchers found that veterans who had suffered a moderate head injury during their service 50 years earlier were twice as likely to develop Alzheimer's disease in later life as veterans who had not. What is more, men who had suffered a severe brain injury were four times as likely to develop the disease.

In an attempt to rule out alternative explanations for the association between head injury and Alzheimer's, the researchers looked at the role of other factors, such as education, genetic abnormalities, and family history of dementia. But even after weighing these factors, the relationship between head injury and later dementia remained strong.

The second study, directed by Scottish researchers Lawrence Whalley of the University of Aberdeen and Ian Deary of the University of Edinburgh, found a link between scores on an intelligence test taken at age 11 and the likelihood of developing dementia more than 60 years later. Children with low scores on the test were much more likely to develop Alzheimer's late in life. These findings corroborate earlier research that involved a study of a group of elderly nuns, which suggested a connection between verbal ability in young adulthood and later risk for dementia.

It remains unclear why intelligence-test results and head injuries among young people are related to the later development of Alzheimer's disease and other forms of dementia. The recent findings have bolstered the suspicion among some scientists that Alzheimer's disease may be a chronic illness whose origins can be found early in life. If this is the case, researchers say, understanding early risk factors for dementia, including head injuries and mental ability, will be critical in identi-

fying ways to combat the disease before it ever manifests symptoms.

HANDSHAKES AND IMPRESSIONS

The etiquette books, old-fashioned as they may sometimes be, appear to be correct on at least one point: a firm handshake is an important part of making a positive first impression. Such was the conclusion of a study of 112 college students directed by psychologist William Chaplin at the University of Alabama, Tuscaloosa, which also found that a person's handshake "style" is consistent over time and is associated with aspects of his or her personality.

The students in the study, 48 men and 64 women, completed four personality tests, each administered by a different monitor in a different laboratory room. The monitors shook hands with each participant as he or she entered and left each room. After greeting a participant, the monitors met in private and evaluated the many possible characteristics of the participant's handshake—including such factors as hand dryness, temperature and texture, strength, vigor, completeness of grip, and duration—

A handshake can convey many messages. In the case of Al Gore and George W. Bush, it symbolized unity and the end of the hotly contested 2000 U.S. presidential election.

and indicated their initial impressions of every participant's personality.

Participants' handshake styles were found to be consistent across the four monitors, regardless of any individual monitor's gender. In addition, participants who had a firm handshake made a more positive first impression on the monitors than did those with a limp handshake.

The results also showed that women who described themselves as more liberal, intellectual, and open to experience had a firmer handshake and made a more favorable impression than did women who perceived themselves as less open and had a less firm handshake. Handshake style was less closely related to personality among male participants; in fact, men who described themselves as more open to experience had a slightly less firm handshake and made a somewhat poorer impression than did men who considered themselves less open.

The finding that women with a firm handshake are perceived more favorably than women with a limp handshake runs counter to other research, which has indicated that confident, assertive women tend to be categorized more negatively than their male counterparts. One possible reason, the study's authors suggest, is that having a firm handshake may communicate competence subtly enough to circumvent the kinds of negative reactions that have been observed in other research.

TEEN SMOKING AND MENTAL HEALTH

In the past, most psychologists believed that mental health problems increased the likelihood that an adolescent would smoke. Two studies published in the past year arrived at quite an opposite conclusion: smoking is more likely to cause depression and anxiety in teens than the other way around.

The first study, carried out by Elizabeth Goodman of Ohio's University of Cincinnati College of Medicine and John Capitman of Brandeis University, Waltham, Massachusetts, used information from two extensive interviews—conducted one year apart—with adolescents between the ages of 11 and 21. Among teenagers who were not depressed at the time of the first interview,

Smoking appears to do more than just cause physical illness; recent studies have shown that it may negatively affect the mental health of many teenagers.

those who had smoked within 30 days of the interview were about four times as likely to experience depression one year later than were nonsmokers. Conversely, nonsmoking teenagers who showed signs of depression during the first interview were no more likely than their peers who were not depressed to take up smoking.

The second study, led by Jeffrey Johnson of Columbia University, New York City, and the New York State Psychiatric Institute, showed a similar link between heavy smoking during adolescence and anxiety disorders during adulthood. In that study, 688 teenagers from upstate New York were interviewed when they were 16 years old, and again about six years later. The researchers found that teens who had an anxiety disorder were no more likely to be smokers in adulthood than were those who had no such disorder. But teens who smoked at least 20 cigarettes per day were far more likely than nonsmokers to develop one of three forms of anxiety: agoraphobia, generalized anxiety disorder (GAD), or panic disorder. Of the 69 teens with anxiety who smoked, more than twice as many said they had begun smoking before being diagnosed than those who reported the opposite.

Although the reasons for the connection between smoking and anxiety disorders are unclear, the researchers speculate that smoking may trigger anxiety by impairing respiration. Another possibility, they suggest, is that sustained nicotine intake can directly promote anxiety.

Siri Carpenter

BIOLOGY

FISH EYES

Scientists have discovered that it is possible to grow a new eye—at least for a certain type of blind cave-dwelling fish that lives off the coast of Mexico. Yoshiyuki Yamamoto of the University of Maryland, College Park, and biology professor William Jeffery tested fish of the same species *(Astyanax mexicanus)*, whose environment and behavior differed. The sighted fish that live near the surface develop eyes, while the eyes of the blind fish that live in caves degenerate soon after the fish begin to grow in the egg.

Two months after a lens was implanted, the cave-dwelling fish had grown a large eye with a pupil, cornea, and iris. The scientists are not sure how the lens stimulated growth of an entire eye, but they do know that lenses can secrete a variety of growth factors or compounds that stimulate cell development. This finding could ultimately provide researchers with information on how eyes evolve and develop. Jeffery believes this study offers clues to what sort of molecules are involved in the eye growth of vertebrates.

BACTERIA, BACTERIA EVERYWHERE

Microorganisms, it seems, can live just about anywhere—from the freezing underside of glaciers to the sky's mile-high clouds. Canadian researchers together with others from the United Kingdom have confirmed that bacteria do indeed grow beneath glaciers, while Austrian scientists have found that bacteria also grow in the equally inhospitable environment of clouds.

Researcher Martin Sharp of the University of Alberta at Edmonton and associates were motivated to find out what was causing chemical reactions beneath a Swiss glacier. When they discovered nitrate in the water that was flowing into the glacier, but found none in the water exiting beneath it, the team took samples of ice, water, and sediment from two mountain glaciers. Surprisingly, they found that sediments beneath the glaciers contained more bacteria than did the ice from the glaciers' surface or interior. This meant that the bacteria they found

were growing at the bottom of the glacier and were not contaminants washed in from the scientists' drilling. The team observed in the lab that the bacteria collected were dividing and further ruled out the possibility that the bacteria may have settled in the glaciers from frozen cells blown in by the wind. Sharp and his team suggest that over time, the northern ice sheets blanketed large quantities of the carbon-rich forest vegetation and tundra, and that bacteria could have slowly decomposed organic matter. Before this discovery, climate researchers had been unable to determine the whereabouts of more than 150 billion tons of carbon whose levels had fallen during the last Ice Age. As subglacial microbes munched away at the glacier during past ice ages, Sharp suggests, dead vegetation and soil were converted into CO_2 and possibly methane. When the climate then warmed up, these gases would have been released, which in turn accelerated the changes occurring in the climate.

Clouds are microbial habitats, too, at least according to findings published by Austrian researchers. Although scientists have been aware for some time that bacteria are known to be blown high into the atmosphere, they did not know that bacteria could actually grow and reproduce in clouds—until now. After Birgitt Sattler of the University of Innsbruck and colleagues took sample water droplets from clouds near Salzburg, they froze them on Teflon plates. The researchers then melted the samples, monitoring them at temperatures typically found in clouds. Sure enough, round, rod-shaped, and long, filament-like bacteria were alive and thriving. Because bacteria multiply over a span of several days—shorter than the "life" of a cloud—Sattler's team knew that the microbes reproduced while inside the cloud. Now that scientists know *where* these bacteria are, they will attempt to learn exactly *what* species are "cloud dwellers." They will also attempt to answer *how* these species survive the subzero temperature, intense ultraviolet radiation, and limited nutrients available, as well as whether they come from plants, surface water, or soils.

FANCY FOOTING

For hundreds of years, scientists have speculated about the gecko's "secret power" to scamper up slippery windows and walls or cross ceilings upside down. And for a long time, it was believed that these reptiles sported suction cups on five-toed, self-cleaning feet. Not so, say researchers who call themselves the Gecko Team. Last summer, two biologists, Kellar Autumn of Lewis & Clark College, Portland, Oregon, and Robert Full of the University of California at Berkeley, published a surprising scientific conclusion—that is, that the "secret" to a gecko's holding power lies at the molecular level, far beyond theories of suction cups and glandular foot goo. These scientists joined Tom Kenny of Stanford University, Palo Alto, California, and Ron Fearing at UC Berkeley for an electron-microscopic scrutiny and micromechanical measurement of the components of gecko feet. They found that the gecko's ability to hang on to just about anything involves molecular forces generated by the interplay between the atoms of the animal's climbing surface and its feet. The team also discovered that the greater the contact area, the greater the forces, and therefore the better the gecko's ability to climb.

A gecko's foot contains about 500,000 setae ("see-tee"), or hairs, each only one-tenth the diameter of a human hair. Each seta branches at the tip into hundreds of projections with tiny, fly-swatter-shaped structures at their ends, called spatulae. Unlike a human hand or foot pressed against a wall—which at the atomic level is jagged, and unable to make an even, intimate contact with the wall—the huge numbers of spatulate tips on every seta of each gecko toe get so close to the surface that they act as a sort of glue. A gecko's toes, although naturally curling backward, can conform to a bumpy surface, increasing the area with which the hairs (setae) make contact with the molecules of the surface. The individual molecular force generated by a single seta is weak; but many setae together can produce an impressively strong force. Indeed, a single seta can lift the weight of an ant—and 1 million setae could lift the weight of a child.

A gecko (above) does not depend on fancy foot glue or miniature suction cups for a steady foothold. Instead, researchers have determined, after decades of pondering, that its amazing antics likely involve molecular forces generated by the interplay of its foot elements (right) and the climbing surface.

When the scientists observed the geckos climbing in the lab, they noted the bizarre manner in which these creatures would place their tiny feet. The palm-shaped area of the foot was set down first, and then each small toe uncurled. These movements revealed that the gecko's microscopic foot hairs adhere only when they contact the surface from a particular direction. As the Gecko Team concluded, should a gecko wish to let go, all it needs to do is to recurl its toes and pull slightly downward. In doing so, the animal changes the angle at which a seta meets the surface, steadily increasing the distance between the spatulae and points of contact. The action is not unlike that of a noisy, hornlike party favor that is blown out and then allowed to roll back into a curl.

Researchers are now looking for anoles, skinks, some insects, and other animals that have setaelike structures on their feet. What lies ahead, based on the Gecko Team's core research, are artificial setae used in multiple applications—from manufacturing highly mobile robots for search and rescue to scratch-free computer chips.

Karen Liljedahl

Book Reviews

Animals and Plants

- Alexander, Shana. *The Astonishing Elephant.* New York: Random House, 2000; 304 pp.—Elephant history, mythology, physiology, and biology, emphasizing the relationship between elephants and humans.
- Montgomery, Sy. *Journey of the Pink Dolphins: An Amazon Quest.* New York: Simon & Schuster, 2000; 317 pp., illus.—A mesmerizing journey through the rain forest in search of the rare, prehistoric *Inia geoffrensis.*
- Nixon, Rob. *Dreambirds: The Strange History of the Ostrich in Fashion, Food, and Fortune.* New York: St. Martin's Press, 2000; 256

how animals manipulate their environments provides the reader with a unique look at how organisms evolve.

- Waldbauer, Gilbert. *Millions of Monarchs, Bunches of Beetles: How Bugs Find Strength in Numbers.* Cambridge, Mass.: Harvard University Press, 2000; 272 pp., illus.—A charming and often surprising look at how insects use numbers in self-defense, reproduction, the creation of microclimates, and much more.
- Zimmer, Carl. *Parasite Rex: Inside the Bizarre World of Nature's Most Dangerous Creatures.* New York: Free Press, 2000; 304 pp., illus.—An evolutionary history of the complex life cycles and defenses of a variety of bizarre parasites.

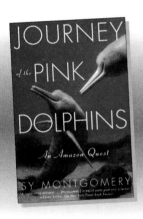 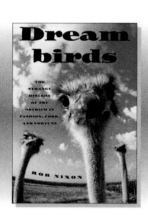 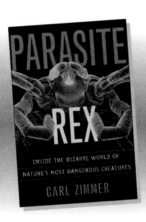 

pp.—A recount of the history of this flightless bird that is part science, part commerce, and part memoir.
- Sapolsky, Robert M. *A Primate's Memoir.* New York: Scribner, 2001; 304 pp.—A natural-history writer and animal behaviorist wittily describes his 20 years of fieldwork among the baboons of southwestern Kenya.
- Tudge, Colin. *The Variety of Life: A Survey and a Celebration of All the Creatures That Have Ever Lived.* New York: Oxford University Press, 2000; 528 pp., illus.—A fascinating study of plant and animal classification.
- Turner, J. Scott. *The Extended Organism: The Physiology of Animal-Built Structures.* Cambridge, Mass.: Harvard University Press, 2000; 384 pp., illus.—This study of

Astronomy and Space Science

- Levy, David, ed. *The Scientific American Book of the Cosmos.* New York: St. Martin's Press, 2000; 416 pp., illus.—A guide by eminent authorities to what we know about the size, age, and nature of our universe.
- Owen, David. *Into Outer Space.* Los Angeles: Lowell House, 2000; 144 pp., illus.—A visual history covering both astronomy and space exploration.
- Standage, Tom. *The Neptune File.* New York: Walker, 2000; 256 pp.—How 19th-century scientists discovered the existence of an unseen planet by studying the effects of its gravity on the orbit of Uranus.
- Tyson, Neil de Grasse. *The Sky Is Not the Limit: Adventures of an Urban Astrophysicist.*

New York: Doubleday, 2000; 208 pp.—The memoirs of the director of the American Museum of Natural History's Hayden Planetarium range from a look at the universe to the problems faced by black scientists.

- Tyson, Neil de Grasse, Charles Tsun-Chu Liu, and Robert Irion. *One Universe: At Home in the Cosmos*. Washington, D.C.: Joseph Henry/National Academy Press, 2000; 224 pp., illus.—An overview of the current state of knowledge of the universe, from its tiniest particles to its grandest theories, with many useful illustrations.

EARTH AND THE ENVIRONMENT

- Alley, Richard B. *The Two-Mile Time Machine: Ice Cores, Abrupt Climate Change,*

Books, 2000; 255 pp.—A look at what might trigger a global weather catastrophe, what it would be like, and what its long-term effects might be.

- Lanting, Frans. *Jungles*. New York: Taschen America, 2000; 260 pp., illus.—Tropical rain forests and the flora and fauna that thrive there, from one of the world's foremost wildlife photographers.

- McNeill, J.R. *Something New Under the Sun: An Environmental History of the Twentieth-Century World*. New York: Norton, 2000; 416 pp., illus.—A lucid look at how humans have altered Earth since the 1890s.

- Souder, William. *A Plague of Frogs: The Horrifying True Story*. New York: Hyperion, 2000; 304 pp., illus.—The ecological detec-

  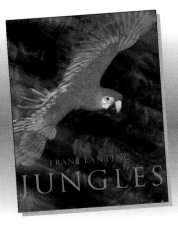 

and Our Future. Princeton, N.J.: Princeton University Press, 2000; 299 pp.—The author contends that the past 10,000 years have been a period of unusual climatic calm compared to the climatic history of the 100,000 years before it, and tells how humans may be able to avoid bringing about undesirable rapid swings in climate in the future.

- Ball, Philip. *Life's Matrix: A Biography of Water*. New York: Farrar, Straus & Giroux, 2000; 400 pp.—A lively exploration of the physical and chemical properties of water, its role in the development of civilization, its presence in space, and the dangers of pollution and overuse of this valuable resource.

- Bell, Art, and Whitley Strieber. *The Coming Global Superstorm*. New York: Pocket

tive hunt spurred by the discovery of a disturbing environmental happening.

- Wolfe, Art. *The Living Wild*. Seattle: Wildlands Press, 2000; 256 pp., illus.—Stunning photographs of the world's diversity, with a plea for habitat preservation.

- Woodard, Colin. *Ocean's End: Travels Through Endangered Seas*. New York: Basic Books, 2000; 320 pp.—A whirlwind tour of the world's imperiled rivers and seas and the crises they face.

HUMAN SCIENCES

- Greaves, Mel. *Cancer: The Evolutionary Legacy*. New York: Oxford University Press, 2000; 276 pp.—A British cancer researcher explains cancer at the cellular level and explains why fighting cancer is actually fighting evolution, which is based upon the ability of cells to mutate.

● Humes, Edward. *Baby ER: The Heroic Doctors and Nurses Who Perform Medicine's Tiniest Miracles.* New York: Simon & Schuster, 2000; 384 pp.—A lucid examination of the incredible progress that has been made in the care of sick and premature infants.

● Nuland, Sherwin B. *The Mysteries Within: A Surgeon Reflects on Medical Myths.* New York: Simon & Schuster, 2000; 286 pp.—A very clear review of the expansion of medical knowledge since the times of Hippocrates and Aristotle.

● Robbins, Jim. *A Symphony in the Brain: The Evolution of the New Brain Wave*

PAST, PRESENT, AND FUTURE

● Ewald, Paul. *Plague Time.* New York: Free Press, 2000; 288 pp.—An evolutionary approach to the role played by viruses, bacteria, and other microbes in cancer, heart disease, mental illness, autoimmune problems, and a wide range of other diseases.

● Fortey, Richard. *Trilobite! Eyewitness to Evolution.* New York: Knopf, 2000; 284 pp.—Tales of creatures that dominated the seas hundreds of millions of years ago.

● Haines, Tim. *Walking with Dinosaurs: A Natural History.* New York: DK Publishing, 2000; 288 pp., illus.—Photography and computer graphics bring dinosaurs to life.

● Jones, Steve. *Darwin's Ghost: "The Origin of Species" Updated.* New York: Random

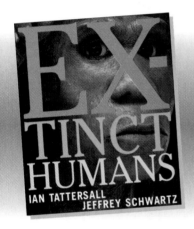

Biofeedback. New York: Atlantic Monthly Press, 2000; 256 pp.—Describes the evolution of neurofeedback as a treatment for hard-to-control medical conditions.

● Schlosser, Eric. *Fast-Food Nation: The Dark Side of the All-American Meal.* Boston: Houghton Mifflin, 2001; 356 pp., illus.—A look at the consequences of fast-food restaurants on the marketing and processing of livestock and produce in America, including the increased health risks.

● Vertosick, Frank T., Jr. *Why We Hurt: The Natural History of Pain.* New York: Harcourt Trade, 2000; 304 pp.—A surgeon's provocative and edifying look at types of human pain and how various cultures have viewed and dealt with the experience.

House, 2000; 377 pp.—The enormous strides made by evolutionary biologists since the 1859 publication of Darwin's pioneer work on the theory of natural selection.

● Tattersall, Ian, and Jeffrey H. Schwartz. *Extinct Humans.* New York: Westview Press, 2000; 224 pp., illus.—The authors contend that there have been more than 15 human species (all but *Homo sapiens* now extinct), many of which coexisted with one another; beautifully illustrated.

● Weinberg, Samantha. *A Fish Caught in Time: The Search for the Coelacanth.* New York: HarperCollins, 2000; 240 pp.—The riveting tale of the search for a fish believed to have become extinct about 65 million years ago.

PHYSICAL SCIENCES

- Bodanis, David. *E=mc²: A Biography of the World's Most Famous Equation.* New York: Walker, 2000; 224 pp.—The history and meaning of the equation behind the atomic bomb, scanners, and how stars ignite.
- Close, Frank. *Lucifer's Legacy: The Meaning of Asymmetry.* New York: Oxford University Press, 2000; 259 pp., illus.—A clearly delineated explanation of one of the key ideas in modern particle physics.
- Garfield, Simon. *Mauve: How One Man Invented a Color That Changed the World.* New York: Norton, 2001; 222 pp., illus.—In 1856, a British teenager's invention brings chemistry to commerce, paving the way for future generations of industrial chemists.

TECHNOLOGY

- Davis, Martin. *The Universal Computer: The Road from Leibniz to Turing.* New York: Norton, 2000; 256 pp.—The development of symbolic logic, which reduced any kind of deductive reasoning to a series of math computations and made computers possible.
- Jardine, Lisa. *Ingenious Pursuits: Building the Scientific Revolution.* New York: Doubleday, 2000; 320 pp., illus.—The genealogy of 17th-century science, and how chance dramatically shaped the modern world.
- Macaulay, David. *Building Big.* Boston: Houghton Mifflin, 2000; 192 pp., illus.—A fascinating look at how some of the world's greatest engineering projects were built, by the author of *The Way Things Work.*

- Goff, M. Lee. *A Fly for the Prosecution: How Insect Evidence Helps Solve Crimes.* Cambridge, Mass.: Harvard University Press, 2000; 224 pp.—A forensic entomologist talks about the science of true crime.
- Seife, Charles. *Zero: The Biography of a Dangerous Idea.* New York: Viking, 2000; 248 pp., illus.—Entertainingly traces the history of the elusive zero, from more than 30,000 years ago to the contemporary cosmological theory.
- Trinh Xuan Thuan, trans. by Axel Reisinger. *Chaos and Harmony.* New York: Oxford University Press, 2000; 366 pp.—An eloquent tour of cutting-edge physics and intriguing theories, such as gravity and chaos contrasted with beauty, harmony, and truth.

- Perkins, David. *Archimedes' Bathtub: The Art and Logic of Breakthrough Thinking.* New York: Norton, 2000; 288 pp., illus.—Tricky puzzles explore the often-hidden mechanisms of innovations such as perspective drawing and the creation of the laser.
- Schaaf, William E., et al. *A History of Invention.* New York: Facts on File, 2000; 352 pp.—Ranges from the most primitive tools to the latest technology.
- Wright, Michael, and M.N. Patel, eds. *Scientific American: How Things Work Today.* New York: Crown, 2000; 320 pp., illus.—A spectacular guide to modern technology, with subjects ranging from Hollywood-style effects to how the space station works.

Jo Ann White

BOTANY

NUTTY CANCER FIGHTER

Oregon scientists have discovered an important cancer-fighting chemical in the common hazelnut, or filbert, tree. Though no one will be able to cure cancer by simply munching a handful of nuts, the discovery could lead to a less expensive version of the drug Taxol, the leading chemotherapy treatment for breast cancer, ovarian cancer, and Kaposi's sarcoma, a form of cancer most frequently seen in AIDS patients.

Soon after it was approved as a cancer treatment in 1992, Taxol became the nation's top-selling cancer drug. But its popularity concerned environmentalists because the only source for its active ingredient, paclitaxel, was the bark of the Pacific yew tree (*Taxus brevifolia*). Fortunately, before demand stripped U.S. West Coast forests of their Pacific yews, biochemists found ways to extract paclitaxel from the needles of many other kinds of yew trees. Still, the cost of growing the yews, harvesting them, and extracting the chemical has remained quite high. As a result, a typical course of Taxol treatment costs about $12,000.

But that figure may well come down in the years ahead, thanks to the discovery of paclitaxel in filberts. The discovery was a lucky one, says horticulturist Larry Daley of Oregon State University, Corvallis. Daley and his fellow researchers stumbled upon the chemical while trying to determine why certain filbert trees resisted a normally fatal fungal disease called eastern filbert blight. But the scientists were not sure of exactly what they had discovered until they showed their results to Angela Hoffman, a chemist at the University of Portland in Oregon. Hoffman had already made a career of finding new botanical sources of the drug. According to Hoffman, the chemical is extremely difficult and far too expensive to synthesize in the laboratory, which is why botanical sources remain so important.

Although filbert trees contain relatively small amounts of paclitaxel, the researchers found the chemical in virtually every part of the plant, even the shells that nut growers discard by the ton after harvest. "It is relatively easy, chemically, to extract paclitaxel from the tree," says Hoffman. And that's good news for the cancer patients and insurance companies who now spend more than $1 billion a year for the drug. Eating filberts won't have a cancer-fighting effect, unfortunately, because the digestive process completely breaks down paclitaxel before it can enter the bloodstream.

HUMONGOUS FUNGUS

The record for the world's largest living organism was shattered in the year 2000. The discovery came after U.S. Forest Service biologist Catherine Parks received reports of an expansive tree die-off in the Malheur National Forest of eastern Oregon. Once she had determined the outer limits of the tree die-off, Parks traced its cause to an enormous underground mat of a tree-killing fungus known as the honey mushroom (*Armillaria ostoyae*). Through genetic testing, Parks determined that all 2,200 acres (891 hectares) of the fungus—the equivalent of 1,665 football fields—were part of the same organism. In other words, when it first began growing an estimated 2,400 years ago, the entire interconnected web of underground fungus arose from a single microscopic spore.

The only parts of the fungus visible above ground are clumps of golden mushrooms that sprout at the base of infected trees each fall. To call these the "tip of the iceberg" is an understatement, says Parks. The organism, with a weight that has yet to be determined, extends into the ground an average of 3 feet (1 meter). The fungus spreads via long black filaments called rhizomorphs that stretch as far as 10 feet (3 meters) through the soil to invade tree roots and rob them of water and other nutrients.

Not surprisingly, foresters feel no love lost on this "king" of destructive organisms. Wisely, however, they have no plans to eradicate it. Instead, they hope to reduce tree deaths around the fungus by planting western larch and ponderosa pine, which can withstand its attack.

This newest discovery is the latest in a series of record-breaking fungus finds, including another honey mushroom—this one covering 1,500 acres (600 hectares)—found in eastern Washington in 1992. In terms of weight, however, these enormous mushrooms may be dwarfed by a 106-acre (43-hectare) grove of interconnected, genetically identical quaking aspens (*Populus tremuloides*) growing in Utah. Weighing an estimated 6,600 tons, the entire aspen grove sprouts from a single, shared root system.

PLANTS WARN NEIGHBORS OF ATTACK
The year 2000 brought the discovery of two fascinating cases of plant communication, including one that supports the much-debated possibility that plants of different species can "understand" each other. The first report, in August, came out of Germany and Japan, where botanists collaborated on a study showing that lima-bean plants attacked by spider mites send out a warning signal to neighboring lima-bean plants. Specifically, their leaves release chemicals known as terpenoids. The terpenoids taste bad to spider mites and also drift through the air to reach surrounding lima-bean plants, signaling them to produce chemical

A recent study has detected "communication" among lima-bean plants. When threatened, the plants release chemicals that repel attacking organisms while alerting nearby plants to marshal their own defenses.

defenses of their own. As an added bonus, the terpenoids attract larger, predatory mites that arrive to eat the tiny but troublesome spider mites.

In a related report, researchers at the University of California found that when they clipped the leaves and stems of sagebrush, nearby wild tobacco plants began boosting their natural chemical defenses against grasshoppers and cutworms. Analyzing the air between the wounded sagebrush and surrounding tobacco plants, the scientists detected a gaseous plant chemical, methyl jasmonate, which appeared to be the "smoke signal" in question. In the laboratory, puffs of methyl jasmonate prompt tobacco plants to produce natural pesticides in their leaves.

Although such reports often get dubbed as examples of "talking" plants, scientists say it would be more accurate to describe them as examples of good "listeners." In other words, the chemicals released by a plant being attacked by insects (or scientists with clippers) are probably an inadvertent by-product of its battle for survival. On the other hand, being sensitive to such airborne chemicals would be a great advantage to a plant that could then arm itself long *before* it is ever attacked.

CULPRIT IN SUDDEN OAK DEATHS
After five years of mystery, plant pathologists have discovered the culprit behind a plague that has killed thousands of oak trees along the California coast. More than just a West Coast problem, Sudden Oak Death has been worrying arborists across North America and Europe, for fear that it could spread to their forests.

The good news is that researchers have at last identified the killer, a newly discovered species of fungus with a huge appetite for oak bark. The bad news is that fungi of this type have a nasty habit of hitchhiking, and not just in contaminated wood and soil. Their spores can also stick to the tires of cars and bicycles, even the shoes of hikers and the furry paws of their four-legged friends. Controlling the spread of the fungus—a swimming, two-tailed member of the genus *Phytophthora* (pronounced fy-TOFF-thor-uh)—could prove difficult. Its nastier relatives include the fungus that caused the infamous Irish potato famine of the 19th century and the 20th-century deaths of cedar trees in California and Oregon, eucalyptus forests in Australia, and oak forests in Mexico, Spain, and Portugal.

Yet to be named, the new species attacks the bark of oak trees, creating cankers up to 2 feet (6 meters) long that ooze burgundy-red to tar-black sap. Eventually the cankers can girdle a tree and kill it. California foresters and residents began noticing Sudden Oak Death in 1995, but did not pay too much attention, as it was killing primarily tan oak (*Lithocarpus densiflora*), a gangly tree many people consider a weed. Concern grew when the fungus began killing the magnificent and much-loved coast live oak (*Quercus agrifolia*) in 1998. Since then, it has likewise spread to the rare California black oak (*Q. kelloggi*).

Still, no one is panicking *just yet*, says David Rizzo, a member of the University of California oak-research team that identified the fungal killer. "Sometimes this sort of thing mysteriously vanishes as quickly as it appeared," he explains. "It may be that this fungus was here all along, but remained relatively harmless until some other kind of environmental stress weakened the trees." Another possibility is that the fungus was introduced from another region or even from a different continent where the trees were more resistant to its destructive tendencies. Yet a third possibility is that the fungus itself recently evolved in a way that made it more lethal, resulting in the kinds of damage currently seen in the affected areas.

In any case, experts are urging visitors to California's coastal forests to thoroughly clean their tires, shoes, and the feet of their pets before leaving infected areas, and not to remove any wood that might be infected. Construction workers are being asked to wash their equipment and avoid moving dirt from one area to another. Officials in the state of Oregon, in turn, are considering a quarantine that would place a ban on the importation of nursery stock, lumber, and firewood from forests along the central and northern coasts of California.

Jessica Snyder Sachs

CHEMISTRY

NANOTUBES AS CHEMICAL SENSORS

Carbon nanotubes, tiny molecule-sized pipes made from sheets of carbon atoms, show great promise as miniature chemical sensors. Twisting the tube in different ways alters its electrical properties, changing it from an insulator to a conductor and vice versa. Now a research team led by Hongjie Dai of Stanford University, Palo Alto, California, has discovered that a nanotube's electrical properties also change radically when it is exposed to different gases. When exposed to nitrous oxide, for example, carbon nanotubes become up to 1,000 times more conductive.

Most chemical sensors now available lack portability and are expensive to build; many also require high operating temperatures. Nanotubes operate at room temperature and are small enough to be used as "labs on a chip." Dai's experiments show that nanotube sensors, manufactured on a large scale, would be comparatively inexpensive and small enough to have many uses, from testing for pollutants in automobile and factory emissions to analyzing the atmospheres of distant planets.

Still, several major problems must be resolved before such sensors can be put into general use. Due to the required twists, each nanotube can detect only one specific chemical at a time. Also, nanotubes currently have a slow response time, on the order of one or two minutes—far too slow for commercial use. The tubes can also take up to 12 hours to recover their original conductivity, or to recalibrate, after exposure to a gas. Dai and his colleagues are continuing their work to upgrade the nanotubes in order to improve response and recovery times.

BOOM TO COME

After more than 25 years of effort, Philip Eaton and Mao-Xi Zhang, organic chemists at the University of Chicago, reported the first successful synthesis of a superexplosive compound called octanitrocubane.

Eaton created cubane, a hydrocarbon with a unique molecular structure, in 1964.

A cubane molecule is made up of eight carbon atoms, each forming the corner of a cube, with a single hydrogen atom bonded to each of the carbons. Due to stresses from its 90-degree bond angles (which are unusually small), cubane is highly strained. While stable under normal conditions, when the molecule breaks down, it releases a powerful burst of energy. Eaton realized that cubane could release even more energy if the hydrogen atoms were replaced with a nitrogen atom bonded with two oxygen atoms.

Organic compounds that contain reactive-nitrogen groups make excellent candidates for explosives. The best known is trinitrotoluene—TNT—invented in 1863 and still used today. The most powerful nonnuclear explosive in current use is HMX, made from TNT and other explosives, and used only in military applications. Calculations show that a cubane-based explosive could be up to 30 percent more powerful than HMX.

Creating the octanitrocubane molecule was a far from trivial task. The high-strain energies of the cubane molecule's bonds made replacing hydrogen atoms with reactive nitrogen compounds a tricky process. Because of this, no one has yet synthesized enough of the new explosive to actually explode it. Calculations show, however, that octanitrocubane will easily top the power of any other explosive used today.

COOLEST FUEL CELL OF ALL

Because they generate electricity without creating unwanted pollutants, fuel cells seem to be the ideal energy source. Japanese researchers, led by Takashi Hibino of the National Industrial Research Institute in Nagoya, Japan, have built a prototype fuel cell powered by natural gas that works at lower temperatures than any other design.

Fuel cells resemble batteries, with a negatively charged anode, a positively charged cathode, and a conducting electrolyte in between. Fuel is drawn from anode to cathode through a membrane, where it reacts with oxygen in the presence of a catalyst and produces electricity as it is broken down.

The first fuel cells were designed to run on hydrogen, but because that element is

Ford will produce a fuel-cell vehicle using hydrogen by 2004, applying the same principles to create electricity as Takashi Hibino did for his ethane-fed cell.

both expensive and dangerous to refine, store, and transport, it is not a good candidate for everyday use. Newer designs use fuels such as ethane, methane, or propane, but the high operating temperatures of these hydrocarbon cells (typically as high as 1,832° F or 1,000° C) create soot that can clog the membrane and shut down the cell.

Hibino's ethane-fed fuel cell runs at around 930° F (500° C). It operates at cooler temperatures than the next-best design, which runs at 1,112° F (600° C). The Nagoya cell uses a cerium oxide membrane doped with samarium that allows ions to pass through at lower temperatures, thus avoiding the problems associated with soot buildup. An additional benefit of the lower operating temperatures is that the other cell components can be made of steel rather than more-expensive, heat-resistant alloys.

While it may take a few years to "scale up" Hibino's groundbreaking design for common use, the new fuel cell should ultimately lead to more-efficient, less-expensive ways to generate clean energy.

NANORIBBONS ENHANCE PLASTICS

Samuel Stupp, a materials scientist at Northwestern University in Chicago, has found a novel way to improve polymers. Stupp and his colleagues were studying three-part molecules called "dendron-rodcoils," or DRCs. When his team dissolved DRCs in a liquid organic solvent, the solvent turned into a gel. This indicated that the DRCs were sticking together—not in chains as the researchers expected, but in orderly molecular ribbons Stupp dubbed "nanoribbons."

When Stupp replaced the original solvent with styrene, the liquid precursor to polystyrene, the molecular orderliness remained even after the styrene was linked into polymer chains. Fibers made from the modified polystyrene, with nanoribbons and polymer chains all lined up in the same direction, were much stronger than threads of randomly oriented polystyrene.

Polystyrene, an inexpensive polymer perhaps most often seen as packing material in "peanut" and "popcorn" forms, is one of the most common industrial polymers in the world. Manufacturers use it to package everything from toys to computers, but polystyrene's relative structural weakness means that it had to be replaced with more-expensive materials when stronger packaging was needed. With a ratio of 0.3 percent nanoribbons to 97.7 percent solvent, Stupp's DRC-enhanced process creates stronger polystyrene with little increase in cost.

Stupp's team has since used nanoribbons with rubber and other plastics, with similar results. They also managed to deposit semiconductors on the ribbons to create nano-sized wires that might someday be used in miniature electronic chips.

POLYMERS AID SCARLESS HEALING

In the United Kingdom, Ronald L. Coffee, a University of Oxford biochemist and president of the Oxford-based biotech company Electrosols, has created a spray-on polymer bandage that encourages skin to heal without scarring.

When skin is damaged, the body quickly mobilizes cells called fibroblasts to the injury site. The fibroblasts lay down thin strips of collagen to temporarily seal the wound and prevent blood loss and infection. Skin cells eventually grow back over the collagen, but the new skin is paler and less flexible: a scar. Current research has focused on using various materials as biodegradable "scaffolds" to supplement the collagen framework. Coffee's method is notable for its use of polymers instead of lab-cultured tissue.

The spray-on bandage is made from ethanol and a biodegradable plastic called polylactic acid. By applying an electrical field to the spray container, the polymer develops a charge and is attracted to the skin, which has a lower electrical potential. As the spray leaves the bottle, it turns into thin, light fibers, about 2 microns, or 0.002 millimeter (0.000078 inch), in diameter. Because the fibers all have the same charge, they tend to repel each other, creating a regularly spaced weave over the wound. Collagen-forming fibroblasts are attracted to the charged fibers, which become a framework for the body's healing processes.

Experimental trials are still needed to test the idea, but researchers hope the spray-on fibers eventually will be used to treat everything from minor cuts and scrapes to serious burns.

NANOWIRES IMPROVE MEMORY

In a multigroup effort, researchers at the University of Massachusetts, Amherst; IBM's Watson Research Center in Yorktown Heights, New York; and the Los Alamos National Laboratory, New Mexico; have developed a novel method to improve the storage capacity of computer hard drives.

Standard hard disk drives store data in tiny patches of magnetic material arranged in an orderly fashion on the surface of a flat plastic platter. In the past, improvements in storage depended on decreasing the size of these magnetic patches, so that the same amount of space could accommodate more data. The trouble with this method is that many magnetic materials lose their magnetism when they are shrunk to sizes smaller than approximately 10 nanometers, or 0.00001 millimeter (0.0000003 inch).

The IBM-led effort focused instead on changing the structure of the disk itself. They replaced the standard hard disk with a plastic template full of pores, then packed the pores with magnetic material to create small magnetic poles, or nanowires. Thus, while the amount of magnetic material on the surface of the disk is very small, there is still enough material in the embedded wire to maintain the magnetic field necessary to store information. Researchers estimate this new style of disk could increase computer memory by as much as 300 times over what is now currently available.

Charlene Brusso

CIVIL ENGINEERING

The turn of the century called for big celebrations and big projects—from housing a world of athletes to sheltering a universe of plant life, from mapping Earth to preparing for unforeseen, massive earthquakes. Along the way, engineers met a seemingly endless array of unique challenges head-on with innovative 21st-century solutions.

EDEN PROJECT
Cornwall, in southern England, has suffered economically in recent decades, but a new attraction is causing curious tourists to flock to the region. The draw is one impressive engineering feat: the Eden Project, a massive botanical garden that contains 80,000 plants from faraway climates. The two conservatories—identified as Humid Tropics and Warm Temperate—house entire biomes under the highest and the largest geodesic (self-supporting) domes in the world. More than 984 feet (300 meters) long and up to 148 feet (45 meters) high, the conservatories could easily hold the Tower of London—and 35 soccer fields.

Dreamed up by a team of local botanists, the Eden Project domes are nestled in the crater of a defunct clay quarry. Over a six-month period, builders took 43 feet (13 meters) of earth from the top of the 197-foot (60-meter)-deep crater and filled in 66 feet (20 meters) in the bottom; then they built a drainage system vast enough to handle the 43 million gallons (163 million liters) of water that flooded the site during two months of rain. After the pit was stable enough, construction began on the domes. The project's geodesic design is perfect for the irregular site. Domes can adapt to the imperfect terrain; they are roomy inside because they don't require internal supports; and their panels

can collect solar energy for the biomes' use. The domes were designed using 3-D computer models, then a scaffolding was built with 46,000 galvanized-steel poles. For the two layers of hexagonal, pentagonal, and triangular panels (831 in all), engineers chose a material called ETFE (ethyltetrafluoroethylene). ETFE is more transparent and more lightweight than glass, and is antistatic, self-cleaning, long-lasting, and recyclable. Each panel of ETFE plastic foil is custom-cut by computerized machines and inflated to a thickness of 6 feet (2 meters).

Over the past two years, botanists made 85,000 tons of soil and grew plants for the conservatories in nearby nurseries. The $120 million Eden Project also includes a visitors' center, restaurant, amphitheater, and classrooms. The 35-acre (14-hectare) complex opened for visitors in 2001.

During construction (above), the Eden Project's massive geodesic domes presented an almost endless series of challenges to the engineers. Today, the domes hold botanical gardens of great diversity.

BRIDGE SAFETY
Construction is nearly complete on the first phase of a three-stage plan to retrofit San Francisco's famous Golden Gate Bridge. The plan was drafted after a computer-model study showed a potential risk to the bridge should a 7.0-magnitude-or-larger earthquake originate from the nearby San Andreas fault. Rather than simply strength-

The Golden Gate Bridge, the San Mateo Bridge (above), and dozens of other spans in California are being retrofitted to guard against damage during earthquakes.

en the bridge, engineers want to free its elements to move more independently of one another. Energy-absorbing materials are also being used to replace components of the bridge. The first phase focused on the north approach to the bridge. When the retrofitting of both approaches and the span itself is complete, the bridge should be functional as soon as a few days following a major seismic event. During the work, engineers and contractors have taken care to disturb traffic patterns as little as possible; to preserve the aesthetic beauty of the bridge; and to honor environmental concerns, such as the preservation of the nearby habitats for the endangered mission blue butterfly.

London's new Millennium Bridge, on the other hand, suffered from a structural snafu, and was closed two days after its June 2000 opening. The 1,050-foot (320-meter) footbridge spans the Thames River; during its opening, large crowds crossed it at one time, and the bridge began to sway considerably. Engineers had not realized that a slight sway caused by high winds would cause pedestrians to compensate by walking in step, and

that this would lead to an "S-shaped lateral wobble," a strong horizontal force resulting in even more sway. (Military troops break step when they cross bridges to prevent this very occurrence.) The Arup engineering firm, which built the bridge, plans to refurbish it by installing shock-absorbing energy dampers. The six-month repairs have a $5 million price tag—or one-fourth of the original cost to build the bridge.

WINTER GAMES

Salt Lake City, Utah, slated to host the XIX Winter Olympic Games in 2002, built its brand-new Olympic facilities both to impress a worldwide audience and to serve American athletes and its state's citizens for years to come. One of the venues planned for the big events was the Soldier Hollow cross-country-skiing and biathlon course. The sprawling 250-acre (101-hectare) site, located in a state park, contains 14 miles (23 kilometers) of looping, undulating trails and will host 22 medal events over a 16-day period. To meet Olympic specifications for track lengths and shapes, local contractors moved 110,000 cubic yards (84,100 cubic meters) of earth, and built a $1.5 million snowmaking system complete with its own water-storage pond. In addition, 2,000 trees were transplanted to give the finish line a picture-perfect, ready-for-television appearance.

The biggest project at the 389-acre (157-hectare) Utah Olympic Park was a pair of world-class ski jumps: the 90-meter and the 120-meter. Engineers carved the ramps right into the mountainside, allowing the natural ridgeline to buffer the crosswinds that often play havoc with ski jumpers. Building on a 35-degree slope brought its share of challenges. Engineers whipped up a complex combination of rock, steel, and concrete to ensure that the ramps would not slide down the mountain, and that the two ramps would share a common outrun.

The $27 million Oquirrh Park Speed Skating Oval is designed to provide the fastest ice in the world. Its seamless concrete slab, covered with a layer of perfectly smooth ice, will allow speed skaters to take advantage of Salt Lake's thin air, increasing their odds of shattering world records. A handsome and efficient cable-suspended roof, one of the first in the American West, covers the facility and reduces the arena's inside volume for maximum temperature control. In November, with the roof in place, engineers poured the slab for the 1,300-foot (400-meter) oval rink with two concrete-leveling machines called screeds. The screeds started in the same spot and inched along in opposite directions around the oval's perimeter for nine-and-a-half hours. When they finally met, they had created a 7-inch (18-centimeter)-thick slab and used 1,100 cubic yards (840 cubic meters) of concrete. But the monolithic surface turned out to be imperfect; cooling tubes had moved below and caused irregularities that could slow down skaters. Twenty-two days after the original pouring, engineers tore up the oval. Then, on December 21, engineers filled the cooling tubes with water to keep them from shifting, and repoured the surface; the rink should be ready for the first spring trial runs.

REMOTE SENSING

Satellites designed to look at Earth have had limited use in the past, but new technologies have increased their capacity for taking high-resolution photographs from space. Leading the way is IKONOS, a privately owned satellite launched in September 1999. IKONOS is about the size and weight of a Volkswagen Beetle, it circles Earth every 98 minutes, and it can take black-and-white images with a resolution of 3 feet (1 meter) across or larger. During its first year in space, IKONOS photographed 9.2 million square miles (24 million square kilometers) of Earth's surface.

Satellite pictures can help engineers design efficient paths for pipelines; plot locations for wireless-communications towers; study traffic patterns; monitor crop failures, deforestation, and natural-disaster fallout; and scout project locations in foreign countries that have poor map data. Another promising technology in the remote sensing field is *lidar*—an airplane-mounted, radarlike system that makes three-dimensional maps by bouncing a laser beam off the ground below it.

Matthew Longabucco

COMMUNICATION TECHNOLOGY

Significant developments in 1999 and 2000 in communication technology included the growing residential use of digital-subscriber-line (DSL) and cable modems to access the Internet. Through 2000 and into 2001, wireless-communication technologies continued to gain general consumer acceptance in the electronics marketplace.

DSL AND CABLE MODEMS

The use of DSL technology boosts the capacity of copper phone lines, enabling Internet connections to be made at much faster speeds than with standard modems. Maximum download and upload speed can reach 256 kilobits per second (Kbps), as opposed to 56 Kbps for a standard modem. In 2000, DSL finally caught on with residential consumers—but for many disappointed users, the promised path to a fast Internet connection was not always as smooth as they would have liked.

Although the average monthly cost for residential DSL service had decreased to approximately $40 to $60 per month, many consumers found themselves unable to take advantage of the desirable technology, since a residence generally must be within 3 miles (5 kilometers) of a phone-switching center to receive DSL service. The availability of DSL also depends on the condition of phone lines both within a home and between the home and a central office, as older lines may hinder performance.

Nevertheless, it was estimated by the Yankee Group, a Boston-based technology-research firm, that there were some 1.5 million residential DSL subscribers by the end of 2000. This number was projected to increase to 8.4 million by 2004.

Also quickly growing in 2000 was the use of cable-modem technology. Cable modems can be significantly speedier than even DSL: downloads can reach 2,000 Kbps, with uploads taking place at speeds of up to 300 Kbps. The Yankee Group estimated that some 2.4 million cable modems were in use

in U.S. households by December 2000. As more people discover this steadily expanding technology, the number of users could increase to 9.6 million by 2004.

WIRELESS DEVELOPMENTS

The so-called Bluetooth standard—a wireless-networking method based on short-range radio frequencies—was first proposed in 1998 by several communications corporations: Ericsson, IBM, Intel, Nokia, and Toshiba. These corporations formed the Bluetooth Special Interest Group, which has since grown to include a total of nearly 2,000 companies worldwide.

The year 2000 saw a jump in the number of manufacturers and corporate users supporting the Bluetooth standard. Observers had expected Bluetooth technology to hit the mainstream sooner, but products have been plagued with various difficulties regarding compatibility with existing technologies, radio-frequency interference, and security concerns.

In 2000, Epson, Xerox, and Compaq demonstrated wireless printing that used the standard, allowing notebook computers to print to a printer located no more than 30 feet (9 meters) away from the wireless device. Printer manufacturer Hewlett-Packard announced in the fall that it planned to join with Ericsson to create a Bluetooth-based peripheral. IBM, Compaq, and Dell all plan to use the technology in notebook computers to be introduced in 2001. Another wireless solution, the Institute of Electrical and Electronics Engineers' IEEE 802.11b standard, was also being incorporated into various products, often in combination with the Bluetooth technology.

Unveiled at the 2001 Consumer Electronics Show held in Las Vegas was the "Infostick," by Sony—an expansion module using Bluetooth technology. It could be inserted into any PC, digital camera, or cellular telephone supporting Sony's Memory Stick module, and would allow wireless data transfer between these devices.

HIGH-TECH "MAGIC WANDS"

Someday soon, consumers may be able to pay for fast food and other purchases in seconds, using a high-tech "magic wand."

Speedpass, a technology in use since 1997 at ExxonMobil stations across the United States, is the first embodiment of this "magic-wand" technology—more formally known as radio-frequency identification (RFID). A Speedpass—usually a plastic tag affixed to a key ring or car window—contains a computer chip in which a unique customer-identification number is embedded. This number enables a scanner to link instantly to the customer's credit or debit account. Transactions using RFID technology can be authorized and completed in as little as five seconds, as opposed to about 30 seconds for credit-card transactions.

Seeing vast potential in RFID technology, ExxonMobil Corporation launched a joint test with McDonald's Corporation in April 2000 to see if the fast-food giant's customers would take to paying for their fries with the wave of a plastic tag. McDonald's has tested the Speedpass at nine outlets in the Chicago area. Customers apparently find the technology appealing, and ExxonMobil projects that there will be as many as 30 million Speedpass users by 2006. Franchisers are testing the technology at other fast-food outlets, and hope to extend its use to all types of retail outlets within the next few years. Although some industry analysts feel such predictions are overly optimistic, they do admit the technology has potential.

Robert C. Fiero, Jr., and Meghan O'Reilly Fiero

COMPUTERS

COMPUTING IN THE COURTROOM

Although the Internet in many ways has changed the way people interact, several companies, and even the Federal Bureau of Investigation (FBI), have learned that some old rules still apply. In April 2000, U.S. District Court Judge Thomas Penfield Jackson ruled that Microsoft, the world's largest software company, had violated the Sherman Antitrust Law. The ruling ended a case brought against Microsoft in May 1998 by the U.S. Department of Justice and attorneys general from 19 U.S. states and the District of Columbia. Jackson found that Microsoft had used anticompetitive methods to monopolize the Internet-browser market. Two months later, Jackson ruled that Microsoft be broken into two companies and regulated to prevent further anticompetitive behavior. Microsoft has appealed the decision. No one expects a final verdict anytime soon.

Two other companies planning on making money on the Internet went head-to-head with U.S. copyright law in court. In April, U.S. District Court Judge Jed Rakoff found that MP3.com had willfully violated copyright law with its "music locker" service called My.MP3.com. MP3.com had copied music from 80,000 compact discs (CDs) onto its databases, so listeners who owned any of these CDs could listen to that music through the on-line service. In response, five major record companies—Warner Music, EMI Music, BMG Entertainment, Sony Music, and Universal Music Group—sued MP3.com for copyright infringement.

Following Rakoff's decision, MP3.com reportedly paid four of the five companies $20 million each to settle. Universal, however, argued for much higher penalties, and it was November before MP3.com and Universal finally settled out of court for $53.4 million. MP3.com has restarted its service with a limited free version and a subscription service for larger users. However, on November 16, several smaller music companies followed up with a similar class-action complaint against MP3.com.

Napster, an on-line service that allows users to share and exchange MP3 files, also "faced the music" in court. Starting in 1999, artists, who included Metallica and Dr. Dre, sued Napster for encouraging illegal copying and distribution of their music. A U.S. federal court decided in July 2000 that Napster had infringed on the copyrights of the musicians, and ordered the company to close down. Although Napster stayed on-line through the appeals process, the company was fighting a losing battle. In February 2001, an appeals court ordered Napster to shut down while it settled the legal chal-

Shawn Fanning, the youthful founder of Napster, a controversial on-line song-swapping service, meets reporters after a U.S. federal court rules that Napster encourages illegal copying of copyrighted music.

lenges. In compliance with the decision, Napster installed software to block users from exchanging copyrighted songs.

The FBI's need to conduct investigations on the Internet ran headfirst into privacy concerns when word got out in July 2000 that the agency had created digital-wiretap software, nicknamed "Carnivore." Just like the wiretaps used to listen in on phone conversations, Carnivore allows law-enforcement officials to sniff out a targeted person's e-mail once the FBI has a warrant. However, the American Civil Liberties Union (ACLU) and Internet-privacy advocates alleged that the Carnivore software could abuse the access and snoop in on just about anybody's e-mail. To address these serious concerns, the U.S. Justice Department had an outside organization review Carnivore; the contracted review concluded that the software worked appropriately. Opponents, however, argue that the inspection was not thorough enough, and that it did not adequately address all relevant privacy issues.

INTERNET GROWING PAINS

The Internet experienced burgeoning growing pains in 2000. For starters, the Internet was running out of names. Internet domain names ending in .com, .org, and .net were growing scarce, so the organization that monitors Internet names, the Internet Corporation for Assigned Names and Numbers (ICANN), announced in mid-2000 a plan for defining new endings for Internet names by the beginning of 2001. ICANN asked for proposals from companies that wished to sponsor new endings, and in November, ICANN selected .aero, .biz, .coop, .info, .museum, .name, and .pro. The opportunity for registering domains with these endings was expected to begin in early 2001.

At the same time, many Internet businesses—better known as dot-com companies—had to close up shop when the Internet-based economy faced some harsh realities. Despite stock prices that had skyrocketed in 1999, many dot-coms had failed to make a profit. Hundreds of ventures launched in 1998 and 1999 during the Internet gold rush filed for bankruptcy, laid off employees, or were forced to close down altogether. Web-based retailers such as eToys.com, PlanetRX.com, Petopia.com, Pets.com, Mercata.com, FreeInternet.com, and many others crashed and burned in 2000. Even the popular Amazon.com and Yahoo! were having a difficult time managing in 2000 and early 2001.

Y2K NOT A PROBLEM

The most widely feared and potentially disastrous computer issue of the year 2000 was over in a second and caused barely a ripple. The Y2K problem, as it was called, harbored the potential for computers to think that the year 2000 was instead the year 1900 because old software abbreviated years in two-digit numbers and assumed that the first two digits were "19."

Billions of dollars were spent updating older software that would help to recognize the year 2000 correctly. The news media broadcast dire worst-case scenarios, going so far as to suggest that the world's electrical, transportation, financial, and communications systems were ripe for disaster, especially in several less-developed nations.

By the end of New Year's Day 2000, however, it was clear that none of the major Y2K fears, and very few of the minor ones, were coming true. This may have been because of the extensive effort and money that the world had spent to head off the Y2K problem. More surprisingly, a few minor Y2K problems popped up a year later, on January 1, 2001. It seems programmers had been so focused on fixing computer software for the year 2000 that they had not bothered to check it for any other year.

HARDWARE AND SOFTWARE

Despite being a rocky financial and litigious year for Internet and technology companies, computer technology continued to advance in 2000. Intel, the world's largest processor manufacturer, broke the gigahertz barrier when it released the first Pentium III chip that ran at 1 gigahertz (GHz), or performed 1 billion computer instructions per second. In November, Intel pushed the envelope still further with the Pentium 4, which can run even faster, at 1.5 GHz.

Intel also gained a new competitor in 2000. Transmeta Corporation unveiled its Crusoe processor in January. The Crusoe chip is compatible with Intel's popular processors, but consumes a small fraction of the power needed by a comparable Intel chip. For consumers, the Crusoe chip makes building a laptop or mobile computer able to run much longer on a single battery charge a reality.

Transmeta is also notable for being the employer of Linus Torvalds, the originator of the Linux open-source operating system. Linux, which is a variation of Unix, has emerged from being an upstart operating system to a serious competitor of Microsoft Windows. In mid-2000, Linux had a market share of 24 percent compared to the 36 percent claimed by Windows. Linux and Unix combined held 39 percent of the server market. And for server computers, Microsoft released Windows 2000 in February, but it is being adopted slowly.

On the other hand, Microsoft's operating systems run on nearly 90 percent of personal computers, and the company released a new Windows version for mobile, handheld computers. Microsoft's Pocket PC operating system is designed specifically for the popular personal digital assistants (PDAs) and other small, mobile computers.

Apple Computer continued to lead in computer design with its G4 Cube desktop and its newest PowerBook laptops—1 inch (2.5 centimeters) thick, with an outer casing of titanium. Apple also delivered a public beta release of its next-generation operating system, the long-awaited Mac OS X, released in March 2001. The Mac OS X combines the ease of use of its predecessor, the Mac OS, with advanced features under the hood from the Unix operating system that will make the Mac OS X almost crashproof.

For sheer computing power, the most powerful computer in 2000 was ASCI White, an IBM system at Lawrence Livermore National Laboratory, California, that can perform more than 12 trillion operations per second. The U.S. Department of Energy installed ASCI White to run simulations that will help test the reliability of nuclear weapons. And they are not stopping there. The Department of Energy has awarded Compaq Computer a contract to build a still more powerful computer to run more-detailed simulations, possibly replacing the need for underground nuclear testing. The computer, code-named "Q," will have almost 12,000 processors in a space equivalent to the size of five basketball courts, and will be capable of conducting 30 trillion calculations per second when it is operational in 2002.

David L. Hart

CONSUMER TECHNOLOGY

AT WORK

● *Look Out, Dick Tracy.* Fingerprinting has long been one of the most important tools for detectives, providing indisputable proof of a person's identity. As an identifier, the human iris is equally effective. What once seemed like wizardry from *Mission: Impossible* or *Star Trek* and completely out of reach for the everyday consumer is now readily available. Iridian Technologies, Inc., of Moorestown, New Jersey, and Geneva, Switzerland, has developed the Authenticam, the first iris-recognition camera available as a computer peripheral. It is a security windfall for those concerned with guarding their workstations, networks, and Internet access from unauthorized users. The Authenticam scans the human eye in less than two seconds and within a distance of only 20 inches (50 centimeters). The "iris print" is then run through a database in search of a match, just as it is in the movies.

● *Office Wear.* Levi Strauss & Co. of San Francisco, in collaboration with electronics manufacturer Philips, has developed what might soon be a sheer necessity for the cell-phone-toting, pager-hugging, MP3-listening executive—or teenager, for that matter. The new Levi's ICD+ jacket eliminates the need for 10 separate devices and 14 pockets—it has a cellular phone and MP3 player built right in; both are tucked away in small pockets and operated via remote control. The jacket features headphones and a microphone near the collar for easy, hands-free access, plus plenty of actual pockets for storing a variety of other devices.

● *High Technology.* Remember the days when pens were merely writing tools, with plastic caps perfect for gnawing on by pensive students? Well, those days are definitely over. The revolutionary Cross Convergence Ball-Point Pen from A.T. Cross, headquartered in Lincoln, Rhode Island, may look like a typical pen, but in reality, it is a translucent-blue writing instrument that integrates a wireless scanner. When swiped

The Goliath coaster at the Six Flags theme park in Los Angeles takes screaming passengers on a high-speed, three-minute tear along its 225-foot-tall track.

over a bar code on a product or in a magazine or catalog, the integrated scanner saves the code. The user can then simply upload the code to his or her computer via the pen's Optolink Coupler. Software included with the pen matches the bar-code information to the correct Internet address and sends consumers to that site. The pen can save up to 300 addresses.

AT HOME

● *So Long, Salmonella.* Kitchen sponges, despite their designated duty, are often less than pristine. In fact, *E. coli* and salmonella bacteria adhere to sponges long after the dishes are done. A near-perfect solution is now available. The Otres Kitchen Sponge Sanitizer uses ozone to eliminate up to 99.99 percent of bacteria. The sponge fits comfortably inside a small, soap-dish-sized container equipped with a fold-down lid. Once activated, electricity converts oxygen to ozone in the container. As the ozone becomes unstable, its extra oxygen molecules cling to bacteria, killing them off for good.

● *Open Sesame!* It is comforting to come home from an evening out to a well-lit, safe house. Stanley Works, headquartered in New Britain, Connecticut, has made that possible with the Stanley brand Welcome-Watch doors. The WelcomeWatch features a built-in, remote-controlled locking and lighting system. A handy key fob turns on the outside lights, unlocks the door, and illuminates those interior fixtures connected to the system—no more fishing around for the proper key. The fob's range is about 30 feet (9 meters), and it can operate two separate doors. Moreover, the door can be installed as an upgrade to any Stanley door system. The apparatus can also flash outside lights on and off in an emergency.

● *Bug Off.* Big Brother may or may not be watching, but consumers need not worry about that anymore, thanks to the Privatel 168-bit voice-encryption system from L-3 Communications Systems-East in Camden, New Jersey. The device—shaped like a regular phone—protects calls from being intercepted by a third party. It is rather simple to use: when both the caller and receiver press the "secure" button on their Privatel devices, any subsequent conversation becomes absolutely indecipherable to "spies."

● *Not Your Dad's Recliner.* Billed as an "e-cliner," the innovative Explorer chair from La-Z-Boy Incorporated (headquartered in Michigan) and Microsoft WebTV Networks, Mountain View, California, is a recliner fit for the new millennium. Weary ones can kick back, relax, and connect to the Internet from a comfy chair. The left arm of the recliner houses a foldout table embedded with a removable Sony wireless keyboard, and a Sony WebTV Plus Internet receiver that accesses the Internet directly through a television set; e-mail and instant-messaging capabilities, simplified VCR recording, and interactive television programs are also accommodated by the "electronic armrest." The recliner's right armrest conceals a beverage holder and a storage area with space for remotes, videos, and magazines.

AT PLAY

● *Shoot the Moon.* Driveway hoops will now serve players long into the night.

A 72-volt battery powers GEM, an automobile designed by a DaimlerChrysler subsidiary. If fuel costs continue to soar, electric vehicles may become the cars of choice for motorists.

Huffy's new Twilight basketballs and footballs, from Huffy Sports, Sussex, Wisconsin, are the first balls to glow from the inside. A light-emitting diode (LED) along the ball's inner wall is powered by a trio of replaceable 3-volt batteries that power the single LED for about three months. When the Sun sets, a standard inflating needle is used to illuminate the ball, which will stay aglow during play. The inner glow diminishes once the ball is inactive for five consecutive minutes.

● *Goliath Wins This One.* Engineers know that thrill seekers are always seeking the next great ride. It looks as if it has arrived. Coney Island's Cyclone is a swim in the pool compared to the Goliath roller coaster at Six Flags Magic Mountain in Los Angeles. Measured as the world's tallest and fastest amusement-park ride, the Goliath pulls passengers up a 26-story climb, and drops them more than 250 feet (76 meters) at a 61-degree angle at speeds of up to 85 miles (137 kilometers) per hour.

● *Ignoring Winter.* Completely redefining expectations for a "winter jacket," Italian fashion company Corpo Nove incorporated National Aeronautics and Space Administration (NASA) technology into its new cold-weather shells. When insulating one of their multimillion-dollar space probes, NASA used a material called aerogel, which can withstand temperatures from −50° F to +3,000° F (−45° C to +1,650° C). Corpo Nove has made this space-age product available to the consumer by designing the jacket with aerogel as its insulator. This lightweight overcoat is made to order.

TRAVEL

● *Ready for Takeoff.* "Folks, we are waiting for a few planes to clear the runway. It will just be about 20 minutes." These dreaded words may become a thing of the past now that the National Aerospace Laboratory of Japan is designing a passenger aircraft equipped with tilt wings. This innovation means that propellers can reposition themselves toward the sky during takeoff—similar to a helicopter's—and then rotate forward during flight. While there are no specific production plans as yet, designers are encouraged by the U.S. military's special-operations aircraft, Osprey, which applied similar propeller designs. The Japanese passenger craft features a wide, winglike body designed to increase lift and provide generous seating space.

● *The Sunday Driver's Delight.* While it looks like an egg on wheels, the GEM vehicle, created by Global Electric Motorcars, LLC, a DaimlerChrysler subsidiary based in

Sony's lightweight and portable Network Walkman can store up to 64MB worth of MP3 files, or 80 minutes of music—a remarkable amount in such a tiny package.

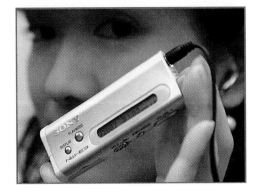

Fargo, North Dakota, is the real thing on the road. It runs on a 72-volt battery, and coasts along at speeds of up to 25 miles (40 kilometers) per hour. The car features two seats, seat belts, a safety-glass windshield and wiper, head and tail lights, and, according to its designers, rolls along at a cost of less than 1 cent per mile (1.6 kilometers). The GEM is legal in 32 states, but do not expect to see it tearing down the slow lane of the interstate just yet—it is allowed only on roads with a speed limit of 35 miles (56 kilometers) per hour or less.

PORTABLE WONDERS

• **The Essence of the Sony Walkman.** It used to be that the Sony Walkman was about as portable as a brick, but Sony has designed a little number that is less invasive than a wallet. The Network Walkman does not use tapes or CDs; instead, it comes equipped with 64MB of embedded memory, able to store more than an hour of music. A fresh AAA battery powers the unit for about five hours of MP3 listening. Weighing in at 1.6 ounces (45 grams), and looking like the offspring of a remote control, the Network Walkman is perfect for runners—or anybody too busy to tote around a brick.

• **Check the Coordinates, Chewie!** The era of bulky, foldout road maps has ended. Owners of the Palm

III and Palm V PalmPilots from Palm, Inc. have finally found a trusted copilot. Rand McNally's new StreetFinder GPS (Global Positioning System) snap-on receiver monitors an individual's exact location to within yards, and displays detailed street maps on its screen. If its user becomes lost, the StreetFinder will promptly map out and display precise directions.

• **Breathalyzer for Bad Breath.** Why did the person who was on a promising date hit the road? Could it have had something to do with those onion rings at dinner? Hint: next time you're cupping your hand over your mouth in an attempt to check your breath, consider using the BreathAlert from Tanita, headquartered in Tokyo. This handheld, pocket-sized device tests the quality of one's breath by measuring sulfur compounds released by bacteria in the mouth. The BreathAlert is equipped with a graphic display that tells the whole truth about slight, moderate, or strong halitosis.

• **Watch It.** Samsung Electronics Co., Ltd.'s Watch Phone—the lightest and smallest wireless terminal ever produced—looks like a small wristwatch, and yet it houses a mobile telephone. Besides exceptional portability, Samsung's Watch Phone offers a speakerphone, a headphone jack, and a custom-colored backlight in green, blue, pink, or yellow, among other colors. An innovative voice-command feature even allows users to dial telephone numbers in their electronic address book and to operate the Watch Phone through spoken commands.

Marc E. Sessler

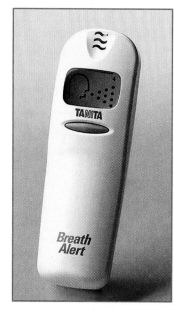

Electronics

Toying with Light

Computer chips that run on light instead of electricity came closer to becoming reality with three developments in 2000.

Electronic devices use the flow of electrons to move energy from one place to another and to harness that energy for lights, clock radios, and other appliances. In computer chips, electrons also move and store information through complex circuitry. But even microscopic electronic switches take up some space, and engineers are running out of room for any more of these switches on today's computer chips.

In a determined effort to use light in circuits, physicists are discovering some surprising ways to stop and store particles of light, called photons, to steer the photons around corners, and to use them in tiny on-off switches. Together, these latest developments are the building blocks engineers need to create the circuits used in tiny computer chips. When photons replace electrons in such circuits, researchers use the term "photonics" to describe the applications.

Engineers know how to stop and restart an electron, but in January 2001, two groups of physicists managed to slow light to a dead stop and restart it. A Harvard University research team led by Lene Hau, and a second group led by Ronald Walsworth and Mikhail Lukin at the Harvard-Smithsonian Center for Astrophysics in Cambridge, Massachusetts, both managed to do this at about the same time using different methods. When Hau's team shot a photon into a cloud of ultracold atoms, the photon dimmed and appeared to get snuffed out. But by flashing a laser into the cloud, the photon emerged at full speed and brightness. Hau is already planning to make a light-stopping device the size of a human fingernail. The Walsworth-and-Lukin team also trapped the light in a cloud of atoms, but they did not use such cold temperatures. In their experiment, only half of the stopped light was recovered from the system.

Stopping and restarting light solves part of the circuitry problem, but to use light in photonic circuits, engineers must also be able to turn a photon. A team led by John Joannopoulos at the Massachusetts Institute of Technology (MIT) in Cambridge designed a new type of coaxial cable—the type used to carry cable television signals—that can efficiently send light over long distances and even turn around sharp bends. Regular coaxial cable is good for carrying radio waves and microwaves, but not for transmitting visible light.

The MIT team's innovation was to design the cable from dielectric materials. Dielectric materials are insulators—they do not conduct electricity. Layers of dielectric materials can be fashioned into a mirror that reflects all of the light that hits it. In addition to a coaxial cable, a tube of the mirror, or waveguide, can also be used as a device to steer light. Conventional waveguides for visible light need to make wide turns so light does not escape. MIT's waveguide can turn light quickly in small spaces, which is critical for designing optical chips.

Other researchers have designed materials that can both steer photons and be used as photonic on-off switches. Sajeev John and his team at the University of Toronto invented a crystal material through which only certain wavelengths of light can travel. By applying an electrical field to the crystal, the researchers can stop all traveling light by turning the switch off or by steering the light around a corner.

So You Want to Be in Pictures?

The incredible shrinking world of electronics is dramatically changing how people use computers to solve problems in science, health, and everyday life. Take, for example, the tiny camera and transmitter that Given Imaging Ltd., in Israel, has developed. At just over 1 inch (2.5 centimeters) long, this pill that encapsulates them can be a rough swallow, but afterwards, it can take an invaluable ride through a patient's digestive tract. On its journey, the coated camera snaps two pictures per second and transmits them to a receiver attached to the subject's belt. In just a day or two, a doctor can download images from the receiver and create a video of the amazing trip.

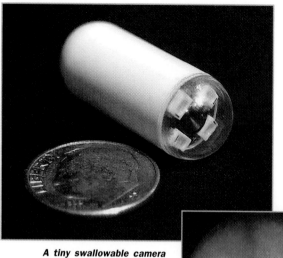

A tiny swallowable camera (above) can transmit an image of an ulcer (right) or other abnormality to help doctors diagnose various disorders of the digestive tract.

The camera-pill is now undergoing trials through the U.S. Food and Drug Administration (FDA). If approved for clinical use, the device could provide more-accurate internal-body images than the only alternative procedure, the endoscopy. More than 8 million endoscopic procedures are performed every year. During an endoscopy, the patient is sedated while a doctor threads a fiber-optic cable through the intestines. Unlike the endoscopic fiber-optic cable that never reaches two-thirds of the small intestine, the camera-pill travels through the entire digestive tract.

It is easy to imagine future offsprings of the pill-sized device replacing other invasive medical procedures. Future devices might deliver a dose of medication to a targeted spot inside the body or use miniature scissors to take a tissue sample that could otherwise be reached only with surgery.

MOLECULAR ELECTRONICS

Although engineers would like to use light instead of electrons in computer chips and other circuits, they still need roomfuls of equipment to control a single photon with today's level of technology. Scientists are trying many different approaches to make conventional electronic circuits smaller and smaller. The space problem is not so much

the tiny electrons; chip designers are simply running out of room on the chips for additional wires and switches.

Consequently, scientists are experimenting with building electronic circuits out of even smaller parts—individual molecules, some with as few as a dozen atoms. If the experiments are successful, computer chips could hold 10,000 times as many electronic switches within the same amount of space.

The leading candidates are carbon nanotubes, DNA strands, and also custom-tailored molecules. Chemists James M. Tour of Rice University, Houston; Mark Reed of Yale University, New Haven, Connecticut; and their colleagues have created molecules of only a dozen atoms that behave like electronic switches when stretched between two electrical connectors. When the voltage between the connectors is 2 volts, the molecular switches turn on. Above or below 2 volts, the switches remain off. The wires on a typical computer chip are bigger than those needed for molecule-sized circuitry. Therefore, scientists now need to find a way to construct smaller wires.

Molecular wires and switches might be made from carbon nanotubes. Carbon nanotubes are constructed from pure-carbon atoms arranged into hexagons and formed into long, seamless tubes, millions of atoms long. It would take 50,000 nanotubes laid side by side to reach the width of a human hair, yet each tube would be 100 times stronger than the same amount of steel. A single nanotube molecule can conduct electricity as a metal such as copper does or as a semiconductor such as silicon does. Conductors and semiconductors are the ideal materials to make computer circuits, so nanotubes have the potential to serve double duty.

Cees Dekker of the Delft University of Technology in the Netherlands, Alex Zettl of the University of California at Berkeley, and Charles Lieber of Harvard are a few of the researchers exploring different ways to build circuits from nanotubes. Dekker is designing circuits as if the nanotubes were tiny wires; Zettl is attempting to create circuits from a jumbled pile of nanotubes; and Lieber is using neatly stacked, crisscrossed layers of tubes. John Cumings, a graduate student who works in Zettl's laboratory, has also built nearly frictionless bearings and tiny springs out of nanotubes nested within one another. Combined with their electrical properties, the ability to use nanotubes as springs or bearings suggests that incredibly useful small machines or tools could be built from them.

Deoxyribonucleic acid, or DNA, which makes up the genetic material inside every cell of living things, is also being examined as a potential electrical component. DNA is made from two strands of amino acids that spiral around each other, with the amino acids in one half attaching exactly to complementary amino acids in the other half, fitting somewhat like a zipper's teeth. The genetic blueprints for a living creature are recorded in strands of DNA with billions of amino acids, but scientists can also fabricate DNA strands with specific sequences.

Bernard Yurke of Bell Laboratories, Murray Hill, New Jersey, and Andrew Turberfield from the University of Oxford in England created molecule-sized tweezers from DNA. They created two strands of DNA that would zip together at one end, but not at the other. When mixed in a test tube, the strands formed a "V." To close the tweezers, a third added "bonding" strand latches onto the loose ends and zips them together. A fourth "anti-bonding" strand removes the latch, opening the tweezers.

All of these possibilities face a common obstacle: the pieces are so small that researchers cannot use traditional methods to turn them into circuits. Therefore, all of the research teams are looking at ways for these pieces to assemble themselves into circuits or tiny machines. DNA has the advantage of naturally self-assembling from complementary strands; scientists just have to specify the strands correctly. What remains unknown is how to use chemical reactions to get other molecules and nanotubes to assemble themselves into circuits.

David L. Hart

ENDANGERED SPECIES

There were some encouraging developments in 2000, but victories are tenuous when weighed against alarmingly sad statistics. The U.S. Fish and Wildlife Service delisted 16 species from endangered status in 2000, either because they had recovered, or because new information was discovered to show they were no longer at risk. Among these were the bald eagle, the gray wolf, and the gray whale. But in Africa, following a six-year survey conducted by the Wildlife Conservation Society (WCS) of New York, the primate subspecies known as Miss Waldron's red colobus (*Procolobus badius waldroni*) was pronounced extinct due to hunting by humans and disruption of habitat. The last confirmed sighting of this primate, discovered in the rain forests of Ghana in 1933, occurred more than 20 years ago. It was the only primate to vanish in the 20th century, although many others are considered critically threatened. In view of this loss, the World Wildlife Fund (WWF) applauded the U.S. Senate's passing of the Great Ape Conservation Act, which became law in October 2000.

Dedicated scientists and conservationists who try to slow the dwindling of species are for the most part grim in their predictions. Estimates vary, but out of a total of between 10 million and 30 million species—includ-

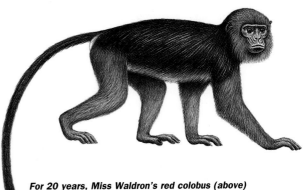

For 20 years, Miss Waldron's red colobus (above) was unseen in its habitat—West Africa's rain-forest canopies—before finally being declared extinct.

ing everything from mammals, fish, and birds to reptiles, insects, plants, and fungi—it has been claimed that worldwide perhaps 100 species per day are becoming extinct. Every time a forest is logged, a field lost to development, a river dammed, a wooded area cleared, or a road or house built, an ecosystem is disrupted. Any species peculiar to that ecosystem that is unable to adapt or find a new habitat may disappear forever. Although they differ on exact numbers, conservationists and biologists agree that radical changes in managing the environment globally are critically needed. If changes in both public attitude and economic/political influence are not immediate, scientists believe it is probable that Earth could lose nearly half of its living species by 2050.

IUCN Launches 2000 Red List

The International Union for Conservation of Nature and Natural Resources (IUCN), better known as the World Conservation Union, based in Gland, Switzerland, includes 112 national government agencies and 735 nongovernment groups. The IUCN Species Survival Commission, established to assess the conservation status of all species, set up an international notation system in 1994 called the Categories of Threat. Using defined categories, the IUCN then launched the IUCN Red List in 1996. For the first time, all known mammal and bird species were centrally assessed, drawing on worldwide data from governments, private groups, and research institutions. The Red List of Threatened Plants followed in 1997. The IUCN brought out the 2000 Red List in September, the first single record of all known animals and plants, with assessments for more than 18,000 species to be updated each year. The 2000 IUCN Red List records 11,046 plants and animals facing a high risk of extinction, in almost all cases as a result of human activities. This list includes the 200 animal species classified as "most critically endangered" in the past four years. The 5,611 plant species appearing on the 2000 IUCN Red List are believed to represent only a fraction of those at risk, since the IUCN estimates that only 4 percent of all plant species have so far been classified and evaluated.

Whale Hunting

Since the start of the International Whaling Commission's 1986 moratorium on whale hunting, much controversy has raged over how best to enforce it—amid allegations of breaches by such whaling countries as Japan, Norway, and Russia. In spite of the moratorium, Japan has continued to hunt whales, exploiting a loophole in the law that allows for a limited take of whales for scientific research. In August 2000, Japan expanded its whale hunt to include two previously protected species of whale: the sperm whale and the Bryde's whale. The whales killed by the Japanese fleet—up to now, officially confined to about 450 of the smaller, minke whales per season—are in fact being sold to the luxury-food market. In spite of displeasure expressed by the United States, the United Kingdom, and 14 other nations, the summer 2000 hunt brought in more than 80 protected whales—and Japan announced that it intends to conduct another such hunt in the summer of 2001. Conservationists now fear that other nations interested in whaling are poised to follow if Japan suffers no repercussions. The International Whaling Commission has been trying since 1994 to draft an acceptable Revised Management Scheme as a proposed replacement for its compromised moratorium, but to no avail.

Black-footed Ferrets Rescued

The black-footed ferret, on endangered-species lists since the 1960s and feared extinct in 1980, suffered from the loss or disruption of its prairie habitat and aggressive control by ranchers of prairie dogs, the ferret's primary prey. In 1981, however, a small population of ferrets was discovered near Meeteetse, Wyoming. But when epidemics of sylvatic plague and canine distemper threatened to wipe out the colony in 1986, Wyoming's Game and Fish Department took the surviving animals into captivity, inoculated and quarantined them, and then placed them in captive-breeding programs. One such program that is proving particularly successful is based at the Smithsonian Conservation and Research Center in Virginia, where the ferrets are bred naturally and/or artificially inseminated, with particular attention given to maintaining as diverse a gene pool as possible to minimize the weakening effect of inbreeding. The resulting litters are raised in open—albeit scrupulously protected—pens, in as close to a wild habitat as possible. Only when a colony becomes strong and well conditioned, is it transferred to a wild habitat.

In 2000, the U.S. Fish and Wildlife Service reintroduced black-footed ferrets from this program into the wild along the Cheyenne River in South Dakota on Sioux tribal land. Together, biologists, members of the tribe, and other agency partners will monitor the progress of the freed animals, while the captive-breeding programs continue to build up numbers for future release.

Oyamel Firs and Monarchs

As scientists continue researching endangered species, they are finding more evidence every day that supports what conservationists have been saying for years: species are linked, and if one or more of the species in an ecosystem become critically endangered, all of the other species feel the impact. Indeed, it is essential to pay attention to the extinction of a species, as it may be a warning that the whole fabric of an ecosystem is at risk.

Such is the case with monarch butterflies—crucially important pollinators across vast expanses of the United States and Mexico. The amazing monarchs begin life in various locations in North America, but all of them migrate thousands of miles in the autumn in order to winter in cool mountainous areas, pollinating as they go, and clinging by the thousands to a particular type of fir tree. Some migrate to California, but the majority head for forests of *Abies religiosa*, or oyamel trees, a species of balsam fir found in the highlands of Mexico. Scientists are not entirely sure what makes these particular oyamel forests so desirable to the monarchs. They do know that the location has optimal climatic conditions—cold but not too cold. The forests also protect the butterflies during hibernation, and provide proximity to water and nectar in the highlands' early spring. During the long winter months, the monarchs' metabolism is slowed by the cold, thereby conserving energy. While clinging to the rough bark of the oyamel firs, the butterflies are protected under sheltering branches from wind and snow. But if the forest is thinned and loses its density, the monarchs will be vulnerable to the elements.

In 1977, Lincoln Brower, Ph.D., a butterfly biologist from Sweet Briar College in Sweet Briar, Virginia, noticed that logging had begun in these oyamel forests. Brower has documented, with aerial photographs taken in the 1970s, 1983, and 1999, how the forests have suffered increasing fragmenta-

Thousands of monarch butterflies cling to the bark of an oyamel tree, instinctively seeking refuge from the cold as they migrate to Mexico to hibernate.

tion from logging and clear-cutting despite a decree from Mexico's president designating the area a protected preserve. Brower's photographs, recently submitted to the Mexican government as part of a study, showed that 44 percent of the forests have been damaged or destroyed, and that only 90 percent of the area supposedly designated a preserve still remains. As a result, the World Wildlife Fund and the Fondo Mexicano para la Conservación de la Naturaleza (FMCN) have worked together in an effort to establish the Monarch Butterfly Biosphere Reserve. It will reinforce the existing preserve by reconnecting the now-separated butterfly sanctuaries with a contiguous corridor, compensating the local people for their lost logging rights, and enlisting their aid in reforestation efforts. The private Packard Foundation donated a $5 million trust fund to support long-term conservation of this essential monarch winter sanctuary.

JAGUARS REIGN AT CALAKMUL

Since Mexico's Calakmul Biosphere Reserve was first established in 1989, the reigning species on its 1.8 million acres (729,000 hectares) has been the mysterious and endangered Mexican jaguar (*Panthera onca*). Until recently, this magnificent big cat has remained elusive and unknowable. Now, ecologists, biologists, veterinarians, and others associated with a major conservation effort at Calakmul hope to use data collected from a study of the world's third-largest cat to shore up the species' declining numbers. The principle that governs the Calakmul jaguar project is somewhat paradoxical—hunting jaguars in order to save jaguars. On the other hand, the project's execution is much more complex.

Gerardo Ceballos, an ecologist and professor at Universidad Nacional Autónoma de México (UNAM), who has also served as codirector of the Calakmul jaguar project for several years, and Carlos Manterola, director general of Unidos para la Conservación, lead the ambitious undertaking. Their plan includes fitting the few remaining jaguars that inhabit the remote Maya heartland area with radio collars. Then the jaguars can be tracked, and information on their social behavior and habitat requirements can be analyzed.

Vital to the conservation plan are teams of hunters (generally local men) who, led by trained dogs, charge through the rain forests after fleeing jaguars. However, these hunters are not killing jaguars. As their dogs close in on a sleek, spotted cat, team members move close enough to shoot a sedative dart and fit the animal with a radio collar. Since the project's inception, more jaguars have been collared at Calakmul than in any other study. The collared animals are monitored several times a week via tall radio towers high atop hills and by aerial surveying. Researchers learn about their territorial range, breeding seasons, movement patterns, and social interactions. Pumas have been included in the study for the added dimension of learning how the two cats share a habitat. There are an estimated 240 to 480 jaguars in Calakmul, or one cat for every 6 to 11.5 square miles (16 to 30 square kilometers).

Jaguars once ran free through the southwestern United States, from Louisiana to California (passing through Mexico), but their range has slowly yet drastically fragmented. The cats have been wiped out by predator-control killing in the U.S. Southwest. They are no longer found in El Salvador and Uruguay, and are nearly extinct in several other Latin American countries. Similarly, hunting and habitat destruction have caused the jaguar to largely disappear in northern Mexico. Although jaguars have lost much of their original habitats in the United States, Mexico, Central America, and South America, they still maintain a stronghold in the Amazon Basin and the Pantanal—an immense area of wetlands shared by Brazil, Bolivia, and Paraguay. The few reserves that do exist, however, will not guarantee the species' survival if the jaguar's habitats continue to diminish outside protected areas.

PRESERVING ECOSYSTEM NETWORKS

Botanists, biologists, zoologists, and environmental scientists claim to have gathered conclusive evidence that in order to preserve endangered species, it is crucial to protect entire habitats and ecosystems. David Hawksworth, former director of the International Mycological Institute, Egham, England, estimates that every time one plant becomes extinct, at least 15 other organisms also vanish. As a result, concerted efforts are being initiated to protect not only the large forests, prairies, oceans, and wetlands, but also to reclaim as many as possible of the networks of smaller, diverse but interwoven ecosystems. This includes native plant and animal life that suffers from or is eradicated by urban development and factory farming, or is degraded by influxes of nonnative species that have taken aggressive hold. As of June 2000, out of a total 738 plants listed with the U.S. Fish and Wildlife Service as threatened or endangered, scientists have developed and received approval for recovery plans for 530 of them.

Additionally, scientists are training specialists to work with farmers to restore land that has been depleted or stripped by chemical fertilizers, pesticides, and overfarming. One way is to replant the native vegetation in the areas around where the crops are being cultivated. It has been found that certain native species planted near crops will attract insect and bird life that, rather than undermining the crop, assist the farmer by feeding on crop pests. Alternatives, such as pesticides and bioengineering pose grave dangers to more than the targeted pests. There is growing concern that the use of genetically altered corn could have a devastating effect on butterflies. For example, monarch caterpillars can die by ingesting toxins from the corn plant's pollen that settles on their favored milkweed.

There are many regional programs under way to plant highway verges and median dividers with native plants and wildflowers in order to replenish at least a bit of the disturbed ecosystems. It is especially helpful to migrating birds and butterflies if at least a chain of supportive habitat can be maintained along the routes they travel. With a similar end in sight, the National Audubon Society sponsors efforts to assist people in rebuilding their land after clear-cutting or chemicals have wiped out any semblance of a working ecosystem. Native ground cover, trees, flowering plants, and shrubs attract and support naturally occurring wildlife that is displaced as human habitation spreads out farther and farther. Rather than causing an influx of pests, such a renewed habitat tends to foster a better self-regulating balance of native species.

Cassia Farkas

ENERGY

OIL

Gasoline and heating-oil prices continued to rise in 2000, to $34 a barrel—the highest crude-oil prices in a decade. The Organization of Petroleum Exporting Countries (OPEC) had reduced production in response to 1998's low price of $10 a barrel; but, as the world's supply shrank, demand from Asia grew. Worldwide refinery capacity and exploratory drilling, which both had been cut back when oil prices were low, lagged behind as well. Nevertheless, Americans drove as much as ever in 2000, and continued buying energy-inefficient automobiles and sport-utility vehicles (SUVs).

Of particular concern was the price of heating oil in the Northeast; the U.S. Department of Energy predicted that home-heating costs for the winter of 2000–2001 would increase an average of $200 per household. To help offset escalating consumer costs, in September, President Clinton released 30 million barrels of oil from the nation's 570-million-barrel Strategic Petroleum Reserve.

Meanwhile, plans moved forward for a major oil pipeline in the Caspian Sea region. Seven oil companies began planning the pipeline, which would connect Baku, Azerbaijan, to the Mediterranean port of Ceyhan, Turkey. Planning also began for another pipeline, from Chad to Cameroon. In Angola, oil companies bid for the rights to offshore reserves despite the fact that they still lack the technology it will take to actively pursue them.

U.S. President George W. Bush has also endorsed an energy plan that would open oil drilling in Alaska's Arctic National Wildlife Refuge, a move environmentalists strongly oppose. On the other hand, supporters point to the economic security that comes with producing up to 1 million barrels of oil a day domestically.

The best news of the year came from the U.S. Geological Survey (USGS), which revised its estimate of the world's oil reserves upward to 649 billion barrels—a 20 percent increase from its last published figure.

NATURAL GAS

Prices for natural gas skyrocketed in 2000, to $5 per million British thermal units (BTUs)—the highest price in 15 years. Many U.S. electricity plants and home-owning consumers had slowly committed to gas, but low oil prices discouraged exploration of further gas resources. When oil prices rose, the demand for gas followed, pushing drilling to capacity in fields already past their prime. Strained U.S. resources cannot be supplemented much by imports, since natural-gas production is overwhelmingly domestic. Overseas transport of gas requires an expensive liquefaction process, whereas domestic gas (including imports from Canada) is transported through an extensive pipeline network. Household consumers in the largely gas-dependent Midwest were expected to face a 44-percent price increase.

CALIFORNIA POWER CRISIS

The year's most startling energy news came from California, where the deregulation of electricity resulted in an expensive and as-yet-unresolved fiasco. The state's deregulation process began with a 1996 law designed to foster free-market competition among electricity providers. According to the plan, consumers would choose from hundreds of provider companies, while the existing utilities—Pacific Gas and Electric (PG&E) and Southern California Edison—would maintain the 40,000 miles (64,000 kilometers) of transmission lines that distribute power. According to policy makers, the competition would then lower rates and provide all consumers with the opportunity to choose providers committed to environmentally responsible production.

But the hundreds of companies that were to provide the competition did not materialize; investors were waiting to see what would happen in the newly charted territory of deregu-lation. Only about 10 companies, mostly from out-of-state, bought the utilities' old plants and started selling power. Then, in August, heat waves suddenly threatened the power grid that serves 24 million California residents. What happened? An unforeseen surge in California's economy, centered primarily in electricity-hungry, high-technology and Internet companies, increased demand for power. Meanwhile, no new plants had been built in the state for a decade (one goal of deregulation was to create the incentive to build new plants). As demand increased on a limited supply, the few existing providers found that they could withhold their power from the California Power Exchange, where prices are set, until the California Independent System Operator (CalISO, which maintains the state's grid) was forced to pay high prices to keep the system operational.

Consumer electric bills doubled, then tripled. PG&E and Edison, forced to make up the rising costs of power, plunged $12 billion into debt. The federal government had to force the generating companies to continue selling power to the beleaguered utilities. Finally, in early 2001, there simply wasn't enough power to maintain the grid. CalISO went to a precarious Stage 3 alert, instituting rolling blackouts that denied

In mid-January, a Santa Ana, California, retail establishment found itself lit only by emergency lights and flashlights when one in a series of "rolling blackouts" left the area temporarily without electricity.

power to more than half a million customers at any given time. Traffic signals and medical equipment were carefully maintained, as schools, businesses, and residences were forced to accept the first mandatory cuts since World War II. Government officials pleaded for conservation measures, while California spent $45 million a day buying energy from other states. By late spring, no solution had been formulated, although proponents of deregulation maintained that the system would work eventually. True or not, 25 states, all of which had looked to California for guidance as they, too, moved toward deregulation, now saw the fiasco as a prime example of what not to do.

ALTERNATIVE SOURCES

Promising research emerged in 2000 to create cost-efficient fuel cells—devices that change chemical energy into electrical energy. A Japanese firm introduced a cell that runs on natural gas and an oxidant, but the most-recent efforts have concentrated on developing a cell that would use hydrogen—one of Earth's most abundant elements.

Until hydrogen fuel cells are made efficient, automobile manufacturers are betting on hybrid cars that use gasoline motors to charge electric batteries. Simultaneously, the federal government is pursuing its goals for cleaner emissions by continuing to subsidize production of corn, soybeans, and other products that can be used to create alternative fuels. A new bill has been signed to offer economic incentives to companies willing to invest in producing ethanol, biodiesel, and other green fuels.

Advances in energy efficiency in 2000 also included the development of microwave lightbulbs with long-life potential. Additionally, a new composite containing "nanomagnets"—8 nanometer-wide particles embedded in a solid matrix that can turn freely with changes in the direction of a magnetic field—could make transformers at electricity substations significantly more efficient. And new solar collectors are being introduced that gather visible and nonvisible light to provide more heat, light, and electricity than earlier solar cells.

Matthew Longabucco

ENVIRONMENT

ENVIRONMENT MELTDOWN

During the summer of 2000, tourists cruising the Arctic Ocean aboard a Russian icebreaker were startled to find a patch of open water at the normally ice-covered North Pole. Their alarm led to a flurry of press reports warning that the polar ice cap was melting. In fact, summertime gaps in the polar ice pack are not unusual. But there is plenty of evidence that the Arctic region has grown steadily warmer in recent decades—and is actually warmer than it has been at any time in the past 400 years—according to researchers who have studied the region's climate. Measurements taken by submarines show that about 40 percent of the ice cap has melted away since 1958. The Arctic permafrost (the permanently frozen earth that underlies Arctic land regions) has indeed begun to thaw. At the opposite pole, Antarctic ice has been melting, too. And researchers have noted shrinking glaciers in mountain ranges all around the world, from the Andes of Peru to the Himalayas of Tibet.

The widespread melting was among a number of signs that raised concern about global warming during 2000. Worldwide, the year was the fifth warmest on record; all 10 of the warmest years on record have occurred since 1982. The climate change has been linked to an atmospheric buildup of carbon dioxide, methane, and other so-called greenhouse gases (gases that act like the glass in a greenhouse, trapping heat from the Sun). Most scientists agree that humans are largely responsible for the greenhouse effect—massive amounts of carbon dioxide are released through the burning of gasoline, oil, coal, and other fossil fuels, while methane is produced in farming, mainly by rice fields and cattle.

Late in the year, a United Nations (UN) report predicted that average temperatures might rise anywhere from 2° to nearly 11° F (1° to nearly 6° C) in the next century. A separate forecast prepared for the U.S. Congress predicted that average temperatures in the United States might rise 5° to 10° F (3° to 6° C) in the next 100 years. The effects of global warming are being seen first at the poles, researchers say. And because Earth's poles help drive the global climate, changes there will have widespread repercussions. Melting polar ice will cause sea levels to rise worldwide, and warming temperatures will change ocean currents, prompting shifts in weather patterns. For some areas, the results may well be devastating.

Rising sea levels will flood low-lying islands and coastal areas. Climate-related disasters such as droughts, floods, and violent storms are expected to increase. Plant and animal species may die out as climate changes destroy their habitats. Malaria and other tropical diseases may spread. And changing rainfall patterns are likely to affect water supplies and crop yields, in some places severely enough to force people to move in search of a more favorable climate. Many of these effects are expected to hit hardest in developing nations, which are least prepared to deal with such extremes.

In 1997, the United States and about 100 other countries signed the Kyoto Protocol, an agreement aimed at reducing emissions of greenhouse gases. However, the signers have not agreed upon a formula for cutting the levels of gases. Negotiators met several times in an effort to firm up the pact, without success. Then, early in his term, President George W. Bush withdrew U.S. support for the treaty, citing several of its provisions as not being in the U.S. public interest.

VANISHING CORAL REEFS
Global warming was one factor blamed during 2000 for ongoing damage to coral reefs worldwide. A report released in December by the U.S. government and the Global Coral Reef Monitoring Network (GCRMN) said that more than one-fourth of the world's coral reefs have been lost to a combination of rising water temperatures, pollution, overfishing, and other threats. If reefs are not protected, the report's authors warned, 70 percent may be gone within the next 50 years.

Coral reefs play a key role in the chain of ocean life, providing habitats for 25 percent of all known types of ocean plants and animals. They also help shelter many islands

Coral reefs that take centuries to grow can be wiped out instantly by human thoughtlessness. If not protected, 70 percent of reefs could be gone in 50 years.

and some mainland coasts from the erosive effects of the sea. The reefs are built over the centuries by colonies of coral polyps, tiny animals that leave behind hard limestone skeletons when they die. Each generation of polyps builds on the skeletons of preceding generations, and so the reefs grow. But since the mid-1980s, reefs—and the life-forms that depend on them for survival—have been dying.

Warmer-than-usual ocean temperatures are one cause. Coral polyps are sensitive to temperature, and when the water is too warm, they "bleach" (lose their color), stop reproducing, and ultimately die. In 1998, the worst year on record, bleaching killed 16 percent of reefs worldwide. In parts of the western Pacific, 90 percent of the corals in shallow waters died. In addition, research indicates that coral growth slows when levels of atmospheric carbon dioxide are high. Reefs have also been damaged by pollution—by oil and other toxic materials spilled into the water by ships, and by runoff from land that carries sediments, fertilizers, pesticides, and industrial wastes.

Reefs are an important economic resource in some tropical nations, and economic exploitation has had damaging effects. Boats scrape the reefs, killing off coral, and divers "harvest" coral formations as souvenirs or to supply hobbyists who keep saltwater aquariums. The tropical fish that live in the reefs are in great demand for aquariums, and divers have been known to use dynamite or cyanide to stun the fish so they can be easily caught—destroying large sections of reef in the process.

National governments and environmental groups are taking steps to protect coral reefs, banning harmful practices and setting up ocean reserves where fishing, pleasure boating, and freighter traffic are restricted. In December 2000, U.S. President Bill Clinton created an 84-million-acre (34-million-hectare) underwater reserve to protect coral reefs in Hawaii. The Northwestern Hawaiian Islands Coral Reef Ecosystem Reserve includes almost 70 percent of U.S. coral reefs and is the country's single largest nature preserve. The United States is also setting up a "no-anchoring zone" off Houston to keep large ships from damaging reefs in the Gulf of Mexico. A government task force is mapping the reefs off U.S. coasts so that the health of the ocean's invaluable life-forms can be monitored more closely.

THE DIRTY DOZEN

A group of 12 toxic chemicals known as the "dirty dozen" will no longer be used or produced, as a result of the signing in May 2001 of an international treaty that banned their use. The contract, which took more than two years to negotiate, was agreed upon in December by representatives from 122 nations, including the United States.

The chemicals in question linger in the environment and are easily absorbed by living things. They have been linked to cancer, immune disorders, birth defects, and various genetic abnormalities. They include DDT and several other pesticides, along with polychlorinated biphenyls (PCBs), dioxins, furans, and other by-products of industrial processes and waste burning. A number of the chemicals have already been outlawed by developed nations. Under the treaty, industrialized nations will pay about $150 million a year to help developing countries meet the terms of the agreement.

PCBs were prominent in the news in the United States, where cleanup continues at sites contaminated years ago. In December 2000, the Environmental Protection Agency (EPA) announced an ambitious plan to restore the Hudson River, long contaminated by these chemicals. The contamination dates back to a 30-year period ending in 1977, during which the General Electric Company (GE) discharged as much as 1.3 million pounds (0.6 million kilograms) of PCBs into the river. The chemicals persist in the river mud, posing a potential risk through the food chain to fish, wildlife, and people. Under the EPA plan, GE would be required to dredge the river's bottom, at an estimated cost of $500 million, to remove the toxic threat.

Two common pesticides, chemicals not on the "dirty dozen" list, were pulled off the shelves of U.S. stores during 2000. In June, the EPA announced a ban on most uses of chlorpyrifos (sold as Dursban and other trade names). An ingredient in many home-and-garden bug sprays and some termite treatments, this organophosphate was the most widely used household pesticide in the United States. The EPA cited risks to children in halting nearly all use in homes and in public locations such as schools, day-care centers, parks, hospitals, nursing homes, and shopping malls. In December, the agency ordered another widely used pesticide off the market. Home and garden use of diazinon (an ingredient in Spectracide, Real-Kill, and other products) was to be phased out by 2004, allowing time for reliable alternatives to be introduced. EPA officials said diazinon was a leading cause of pesticide poisoning, producing nausea, headaches, diarrhea, and other symptoms in people who touched it or inhaled its fumes. It was also proved to be harmful to pets and wildlife, especially birds. However, the agency said the pesticide posed no immediate danger if used according to directions.

TAKING ORDERS

There was some question as to how—or whether—Clinton's Republican successor, George W. Bush, would enforce rules approved by the previous administration.

Tough standards for vehicle emissions were among the legacies Clinton hoped to leave. In December 1999, the EPA set stricter tail pipe standards for passenger cars, minivans, sport-utility vehicles, and pickup trucks. And in December 2000, Clinton signed off on restrictions designed to cut back emissions from heavy-duty trucks and buses. These behemoths, which one EPA official called "smudge pots on wheels," account for just 6 percent of highway miles driven on U.S. roads each year. But with their powerful diesel engines, they are responsible for half the soot, or particulate matter, and one-fourth of smog-causing nitrogen oxides.

The new directives were formulated to reduce the amount of soot released by trucks and buses by 90 percent, and cut nitrogen oxides by 95 percent, over a 10-year period. A key component of the plan was a requirement for cleaner diesel fuel, with 97 percent less sulfur. The sulfur in diesel fuel yields soot, which has prevented trucks and buses from being fitted with antipollution devices such as the catalytic converters installed in cars. In the timetable outlined by the Clinton administration, 80 percent of all diesel fuel would have to meet the sulfur requirement by 2006, and the rest by 2010. The rules also called on truck makers to put pollution controls on new engines. By 2007,

New standards should reduce the soot and smog-causing pollutants produced by diesel-engine trucks and buses—so-called "smudge pots on wheels."

half of new engines would be required to have the controls. By 2010, *all* new engines would be so equipped.

The EPA and the Army Corps of Engineers also issued rules designed to close a loophole in the Clean Water Act. By taking advantage of unclear language in that law, the agencies said, developers had destroyed some 20,000 acres (8,000 hectares) of envi-

ronmentally sensitive wetlands and 150 miles (240 kilometers) of streams since 1998. The new regulations detail the types of wetlands development that requires governmental review.

Just two weeks before leaving office, Clinton issued a powerful order that placed nearly one-third of national-forest land off-limits to logging and road building. By halting road construction, the order effectively barred drilling for oil and natural gas in the covered areas, which included the Tongass National Forest in Alaska. In all, more than 58 million acres (23 million hectares) in 39 states were affected. The oil and timber industries, several governors from the western states, and Republican leaders were adamantly opposed to the restrictions. President Bush announced that he would review this and other last-minute Clinton-era orders before they went into effect.

ALIEN INVASION

Marine biologists were alarmed to see a living green mat rippling on the floor of a coastal lagoon near San Diego in June 2000. They discovered *Caulerpa taxifolia* alga, a fast-growing species notorious for smothering native sea plants and upsetting coastal ecology. Originally cloned as a decorative accent for fish tanks, this *Caulerpa* variant escaped into the Mediterranean Sea from an aquarium in Monaco in 1984. In five years, it had spread to cover 2.5 acres (1 hectare), soaking up nutrients and choking out all other plants. Today, the plant is creating what some biologists call a "carpet of AstroTurf" wherever it takes hold.

The sudden appearance of *Caulerpa* in California called attention to the problems created when nonnative species are transported to new areas. Imports of the plant have been banned in the United States since 1999; still, some fish fanciers have it in their aquariums. Officials of the U.S. National Marine Fisheries Services eradicated the green invader by covering it with tarpaulins and dousing it with herbicides. They say that someone might have emptied a fish tank down a storm drain, giving the noxious weed a shot at the Pacific.

Elaine Pascoe

FOOD AND POPULATION

PREMATURE CELEBRATION?

Celebration of the United Nations World Food Summit's fifth anniversary in November 2001 appears premature. According to the Food Insecurity and Vulnerability Information and Mapping System (FIVIMS), a product of the summit's commitment to develop a new way to measure food insecurity and gauge progress in reducing it, the world community lags far behind the pace required to achieve the summit's central goal—to cut global food insecurity in half within two decades, that is, by 2015.

FIVIMS published its estimates for 2000, noting that 792 million people in developing countries are not getting enough food, and that 34 million are similarly at risk in the industrialized world and in the transition states of Eastern Europe and the former Soviet Union. Instead of the planned reduction in food insecurity of 20 million people per year, the FIVIMS reports that since the summit, the actual reduction has been no more than 8 million annually.

FOOD-POPULATION EQUATION STEADY

According to the United Nations (UN), aggregate production of wheat, corn, and rice fell by a little less than 2 percent in 2000. But with carryover from previous years, there was enough to feed the year's estimated global population increase of 75 million to 80 million people. Global stocks of food, however, decreased by approximately 4 percent; and the output of crops, meat, and fish is declining.

The situation is precarious in sub-Sahara, where drought, war, and AIDS have contributed to food shortages. The impact of the January 2001 earthquake on western India's food supply is unpredictable. Storms and floods have weakened Bangladesh, Cambodia, and Vietnam, and malnutrition threatens Afghanistan's population. The food supply continues to be inadequate in North Korea. Likewise, the outlook in such countries as Nicaragua, Belize, Honduras, and El Salvador remains unclear in the aftermath of recent earthquakes, hurricanes, and mud slides. Rain and cool weather in Canada, dry conditions in the United States, and deteriorated crop prospects in Australia have also contributed to the general uncertainty. Yet, at the same time, food security, defined as access to an adequate human diet through production or purchase, remains high on the agenda of several UN agencies.

WHERE WILL FOOD COME FROM?

Nearly all analyses indicate that increases in food will have to come from land now under cultivation. The global fish catch appears to have reached its limit, and overfishing is a continuing threat. Although forage for cattle is adequate overall, feedlots in the industrialized world continue to use grain that could feed people.

The challenge is to increase yield, and research, science, and technology have major roles. Research-generated seeds brought about the miracle in Asia called the Green Revolution. But that production increase seems to have run its course. Agricultural biotechnology, whose promise lies more in improving crops than in increasing yield, has sparked worldwide controversy.

This new technology tends to pit the United States and Canada—where there has been little resistance to genetically modified (GM) foods—against Japan and Europe. Europe, in light of its scare with hoof-and-mouth and mad-cow diseases, resists consuming beef produced with the help of bovine-growth hormones (BGHs), and has extended its concern to GM corn, soybeans, and cotton. This reluctance reflects the fact that Europe is behind the curve in this type of crop development.

In the Third World, opposition to GM foods focuses more on the foreign corporate ownership of the seeds and/or the processes promoted—even when corporations provide free seeds. The expressed view is that poor subsistence farmers will get "hooked" on new seeds that not only cannot be saved from year to year, but improve quality rather than increase yield. Also, biotech companies located in industrialized nations have shown little interest in such crops as millet and cassava, the staples of many Third World subsistence farmers. The argument escalates when ethical considerations are added—for example, the patenting of life-forms; "biopiracy" of indigenous knowledge by profit-seeking corporations; and the lack of any systematic improvement from the use of biotech applications.

THE U.S. SITUATION

Last year, the U.S. National Food Plan estimated there were about 32 million food-insecure people, and had a wide variety of programs to meet some of their needs. Although these people count in the global figures noted, they have little impact on the world food situation.

Because of the leading role the United States plays in the global food system, however, U.S. policy is crucial for the existing 800 million food-insecure people. The current basic farm legislation—the Federal Agricultural Improvement and Reform Act (FAIR) of 1996 runs out in 2002. The legislation deals with a dozen specified crops, as well as subsidies, emergencies, farming practices, and international trade. It will be the subject of lively debate and intensive lobbying—by all stakeholders.

Martin M. McLaughlin

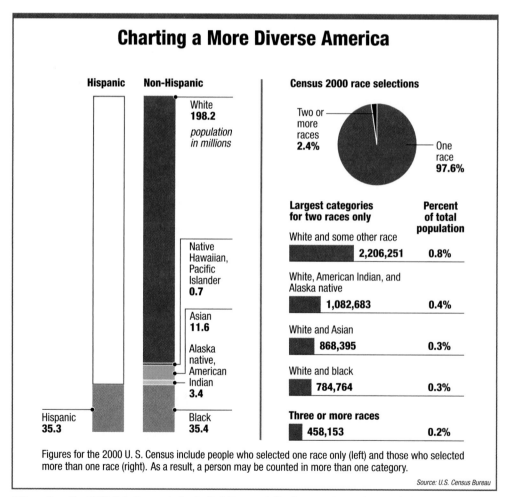

Charting a More Diverse America

Hispanic **Non-Hispanic**

White
198.2

population in millions

Native Hawaiian, Pacific Islander
0.7

Asian
11.6

Alaska native,
American Indian
3.4

Hispanic
35.3

Black
35.4

Census 2000 race selections

Two or more races
2.4%

One race
97.6%

Largest categories for two races only		Percent of total population
White and some other race	2,206,251	0.8%
White, American Indian, and Alaska native	1,082,683	0.4%
White and Asian	868,395	0.3%
White and black	784,764	0.3%
Three or more races	458,153	0.2%

Figures for the 2000 U. S. Census include people who selected one race only (left) and those who selected more than one race (right). As a result, a person may be counted in more than one category.

Source: U.S. Census Bureau

Figures from the 2000 U.S. Census indicate that the population increased more in the 1990s than in any other 10-year period in the nation's history. This explosive growth can be attributed to waves of new immigrants that increased ethnic diversity, coupled with a steady birth rate that outpaced the number of people who died.

Genetics

Sequencing the Human Genome

The year of the millennium brought one of the greatest accomplishments in genetics, second perhaps only to geneticists James Watson and Francis Crick's discovery of the structure of deoxyribonucleic acid, or DNA. In February 2001, two teams of researchers—one public and one private—announced that they had deciphered the human genome, the complete set of blueprints necessary to make a person. Their feat offered some surprising insights into both what it takes to put together a human and how we came to be what we are. Researchers are also confident that the achievement will provide many new ways to attack the diseases that afflict humans.

The human genome is composed of 3.2 billion individual chemicals, called bases or nucleotides, strung together like beads on a string. Four distinct chemicals, labeled A, T, C, and G, serve as the genome's alphabet. Just as the 26 letters of the English-language alphabet can be combined in an infinite number of ways to produce words, sentences, paragraphs, and books, the four chemical bases can be combined to specify the formation of all the proteins, fats, enzymes, hormones, and other components of the body. Each of the body's 100 trillion cells contains this full set of instructions.

Celera Genomics of Rockville, Maryland, and the federally funded U.S. Human Genome Project each reported that they had sequenced—determined the precise order of the bases of—more than 90 percent of the genome. As just one measure of that effort, if all 3.2 billion A's, T's, C's, and G's were printed in standard-sized type, the complete sequence would occupy the space of 75,490 newspaper pages.

The biggest surprise was the number of genes that the two groups found. Although the exact total has not yet been determined, both groups say that there are probably 30,000 to 40,000 genes in the human genome. Based on earlier studies of other organisms, most scientists had believed that the human genome contained at least 100,000 genes. The new number is only a few more than the number in a mouse genome, and only twice as many as in a simple worm. Researchers are perplexed at how such a small number of genes can produce the complex human organism. One possible explanation is that many human genes are more complex than those of their animal counterparts. Perhaps more significantly, the proteins specified by each human gene can be cut apart and spliced together in a variety of ways to produce two, three, four, or more different products.

Sequencing the genome has also provided some important evolutionary clues. Researchers so far have discovered 223 genes that are bacterial in origin, but that were captured long ago by some distant human ancestor and subverted for our own purposes. They have also found many transposons, the so-called "jumping genes" that move from place to place throughout a DNA molecule and carry bits and fragments of DNA with them, reorganizing and reediting genes in the process. Scientists believe that some of the genes altered in this fashion have adopted new roles over the millennia.

In a few cases, researchers have identified four or more separate copies of a single gene, with the extra versions presumably produced by transposons. Such repetitive sequences make up as much as 50 percent of the human genome, while genes themselves account for only about 1.5 percent. Researchers had previously believed that the 98.5 percent of the genome that does not serve as gene blueprints was simply junk DNA with no purpose, but the small number of genes they have actually found suggests that at least some of these other materials may play a regulatory role.

The location of genes themselves has also proved surprising. Biologists had assumed that most genes were scattered evenly across the genome, but that is not the case. Instead, they appear to cluster in small groups whose significance is yet to be determined. Even more surprisingly, at least 500 genes have been found to reside in telomeres, the long stretches of DNA found on the ends of each of the 23 pairs of chromosomes that organize the genome. That seems a rather unlikely place to keep genes, because a small section of the telomere is cleaved from the chromosome each time the cell replicates. Some geneticists now speculate that this loss of genes could be responsible for some of the infirmities associated with aging.

The next step for researchers is to figure out what each gene is doing. Geneticists now

As the representatives of the two teams that cracked the human genetic code, Dr. J. Craig Venter (left), head of Celera Genomics, and Dr. Francis S. Collins (right), leader of the U.S. Human Genome Project, shared the spotlight at a White House ceremony marking the scientific milestone.

know the function of about 42 percent of the known genes, and are trying to deduce the role of others. One approach to that task is being carried out by the International Mouse Mutagenesis Consortium, whose ultimate goal is to produce a mutant strain of mice for each of the 30,000 identified mouse genes. Such mice would lend insight into how the genes function, and would provide inroads for future investigation of genetic diseases for which causes have yet to be determined. So far, the team has produced 5,000 such mouse variants.

The findings emphasize both our differences from, and our similarities to, other forms of life. Humans share about 40 percent of their genes with nematode worms, 60 percent with fruit flies, and 90 percent with mice. We differ from our closest relatives, chimpanzees, by only about 1 percent.

The differences between individual humans are smaller still. Those differences are produced by single base changes in the genome, so-called single-nucleotide polymorphisms, or SNPs. The Human Genome Project has identified about 1.3 million SNPs that characterize individual human beings; Celera, about 4 million. This means that approximately 0.1 percent of the human genome accounts for the differences between one individual and another.

While they are deciphering the human genome, researchers are also sequencing the genomes of a variety of other organisms. That of the fruit fly, a laboratory-research mainstay, was reported in March 2000. Other geneticists are almost finished with the genome of the mouse, another key research animal. Simpler organisms that have also had their genomes sequenced include the bacterium *Pseudomonas aeruginosa*, which often causes pneumonia in burn victims, patients with cystic fibrosis, and others with impaired immune systems; and *Mycobacterium leprae*, which causes leprosy. The latter sequence, announced in February 2001, also surprised researchers. *M. leprae* shares approximately 93 percent of its genes with the bacterium that causes tuberculosis, but it seems to have lost nearly half of its nonessential genes over the millennia—more than any other organism studied so far. But because *M. leprae* has so few genes, it will be considerably easier for geneticists to study.

GENE-THERAPY DEATH

Pennsylvania State University researchers believe they have discovered what caused the death of Jesse Gelsinger. The 18-year-old Arizonan, who suffered from a rare liver disorder—resulting from a defective gene—died in September 1999 while undergoing gene therapy at the University of Pennsylvania,

Philadelphia. Gelsinger's death led the U.S. Food and Drug Administration (FDA) to suspend further gene-therapy trials at Penn State indefinitely. The case has reverberated throughout the community since Gelsinger was in relatively good health at the time of the experiment, and could have survived without the therapy.

Geneticist James Wilson and his colleagues attempted to replace a defective gene in Gelsinger and other patients by incorporating a normal gene into an adenovirus, a form of cold virus (whose own pathogenic DNA had been removed). Then they injected the modified adenovirus containing the gene into Gelsinger's liver, anticipating that the gene would ultimately begin manufacturing the needed enzyme.

New studies in monkeys, Wilson reported at a January 2001 meeting, demonstrated that the viral coating itself could trigger a massive immune response that damages internal organs, which is what had happened to Gelsinger. But researchers do not understand why the dose Gelsinger received triggered a fatal immune response while another patient who received the same dose was not affected. Researchers are understandably concerned, because many other individuals and companies are also using a variety of adenoviruses as vectors to introduce replacement genes.

ONE GENE LINKED TO ASTHMA

British scientists announced in February that they had discovered a single gene that could be responsible for as much as 40 percent of all cases of asthma. The discovery offers potential for the development of new drugs, and provides a way to screen for children who are susceptible to the disease. Asthma specialists were surprised by the report, because most had assumed that several genes are responsible for triggering asthma, with each playing only a small role.

Stephen Holgate of the University of Southampton in England screened 342 families in which at least two children had asthma, and narrowed down the search to five suspicious genes. With information from the Human Genome Project, his team was able to focus on one, which proved to be strongly linked to the disorder. Testing in 110 American families then confirmed the discovery. Holgate has neither identified the gene publicly nor described what it does, but he did say that it plays a role in lung function. The companies that sponsored the research are seeking a patent, and plan to publish their findings in a scientific journal.

DIABETES-GENE CONTROVERSY

An Illinois team has discovered a gene that plays a key role in triggering type 2 diabetes in Mexican-Americans, Native Americans, and African-Americans. Type 2 diabetes, also known as non-insulin-dependent diabetes mellitus (NIDDM), or adult-onset diabetes, affects about 4 percent of the population—and, notably, 11 percent of the Mexican-American population. The new gene may explain why, and may also present new targets for therapy.

Researchers believe that a dozen or more genes play a role in diabetes, but identifying them has been difficult. In 1996, geneticists Graeme Bell of the University of Chicago Medical Center and Craig Hanis of the University of Texas, Houston, reported that a crucial gene for diabetes appears to lie in a small region of chromosome 2. They named it NIDDM1. But other groups have failed to reproduce Bell's and Hanis' finding, and the putative existence of NIDDM1 has been quite controversial.

In September 2000, Bell's team reported that in a study of DNA from 330 pairs of Mexican-American brothers and sisters from Starr County, Texas, they finally identified NIDDM1. To their surprise, it turned out to be a previously known gene that serves as the blueprint for a protein called calpain-10. Calpain-10 is a protease, a protein that breaks down other proteins, snipping them into smaller segments. Although calpain-10 is found in tissues throughout the body, no one knows the protein's precise function, nor has it ever been implicated in any pathways for insulin secretion or use. The team found that people with the newly discovered mutation produce less calpain-10 than do other individuals. Bell's group estimates that the gene is responsible for about 14 percent of type 2 diabetes cases among

Mexican-Americans, but studies in Caucasians from Finland and Germany showed that the gene played a role in less than 4 percent of cases—which explains why researchers had difficulty reproducing the original findings. Other studies now under way suggest that calpain-10 is also responsible for about 15 percent of type 2 diabetes in Pima Indians, who have the world's highest incidence of the disease, and as much as 25 percent of cases among African-Americans.

OTHER DISEASES

Researchers identified genes responsible for several other rare disorders in the past year, and two of these genes seem particularly intriguing. In January 2001, a team from the National Institute on Aging (NIA) identified one gene that causes blepharophimosis, which is characterized by drooping eyelids. The newly discovered gene, called FOXL2, is required for normal development of the eyelid in newborns. It is also responsible for the development of a full complement of eggs in the ovaries of female fetuses before birth. Women who do not acquire the full complement often develop a condition called premature ovarian failure, which usually accompanies early menopause. The discovery means that women at high risk for this condition can now be identified at birth by the presence of blepharophimosis.

And in February 2001, three groups of researchers independently reported that they had identified a second gene, one that causes DiGeorge syndrome and affects one in every 4,000 babies. The disease has a wide range of symptoms, including facial abnormalities, heart defects, immune malfunctions, and learning disabilities, and its severity varies widely. Some victims die shortly after birth, while others have symptoms so mild that the disorder is virtually unnoticeable.

DiGeorge syndrome has long been known to be caused by the deletion of a segment of chromosome 22, but the deleted segment contains several genes, and researchers were not certain which was important. The three teams found that the crucial gene was Tbx1, which plays a major role in regulating development.

Thomas H. Maugh II

GEOLOGY

A BAD DAY FOR DINOSAURS

The speed with which the dinosaurs died out is key to understanding the cause of their extinction. Did they disappear gradually over the course of hundreds of thousands of years due to global climate changes, or were they wiped out suddenly in the wake of a single catastrophic event?

One piece of evidence that apparently supported the theory of gradual extinction was the so-called three-meter gap. In a study of the Hell Creek Formation in North Dakota and Montana published more than 20 years ago, scientists reported the existence of a layer of sediment about 9 feet (3 meters) thick that contained relatively few fossils of the last known dinosaurs. According to the study, this layer, which accumulated over the span of 2.2 million years, separates an abundance of fossils from the remnants of a large asteroid that is now widely believed to have struck Earth 65 million years ago. The scarcity of fossils in this layer suggests to some scientists that the dinosaurs were already dying out before the asteroid hit.

Unconvinced by this study, Peter M. Sheehan, curator of geology at Wisconsin's Milwaukee Public Museum, led a three-year survey of the Hell Creek Formation to compare the number of dinosaur fossils within the "gap" with the number in older layers. Contrary to the earlier study, Sheehan found just as many fossils in the "gap" as he did in the lower layers. He therefore concluded that there was no decline in the dinosaur population prior to the impact of the sizable asteroid, and that the end of the dinosaurs was anything but gradual.

A GIANT GEODE

Anyone who has visited a natural-history museum is more than likely familiar with geodes. These globe-shaped mineral bodies look like rough, round rocks, but more often than not, their hollow insides are lined with masses of glittering, inward-pointing crystals. Geodes generally begin as "bubbles" in volcanic rock, as animal burrows, tree roots, or mud balls most commonly found in regions with limestone. In time, an outer shell forms and hardens, and silica precipitation containing dissolved minerals (most commonly quartz) forms on its inside walls. Especially desirable are geodes that house amethyst crystals, a violet-colored type of quartz known for its wide range of purple shades and unique formations.

Geodes vary in size, but it is unusual to find one bigger than 12 inches (30 centimeters) in diameter. Imagine the astonishment of Javier Garcia-Guinea, a geologist with the National Museum of Natural Sciences, Madrid, Spain, when he encountered an entire cave full of sparkling gypsum crystals in an old silver mine near Almería on Spain's southern coast. The cave measures 26 feet (8 meters) long, 6 feet (2 meters) wide, and 6 feet high—large enough to hold 10 people. Naturally, this giant geode's inner crystals are also large, about 20 inches (0.5 meter) in length and each several inches across.

Garcia-Guinea believes that the origin of the giant Almería geode dates back about 6 million years, when the Strait of Gibraltar closed up and the Mediterranean Sea, which once covered the cave, evaporated. The retreating sea left behind several salty deposits that, along with ideal temperatures and humidity, favored the growth of the brilliant-looking crystals.

To protect his discovery from souvenir hunters and mineral collectors, Garcia-Guinea sealed the cave with several tons of rock. He hopes one day to turn the site into a tourist attraction, so that others can see this amazing natural phenomenon.

VOLCANOES AND SATELLITES

Can satellite imagery tell us enough about volcanoes to protect us from them? Satellites have already been used to locate volcanoes, as well as to estimate the amount of damage they might cause. For example, geologists Pierre Wiart and Clive Oppenheimer of the University of Cambridge, England, used satellite imagery to reconstruct the size of the 1861 Dubbi eruption in Eritrea, the largest eruption ever in Africa. Using Landsat images, they were able to trace the extent

Researchers marvel at the abundance of transparent gypsum crystals lining the walls of a giant geode discovered in an abandoned silver mine on the southern coast of Spain.

of the slow-moving lava flows and compare the various data to the volcano's dramatic historic aftermath (ships in the Red Sea were showered with pumice, coastal cities were plunged into darkness, and explosions were heard 200 miles [320 kilometers] away).

Despite conventional wisdom, in many cases it is not a volcano's lava flows that take lives and property; rather, it is the often vast amount of mud from the volcano's flanks that streaks down into valleys and buries anything in its path. In light of this knowledge, imagine, then, if the topography, size, and vegetation of an active volcano could be taken into account so that the extent of mudflows, or lahars, could be predicted.

That is exactly what volcanologist Peter Mouginis-Mark, professor at the Hawaii Institute of Geophysics and Planetology of the University of Hawaii, Honolulu, and his colleagues have attempted. These scientists developed specialized computer programs to account for all of the variables that might affect lahar flow. Using the 1991 eruption of Mount Pinatubo in the Philippines as a test case, they compared their models against what actually happened in the eruption. Their technique holds promise as a means of predicting the occurrence of future lahar flows around the world.

ARCHAEOLOGY MEETS GEOLOGY

One of the great mysteries of ancient Greece is the unexplained quick disappearance of the Minoan civilization sometime around

1300 B.C. A team of scientists led by Koji Minoura of Tohoku University, Sendai, Japan, recently unraveled the mystery when the researchers identified tsunami deposits associated with the late-stage eruption of Thera, a powerful volcano located north of the island of Crete. Thera has been implicated in the destruction of the Minoan civilization, but considerable evidence suggests that the civilization survived despite repeated eruptions between 1600 and 1300 B.C. Nonetheless, Minoura and his colleagues note that previous archaeological studies have documented the bending and movement of walls in late Minoan settlements, as well as the deposition of archaeological artifacts by water. These observations, in concert with the newly discovered sedimentary evidence for a tsunami, suggest that Knossos, the Minoan capital, was battered by tsunamis toward the end, if not at the end, of its existence. The scientists reconstructed a train of tsunami waves striking the northern shore of Crete within 24 hours of the eruption of Thera.

While volcanic activity may have had a hand in the destruction of the Minoan civilization, climate change appears to have brought about the ultimate demise of the prosperous Akkadian Empire. The Akkadians ruled Mesopotamia from the Tigris and Euphrates Rivers to the Persian Gulf from 4300 to 4200 B.C. Archaeologists have determined that the civilization disappeared rather abruptly, perhaps because of a sudden shift toward more-arid conditions.

To test this hypothesis, a team of researchers led by Heidi Cullen at the Lamont-Doherty Earth Observatory of Columbia University, Palisades, New York, studied a marine-sediment core from the Gulf of Oman. Just above a cultivated layer attributed to the Akkadian civilization, the core shows a thick, 39-inch (99-centimeter) interval of windblown dust deposits that dates to 4025 ± 125 years B.C. The researchers linked the presence of the windblown dust to an increase in aridity in the region, and confirmed that the Akkadian civilization fell prey to a short-lived but extremely intense drought.

David E. Fastovsky

HEALTH AND DISEASE

CARDIOVASCULAR DISEASE
Chest pain has long been considered characteristic of a heart attack, but a study led by John G. Canto of the University of Alabama, Huntsville, of 434,877 heart-attack patients found that one-third did not experience chest pain. As a result, these patients arrived at the hospital three hours later than those with the telling pain. Since they may have complained of nausea, arm pain, or breathing difficulty, doctors were less likely to diagnose them as having a heart attack upon admission. Perhaps because of this failure to receive rapid treatment, the patients under study were more than twice as likely to die in the hospital than patients with chest pain.

Brief interruptions of blood flow to the brain cause transient ischemic attacks (TIAs), or ministrokes, that last anywhere from a few seconds to 24 hours. Symptoms, such as weakness or numbness, are variable and easily ignored by patients. TIAs seldom cause permanent damage, but they often presage a major stroke, as demonstrated by a study conducted at the University of California, San Francisco. The study found that 180 of 1,707 TIA patients had strokes within three months of a TIA, with half of the strokes occurring within two days. The researchers stressed that both patients and doctors need to take TIAs "very seriously."

Approximately 500,000 bypass operations are performed annually in the United States. A study of 261 bypass patients at Duke University, Durham, North Carolina, found that five years after surgery, 42 percent of the patients scored significantly lower on tests of mental ability than they had before the surgery. The reasons are unknown. One possibility is that clamping the aorta during the bypass operation breaks off fat deposits that then travel to the brain and block the flow of blood. Another possibility is that as a patient's blood moves through a heart-lung machine during the operation, the blood picks up air bubbles that reach the brain and block blood flow.

AN EPIDEMIC OF DIABETES

Diabetes is a disease in which the body does not produce or properly use the hormone insulin, and therefore cannot regulate levels of blood sugar (glucose). It is the sixth-leading cause of death by disease in the United States, and a major cause of blindness, heart attacks, kidney failure, and limb amputations. At least 16 million Americans have been diagnosed with the disease, a number expected to increase to 22 million by 2025. The Centers for Disease Control and Prevention (CDC) reported that the incidence of diabetes jumped from 4.9 percent to 6.9 percent of the population between 1990 and 1999. "This dramatic new evidence signals the unfolding of an epidemic in the United States," says Jeffrey P. Koplan, director of the CDC.

More than 90 percent of U.S. diabetics have type 2 diabetes, in which the body fails to use insulin properly. Once known as adult-onset diabetes, type 2 was typically found among older people. But it is closely associated with obesity, which in the United States has increased 57 percent since 1991. An American Diabetes Association (ADA) panel reported that the percentage of childhood-diabetes cases that were type 2 rose from fewer than 4 percent in 1990 to approximately 20 percent in 1998, and that of these diabetic children, 85 percent were obese.

A Finnish study involving 523 adults, average age 55, with impaired glucose tolerance—a condition between "normal" and "diabetic"—demonstrated that changes in eating and exercise habits can prevent type 2 diabetes. "Our intervention was relatively inexpensive compared to the high costs of having diabetes," says Jaakko Tuomilehto of Finland's National Public Health Institute. "It showed that a modest weight loss of less than 10 pounds [4.5 kilograms], combined with a healthy diet and regular moderate exercise, can produce major benefits in people with impaired glucose tolerance."

Type 1 diabetes, in which the body produces little or no insulin, typically develops in children or young, slim adults. Scientists at the University of Alberta in Canada reported that they had successfully transplanted insulin-producing cells into eight patients with severe type 1 diabetes. At the time of the report, the patients had been free of symptoms of the disease for up to 14 months, and no longer needed insulin injections to regulate their blood sugar.

DRAMATIC RISE IN ASTHMA CASES

Between 1980 and 1994, the prevalence of asthma, a chronic inflammation of airways in the lungs, increased 75 percent, with a 160 percent increase among children younger than age 4. Today, about 14 million

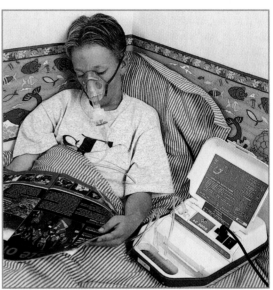

Asthma among young children is clearly on the rise. Attacks appear to be triggered most often by the presence of certain airborne materials, such as pollen, animal hair, and dust.

Americans have asthma, up from about 5 million in 1980; by 2020, the number could reach 29 million. Asthma is the most common chronic disease among children, and the leading medical cause of school absenteeism. But most states lack systems to track people with asthma. A national monitoring program could require $25 million annually, compared to the present $14.5 billion that asthma now costs the national economy each year.

The cause of asthma is unknown, but a variety of factors can set off or exacerbate attacks. These include bronchial diseases and allergens in the air, such as pollen, animal hair, and dust. Scientists at Johns Hopkins University, Baltimore, tested several homes in eight inner-city areas and discovered that 95 percent of them had at least one room which contained mouse urine, dander, or some other type of mouse allergen. The scientists found that 18 percent of the children who lived in these homes were allergic to mice and also tended to suffer from severe asthma.

Recently, a provocative study by researchers at the University of Arizona College of Medicine in Tucson found that very young children who had frequent exposure to other children—in day-care centers, for instance—were less likely to develop asthma later on. Also, those who did develop asthma experienced fewer attacks than did asthmatic children not as frequently exposed to other children. But children in day-care centers suffered more sniffles and ear infections than did toddlers kept at home. The researchers theorized that these infections might play an important role in development of the immune system, helping it become less reactive to allergen exposure.

Inhaling corticosteroids, a common treatment for asthma, reduces inflammation and makes breathing easier. A Canadian study of 30,569 people treated for asthma found that those who regularly used corticosteroid inhalers also decreased their risk of dying from the disease. In August 2000, the U.S. Food and Drug Administration (FDA) approved the use of the corticosteroid inhalant Pulmicort Respules for asthmatic children as young as 1 year—the first corticosteroid ever approved for treatment of asthma patients that young.

PREGNANCY AND CHILDBIRTH

Between 1984 and 1998, the proportion of low-birth-weight babies—those weighing less than 5.5 pounds (2.5 kilograms)—increased from 6.7 percent to 7.6 percent of U.S. births. The number of older women giving birth also increased during this period; and older women have a higher risk of delivering low-birth-weight babies. But researchers attributed most of the increase to the use of fertility aids, such as in vitro fer-

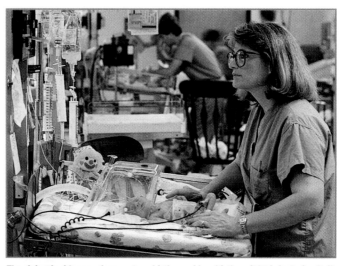

The rising incidence of premature births and low-birth-weight infants is attributed to older women taking fertility drugs. These drugs also help account for the increasing number of twins and triplets born in the United States.

tilization and drugs that increase ovulation (the release of eggs). These practices often result in multiple births, in which babies are more likely to be premature and tiny. From 1980 to 1997, twin births rose more than 50 percent, while the number of triplets in the United States quadrupled.

At the time of delivery, about 4 percent of babies are in the breech position, ready to emerge bottom first rather than headfirst. A study involving 2,083 pregnant women in 26 countries, who all were carrying babies in breech positions, found that a cesarean section (C-section)—a surgical procedure in which the baby is delivered through an abdominal incision—is three times safer than a vaginal delivery in this situation, and greatly reduce the infant's risk of dying or being severely handicapped. In addition, the study found that C-sections were no riskier to the mothers than were natural deliveries. Most mothers and infants recover with few problems. Postoperative abdominal scars are generally minimal for mothers once the stitches are removed.

Some 1 million C-sections are performed in the United States each year. The procedure is chosen in approximately 294,000 of these cases when labor progresses more slowly than expected. Researchers at RAND, a nonprofit research-and-analysis institution, and two universities reported that up to 24 percent of these C-sections may be performed too early, before the cervix is dilated to 4 centimeters or more, as recommended by the American College of Obstetricians and Gynecologists.

DRUG APPROVALS AND WITHDRAWALS

Zyvox (linezolid), the first entirely new kind of antibiotic in 35 years, was approved by the FDA. Designed to attack deadly bacteria that cause pneumonia and other infections commonly found in hospitals and nursing homes, Zyvox was shown to be effective against bacteria resistant to other kinds of antibiotics. Officials urged that Zyvox be used only for the worst infections and those suspected of being resistant to older antibacterial medicines; otherwise, bacteria will quickly evolve resistance to Zyvox, ultimately making the drug useless.

Sixteen years after U.S. clinical trials began, and more than a decade after it became available in Europe, the abortion-inducing pill mifepristone (also known as RU 486) received FDA approval. Mifepristone blocks the action of the female hormone progesterone, thereby preventing successful implantation of a fertilized egg into the lining of the uterus. Thirty-six to 48 hours after taking mifepristone, a woman takes a second pill, the previously approved misoprostol, which induces contractions that expel the embryo. This regimen, an alternative to surgical abortion, is effective only during the first seven weeks after a woman's last menstrual period.

The FDA warned consumers about PPA (phenylpropanolamine), an ingredient in hundreds of over-the-counter cold remedies and appetite suppressants: "We suggest you stop taking the drug immediately and use an alternative." The action came after a five-year study at Yale University, New Haven, Connecticut, showed that PPA—which had been on the market for more than 50 years—increased the risk of stroke, particularly in young women. Months before the FDA ban took effect, manufacturers of affected products offered reformulated versions, replacing PPA with a safer alternative.

Rezulin (troglitazone), an oral agent approved by the FDA in 1997 for treating type 2 diabetes, and used by about 500,000 Americans in early 2000, was withdrawn from the U.S. market after being linked to 90 cases of liver failure, 63 of which resulted in death. Physicians advised that any patients taking two related drugs, Avandia (rosiglitazone maleate) and Actos (pioglitazone hydrochloride), also should be carefully monitored for signs of liver problems.

The FDA began an investigation of Lymerix, the Lyme-disease vaccine approved in 1998 and since received by some 440,000 Americans. The vaccine provides about 80 percent protection against the disease, but it may also cause health problems. More than a dozen physicians reported treating 170 people with Lyme disease and arthritis who developed these illnesses as a result of receiving the vaccine: the vaccine either caused flare-ups of Lyme disease in people who previously had been infected, or triggered a reaction that resulted in arthritis.

The efficacy of new medications is best tested in randomized controlled trials, in which some patients receive a test drug, and others receive nothing or a different drug. A study authored by John P.A. Ioannidis of Tufts University School of Medicine, Boston, and others examined safety reporting in 192 randomized drug trials involving more than 130,000 patients. The study found that researchers underreport or even neglect problems involving drug safety. For example, the study found that the severity of side effects and drug toxicity was adequately explained in only 39 percent and 29 percent, respectively, of drug-trial reports.

Jenny Tesar

MATHEMATICS

THE GOLDBACH CALCULATIONS
Christian Goldbach, an 18th-century Prussian mathematician and historian, made headlines in 2000. When a British book publisher offered $1 million to the person who could prove Goldbach's enigmatic conjecture, that was big news. But when a German mathematician verified Goldbach's conjecture to be true for numbers up to 400 trillion, that was even bigger news.

Goldbach had proposed that every even number can be written as the sum of two prime numbers. (Prime numbers are whole numbers that are evenly divisible only by themselves and 1.) More than 250 years after Goldbach made his conjecture known, Jörg Richstein, a mathematician at the University of Giessen in Germany, used computers to confirm that all even numbers up to 400 trillion obeyed the relationship. While other mathematicians had used a supercomputer in 1998 to verify numbers up to 100 trillion, Richstein's method was notable because it was calculated on a network of much smaller computers.

Richstein's method also allowed him to list all the possible ways that a particular number could be written as a sum of two prime numbers. For example, there are two ways to write 20 as a sum of two primes, and five ways to write 48. Richstein counted all of the combinations for numbers up to 500 million, including all 291,400 ways to write 100 million as the sum of two primes. Calculations such as Richstein's may offer some clues for proving the conjecture, but calculations are not proof in themselves.

Coincidentally published in 2000, the novel *Uncle Petros and Goldbach's Conjecture* by Apostolos Doxiadis describes one man's attempt to find a proof for Goldbach's theorem, and his dreaded fear that perhaps no proof was possible. To publicize the book, Britain's Faber & Faber publishers offered a $1 million prize to anyone who could prove the conjecture before March 15, 2002. While this substantial sum served as little more than publicity for the book, such prizes can provide the incentive for mathematicians to attack extremely difficult problems. Because some math problems appear to have no real-world applications, prizes and a bit of notoriety may be the only rewards some will ever see for their efforts.

SAMPLING THE U.S. POPULATION
Another major mathematics story in 2000 also involved counting. The U.S. Census Bureau conducted its 10-year tally of all residents of the United States. The first results indicated a population of 281,421,906 as of April 1, 2000, an increase of 13.2 percent from 1990.

The U.S. Constitution calls for a head count every 10 years. In 2000, the Census Bureau mailed surveys to every household, and "enumerators," visited every residence that did not return a survey or have a recorded mailing address. The first results were tabulated by the end of 2000 and submitted to the president.

The census ensures that the 435 seats in the House of Representatives can be apportioned properly to the states according to each state's population. In 2000, the most populous state in the country was California, with 33,871,648 residents; the least populous was Wyoming, with 493,782. Nevada had the highest percentage growth in population, climbing 66.3 percent since 1990 to 796,424 people. The reapportionment of congressional districts will spark much debate and discussion since representatives from the reapportioned districts will be elected in November 2002.

Mailed census surveys and data submitted by enumerators can miss some people, resulting in an "undercount." Such undercounts concern many people because census data are also a vital factor for distributing federal funds nationwide for social programs. The Census Bureau proposed adjusting the final 2000 count using complex statistical methods, but it appears that, at least for apportioning congressional seats, the preadjusted total will stand as it is.

The Census Bureau will use statistics for other purposes. For example, one out of every six census surveys mailed was a long form that included many questions about how a family was living in the year 2000.

This information can paint a mathematical picture of life in the United States. Census statistics will show the percentage of people in urban and rural areas; the racial breakdown of the population; the various levels of income; and other characteristics. Demographics, as these factors are collectively known, are used to make economic, social, and political decisions, as well as to show how life has changed since the first U.S. census was conducted in 1790.

EIGHTH-GRADE MATH TEST

In December 2000, the U.S. Department of Education released the initial results from an evaluation designated the Third International Mathematics and Science Study-Repeat (TIMSS-R). Eighth-grade students from 38 countries participated in the 1999 assessment, which will help each country determine how well its education system compares with the rest of the world's. The assessment repeated a 1995 study that evaluated how math and science performance has changed over the four-year period.

The United States ranked 18th in math and 19th in science, scoring above the international average in both subjects. Singapore, the Republic of Korea, Chinese Taipei (Taiwan), and Hong Kong scored highest in math, while Taiwan, Singapore, Hungary, Japan, and the Republic of Korea scored highest in science.

U.S. eighth graders performed better than the international average in such areas of math as fractions; data representation, analysis, and probability; and algebra. In science, U.S. eighth graders exceeded the international average in Earth science, chemistry, life science, environmental issues, and scientific inquiry.

The assessment also probed such factors as study habits, student attitudes, classroom activities, teacher practices, and teachers' professional preparation. The study also considered differences in performance between boys and girls. In math, most countries did not report significant disparity between genders. In science, boys showed higher-than-average achievement in 16 of the 38 participating countries.

David L. Hart

METEOROLOGY

IS THE ARCTIC TURNING TO SLUSH?

As they sailed across the Arctic Ocean, adventure tourists aboard the chartered Russian icebreaker *Yamal* soon expected to set foot on the ice-covered North Pole. Instead, when the *Yamal* reached the Pole in late July 2000, it encountered an expanse of open water several miles across. Such "leads"—long, narrow breaks in an ice pack—are common across the Arctic in the summer, according to satellite photos. Still, reports of an ice-free Pole made world headlines and focused attention on the prospect of a melting Arctic ice pack.

Oceanographer Drew Rothrock and colleagues of the University of Washington, Seattle, have found evidence of dramatic ice-pack thinning across the Arctic. During the 1990s, U.S. Navy submarine crews collected sonar measurements of the ice. These readings were compared to measurements taken during naval exercises conducted between the 1950s and the 1970s. Calculated at its thinnest point of the year, usually around mid-September, the researchers found that the average thickness of the ice pack shrank from roughly 10 feet (3 meters) in the 1958–76 period to just less than 6 feet (2 meters) in the 1990s. From 1993 to 1997, the average thickness dropped by about 10 percent.

The horizontal extent of Arctic ice is shrinking as well, although less dramatically. Since 1978, satellite photos show a 6 percent loss in the winter extent. This drop represents an area almost half the size of Alaska. The year-round zone of ice coverage—as measured by the edge of the summer ice—is shrinking nearly twice as quickly as the winter extent, according to a research team at the University of Bergen, Norway. In its report, titled "Toward an Ice-Free Arctic?", the Bergen team speculates that the Arctic's entire ice pack could completely melt each summer beginning in the middle of the 21st century. Such a scenario would spell trouble for polar bears, walrus, and other high-latitude wildlife that are already having difficulty feeding and raising their young amid the changing conditions. At the same time, the melt could be a boon for industry: new shipping routes would save thousands of miles per trip.

While global warming is a likely factor in the Arctic meltdown, other forces are also at work. Prevailing winds over the past few years have been pushing ice out of the Arctic through the Labrador Sea. Should the long-term weather patterns shift, the ice pack would have a better chance of reconsolidating across the Arctic.

TORNADO PROBABILITIES

Precipitation probabilities have been a part of U.S. weather forecasts since the mid-1960s. Now, along with predicting the odds of rain or snow, the National Weather Service (NWS) is assigning numbers to the likelihood of even-more-threatening weather situations, including tornadoes.

The Storm Prediction Center (SPC) in Norman, Oklahoma, which issues hundreds of tornado and severe-thunderstorm watches each year, is creating new probabilistic outlooks. The forecasts are being released to

Meteorologists can readily track a hurricane (above) and predict where and when it will impact the U.S. mainland. Considerably less precise is their ability to forecast localized severe weather, such as tornadoes.

the public through the center's Internet site, http://www.spc.noaa.gov. Each day, the SPC produces a map with contours showing the chance that a particular severe weather event—a tornado, hail at least 0.75 inch (1.9 centimeters) in diameter, or a wind gust of at least 58 miles (93 kilometers) per hour—

will occur within 25 miles (40 kilometers) of any given point. Because the climatological risk of severe weather occurring in such a small area is quite low, even in the Great Plains' notorious "Tornado Alley," the highest likelihood to be assigned in the new forecasts is 45 percent.

In order to estimate the chances of destructive weather, the SPC's research meteorologists pooled vast bodies of data indicating where severe events have occurred across the United States over the past 50 years, specifically focusing on the period since 1980. The forecasters use this database, together with each day's actual weather setup, to evaluate the chances of meteorologic mayhem across the country. The SPC's climatological database is available on its Internet site, so that Americans can track the odds of severe weather striking near their homes in a typical year.

RECONCILING DATA

One of the most heated areas of debate about global warming has been over the disparity between air temperatures measured at ground level and the readings taken several miles aloft. Greenhouse gases produced by human activity, such as carbon dioxide, are well mixed throughout the troposphere, the lowest layer of the atmosphere, which extends from the ground to roughly 8 to 10 miles (13 to 16 kilometers) above Earth's surface. This suggests that any warming triggered by the added greenhouse gases ought to extend throughout the troposphere. However, the facts dispute such an assumption. Earth's surface temperature has risen between 0.15° and 0.25° F (0.08° and 0.14° C) since the late 1970s, while the air through the layer from the surface up to about 5 miles (8 kilometers) has warmed perhaps only half that much. For a time, satellite readings suggested that the lower to middle troposphere might even be cooling.

In their battle to downplay the risk of global warming, skeptics have long cited the satellite trends. In a January 2000 report, the National Research Council (NRC) took away much of the skeptics' ammunition. This study brought together a blue-ribbon panel of specialists from separate areas in each type of measuring system—surface stations, balloon-borne radiosondes, and microwave sounding devices deployed on satellites—to compare notes and determine what might be causing the disparity. A close look at the satellite readings has found a cool bias that grew over time. The reasons included such long-term trends as a slow downward drift in each satellite's orbit. Meanwhile, surface readings were closely inspected to make sure that urban heat islands and other factors were not biasing the ground-based record.

Even when all known instrument errors were corrected, some difference remained. From its findings, the panel concluded that, in fact, the troposphere actually may have warmed much less rapidly than the surface. No explanation is clear just yet, but at least one familiar culprit may be partially to blame. The unusually frequent and intense El Niño events of the 1980s and 1990s appear to have warmed temperatures in the tropical troposphere more than at the surface. Also, ground-hugging cold-air inversions might have weakened during the period, and the timing of two intense volcanic eruptions (El Chichón in Mexico in 1982 and Mount Pinatubo in the Philippines in 1981) may have affected the trends as well. The reviewers noted that observations are still skimpy across the oceans, including much of the Southern Hemisphere, and more time is needed to identify long-term trends both below and above.

A Wind Profiler's New Home

The *Ronald H. Brown,* operated by the National Oceanic and Atmospheric Administration (NOAA), is among the world's best-equipped ships for weather research. The *Brown* is now hosting the first wind profiler to have a permanent home on a research vessel. The 915-megahertz profiler is an upward-pointing type of Doppler radar that senses wind speed and direction at heights of up to several miles. Its shipboard debut came in the fall of 2000 on a voyage from Dutch Harbor, Alaska, to San Diego.

Ground-based profilers have successfully mapped winds over the central United States and several other locations for more than a

The first wind profiler to operate at sea tracked ocean winds on its debut voyage from Dutch Harbor, Alaska, to San Diego aboard the weather ship Ronald H. Brown.

decade; operating a wind profiler aboard a ship is a different matter. Just as buildings and other ground clutter can impede a standard radar's performance, a profiler that is deployed over an ocean can be degraded by "ocean clutter," unwanted signals from the sea's surface. The profiler's data must also be corrected for interference as well as for the ship's rocking and rolling.

These challenges were tackled by the profiler's builder, the NOAA's Environmental Technology Laboratory in Colorado. The final product accounts for the heaving and rolling of a ship at sea through tiny adjustments in the data, calculated 10 times a second. The process is similar to the image stabilizer in a video camera that corrects for the photographer's shaking hands. Much like its land-based counterparts, the profiler includes a hexagonal plate about 8 feet (2.4 meters) across, sporting an array of 90 identical antenna elements. Each element transmits a sliver of the overall signal. Since the flat plate cannot be pointed like a radar beam, the signal's direction is tweaked by adjusting the departure times of the 90 subsignals. This tilts the collective beam in the direction of the last subsignals that emerge.

With its initial performance gaining high marks, the shipborne instrument may serve as a prototype for other profilers that could be installed aboard fixed buoys. Such a network would greatly enhance the diagnosis of winds in the poorly sampled realm above Earth's oceans.

Robert Henson

The Year in Weather—2000

       U.S. Highlights

SPRING 2000

Overview

Warmth and drought built across the southern and western United States, setting the stage for wildfires. More than 1 million acres (400,000 hectares) were scorched by the end of May. Summerlike heat pushed temperatures above 100° F (38° C) well ahead of schedule across much of the West. Tornadic activity remained on the quiet side, though. From April through June, 515 twisters were reported, a drop of more than 30 percent from the previous two years. By the end of 2000, only 16 tornadoes with winds above 158 miles (254 kilometers) per hour had been recorded, less than half the long-term average. The year's tornadic death toll of 40 was the lowest since 1996.

U.S. Highlights

- A tornado struck downtown Fort Worth, Texas, March 28, killing two people and destroying several high-rise buildings.
- The nation's record high for May was broken when Death Valley, California, soared to 122° F (50° C) on May 29. At Altus, Oklahoma, a new monthly record for the state was set: 112° F (44° C) on May 23.
- Dry conditions caused water levels in the Great Lakes to fall to their lowest point since 1965.
- On the Arctic coast of Alaska, the first thunderstorm ever to move through the town of Barrow shocked residents and obscured the Sun at 11:00 P.M. on June 19.

SUMMER 2000

Overview

The hallmark of the season was a striking continental contrast: hot and dry conditions in the fire-plagued South and West, and one of the coolest and dampest midsummers for the Northeast. Severe thunderstorms plagued Chicago and other airport hubs, throwing flight schedules into turmoil. A freakish heat wave in early September set all-time temperature records across much of Texas and neighboring states. As its second year drew to a close, a weakening La Niña helped foster an active hurricane season in the Atlantic Ocean but the storms had little impact. Only two tropical storms came ashore: Gordon and Helene—both striking northern Florida.

U.S. Highlights

- Albany, New York, had its coolest July since record keeping began in 1826, as temperatures never rose above 85° F (29° C) the entire month.
- Illinois experienced a cool summer, with much of the state failing to hit 90° F (32° C) until mid-August.
- In early September, several Texas cities set all-time records for heat, including 104° F (40° C) in Galveston, 109° F (43° C) in Houston, and 111° F (44° C) in San Antonio.
- Heavy thunderstorms on August 12-13 triggered widespread flash floods across northern New Jersey that damaged more than 2,000 homes.

FALL 2000

Overview

A dramatic change in weather patterns took shape as the nation shifted from its fifth-warmest August on record to its second-coldest November. Even before winter officially began on December 21, parts of the Great Lakes had more than 3 feet (1 meter) of snow. A long drought across the Deep South was only partially dented by spotty rains. Autumn chill and snow helped bring an end to the worst fire season in 50 years across the western United States, but Pacific storms avoided California through most of the fall, allowing for tinder-dry conditions and occasional blasts of Santa Ana wind. The La Niña of 1998–2000 was barely detectable by fall. Calendar year 2000 went into the books as the nation's 13th warmest in the past century.

U.S. Highlights

- One of the nation's deadliest series of tornadoes during 2000 devastated Tuscaloosa County, Alabama, on December 16, killing 11 people. Only a few hours later, temperatures sharply dropped, bottoming out below freezing.
- Four feet (1.2 meters) of water flooded some areas near Miami after 20 inches (508 millimeters) of rain fell on October 2–3.
- A dying tropical storm and a cold front combined on November 1-2 to dump 27.24 inches (690 millimeters) of rain on Hilo, Hawaii, in 24 hours. Despite the torrent, Hawaii remained in a long-term drought.
- In one of Buffalo's worst snowstorms on record, 24.9 inches (632 millimeters) brought the city to a halt on November 20.

WINTER 2000-2001

Overview

One of the rawest, stormiest winters in years settled in across the eastern two-thirds of the country. Missouri, Oklahoma, and Arkansas saw their coldest November–December period on record. The region's worst ice storm downed thousands of trees and left more than half a million people without power during Christmas week. Farther north, a record snowpack built across parts of the northern Great Plains, while Florida's drought became the worst in its history. After a bone-dry start to the rainy season, Southern California was socked in early January by its strongest winter storm in three years. La Niña made a surprise reappearance, but forecasters predicted its demise by summer 2001, with a new El Niño possible in the coming winter.

U.S. Highlights

- It was the chilliest Christmas on record in Green Bay, Wisconsin (-22° F, or -30° C), and Waterloo, Iowa (-29° F, or -34° C). A harsh winter followed in the Great Plains, as Huron, South Dakota, reported its deepest-ever snow cover on February 9: 30 inches (762 millimeters).
- In New York's heaviest snowfall in five years, a blizzard on New Year's weekend dumped more than 1 foot (300 millimeters) of snow on Central Park.
- A freeze nipped much of Florida around New Year's, following the state's driest year on record. Readings fell to 28° F (-2° C) in Orlando and 30° F (-1° C) in Tampa, while Miami hit bottom at 39° F (4° C).

WORLD HIGHLIGHTS

- Dust storms from the Mongolian Plateau that darkened skies across northern China were followed by drought that threatened the water supply of more than 3 million Chinese.
- The worst drought in a century scorched more than 8,000 communities across northern India and parts of Afghanistan, Pakistan, and Iran.
- Floods and mud slides struck Guatemala and the Mexico City area in early June.
- A late-April tornado formed in northeast Bangladesh, killing 19 people, injuring more than 1,000 others, and destroying at least 2,500 homes.

Shocked residents console each other following a devastating tornado that ripped through their neighborhood in Arlington, Texas, in March 2000.

- Southeast Europe endured one of its worst heat waves on record. Readings topped 110° F (43° C) from Italy to Turkey and hit 113° F (45° C) in southern Bulgaria.
- An unusually strong monsoon inundated parts of Southeast Asia with record rains. More than 180 people died, and approximately 4 million lost homes, belongings, or family in and near the Mekong Delta of Cambodia and in Vietnam, Laos, and Thailand.
- Central Japan was socked by a record 24 inches (610 millimeters) of rain during mid-September. The resulting floods forced the nation's largest automobile factory to temporarily halt its production operations.

In July 2000, two weeks of searing temperatures baked Tuscaloosa, Alabama, prompting one innovative 12-year-old to take matters into her own hands.

- Relentless rains produced the worst floods in half a century and the wettest autumn on record across parts of Great Britain.
- Typhoon Xangsane ("elephant" in Taiwanese) killed 62 people and caused more than $2 billion in damage as it tore across Taiwan in late October.
- A fierce storm on October 7 brought deep snow and winds approaching 159 miles (256 kilometers) per hour to Switzerland; meanwhile, high winds and heavy rains battered much of western Europe.
- As La Niña persevered, Indonesia was beset by some of its worst flooding in 40 years. More than 150 people were killed on the island of Sumatra alone.

- A fierce winter killed hundreds of people and more than half a million livestock across China's Mongolian Plateau.
- A rare but dangerous sequence of snowmelt followed by refreezing made the Italian Alps a death trap. Twelve climbers slipped to their deaths in separate accidents the weekend of December 16–17.
- Seoul, South Korea, was blanketed by 8.4 inches (213 millimeters) of snow, the deepest snowfall in 32 years, on February 15. It was the nation's second major snowstorm to strike in a month.
- Weeks of flooding in Mozambique killed more than 70 people and displaced more than 80,000 in February and March.

The heavy spring rains that drenched southern Africa produced the worst flooding ever recorded in Mozambique; thousands of families lost their homes.

Nobel Prize: Chemistry

Research with direct practical applications brought the 2000 Nobel Prize in Chemistry to three scientists. Alan J. Heeger and Alan G. MacDiarmid of the United States and Hideki Shirakawa of Japan shared the prize for the discovery and development of conductive polymers, thin films of plastic that can conduct electricity.

The three scientists made their initial findings in the late 1970s. Since then, the Nobel committee noted, they and others have developed conductive polymers into an important research field with enormous commercial possibilities.

Chance Aids a Discovery

Plastics are polymers, molecules formed into long, repeating chains, like pearls in a necklace. They are known as insulators—that is, they stop the flow of electricity. That is why electrical wires are wrapped with plastic insulation. But Heeger, of the University of California at Santa Barbara; MacDiarmid, of the University of Pennsylvania, Philadelphia; and Shirakawa, of the University of Tsukuba in Japan, found a way to make plastics that carry electricity just as well as metals do. In the 1970s, the trio discovered that a thin film of polyacetylene could be oxidized with iodine vapor, increasing its electrical conductivity a billion times, according to the Nobel citation.

The discovery was made partly by accident. During the 1970s, Shirakawa was working on new ways to synthesize polyacetylene, which is prepared through polymerization of the hydrocarbon acetylene. Once, in error, a research assistant added 1,000 times too much catalyst to the acetylene brew with which he was working. In place of the black polyacetylene film that normally appeared on the inside of the reaction vessel, a beautiful silvery film surfaced. Shirakawa was intrigued. He began to experiment, varying the temperature and concentration of the catalyst to produce other shimmery metallic films.

A chance meeting also played a part in the discovery. While Shirakawa was working with organic polymers in Japan, MacDiarmid and Heeger had produced a metallic-looking film of the inorganic polymer sulfur nitride. MacDiarmid made mention of this work to Shirakawa when he was in Japan. When MacDiarmid heard about Shirakawa's metallic film, he invited the Japanese scientist to come to the United States and investigate the polymer at the University of Pennsylvania in Philadelphia.

There, with Heeger, MacDiarmid and Shirakawa modified polyacetylene by oxidizing it with iodine vapor—a process known as doping—and discovered its amazing conductivity. But how did the plastic become conductive? A metal wire conducts electric current because the electrons in the metal are free to move. Plastics do not normally share this property; the electrons in polymers are bound to their atoms. To conduct electricity, a polymer has to imitate a metal; that is, its electrons must be free to move. Two conditions make that possible. First, the polymer must have alternating single and double bonds (an arrangement known as conjugated double bonds) between its carbon atoms. In other words, the atoms alternately share electrons.

Second, the plastic must be doped—by oxidation, which removes electrons from the material, or by reduction, which adds electrons. By removing electrons, oxidation creates "holes," or electron deficits. In the case of the iodine-polyacetylene reaction, for example, an iodine molecule attracts an electron from the polyacetylene chain, leaving a double bond one electron short. Deserted by its pair, the odd electron of that bond now can move freely. Reduction introduces extra electrons that are likewise free to move. When an electrical field is applied, the electrons travel quite rapidly along the polymer chain. This way, an electric current can travel through the plastic.

A plastic material consists of many polymer chains, and the arrangement of the chains affects the material's conductivity. Because electrons must jump from one molecule to the next to carry a current, the chains have to be packed in ordered rows.

Alan G. MacDiarmid, Hideki Shirakawa, and Alan J. Heeger (left to right) shared the Chemistry Nobel Prize for developing plastics that exhibit electrical conductivity—a property now exploited in countless products.

FOLDING VIDEO SCREENS AND MORE

A promising field of research has opened up since this award-winning discovery. A number of other conductive polymers have since been developed, as well as semiconductive polymers in which the ability to carry electric current can be switched on and off. These new materials are apt to find numerous applications.

Conductive polymers are widely used today to drain away static electricity in various materials. The new polymers are also used to shield computer users from the electromagnetic radiation that is produced by computer screens, and in "smart" windows that block sunlight.

Conductive and semiconductive polymers are finding uses in photodiodes and energy-saving light-emitting diodes (LEDs). Inorganic semiconductors, such as gallium phosphide, traditionally have been used in these devices, but interest is growing in plastic versions because they are relatively inexpensive and easy to produce. Besides mobile-phone displays and similar uses, light-emitting polymer materials may one day become the basis for inexpensive, flat, or even folding video displays, glowing traffic signs, or wallpaper designs that light up.

In addition, inexpensive integrated circuits based on semiconductive polymers are likely to find a growing role in consumer electronic products. Research of these materials has helped give rise to a new field of study: molecular electronics. Studying molecular electronics could lead to the development of integrated circuits so tiny that they would make today's silicon chips look like dinner plates.

Alan J. Heeger, born in 1936 in Sioux City, Iowa, received his Ph.D. at the University of California, Berkeley, in 1961. He became an associate professor at the University of Pennsylvania the next year, and served as a full professor there from 1967 to 1982. Since 1982, he has been a professor of physics at the University of California, Santa Barbara, and directs its Institute for Polymers and Organic Solids. In 1990, he founded the UNIAX Corporation, which makes conducting polymers.

Alan G. MacDiarmid, born in 1927 in Masterton, New Zealand, earned degrees from the University of New Zealand, the University of Wisconsin, and the University of Cambridge in the United Kingdom. He joined the faculty of the University of Pennsylvania in 1955 where he is Blanchard Professor of Chemistry.

Hideki Shirakawa, born in 1936 in Tokyo, received his Ph.D. at the Tokyo Institute of Technology in 1966. That year, he joined the Institute of Materials Science at the University of Tsukuba, where he was a full professor from 1982 until retiring in 2000.

Elaine Pascoe

NOBEL PRIZE: PHYSICS

The 2000 Nobel Prize in Physics was awarded to three scientists whose work helped usher in the age of digital electronics. Zhores Alferov of Russia shared the award with Herbert Kroemer and Jack Kilby of the United States for work that led to today's computers, cellular telephones, and other electronic devices.

Kilby, 76, of the Dallas firm Texas Instruments, received half the prize for his part in developing the integrated circuit, or chip, that drives today's computers. Alferov, 70, of the A.F. Ioffe Physico-Technical Institute in St. Petersburg, Russia, and Kroemer, 72, of the University of California at Santa Barbara, shared the other half of the award for their separate semiconductor research. Their work led to the development of semiconductor heterostructures, the high-speed circuits used in mobile phones, satellite links, CD players, bar-code readers, and fiber optics.

The choice of the three researchers was perceived as unusual for the Royal Swedish Academy of Sciences, which selects the Nobel winners. In recent years, the physics prize has gone to scientists who made their mark in the realm of quantum physics and similar theoretical fields. This was the first time in many years that practical work had been honored. But the importance of the work is clear. The three award winners are responsible for fundamental inventions that underlie today's information technology, allowing the development of devices that can process and transfer huge volumes of information at high speed, and yet are portable enough to go anywhere. This ever-evolving technology is bringing major changes to society.

The pocket calculator was one of the first practical applications of Jack Kilby's integrated circuit.

LAUNCHING THE INFORMATION AGE

The revolution in information processing began with the invention of the transistor in the late 1940s (for which William B. Shockley, John Bardeen, and Walter H. Brattain shared the 1956 Nobel Prize in Physics). Transistors make use of semiconductors—materials whose ability to conduct electricity can be adjusted—to direct the flow of electric current. Transistors are smaller, more reliable, and use less energy than vacuum tubes, which they quickly replaced in radios, early computers, and various other modern electronic devices.

More than 10,000 individual transistors could be soldered together on a circuit board, thus allowing a great increase in the complexity of electronic systems. But as ever-more-complex computers were developed, it quickly became apparent that this would not be enough. Enter the integrated circuit (IC), a device in which many transistors are formed in a single composite semiconductor block. Although researchers realized early on that an integrated circuit would be the solution, it was not until about 1960 that technological advances allowed the various elements to be produced in one piece. The method involves growing silicon crystals that are specially "doped" with selected impurities, slicing the crystals into wafers whose thickness is measured in micrometers, and imprinting circuit patterns through complex techniques based on photolithography.

Two engineers who worked independently of each other—Jack S. Kilby and Robert Noyce—are both considered to be the inventors of the IC. Kilby, at Texas Instruments, was the first to build an IC and the first to file a patent application. He was also the coinventor of the pocket calculator, one of the first applications of the IC. Noyce, who died in 1990, developed the IC as it was later to be manufactured, using silicon and

The scientists who shared the 2000 Nobel Prize in Physics—Zhores I. Alferov (left), Herbert Kroemer (center), and Jack S. Kilby (right)—helped launch the electronics age. Alferov and Kroemer worked to develop the semiconductors used in such items as laser pointers and bar-code readers, while Kilby's efforts led to the microprocessor.

silicon dioxide as semiconductor and insulator elements, and aluminum as the conductive element. He later helped found the Intel Corporation. In making its award, the Nobel committee acknowledged that the integrated circuit was more of a technical invention than a discovery in physics. However, its invention embraced progress by addressing many fundamental questions, including how to produce dense layers that are only a few atoms thick. And the development of the IC prompted enormous investment in research and development in solid-state physics. This has in turn led to significant advances in areas such as semiconductor technology and miniaturization.

By the 1970s, the integrated circuit had evolved into the microprocessor, a chip that carried enough components to run a computer. That led to the development of desktop personal computers. The power of computer chips continues to grow following a remarkable trend known as "Moore's law," which states that the number of components on a chip will double every 18 months, exponentially increasing computer capabilities over relatively short periods of time. Today, there are chips with millions of components, and they are at the heart of a huge array of devices, from washing machines to supercomputers. More-powerful chips continue to be developed, and there is no sign that advances will end anytime soon.

HIGH-SPEED SEMICONDUCTORS

Zhores I. Alferov and Herbert Kroemer kicked communications circuitry into high gear with heterostructures, which are layered (or compound) semiconductor devices. Heterostructures are made up of several thin layers (some as thin as a few atoms) with differing conductivity. The layers consist of materials such as gallium arsenide and aluminum gallium arsenide, selected so that their crystal structures fit one another exactly. Where the layers meet, electrons can move almost freely.

The unique properties of heterostructures have proved useful for research in quantum physics. But the practical applications have so far been even more important. It was in 1957, while Kroemer was working at RCA in Princeton, New Jersey, that he first proposed a heterostructure transistor. He calculated, correctly, that it would be able to handle higher frequencies and produce less noise than ordinary transistors. Low-noise, high-frequency amplifiers utilizing heterotransistors are often used today in satellite communications and for improving the signal-to-noise ratio in mobile telephones.

In addition, heterostructures proved to be the key to the development of small semiconductor lasers that have found dozens of practical applications. Alferov and Kroemer independently put forward the principle for the lasers in 1963. By around 1970, a technological breakthrough allowed them to build practical small lasers that worked continuously at room temperatures. Today, laser diodes built with heterostructure technology send information over fiber-optic cables. They are also used in CD players, bar-code readers, and laser pointers. The same technology is being used to make light-emitting diodes (LEDs) for use in car brake lights, traffic lights, and other warning lights. LEDs may one day even replace electric lightbulbs.

Jack S. Kilby was born on November 8, 1923, in Jefferson City, Missouri, and grew up in Great Bend, Kansas. He earned bachelor's and master's degrees in electrical engineering from the Universities of Illinois and Wisconsin, respectively. In 1958, he joined Texas Instruments, where he used borrowed and improvised equipment to create the first microchip. Kilby developed numerous military, industrial, and commercial applications of microchip technology, and he holds some 60 patents. From 1978 to 1984, he was a professor of electrical engineering at Texas A&M University.

Zhores I. Alferov was born on March 15, 1930, in Vitebsk, Belorussia, in the former Soviet Union. Since 1983, he has directed the Ioffe Physico-Technical Institute in St. Petersburg, where he had earlier earned several advanced degrees, including a doctorate of sciences in physics and mathematics. Alferov is the first Russian to win a Nobel Prize since Mikhail Gorbachev was awarded the Peace Prize in 1990, and the first Russian to win the physics prize since 1978, when Piotr Kapitsa shared the award for work in low-temperature physics.

Herbert Kroemer was born in Germany in 1928, and earned a doctorate in theoretical physics at the University of Göttingen in 1952. After moving to the United States in 1959, he worked at RCA Laboratories in Princeton, New Jersey, and at Varian Associates in Palo Alto, California. In 1968, he joined the faculty of the University of Colorado, Boulder, and in 1976 became a professor at the University of California at Santa Barbara. There, he expanded a small program into a leading research group focused on heterostructure physics and technology.

Elaine Pascoe

NOBEL PRIZE: PHYSIOLOGY OR MEDICINE

The 2000 Nobel Prize in Physiology or Medicine was awarded to three scientists for their studies of how messages are transmitted between brain cells. Arvid Carlsson of Sweden, and Paul Greengard and Eric Kandel, of the United States, shared the prize for their separate discoveries on how brain cells send signals to each other and how this affects mental processes. "These discoveries have been crucial for an understanding of the normal function of the brain," the Nobel Assembly at the Karolinska Institute noted, and for understanding how disturbances in signal transmission "can give rise to neurological and psychiatric diseases."

Carlsson, 77, of Göteborg University in Sweden, studied dopamine, a neurotransmitter (a chemical that is involved in transmitting signals through the nervous system), and traced its importance in controlling movement. His work led to the development of the drug L-dopa for the treatment of Parkinson's disease, a condition in which dopamine is depleted. Greengard, 74, of Rockefeller University in New York City, investigated the complicated effects that dopamine and other kinds of neurotransmitters have on brain cells. His research has helped in the development of better drugs for treating psychiatric disorders, such as the antidepressant Prozac. Kandel, 70, of Columbia University in New York City, has done pioneering research into short-term and long-term memory, using the sea slug and the mouse as research subjects. His studies revealed the complex biochemical changes that take place in brain cells when memories are formed.

THE ROLE OF DOPAMINE

In the brain and elsewhere, nerve cells, or neurons, are arranged in networks—but they do not actually touch each other. Between the axon (signal-sending branch) of one neuron and the dendrite (signal-receiving branch) of the next is a tiny gap called the synapse. When a nerve impulse (actually a tiny electrical current) reaches the end of the axon, it triggers the release of neurotransmitters. These chemicals flow across the synapse to the dendrite, where they lock on to receptors and set off an electrochemical reaction. In that way, the nerve impulse is carried along.

During the late 1950s, Arvid Carlsson identified dopamine as an important transmitter in the brain. At the time, most scientists thought that dopamine was only a precursor of another transmitter, noradrenaline. Through meticulous research, Carlsson found that dopamine was concentrated in areas of the brain where noradrenaline was not present. He later concluded that dopamine was a transmitter in itself.

Carlsson found dopamine in especially high concentrations in the basal ganglia, parts of the brain that play key roles in controlling body movement. In experiments, he discovered that laboratory animals lost motor control when he gave them reserpine, a drug that depletes stores of dopamine. They recovered when he gave them L-dopa, a substance that is transformed into dopamine in the brain.

It was a short jump from Carlsson's conclusive experiment to developing a treatment for Parkinson's disease, which produces symptoms—tremors, rigidity, and loss of motor control—very similar to the effects of reserpine. It turned out that the disease causes degeneration of dopamine-producing cells in the brain, leaving victims with abnormally low levels of the neurotransmitter. L-dopa was found to restore levels of dopamine and allow patients to regain normal motor control. The drug is still the most important weapon available against Parkinson's disease.

A CASCADE OF CHANGES

Paul Greengard received his share of the Nobel Prize for research into the ways neurotransmitters exert their effects on the synapse. Understanding the complex processes by which these chemicals work has led to new drugs for treating a variety of psychiatric disorders.

Transmitters such as dopamine, norepinephrine, and serotonin relay nerve impulses through slow synaptic transmission. They produce changes in the functions of nerve cells that may last from seconds to hours. Slow synaptic transmission is responsible for a number of basic functions of the nervous system, and it is vital to states of alertness and mood. Slow synaptic transmission can also regulate fast synaptic transmission, which is involved in speech, movement, and sensory perception.

Greengard showed that slow synaptic transmission entails a chemical reaction

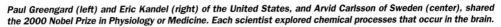

Paul Greengard (left) and Eric Kandel (right) of the United States, and Arvid Carlsson of Sweden (center), shared the 2000 Nobel Prize in Physiology or Medicine. Each scientist explored chemical processes that occur in the brain.

called protein phosphorylation. In this reaction, proteins take on, or shed, small chemical groups known as phosphates, which alter the proteins' form and function. When dopamine or another chemical involved in slow synaptic transmission hits receptors in the membrane of the nerve cell, the neurotransmitter sets off a cascade of changes that trigger phosphorylation in certain proteins. Some of these proteins form what are called ion channels in the membrane, allowing the nerve cell to send electrical impulses. Thus, changes in these proteins alter the excitability of the nerve cell and its ability to send impulses along its branches.

SEA-SLUG MEMORIES

In the 1970s, Eric Kandel studied learning and memory in mammals, but he quickly realized that he needed a simpler research subject. He turned to the lowly sea slug, *Aplysia,* for several reasons: it has a simple nervous system with relatively few nerve cells. It also does not have memory as we think of it; rather, it has a basic reflex that protects its gills. Kandel found that certain stimuli would cause the reflex to strengthen and remain strong for a time. That qualified as a form of learning and made the sea slug a likely subject.

Kandel found that weak stimuli produced a form of short-term memory, lasting from minutes to hours. The mechanism for this involved the phosphorylation described by Paul Greengard. In this case, changes in the proteins of the cell membrane led to the release of more neurotransmitters at the synapse, amplifying the reflex the next time the stimulus appeared.

Stronger stimuli produced a form of long-term memory that could last for several weeks, Kandel found. These stimuli triggered chemical changes that affected the nerve-cell nuclei, causing new proteins to be formed, and changing the number of proteins at the synapses. The altered synapses could release even more neurotransmitters. Kandel showed that this occurrence results in the synapse growing larger, and a long-lasting change of function, actually forming the building blocks of memory. In his many studies on mice during the 1990s, Kandel demonstrated that the same types of changes occur in mammals, and that learning takes place through the strengthening of these nerve-cell connections.

The human brain has some 100 billion nerve cells, with at least 100 trillion synapses. Yet in the synapses, the mechanisms that operate are the same as those in mice and sea slugs. This fact has raised hope for new drugs to treat the memory impairment associated with dementia.

Arvid Carlsson was born January 25, 1923, in Uppsala, Sweden, and earned his medical degree in 1951 at Lund University. He did much of his pioneering research into dopamine at the National Institutes of Health (NIH), Bethesda, Maryland. Carlsson has been affiliated with Göteborg University in Göteborg, Sweden, for most of his career, where he was a professor of pharmacology in 1959, retiring in 1989.

Paul Greengard was born December 11, 1925, in New York City. He studied theoretical physics in college, but later switched to biochemistry. Greengard earned a doctorate in 1953 from Johns Hopkins University, Baltimore, and did postdoctoral studies at the University of Cambridge, England, and other institutions. In the 1960s, he worked for Geigy Research Laboratories, and from 1961 to 1970, he taught at the Albert Einstein College of Medicine, Bronx, New York. From 1968 to 1983, he was a professor of pharmacology and psychiatry at the Yale University School of Medicine, New Haven, Connecticut. Since 1983, he has been on the faculty of Rockefeller University, where he is professor and head of the Laboratory of Molecular and Cellular Neuroscience.

Eric Kandel was born November 7, 1929, in Vienna, Austria, and fled with his family to the United States in 1939, at the start of World War II. Now an American citizen, Kandel attended Harvard Medical School, Boston, to become a psychoanalyst; but a course in neurophysiology sparked his interest in the biology of memory. Since 1974, he has been on the faculty of Columbia University. In addition, he is a senior investigator at the Howard Hughes Medical Institute, Chevy Chase, Maryland.

Elaine Pascoe

NUTRITION

UPDATED DIETARY GUIDELINES

Confused about what are the best foods to eat? Both the federal government and the American Heart Association (AHA) have released updated versions of their respective dietary recommendations.

In May 2000, the fifth edition of *Nutrition and Your Health: Dietary Guidelines for Americans*, developed jointly by the U.S. Department of Agriculture (USDA) and the Department of Health and Human Services (DHHS), was unveiled. Since 1980, these agencies have been required by law to issue updated dietary guidelines every five years. The newest edition features 10 guidelines that outline desirable health goals.

Additionally, the recommendations for grains, vegetables, and fruits have been separated into two guidelines, one for fruits and vegetables and one for grains. And, in light of recent findings that link soft drinks and obesity, a revision on sugar intake now targets beverages.

In October 2000, the AHA released its revised dietary recommendations, reflecting up-to-date findings regarding the link between diet and heart disease, high blood pressure, and stroke. The latest recommendations focus on: (1) an overall healthy eating pattern, (2) a healthy body weight, (3) a desirable cholesterol level, and (4) a desirable blood-pressure level. Departing from previous editions, the guidelines include recommendations aimed at preventing overweight and obesity. The AHA now also encourages the consumption of two servings per week of fish.

FISH SAFETY ISSUES

While the AHA is urging consumers to eat more fish, there are new concerns about the safety of some varieties. The U.S. Food and Drug Administration (FDA) issued warnings in January 2001 that certain kinds of fish may contain excessive levels of methyl mercury, cautioning that this substance may harm an unborn baby's developing nervous system. Citing shark, swordfish, king mackerel, and tilefish—all species of long-lived, larger fish that feed on smaller fish, and therefore are more likely to accumulate higher levels of methyl mercury—the advisory warns pregnant women and women of childbearing age who may become pregnant that they could pass excessive levels of methyl mercury on to their developing fetuses. These women were cautioned to limit their fish consumption to 12 ounces (340 grams) of cooked fish per week. Due to the potential effect of methyl mercury on

While nutritionists recommend that people eat more fish, certain kinds may contain excessive levels of methyl mercury—a substance harmful to the nervous systems of unborn babies and young children.

the maturing nervous systems of young children, the FDA recommends that nursing mothers and young children avoid these fish as well. Instead, the FDA recommends choosing other varieties of fish, including shellfish, canned fish, smaller ocean fish, and farm-raised fish.

The Environmental Protection Agency (EPA) also advised that women and children exercise caution when eating fish caught by family and friends, due to potential mercury contamination in some local waters. The FDA advises the public to check with state and local health departments regarding the safety of fish caught in local waters.

BUTTER VERSUS MARGARINE

Butter or margarine—which one is healthier? When the butter-vs.-margarine debate first hit the press in 1993, Americans stoically were downing margarine, believing that it was the healthier spread. That changed following an editorial that appeared in the *American Journal of Public Health* citing that margarine, with its trans-fatty-acid content, is the cause of major health problems in the United States. Trans fatty acids are produced when liquid fats are subjected to a process called hydrogenation, which changes the structure of fat molecules so as to enhance the solidification process. Some studies have suggested that trans fatty acids may wreak the same havoc as saturated fats, raising blood-cholesterol levels and increasing the risk of heart disease. Consequently, many Americans turned back to butter as the more "natural" fat, now believing it has fewer health risks than margarine. Not so, say researchers at the University of Texas Southwestern Medical Center, Dallas.

In a recent study of 46 families on two diet regimens—five weeks with butter and five weeks with tub margarine—researchers found that the margarine diet lowered the adults' LDL ("bad") cholesterol by 11 percent when compared to those who consumed butter, while the children's LDL cholesterol fell by 9 percent on the margarine diet. So, despite fears about trans fatty acids, when compared to butter, tub margarine may actually be effective at *lowering* blood-cholesterol levels.

Why? The amount of cholesterol-raising fat—the number of grams of saturated fat *plus* the number of grams of trans fatty acids—is significantly higher in butter than in margarine. Butter contains more than 7 grams of saturated fat and nearly 0.5 gram of trans fatty acids per tablespoon—a total of 7.5 grams. Regular stick margarine (82 percent fat) contains 2.3 grams of saturated fat and about 2.4 grams of trans fatty acids—a total of 4.7 grams. Switching to tub (soft) margarine (80 percent fat) lowers the numbers further to 3 grams of combined

saturated plus trans fat. Best of all is soft "light" margarine (40 percent fat), with 1.7 grams of combined saturated and trans fat.

Considering the facts, one way to protect against high blood cholesterol is to limit saturated-fat intake. The most harmful source of trans fatty acids in American diets is not margarine but processed foods, such as premade cakes, candy bars, cookies, crackers, doughnuts, fried foods, microwave popcorn, and pastries. While the FDA ponders proposed regulations requiring food companies to list the number of grams of trans fatty acids on nutrition labels, the consumer's best ally is to read ingredient lists for evidence of "hydrogenated," or "hardened," or "partially hydrogenated" oils. The earlier these words appear on the list, the greater the number of grams of trans fatty acids that are likely to be present.

USDA TO STUDY POPULAR DIETS

As a result of the huge public following for Atkins-type low-carbohydrate, high-protein diets—and the heated controversy these diets have inspired—the USDA plans to probe their effects. In a preliminary study designed to follow 20 dieters for one year, researchers will compare the effects of the Atkins New Diet Revolution with the effects of the LEARN approach to weight loss, a high-carbohydrate, low-fat diet based on behavior modification. Participants will be examined for the effects of the two weight-loss plans; 10 dieters will follow the Atkins diet, and 10 the LEARN program. Groups will be evaluated and compared for changes in blood-cholesterol levels, blood pressure, ketone levels, eating behavior, and the ability to handle sugars. Data from this study will be the basis for a larger study that ultimately should allow researchers to draw more-reliable conclusions about the two types of popular diets.

As a first step, the USDA has issued a summary of the consensus of research on weight loss, which concluded that by eliminating carbohydrates, dieters are simply consuming fewer calories and not invoking a unique metabolic effect that preferentially burns fat, as claimed by proponents of the low-carbohydrate diet. The agency affirms that individuals following a moderate-fat, high-carbohydrate diet, as directed by current U.S. dietary guidelines, are more likely to maintain weight loss. The FDA plans to continue to examine the long- and short-term consequences of popular diets.

BURGER COLOR

Cooking burgers on gas grills until they are brown—rather than using a meat thermometer—does not ensure that the meat is adequately cooked. How meat is handled before cooking can falsely make it appear to be cooked adequately, according to scientists in the Agricultural Research Service's (ARS's) Food Technology and Safety Laboratory in Beltsville, Maryland. Their research has prompted the USDA's Food Safety and Inspection Service (FSIS) to reissue guidelines for food temperatures.

ARS scientists cooked ground-beef patties on a gas grill using a thermometer to determine when the burgers reached internal temperatures of 135°, 151°, and 160° F (57°, 66°, and 71° C). They also cooked burgers until they turned brown without using a thermometer. Using ground beef bought at a supermarket, scientists shaped some into patties and cooked them immediately, shaped some into patties and froze them, and froze some meat in bulk form.

The beef that had been frozen in bulk, thawed, formed into patties, and then cooked right away was the only type that showed brown color at unsafe temperatures. Premature browning was not evident in frozen patties that were thawed and then cooked, or in fresh patties that were cooked without having been previously frozen.

Furthermore, all of the burgers that were removed from the grill with pink centers continued to brown for several minutes. Surprisingly, a burger cooked to 135° F (57° C) and allowed to sit for about four minutes looked the same as a burger cooked to 160° F (71° C), even though it had not reached an internal temperature of 160° F.

The research confirms the current advice to use a meat thermometer and to cook meat to 160° F, the temperature at which *Escherichia coli* (*E. coli*) is killed.

Sue Gebo

OCEANOGRAPHY

OCEAN FERTILIZATION

Carbon dioxide (CO_2) is released when coal, oil, and other fossil fuels are burned, and its atmospheric levels have risen steadily with increased use of these fuels. Because CO_2 is a "greenhouse" gas—it traps heat in the same way as glass does in a greenhouse—its current high atmospheric level has been linked to a warming trend in Earth's climate. The ongoing search for ways to reduce levels of CO_2 in the atmosphere, and in turn slow global warming, has some researchers turning to Earth's oceans.

Because phytoplankton, tiny algae that float freely in the oceans, carry out about half of Earth's photosynthesis, they play an important role in the global CO_2 exchange cycle. Theoretically, an increase in phytoplankton growth could help reduce carbon dioxide levels in the atmosphere. How could this be achieved? In the equatorial Pacific Ocean and the so-called Southern Ocean (the seas surrounding Antarctica to the southern tips of Africa, Australia, and South America), phytoplankton growth is limited by the supply of dissolved iron, a trace element. In 1990, oceanographer John Martin, of California's Moss Landing Marine Laboratories (MLML), suggested that small amounts of additional iron could trigger increased phytoplankton growth in these southerly waters.

Four experiments have been conducted to check Martin's hypothesis, the latest in November 2000 in the ocean south of Africa. Professor Victor Smetacek of Germany's Alfred Wegener Institute (AWI) for Polar and Marine Research led an international study expedition aboard the research vessel *Polarstern* to distribute an iron sulfate solution over a small patch of the ocean.

The researchers planned the expedition carefully because they were aware that vicious storms in the Southern Ocean governed by the strong Antarctic Circumpolar Current could spread the iron solution over a large area, diluting it too much to promote significant phytoplankton growth. To head off that possibility, *Polarstern* hunted for an eddy—a circular current that, as it swirls, prevents the water caught within it from mingling with surrounding waters. Once the scientists found an eddy, *Polarstern* dispensed the iron solution and measured the biological, chemical, and physical properties of the ocean water.

The eddy kept the solution contained, and the area's algae thrived. Within two weeks, measurements showed that chlorophyll—the component responsible for photosynthesis—had tripled. That was a clear indication that the tiny plants were pulling in vastly increased amounts of CO_2.

However, it is still not completely clear whether iron fertilization could be used to reduce atmospheric CO_2. For that, the carbon content in the plants would have to move into the deep ocean and stay there. This can happen through the ocean's food web, when marine animals feed on phytoplankton; otherwise, most of the carbon trapped by the plants eventually returns to the atmosphere as CO_2.

Observing the Deep Ocean

For most of the past century, research vessels have painstakingly collected measurements of ocean temperature and salinity during yearlong expeditions. These efforts have greatly advanced knowledge of the ocean and its circulation, but collecting data this way is a slow process. The 1990s saw a burst of activity, as the international World Ocean Circulation Experiment (WOCE) collected approximately 20,000 oceanic temperature and salinity profiles, as many as had been amassed in the previous 100 years. But still, the data were sparse and uncorrelated.

Now a project headed by Dean Roemmich, chairman of the Argo Science team and professor at the Scripps Institution of Oceanography, in La Jolla, California, will monitor temperature and salinity worldwide with an array of 3,000 free-drifting, computer-controlled floats. Several hundred Argo floats were deployed in 2000.

Like a submarine, Argo descends below the surface, to a depth of about 6,560 feet (2,000 meters). There, it travels with prevailing currents, gathering information. Every 10 days, the float returns to the surface and

Argo floats (above) gather valuable information about ocean temperature and salinity levels to help forecast storms and predict weather patterns.

relays ocean temperature and salinity levels to scientists ashore via satellite link. The floats are designed to repeat this cycle for four to five years, gathering up to 180 profiles each. When all 3,000 are deployed, they will record as much information in three months as was collected during all 10 years of WOCE. Data collected by Argo floats will help in forecasting storms and patterns such as El Niño, which periodically disrupts North American weather patterns. The information will also contribute to a better overall understanding of oceanic circulation and its role in the climate of the planet.

Forecasting a Hurricane's Force

To evacuate or not to evacuate? Citizens and government officials alike ponder this question each year. Apart from the predicted track of the hurricane, its strength is a crucial factor in making the decision. Past forecasts have reliably provided predictions of where these storms will hit, but they have also systematically overestimated the future strength of weak storms and underestimated the potential force of powerful hurricanes.

To overcome these inaccuracies, in June 2000, the U.S. National Weather Service (NWS) included a new computer model in its hurricane-prediction toolbox. Developed by professors Isaac Ginis and Lewis Rothstein of the University of Rhode Island (URI) Graduate School of Oceanography, the model has proved to be 30 percent more accurate than earlier models in predicting maximum wind speed. This difference can amount to a full category in hurricane strength, and therefore can significantly influence the decision to evacuate.

The model succeeds by taking into account the interaction between ocean and atmosphere within the hurricane. Hurricanes gather strength from water vapor that evaporates from the seas over which they travel. Since warm water generates more vapor than cold water, ocean temperature is a crucial parameter for hurricane development. As a rule, hurricanes form only over waters warmer than 79° F (26° C).

However, hurricane-force winds churn the ocean and affect surface water temperatures. Generally, the uniformity of water temperature rapidly decreases with depth. With the hurricane acting as a giant mixer, colder water from below is stirred into the mixed layer. As a result, the surface temperature can decrease 2° to 11° F (1° to 6° C), reducing the rate of evaporation and the amount of water vapor available to fuel the hurricane. This ultimately helps to weaken the advancing storm, causing it to sputter as it literally runs out of gas.

Predicting this interaction between ocean and storm requires knowledge of water temperatures under and in front of the hurricane, and this information is seldom available to forecasters tracking an approaching storm. But the URI scientists solved this problem with their highly accurate computer model, which relies on a database of historical temperature profiles, real-time satellite surface-temperature measurements, and data from the atmospheric hurricane model produced by the National Oceanic and Atmospheric Administration's (NOAA's) Geophysical Fluid Dynamics Laboratory (GFDL). The URI temperature information, in turn, is then fed back into the NOAA model, to help predict further development of the storm.

Olaf Boebel

PALEONTOLOGY

HAVE A HEART

When professional collector Michael Hammer discovered the skeleton of a plant-eating ornithischian dinosaur *Thescelosaurus* (dubbed "Willo") in South Dakota in 1993, the animal's ribs were so well preserved that Hammer wondered if perhaps some internal organs could still be deep inside its chest cavity. Physician Andrew Kuzmitz, who is also an amateur paleontologist, followed up on Hammer's hunch and produced two-dimensional computer-tomography (CT) scans of the 663-pound (300-kilogram), 13-foot (4-meter)-long dinosaur's chest area.

Then, several years after the North Carolina Museum of Natural Sciences in Raleigh acquired the fossilized dinosaur, researchers sent it to a local hospital for further examination. Three-dimensional medical imaging revealed that the rust-colored lump in Willo's chest indeed appeared to be soft tissues that had mineralized over time. They included ligaments, cartilaginous rib attachments, and—most exciting of all—a structure interpreted by the researchers to be a 66-million-year-old heart.

Paleontologists were especially excited to learn that Willo's heart was confirmed to be four-chambered, with a single arched

"Willo," a Thescelosaurus *found in South Dakota, is remarkably well preserved, and the first one ever discovered with a complete skull—and a fossilized heart.*

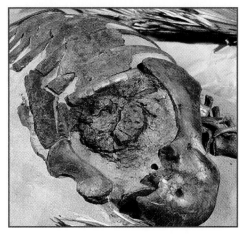

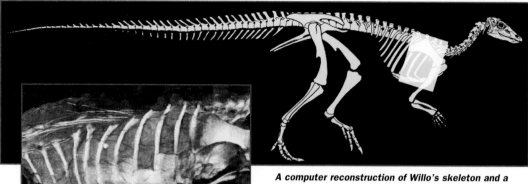

A computer reconstruction of Willo's skeleton and a 3-D image of the dinosaur's chest cavity (inset), both produced via medical-imaging technology, proved invaluable to scientists analyzing the remains.

aorta—a discovery that significantly validates the long-standing hypothesis that there is a close relationship between birds and dinosaurs. Since 1841, paleontologists have speculated on the nature of the dinosaur heart. Sir Richard Owen, the man who coined the word "dinosaur," suggested that the animal's heart should be four-chambered, as is found in birds and mammals with high metabolic rates.

More studies are in store for this skeleton. The find is so well preserved that it is possible that other fossilized organs are present. Its remarkable preservation is attributed to its burial in wet, oxygen-free sand, causing its soft tissues to undergo saponification, a process by which they turn into a soap-like substance and petrify.

Researchers who remain skeptical of the link between dinosaurs and birds will have their chance to study the heart of this pony-sized dinosaur. And whichever side of the argument paleontologists take, one thing is certain: the way they inspect their finds will be changed forever. Instead of chiseling debris away from fossilized animal bones, those who find something as remarkable as Willo's remains will most likely first turn to medical imaging for a closer look.

THE DINOSAUR–BIRD TRANSITION
The idea that dinosaurs, and in particular theropod dinosaurs, might appear in the ancestry of birds also received a boost from a highly detailed study on the microstructure of bone tissues in birds, mammals, and dinosaurs that was published in *Nature* in August 2000. Bone tissue in living birds and mammals "remodels," or redeposits, itself as these creatures grow—the newly formed

bone is known as secondary bone. A similarity between the secondary bone of birds and mammals on the one hand, and dinosaurs on the other, has been known since the late 1970s. This had been viewed as evidence that dinosaurs may have been endothermic (warm-blooded).

In this new study, however, noted paleontologists John M. Rensberger and Mahito Watabe studied canaliculi—microscopic channels that connect bone cells—and the organization of the collagen fibers in the bone. Their results were striking. It turns out that birds and a particular group of dinosaurs—ornithomimids—share a similarly disorganized structure of the microscopic canaliculi, whereas mammals and herbivorous (ornithischian) dinosaurs share a highly organized canalicular structure. The same relationships hold true for the organization of the collagen fibers. Evidently, mammals and ornithischian dinosaurs evolved their similar collagen and canalicular morphologies independently; these two groups are not closely related. On the other hand, in the context of the other important features shared by ornithomimids and birds, Rensberger and Watabe interpreted the similar structure of the canaliculi and collagen as indicative of a close relationship between ornithomimid dinosaurs and birds.

A BIRD OF A FEATHER?
Feathers are key features that are uniquely avian. Because the complex structure of feathers is thought to have evolved only once, anything bearing feathers is presumed to be more closely related to other feather-bearing organisms than to anything else. This is one of the compelling reasons for the

hunt for feathers in nonbird dinosaurs. If one were to demonstrate that a feathered organism was neither a bird nor a dinosaur, it would bring into question the idea that birds and dinosaurs are more closely related to each other than to anything else, and consequently undermine the belief that birds evolved from dinosaurs. Therefore, it was with a full appreciation of the significance of their claim that Oregon State University zoologist Terry Jones and colleagues reevaluated the presence of feathers in the Triassic archosaur *Longisquama.*

Longisquama is not a new discovery. Known since 1970, it is a small, gliding, lizardlike, four-legged animal, discovered in Kyrgyzstan in Central Asia, with a row of tall, featherlike vanes sticking up out of its back. Are these real feathers? The authors claim so, implying that this primitive tetrapod is closely linked to the ancestry of birds. If so, this would bypass dinosaurs as the near ancestors of birds. A number of paleontologists, however, question whether these are real feathers, or, rather, simply highly modified scales that, when viewed as preserved impressions some 200 million years after the animal lived, superficially resemble feathers. The jury remains out on *Longisquama* "feathers," but it is probably safe to say that as more data accumulate linking birds and

Eosimias, the world's smallest primate, lived 45 million years ago. As depicted in this illustration, the tiny anthropoid was no bigger than a human thumb.

dinosaurs, Jones' earnest interpretation of *Longisquama* may be relegated to the view held by a minority.

The discovery in 2000 of another feather-bearing dinosaur fossil in China adds more credence to the idea of a dinosaur-bird connection. The 130-million-year-old dromaeosaur—a small, fast-running relative of the velociraptor—appears to have traces of downy fibers over most of its body. Scientists theorize that if dinosaurs were warm-blooded animals (rather than cold-blooded reptiles), it is conceivable that some would have evolved to grow an insulating coat of feathers. While the latest fossil remains are analyzed further, evidence mounts in favor of an almost indisputable connection between birds and dinosaurs.

"LOWER" AND "HIGHER" PRIMATES

Primates are of particular interest to humans, because even those that are not hominids shed light on our own ancestry. Unfortunately, the fossil record of primates is not particularly reliable, because their bones tend to be poorly preserved in the forested habitats preferred by primates. Until recently, it has been quite difficult to reconstruct the ancestry of the so-called higher primates (anthropoids), the group that includes monkeys, apes, and humans.

Paleoanthropologist D.L. Gebo and his colleagues took an important step toward understanding the early anthropoid primates when they recovered tiny anklebones from a palm-sized middle Eocene creature known as *Eosimias,* earlier known only from a braincase element and a handful of teeth. The anklebones preserved key facets that suggest the animal made more-frequent use of horizontal foot positions than did its antecedents, whose feet were held inverted. A horizontal foot position is a key feature of anthropoid primates; therefore, this discovery sets *Eosimias,* in this specimen at least, squarely between the bulk of early fossil primates and anthropoid primates. While no one would claim that *Eosimias* is the ancestor of all anthropoid primates, the actual progenitor would likely have had the same kind of ankle and locomotory behavior.

David E. Fastovsky

PHYSICS

THE TAU OF NEUTRINOS

Physicists at the Fermi National Accelerator Laboratory (Fermilab) in Batavia, Illinois, announced in July 2000 their detection of the tau neutrino, an elusive subatomic particle whose existence was predicted 25 years ago. Finding the tau neutrino completes the search for all 12 fundamental building blocks of matter associated with the Standard Model, which physicists use to explain the creation of matter and its forces.

An international team of scientists collaborated on the Direct Observation of the Nu Tau (DONUT) experiment at Fermilab. For six months in 1997, researchers fired neutrinos at a target of iron plates alternately layered with sheets of emulsion, which served as a film to record evidence of particle interactions.

The DONUT team hoped to capture a one-in-a-trillion occurrence: a tau neutrino colliding with an iron nucleus to create another subatomic particle called a tau lepton. When the tau lepton decayed, it left a telltale millimeter-long track in the emulsion layers. Researchers at Nagoya University in Japan spent three years sifting through 6 million potential interactions to pinpoint just four tau-neutrino events.

According to the Standard Model, up and down quarks combine to produce protons and neutrons. Together with the electron and electron-neutrino leptons, these particles form the so-called first-generation matter of the everyday world. Strange and charm quarks, together with the muon and muon-neutrino leptons, produce second-generation matter—the more exotic particles found in quasars and cosmic rays. Top and bottom quarks, along with the tau and tau-neutrino leptons, form third-generation matter—the particles that existed for a fraction of a second after the Big Bang explosion that formed our universe.

Although the Standard Model prescribes that neutrinos are massless, a Japanese experiment in 1998 known as Super-Kamiokande suggested otherwise. Neutrinos endowed with mass would be able to change type, or "oscillate," which could explain why detectors always find fewer neutrinos than predicted by theory.

In June 2001, researchers spotting neutrinos at Canada's Sudbury Neutrino Observatory (SNO) in Ontario compared their new data with the Super-Kamiokande data to establish definitively that electron neutrinos produced deep inside the Sun change type before reaching Earth, and therefore have mass. While these findings validate long-standing models for fusion reactions in the Sun, physicists must further quantify neutrino masses and reconcile the Standard Model to these numbers.

BREAKING UP IS HARD TO DO

The idea of electron fission flies in the face of quantum theory, which holds that the fundamental building blocks of matter, such as the electron, quark, and neutrino, cannot be broken down any further.

None of this deters physicist Humphrey Maris of Brown University in Providence, Rhode Island, who has studied experiments that demonstrate how electrons injected in supercooled helium become trapped in individual, tiny bubbles. When light shines

Vittorio Paolone, of the Direct Observation of the Nu Tau experiment, poses inside the huge magnet used to eliminate charged particles from a neutrino beam.

on the helium, the electron bubbles behave in ways that defy explanation. They move through the helium faster or clump together to travel at different speeds, accompanied by a veritable potpourri of unidentified negatively charged particles.

Maris and his colleagues theorize that shining light on the electrons causes them to absorb energy and break up into two or more pieces. His revolutionary theory, first presented at a U.S. conference on quantum fluids and solids in June 2000 (the year many physicists were celebrating the 100th birthday of quantum theory), may force physicists to reevaluate many aspects of quantum theory, particularly the nature of the wave function.

The wave function mathematically describes a particle's position and energy states in terms of probabilities. The wave function for an electron in its lowest-energy ground state is spherical like the electron bubble. The shape of the wave function for the electron's next-highest energy level looks like a dumbbell. Maris argues that at this level, pressure from the surrounding helium could stretch the electron bubble until it breaks in half at the center. The resulting daughter bubbles, which he calls electrinos, would each contain half of the electron's wave function.

Such electrinos would indeed be able to move faster than their parent bubbles because they experience less drag in the helium. And if illuminated, these electrinos would also subdivide, creating clusters of bubbles with whole, half, and quarter charges that travel at different speeds.

Physicists are not used to thinking of the wave function as a physical entity that can be split. And while they regard the notion of electron fragments with skepticism, nobody has yet been able to find a hole in Maris' claims. Meanwhile, Maris and his colleagues are continuing to experiment with electrons in helium and to devise new experiments, perhaps in a race with skeptics, to see if quantum theory can embrace electrinos.

THE ENTANGLED WEB WE WEAVE

Superposition and entanglement are vital quantum-mechanical properties currently being exploited in the quest for quantum computers. Still decades away, these computers have the potential to outperform conventional computers in certain functions, such as factoring large numbers or searching databases.

According to quantum theory, an unobserved photon contains a combination or superposition of all its possible states. The act of observing the photon forces it to be in one particular state. Entanglement describes an almost telepathic relationship between particles sharing a superposition of states— observing one particle of an entangled pair determines the state of the other particle, even if the particles are oceans apart. The future development of quantum computers depends in part on whether we can entangle large numbers of particles, an undertaking that has yet to be successfully accomplished.

Cass Sackett and his colleagues at the National Institute of Standards and Technology (NIST) in Boulder, Colorado, have achieved the first entanglement of four atoms, demonstrating a technique that can be extended to any number of atoms. Based on the ideas of theorists Klaus Mølmer and Anders Sørenson at the University of Århus in Denmark, the new method is called push-button entanglement because it allows physicists to entangle specially prepared particles on demand.

To prepare for entanglement, the NIST team ionized four beryllium atoms—hit them with lasers to knock off electrons— and lined them up in an electromagnetic trap. After cooling the atoms to near absolute zero (–460° F or –273° C), researchers used additional laser fire to make the atoms rock back and forth in the same spin state, either up or down. (Spin is a measure of the atom's angular momentum.) Then a single pulse of laser light that was tuned to specific frequencies fired on the atoms to entangle their oscillations with their spin states. Consequently, the atoms shared a spin-up state and a spin-down state, as well as a superposition of both spin states. When they had observed one member of this newly entangled quartet, the researchers knew the spin states of the remaining atoms.

Therese Lloyd

PUBLIC HEALTH

NEW EFFORTS AGAINST PAIN

New protocols promise improved evaluation and treatment of pain—one of the most distressing aspects of disease, illness, and surgery, yet one that has been grossly undertreated in the United States. Research shows that many health-care providers are unaware of effective pain therapies, dismiss pain as "normal" or "imaginary," or believe that prescribing strong painkillers for their patients is too dangerous.

The Joint Commission on Accreditation of Healthcare Organizations, which accredits most U.S. hospitals, outpatient clinics, and nursing homes, directed such facilities to institute pain-management strategies by January 1, 2001. By February, the commission had begun to evaluate those plans; facilities not following suitable plans faced possible loss of accreditation.

The commission's guidelines specified that doctors and nurses must ask patients to evaluate their pain on a scale of 0 to 10—with 0 indicating no pain, and 10 signifying unbearable pain. Young children were to be shown pictures of expressive faces to evaluate their pain. Then the doctors and nurses were instructed to relieve, or at least alleviate, patients' pain using medications or non-drug treatments such as physical therapy, massage, and relaxation techniques.

In addition to its impact on the quality of one's life, pain has a huge economic impact: each year, an estimated 36 million Americans—27 percent of working adults—miss work due to physical pain.

CANCER CAUSES AND PREVALENCE

A report from the National Cancer Institute (NCI) in May 2000 showed that the rate of new cancer cases and deaths for all cancers combined declined between 1990 and 1997 in the United States. The greatest decline occurred among men, who overall continued to experience higher rates of cancer than do women. The report also noted large differences in cancer incidence by race and ethnicity, with rates generally higher for blacks than for whites.

Non-Hodgkin's lymphomas (NHLs), malignant growths of B or T cells in the lymph system, are becoming more common. The American Cancer Society (ACS) had estimated that there would be 54,900 new cases of the disease, and 26,100 deaths from NHLs in the United States in 2000. The cause of NHLs is unknown. Also on the upswing was skin melanoma, with incidence rates rising about 3 percent annually between 1981 and 1997. The ACS estimated 47,700 cases and 7,700 deaths in 2000. Exposure to sunlight or ultraviolet radiation is a major cause of melanoma.

In January 2001, the U.S. Department of Health and Human Services released the 9th edition of its biennial *Report on Carcinogens*, which identifies several substances that are "known" or "reasonably anticipated" to cause human cancers. The report had 14 new entries among its 218 listings, including some to which large numbers of people are often exposed: environmental tobacco smoke, tobacco smoking, oral use of smokeless tobacco, alcoholic-beverage consumption, diesel-exhaust particulates, ultraviolet solar radiation, and the use of sunlamps and tanning beds. Tamoxifen, widely used to treat breast cancer and to help prevent it in women at high risk, also made the list, based on evidence that the drug increases the risk of uterine cancer. The report noted that tamoxifen's benefit of decreasing the risk of breast cancer outweighs the risks of taking it. One substance, the sweetener saccharin, was removed from the 9th edition after a review of rodent cancer-data was deemed insufficient to meet current criteria for listing as a possible human carcinogen.

CONCERNS ABOUT MAD-COW DISEASE

The anxiety over bovine spongiform encephalopathy (BSE), popularly known as mad-cow disease, heightened in Europe during 2000 following detection of the disease among cattle in a number of countries. BSE has been linked to a strain of Creutzfeldt-Jakob disease in humans; both are degenerative and fatal diseases characterized by a breakdown of brain tissue. The infectious agent is believed to be a type of protein called a prion, which for reasons not

Sheep from two Vermont farms were destroyed in March 2001 when they were suspected of having transmissible spongiform encephalopathy (TSE), a class of illnesses that includes mad-cow disease.

yet understood can be transformed into an abnormal form capable of destroying cells.

It is suspected that people become exposed to the bovine disease by eating beef from infected cattle. Since 1996, when the likelihood that the infectious agents spread from cattle to humans was announced by Britain, new-variant Creutzfeldt-Jakob disease has killed at least 91 people there and two in France. No one knows how many cattle may be infected with BSE, or how many people may have been contaminated, since Creutzfeldt-Jakob disease has a 10- to 40-year incubation period. In an effort to halt the spread of BSE, hundreds of thousands of cattle have been destroyed. According to the U.S. Department of Agriculture (USDA), BSE has never been identified in the United States, although in March 2001, sheep apparently suffering from a related form of spongiform encephalopathy were seized in Vermont, tested, and later destroyed.

UPDATE ON AIDS

Since AIDS was first recognized in 1981, it has killed an estimated 21.8 million people, including 3 million in 2000, reported the World Health Organization (WHO) in a November analysis. The report indicated that in 2000, an estimated 5.3 million people, including 600,000 children under age 15, became infected with HIV, the virus that causes AIDS. A total of 36.1 million people were thought to be infected, divided almost equally between men and women. WHO noted that sub-Saharan Africa accounted for 70 percent of people with HIV or with AIDS, and for 80 percent of the deaths during 2000. Asia and the Pacific nations ranked second, with an estimated 6.4 million infected. Some of the sharpest increases in infections occurred in eastern Europe and Central Asia, with new cases attributed mainly to the injection of illicit drugs.

When the United Nations Children's Fund (UNICEF) conducted a survey in 34 developing countries to evaluate how much young people actually knew about AIDS, the findings revealed alarmingly high levels of ignorance. For instance, more than 50 percent of girls aged 15 to 19 did not know that a person with AIDS can appear to be healthy; in Chad, in central Africa, the figure was 83 percent; in Niger, 81 percent; and in Nepal, 80 percent. In Bangladesh, 96 percent of girls aged 15 to 19, and 88 percent of boys in the same age group, could not name a single method of protecting themselves against HIV.

In the United States, the number of new infections has remained relatively constant in recent years, at about 40,000 annually, according to the Centers for Disease Control and Prevention (CDC). During the 1990s, a steadily growing proportion of AIDS cases occurred in blacks, Hispanics, and women, with a decreasing proportion in homosexual and bisexual men. A CDC analysis concluded that 4 million to 5 million Americans put themselves at high risk of contracting HIV, largely through unsafe sexual habits and use of contaminated needles.

In another report, the CDC noted that more than half of all new HIV infections in the United States occur among blacks. The report estimated that 1 in 50 black men and 1 in 160 black women are now infected with HIV, compared to 1 in 250 white men and 1 in 3,000 white women.

More than a dozen drugs are available to combat HIV and prolong patients' lives, but they are not without complications. Concerns over nerve damage, weakened bones, diabetes, and other serious side effects led the U.S. Department of Health and Human

Services in 2001 to issue new treatment guidelines, which recommend that treatment be delayed as long as possible for people without symptoms. This reverses the approach in effect since 1996, which called for aggressive use of drugs for all HIV patients, regardless of their symptoms.

ILLICIT-DRUG USE

The 2000 National Household Survey on Drug Abuse reported that the use of illegal drugs by people aged 12 to 17 fell sharply from 1997 to 1999, dropping 21 percent among those admitting use within a month prior to the survey. Among 18- to 25-year-olds, usage rose 28 percent. American Indians and Alaskan natives scored highest on drug use (10.6 percent versus 7.7 percent for blacks and 6.6 for whites), and Alaska led the states in drug-use rates.

The National Center on Addiction and Substance Abuse at Columbia University, New York, released a study showing more drug abuse among eighth graders who live in rural areas than among their counterparts in large cities. For example, according to the new study, rural teens were more likely to abuse amphetamines (104 percent likelier), cocaine (50 percent), marijuana (34 percent), and alcohol (29 percent).

A drug growing in popularity among the young is Ecstasy, an addictive psychedelic also known as MDMA, short for methylenedioxymethamphetamine. Sold in pills, it is noted for increasing energy and producing hallucinogenic effects. A nervous-system stimulant, MDMA increases heart rate and blood pressure and can cause panic attacks and paranoia.

Drug abuse is not limited to illegal drugs. The drug OxyContin, a painkiller prescribed for cancer patients, is illegally obtained and inhaled nasally or injected to achieve a feeling of euphoria. Withdrawal symptoms often include nausea, diarrhea, and severe stomach cramps. Another dependency-inducing drug, GHB (gammahydroxybutyrate), is usually taken for its alleged bodybuilding effects. Its prolonged withdrawal, which begins soon after it is discontinued, can lead to psychotic behavior.

Jenny Tesar

SCIENCE EDUCATION

ANIMATED AMBASSADORS

For years, educator Norm Gershenz has used science projects and slide shows to teach children about the importance of protecting endangered ecosystems and preserving their biodiversity. But recently, Gershenz adopted a new teaching method—one that is much more "animated."

Under the auspices of the Center for Ecosystem Survival (CES), in San Francisco, Gershenz and Leslie Saul, his entomologist wife, founded the Insect Discovery Lab (IDL), a program that employs a menagerie of insects—from Arizona's whip scorpions to Madagascar's cockroaches—to illustrate the need to support biodiversity. Gershenz succeeds by traveling to area schools, armed with his arthropod ambassadors that leave a lasting impression on young minds.

Insects are well suited for illustrating the interconnectedness of ecosystems and for inspiring children's interest in the natural world, Gershenz believes. He advocates that children are born naturalists, and works to get them excited early on about nature. Gingerly handling the familiar ladybug, stilt-walking daddy longlegs, or centipede that roller-coasters across the knuckles might represent a child's first step toward a lifelong involvement in conservation.

Gershenz also directs the nonprofit CES at San Francisco State University. Among other conservation projects, CES is involved with a number of innovative fund-raising programs such as Adopt An Acre (which has had at least one participating school from each state), Adopt A Reef, and a clever concept called the Conservation Parking Meter. Strategically placed in areas such as zoos and nature centers, genuine parking meters have been modified with an ecological theme, and accept change as donations for habitat preservation. "A nickel will buy 18 square feet [1.7 square meters] of rain forest," Gershenz says, emphasizing that both young and old can be instrumental in saving endangered ecosystems.

Star Pupils

Every summer for six weeks, roughly 35 teenagers are doused with mathematics, placed knee-deep in astronomy, and served a heavy helping of the scientific method when they attend the Summer Science Program (SSP) in Ojai, California.

Founded in 1959 when the Soviet Union had an apparent edge in the space race, the program caters to academically high-achieving and interested students from all over the world. Working in small teams, students jointly agree on a particular asteroid for study, photograph it with the SSP's 7-inch (18-centimeter) Zeiss astrograph over a period of several nights, develop the plates, and take measurements of the asteroid's movements. The students learn quickly that data do not come in easily manipulated "byte-sized" packages. Scientists must take their own measurements and do the analyses and calculations that yield usable data. SSP students must also write their own computer programs to determine various characteristics of their asteroid, such as its size, shape, and orientation of its orbit.

The SSP faculty live on campus with the students, thereby providing the teenagers with 24-hour access to their knowledge, guidance, and enthusiasm. Students can also mingle with scientists from universities, private industries, and NASA's Jet Propulsion Laboratory (JPL) during twice-a-week lectures. SSP students also take field trips, get involved in sports, and engage in the good-natured pranks that are so often part of the summer-camp experience.

Speedier Information Flow

Before publishing any research, scientists must submit their work for scrutiny to a board of fellow scientists. Only after having withstood such close examination—which typically involves a substantial amount of time—is their written piece published. This process helps to ensure the validity of submissions, but it also slows the progress of other scientists who might find the information applicable to furthering their own research. Now, in what might be considered an "experiment in research," chemists can make their research findings publicly available instantaneously—by posting their papers on the Internet. ChemWeb.com, headquartered in London, operates the Chemistry Preprint Server, under which papers submitted for posting are placed online. Readers can then rate the posted submissions and critique them in spirited on-line discussions.

This fast turnaround has its advantages. But chemists who later hope to submit their on-line papers to traditional journals for publication may be disappointed to discover that some periodicals may not accept their work, deeming it "previously published." Even more critical to scientists is that the lack of review will dilute the accuracy of the pool of information available to them. But according to Bill Town, director of operations at ChemWeb, a number of academic papers previously posted on-line have since been accepted for journal publication.

Turmoil at the Smithsonian

When the Smithsonian Institution's relatively new and first nonacademic secretary, Lawrence Small, proposed budget cuts for the cultural institute in early 2001, he announced plans to close not only its artifact-conservation

Student stargazers may not be able to study astronomy in high school, but hard work could win some a spot tracking asteroids in the Summer Science Program at Ojai, California.

offices—the Center for Materials Research and Education (SCMRE) in Maryland—but also three branches of the Smithsonian Libraries, Smithsonian Productions, and the institution's photographic and imaging office. When Small also announced he would close the National Zoo's Conservation and Research Center (CRC), located near Front Royal, Virginia, public and political outcry was so overwhelming that he bowed to the pressure and called for a review of plans in order to avoid harmful publicity. Instead, Small received approval from the Smithsonian Board of Regents for the establishment of a science commission that will advise him and the board on how to proceed. The commission's task is to survey the entire Smithsonian—all 16 museums and the National Zoo—as well as the National Portrait Gallery and the Tropical Research Institute in Panama. Small's rationale for closing the zoo's research center was to save approximately $2.8 million in expenses, and to redirect the money to what he deemed priority research.

The center currently houses 300 students from around the world and researchers who work with local schools. Equally significant, its 3,200 acres (1,300 hectares) of pasture and woodland are home to more than 30 endangered animal species that include red pandas, Eld's deer, Przewalski's horses, and Guam rails.

Critics who support the SCMRE will not benefit from the congressional or public support that reversed the planned CRC closing, even though the SCMRE is widely considered state-of-the-art in the area of artifact conservation. Its projects have included work on the original "Star-Spangled Banner" flag, research on plant material from the Lewis and Clark expedition, and preservation studies of Apollo space suits. Despite a 9 percent White House budget increase for the Smithsonian for 2002, Small's rationale for the closure of the conservation center was that most museums have their own materials-treatment facilities. Small's career centers on finance, so it is not surprising that his strategies clash with the goals of traditional scientists.

Gayle Wanag

SEISMOLOGY

In 2000, there were 231 earthquake-related deaths throughout the world. That comparatively low number does not mean, however, that there was less seismic activity. In fact, only three times before—in 1994, 1995, and 1996—were more earthquakes with a magnitude of 6.0 or higher recorded. ("Magnitude" refers to the size of an earthquake as measured on a 10-point scale. An increase of one full number represents an earthquake that is 10 times larger and, more significantly, releases about 32 times more energy.) The year 2000 brought three "great quakes"—magnitude 8.0 or more; the average is just one per year. Finally, the world was shaken by 22,313 earthquakes of notable magnitude in 2000, more than in any other year but one since 1970. However, if the world's seismic activity that upset early 2001 is any indication of things to come, by year's end the devastation of 2000 may end up seeming relatively mild.

NORTH AMERICA
North America's most destructive earthquake in 2000 hit early in the morning on September 3 in Napa, California. Despite its relatively low magnitude (5.2), the quake caused considerable damage because the city was built on the soft soil of an ancient riverbed. Exploding transformers lit up the sky, walls cracked, streetlights shattered, cinder blocks toppled, sidewalks split, and water mains ruptured. Forty-one people were injured, and damage was estimated at nearly $50 million.

One of the largest North American earthquakes of the year was a magnitude-6.8 temblor that shook Kodiak, Alaska, on July 10, but caused only minor damage.

The same cannot be said of an earthquake of equal magnitude that struck the Seattle area on February 28, 2001. In the span of just 40 seconds, the quake, which was centered 10 miles (16 kilometers) northeast of Olympia and 35 miles (56 kilometers) southwest of Seattle, caused some $2 billion in damage and resulted in more than 300 injuries, most of them minor.

The largest earthquake to shake the U.S. Northwest in 52 years hit on February 28, 2001. Lasting only 40 seconds, the 6.8-magnitude temblor rocked Seattle, Washington, resulting in some $2 billion in damage.

For all that, people in the Puget Sound region had reason to be grateful. Despite the size of the quake and its proximity to densely populated areas, no one was killed, and the damage, while significant, was nowhere near what it could have been. The reason western Washington got off so lightly is twofold. First, the quake was located deep below the surface—33 miles (53 kilometers) underground—so Earth's crust absorbed much of the shock. Second, stringent building codes adopted in the 1970s and a concentrated effort over the past decade to retrofit older structures and stabilize highways kept damage to a minimum. Buildings that were up to code escaped largely unscathed, while buildings that had not been retrofitted, such as the State Capitol Building in Olympia, were, in many cases, badly damaged.

SOUTHEAST ASIA

Southeast Asia, which is known for frequent seismic activity, experienced a number of noteworthy temblors in 2000. A massive magnitude-8.0 earthquake struck southern Sumatra, Indonesia, on June 4. The epicenter of the earthquake was deep in the Indian Ocean, about 60 miles (96 kilometers) from the coastal city of Bengkulu, which suffered the greatest damage. Deaths numbered 103, more than in any other earthquake of the year, and more than 1,900 were reported injured. The quake was followed 11 minutes later by a magnitude-6.7 aftershock, which threw people into even greater panic and hampered rescue efforts. Buildings in Bengkulu that were not destroyed outright suffered significant damage, and telephone and power lines were knocked out. Up to 260 smaller aftershocks followed over the next few days, causing landslides and leaving people too frightened to return to those houses still standing. Doctors treated patients outdoors, fearing the hospital was not safe. Their fears were justified on June 7, when a second magnitude-6.7 aftershock killed one person and damaged 600 homes.

The second-highest number of casualties from an earthquake in 2000 was sustained in Sulawesi, Indonesia. On May 4, a magnitude-7.6 earthquake was followed by an 18-foot (6-meter)-high tsunami, or tidal wave. Forty-six people were killed, 26 injured, and 30,000 left homeless. On nearby Banggai island, 80 percent of all buildings were destroyed. In the district of Luwuk, dozens of homes were consumed by fire following the quake.

Between November 16 and November 18, a series of linked earthquakes occurred in the Bismarck Archipelago northeast of Papua New Guinea. The first quake, which had a magnitude of 8.1, struck early in the morning on the island of New Ireland. A tsunami and landslides followed, washing away homes, schools, and a church, killing one person and leaving 5,000 homeless. Another temblor, this time of magnitude 7.8, came three hours later, followed by a magnitude-7.2 quake only three minutes after that. The next day, November 17, the island of New Britain was ground zero for a magnitude-8.0 quake. Two more temblors, each of magnitude 6.6, came on November 18, one near New Britain, the other near New Ireland.

The first earthquake-related fatalities in 2000 occurred on January 14 in Yunnan, China. A magnitude-5.8 temblor claimed 11 lives, injured at least 2,500, and destroyed 41,000 homes.

Honshu, the largest of Japan's islands, experienced six strong quakes in 2000, ranging in magnitude from 6.0 to 7.0. On July 1, a magnitude-6.2 earthquake caused a landslide that killed one person, and a magnitude-7.0 quake on October 6 caused more than 130 injuries, destroyed 104 houses, caused seven bridges to collapse, and set off 65 landslides in the Okayama-Tottori area. None of the earthquakes that struck Asia in 2000 compare with the magnitude-7.7 temblor that shook the western Indian state of Gujarat on January 26, 2001. This large shallow quake took the lives of nearly 20,000 people, many of them in the city of Bhuj, where buildings constructed without regard to earthquake codes collapsed like houses of cards. Early reports indicated that more than 60,000 people were injured, and more than 600,000 were left homeless by the disaster, while later reports noted that injuries numbered closer to 160,000.

CENTRAL AND SOUTH AMERICA

Nicaragua suffered the most earthquake damage in Central and South America in 2000, although from less-intense quakes than those felt elsewhere in the region. On July 6, a magnitude-5.1 temblor shook Managua, killing seven people and injuring 42. The destruction of more than 350 homes and serious damage to close to 1,100 others sent crowds of people to refugee centers.

By contrast, the northern border region between Chile and Argentina experienced a magnitude-7.0 quake on April 23, followed by a complex magnitude-7.1 quake on May 12 and a magnitude-6.4 temblor on June 16. One person was killed in the May 12 earthquake, but there were no other casualties, and little damage was reported.

The human toll of an earthquake that struck El Salvador just two weeks into 2001 was far greater. On January 13, a 7.7-magnitude quake near the capital, San Salvador, reportedly left 844 dead, caused more than 4,700 injuries, and destroyed nearly 260,000 homes. Then, one month later to the day, and only 53 miles (85 kilometers) northwest of January's event, a magnitude-6.6 earthquake rocked the region again, taking more than 300 lives, injuring close to 3,000, and destroying or damaging 2,000 homes.

OTHER NOTABLE TEMBLORS

The third-highest number of casualties in 2000 came from a magnitude-6.3 quake that took place beneath the Caspian Sea south of Baku, Azerbaijan, on November 25. Five people died from falling debris, 23 died following heart attacks, and three were killed in an explosion from a gas leak caused by the quake. Eleven days later, on December 6, Baku felt a 7.0-magnitude complex quake from across the Caspian Sea at Balkanabat, Turkmenistan, where 11 people were reported killed and many injured.

Iceland experienced two magnitude-6.6 temblors on June 17 and June 21, the strongest earthquakes there in more than 90 years. A total of 23 houses were reported destroyed and 43 severely damaged.

EARTHQUAKES ON THE INCREASE?

Is the number of earthquakes increasing, or does it just seem that way? Experts tell us that the occurrence of earthquakes of magnitude-7.0 or greater has actually remained fairly constant during the last decade. According to the National Earthquake Information Center (NEIC), the number of seismograph recording stations around the globe has increased more than tenfold since the beginning of the 20th century. In 1931 there were approximately 350 stations operating in the world; today there are more than 4,000. Other factors include a giant advance in global communication. Information is transmitted faster and in more detail because of the advanced capabilities of electronic and satellite communication. Worldwide earthquake tracking organizations are now able to locate and evaluate an average of 35 earthquakes a day. Ever-better methods of communication and greater public interest means that the world is hearing about many more seismic episodes than it used to.

Cassia Farkas

SPACE SCIENCE

The last year of the 20th century saw numerous space successes and failures, a few major anniversaries and milestones, some of the most remarkable discoveries in history, and an impressive launch record.

IN EARTH ORBIT

In October 2000, the National Aeronautics and Space Administration's (NASA's) space-shuttle program celebrated a milestone—its 100th shuttle launch—when the orbiter *Discovery* blasted off for an 11-day rendezvous with the *International Space Station* (*ISS*). The shuttle's mission was to deliver and install a girderlike truss and docking port, making way for the station's first inhabitants. During its 100 missions since April 1981, the shuttle program racked up an impressive list of firsts. They include launching the first spacecraft carrying seven people; deploying the first satellites from a manned spacecraft; recovering, repairing, and redeploying a satellite; and capturing a satellite and returning it to Earth.

Even as *Discovery* celebrated its October mission, the *ISS* had begun taking shape. Then, in February 2001, the shuttle *Atlantis* delivered a $1.4 billion laboratory module known as *Destiny*. The modular lab is not limited to scientific research; it will also provide an environmental-control and life-support system, communication and tracking systems, and command and data-handling capability. And the arrival of the Russian-built *Zvezda* Service Module in July cleared the way for one American and two Russian spacefarers (Expedition One) to make their home aboard the craft. After four months, that weary crew was replaced by one Russian and two Americans (Expedition Two).

Mir. Russian space authorities have ended the life of the Earth-orbiting *Mir* space station. During its 15-year mission as the world's first extended-orbiting station, *Mir* had celebrated many pioneering achievements, offset in recent years by white-knuckle mishaps, including a collision, a fire, and an explosion. Space engineers had sent an unmanned cargo ship filled with fuel to *Mir* in preparation for the station's final fall. Then, after officials commanded three engine bursts from the attached cargo ship, the deteriorating station began its suicidal dive into the South Pacific Ocean, plunging down between New Zealand and Chile on March 23, 2000.

LOOKING BACK

Endeavour. Early in 2000, the space shuttle *Endeavour* served as an Earth observatory and contributed to a breakthrough in the science of remote sensing. With its radar sweeping most of the land surfaces of Earth, the Shuttle Radar Topography Mission (SRTM) gathered enough data in 10 days to produce topographic maps 30 times as precise as the best current global maps.

TOMS. In September 2000, scientists used the Earth-orbiting Total Ozone Mapping Spectrometer (TOMS) to detect the largest ozone hole ever observed in Earth's atmosphere. Over Antarctica, this "ozone-depletion area" is three times larger than the entire landmass of the United States.

IMAGE. The first large-scale images of the hidden workings of Earth's magnetic field were released in early 2001, and they helped confirm a long-suspected, but previously invisible, "tail" of electrified gas. Researchers utilizing NASA's Imager for Magnetopause to Aurora Global Exploration (IMAGE) spacecraft located this tail, which streams from Earth toward the Sun.

PEERING OUTWARD

HST. April 24, 2000, marked the 10th anniversary of one of the greatest telescopes ever constructed. In its first decade, the 12.5-ton Earth-orbiting Hubble Space Telescope (HST) studied 13,670 celestial objects, made 271,000 individual observations, and returned 3.5 terabytes of data, which have been archived as a scientific treasure trove for future generations of astronomers.

SOHO. Solar scientists, who were aided considerably by the Solar and Heliospheric Observatory (SOHO) and a technique called helioseismology, used ripples on the Sun's visible surface to probe its interior and to image its solar-storm regions. With NASA's Transition Region and Coronal

United States Manned Spaceflights—2000

Mission	Launch/Landing	Orbiter	Primary Operation
STS-99	Feb. 11/Feb. 22	*Endeavour*	**Shuttle Radar Topography Mission:** Using *Endeavour*'s radar, virtually all of the targeted mapping area (80 percent of Earth's surface—the area between 60°N and 56°S) was covered, and the necessary data gathered to produce the most-detailed 3-D map of Earth to date. The final product will be useful for civil, military, and scientific applications, such as geology, seismology, geophysics, and volcanology.
STS-101	May 19/May 29	*Atlantis*	***International Space Station* Assembly Flight 2A.2a:** While docked with the *ISS*, the *Atlantis* crew performed various service-related tasks and delivered supplies in anticipation of the Expedition One crew's upcoming arrival. Primary objectives included reboosting the station's orbit from 230 miles (370 kilometers) to 250 miles (402 kilometers) and replacing nonfunctioning batteries and other electronic equipment in *Zarya*.
STS-106	Sept. 8/Sept. 20	*Atlantis*	***International Space Station* Assembly Flight 2A.2b:** The seven-member crew continued preparations for the first *ISS* residents and performed general maintenance on the *Zvezda* Service Module, such as moving equipment, cleaning, plumbing, and electrical work.
STS-92	Oct. 11/Oct. 24	*Discovery*	***International Space Station* Assembly Flight 3A:** Using *Discovery*'s robotic arm, the crew installed two large components to the *ISS*—the Integrated Truss Structure (ITS) Z1 and the Pressurized Mating Adapter 3 (PMA 3). The (ITS) Z1 is an exterior framework that will allow future shuttle crew members to temporarily attach the first U.S. solar arrays set to provide early power on *Unity*. The PMA 3 will provide a shuttle docking port for the planned solar-array installation.
STS-97	Nov. 30/Dec. 11	*Endeavour*	**International Space Station Assembly Flight 4A:** The *Endeavour* crew delivered equipment, supplies, and the first set of U.S. solar arrays, which will increase the power available to the complex. The crew also installed a camera cable outside the *Unity* module that will transmit television images and help the next shuttle crew to attach the U.S. laboratory *Destiny*.

REMARKS

- Largest rigid structure flown in space—a 200-foot (61-meter)-long deployable mast used as part of the imaging radar system.

- First fixed-baseline, single-pass spaceborne interferometric Synthetic Aperture Radar (SAR).

- First dual-frequency (C-band and X-band) interferometric SAR.

- Experiments planned included testing new technology developed for the BioTube magnetic field apparatus (MFA), a device designed to grow seeds in microgravity.

- Demonstration of two versions of the Micro-Wireless Instrumentation System (Micro-WIS)—miniaturization technology that is hoped to significantly reduce weight and improve space and energy use.

- The 23rd consecutive landing of a shuttle at the Florida spaceport and the 30th landing of a shuttle at the Cape in the past 31 flights.

- Space walk was conducted to connect power, data, and communications cables to the *Zvezda* Service Module and the *ISS*.

- Mission marked the 22nd space flight for *Atlantis*.

- The 100th shuttle launch.
- Crew performed four space walks to assemble the (ITS) Z1 and the PMA 3.
- Crew spent two extra days in space due to inclement weather at the Kennedy Space Center in Florida and Edwards Air Force Base in California. Ultimately *Discovery* landed at Edwards.
- The 28th mission for *Discovery*.
- Crew demonstrated the use of a backpack for helping to rescue drifting astronauts.

- Fifth space-shuttle mission dedicated to the preparation of the *ISS*.
- The 25th night launch.
- The 16th night landing.
- The 15th mission for *Endeavour*.
- Crew performed three space walks to attach solar arrays.

During the first space-shuttle flight of 2000, Endeavour astronauts Janet Kavandi and Gerhard P.J. Thiele found time to pose with a few worldly effects.

The crew of Atlantis STS-101, including Susan J. Helms (above), spent much of its time transferring equipment and supplies to the Zarya and Unity modules.

Tethered to a robotic arm, Discovery mission specialist Michael Lopez-Alegria puts some final touches on the ISS to help ready it for permanent occupancy.

2000 SPACE LAUNCHES

Country	Number of Launches	Number of Failures	Number of Attempts	Success Rate
United States	30	1	31	97%
Russia	34	2	36	94%
Europe (ESA)	12	0	12	100%
China	5	0	5	100%
Japan	0	1	1	0%
Total	**81**	**4**	**85**	

Explorer spacecraft (TRACE), scientists have captured dramatic giant-fountain images of fast-moving, multimillion-degree gas in the Sun's outer atmosphere, or corona. These "coronal loops" may be the key to understanding why the Sun's corona is 300 times hotter than its visible face.

TO WORLDS BEYOND

In October 2000, NASA unveiled its plans for the next two decades of Mars exploration. Scientists hope to unravel the secrets of the Red Planet's past environments, the history of its rocks, its watery legacy, and, perhaps, its past or present life.

Mars Global Surveyor. NASA's Mars Global Surveyor (MGS) spacecraft, which has collected more information about the Red Planet than all previous missions combined, completed its primary science mission in January 2001. By then, the spacecraft had made 8,505 orbits of Mars and had taken more than 58,000 images, 490 million laser-altimeter shots to measure topography, and 97 million spectral measurements. One of its greatest discoveries in 2000 was solid evidence for the presence of liquid water on the Martian surface.

Galileo. The Galileo spacecraft has been orbiting Jupiter since late 1995, and completed its 29th orbit as it flew by the moon Ganymede on December 28, 2000. Galileo's recent data transmissions seem to suggest that two of Jupiter's large moons, Europa and Ganymede, may have oceans beneath their frozen surfaces. On its way toward Saturn, the spacecraft Cassini also flew past Jupiter at the end of December 2000. This was the first time ever that two spacecraft explored an outer planet together.

NEAR Shoemaker. On February 12, 2000, after completing a yearlong 2-billion-mile (3-billion-kilometer) orbit of the asteroid Eros and producing 160,000 images, the NEAR Shoemaker (Near Earth Asteroid Rendezvous) spacecraft made an improbable, gentle landing on the asteroid—with no landing gear. The set down was NASA's afterthought for the fund- and fuel-exhausted probe, which continued to collect data and transmit unprecedented images—the closest only 394 feet (120 meters) away from the asteroid's surface. NASA had originally planned to pull the plug on NEAR Shoemaker's $200 million mission on February 14, but then extended its life, hoping to collect further information on the asteroid's composition. The change of seasons on Eros should end the life of NEAR Shoemaker when the craft's solar panels will receive decreasing amounts of sunlight as the asteroid's winter darkness sets in. Should it survive, engineers might try to revive it during an Eros summer.

Stardust. On January 15, 2001, the Stardust spacecraft swung past Earth and the Moon, picking up speed as it headed toward a rendezvous with Comet P/Wild-2. Nearly a year earlier, the spacecraft had opened its specially designed particle collector and had scooped up interstellar dust particles from our solar system. A similar collection was planned for mid-May 2002.

Pioneer 6. On February 16, 2001, NASA scientists successfully contacted the Pioneer 6 spacecraft—35 years to the day when the space agency's oldest working spacecraft was launched into solar orbit on what was to have been a six-month mission.

Dennis L. Mammana

TRANSPORTATION

NEW SUB INNOVATIONS

One hundred years after the U.S. Navy commissioned its first submarine, creative new technological innovations are dramatically reshaping the capabilities of the military's submarine fleet. The latest innovations will allow the submarines to carry larger and better weapons, to operate safely in shallow coastal waters, and to serve as an operations center for special forces.

Helping to prompt these innovations is a federal mandate that the navy reduce by four its fleet of Trident nuclear submarines in the next three years. Instead of scrapping the boats, the navy plans to replace their nuclear missiles with as many as 154 conventional cruise missiles. Each nuclear missile would be replaced by a seven-pack of cruise missiles—more missiles than an entire aircraft-carrier battle group can carry. The navy also plans to retrofit some of the missile tubes on these subs so that they can be used to deploy special-operations forces, such as Navy SEALS. To do this, four to eight of the missile tubes would be converted into storage areas for weapons, ammunition, and gear for 66 to 102 special-forces soldiers. Two tubes, connected to each other, would be redesigned to allow forces to exit the submarine, with divers either leaving on their own via a dry dock or exiting via a minisub. The navy is currently testing a 65-foot (20-meter) minisub, which is slated for use on the U.S.S. *Virginia.*

The navy is working on these and other innovations to increase submarine maneuverability in shallow areas. For instance, more small propellers on either side of the main propeller would make the submarines more agile. In addition, the sonar system of a sub in deep water may not always detect the presence of a ship on the surface. So submarines that regularly operate in coastal waters will need some sort of warning system to better detect and identify surface vessels. One such system currently under development would detect electromagnetic radiation emitted by radar.

Funding for the renovation and missile-conversion program should come in 2001, and the program is expected to be completed by 2004. The cost to convert four submarines is estimated at $2.5 billion, but that figure is subject to revision.

AMTRAK SPEEDS IT UP

Amtrak increased the top speeds of its trains in 2000, running trains from New York City to Boston at 150 miles (240 kilometers) per hour. Previously, the top speed on that route had been 110 miles (177 kilometers) per hour; the top speed on trains between New

Amtrak's technologically advanced, high-speed Acela train pulls into New York City's Pennsylvania Station through one of the six 90-year-old tunnels badly in need of costly repairs.

York and Washington, D.C., had been 125 miles (200 kilometers) per hour.

Along with the speed increase, Amtrak began installing computerized safety equipment designed to decrease human error and the chance of an accident. Although traveling by train poses somewhat (about one-tenth) less of a risk of dying in an accident than does traveling by car, rail transportation is not as safe as air travel. In part, this is because trains travel across street-level crossings at 85 miles (137 kilometers) per hour and need 1 mile (1.6 kilometers) to stop at that speed.

In January 2000, Amtrak began offering service on its Acela Regional trains between New York and Boston. The trains are refurbished Metroliner cars with new engines that can make the New York–Boston trip in four hours instead of six. The Acela Regional features all-electric service, eliminating a former (and usually prolonged) stop in New Haven, Connecticut, to change to diesel engines. Amtrak planned to begin running new cars on the line as well; those trains will travel 150 miles (240 kilometers) per hour.

To reduce the chance of accidents occurring at the street-level crossings that still exist on the New York-to-Boston run, Amtrak is installing several safety devices. First, gates on the crossings will be changed so that drivers cannot zigzag their way around them. In addition, sensors will automatically detect the presence of a vehicle on the tracks, and send a signal to the train while it is 1.5 to 2 miles (2.4 to 3.2 kilometers) away. If the train engineer does not respond, the system will automatically brake the train. Crossing gates will also descend 90 seconds before a train comes through, even though Connecticut state law requires only 29 seconds. Finally, radio beacons buried in the tracks along the route will broadcast the speed limit as the train passes; trains over the limit will be slowed automatically. Despite the new safety features, some analysts have actually predicted more accidents because of the increased number of trains that will use the route.

In addition to safety features en route, the new railroad cars were designed to increase passenger safety during a collision. The cars feature "crumple zones" that prevent passenger compartments from being crushed; inside the passenger compartments, sharp edges are eliminated or padded, and overhead luggage racks are enclosed.

NEW YORK CITY TUNNEL ISSUES

The six biggest train tunnels that connect New York City's Pennsylvania Station with New Jersey Transit and New York's Long Island Rail Road trains have serious safety problems. Furthermore, they are badly in need of substantial repair, according to a report published in December 2000 by the U.S. Department of Transportation.

Of critical importance are the two issues of fire safety and overall safety, according to the report. The report also noted that unless $898 million could be budgeted for the project, it will likely take 30 years to complete the repairs; with the extra money, the repairs could be finished by approximately 2010. Some railroad officials, however, have disagreed with these estimates, stating that the repairs could be finished by 2014 without appropriating additional funds.

Among the major safety concerns that the report found was the inadequate ventilation system in the tunnels. The system needs to be updated so that, in the event of a fire, fresh air can be pumped into the tunnels and smoke pumped out. The tunnels also need standpipes along their entire length to provide water for fire fighting. Currently, the standpipes are found only in parts of the tunnels; elsewhere, there are dry-chemical fire extinguishers, but these are not always effective in fighting a large fire. The escape routes—including narrow spiral staircases and raised platforms that run next to the tracks—are inadequate or in poor shape. And lastly, the tunnels do not have a uniform communications system.

The tunnels, which run under the Hudson and East Rivers, are more than 90 years old. Each day, approximately 300,000 passengers ride the trains that use these tunnels.

In another, unrelated, study, the New York City Economic Development Corporation recommended the construction of a new tunnel for freight trains to connect Brooklyn with either New York's Staten

A new Los Angeles traffic system shortens some commutes by as much as 25 percent. Working together, sensors embedded in the road "communicate" with transmitters (inset) mounted in specially equipped municipal buses to trigger traffic signals to stay green longer, thereby expediting bus runs.

Island or with New Jersey. The tunnel would allow the freight-train network that exists in the rest of the country to connect with New York City, and therefore reduce the volume of large commercial trucks that drive into the metropolitan area by perhaps 1 million per year. The ambitious undertaking could have the further benefit of stimulating the local economy and revitalizing the Brooklyn waterfront.

The 10-year tunnel project would cost an estimated $2.3 billion, but according to the report, the increased business on the Brooklyn waterfront would be worth the investment. Critics of the proposed tunnel said that the project is too expensive and that it may never even get started because of the complex federal and state review process required for approval. In addition, some critics said that by the time the project would be completed, the tunnel could be outdated, since it is difficult to predict what the needs of the freight market will be a decade or two from now.

BUSES GET A GREEN LIGHT

A new traffic system in Los Angeles is shortening commuting times by keeping traffic lights green for an extra 10 seconds as specially equipped buses approach designated intersections. The system has cut travel time on some bus trips by as much as 25 percent.

Los Angeles officials installed the system in response to commuter complaints about slow bus speeds. Prior to the new system, the average bus speed had been just 10 miles (16 kilometers) per hour. One of the most frustrating problems was that the buses spent an extraordinary amount of time simply waiting for the traffic lights to turn.

The city began using the system in June 2000, installing it on two Metro Rapid express-bus routes used by approximately 70,000 commuters per day. As a bus passes over sensors embedded in the road along its route, an onboard transmitter sends a signal to the traffic light's control box at the next intersection. As a result, the light stays green for up to 10 additional seconds, so that the bus is less likely to have to stop at a red light. A software program prohibits the light from being delayed for more than 10 seconds, preventing the traffic on cross streets from building up.

Los Angeles officials made some other changes to ease travel times. Routes have been simplified, buses are tracked via the street-embedded sensors, and dispatchers tell bus drivers to slow down or speed up (without exceeding posted limits) in order to keep buses from "grouping" together. Officials estimate that these changes, coupled with more-efficient connections to subway schedules, have cut commuters' travel time by 30 to 40 percent.

Devera Pine

VOLCANOLOGY

ROWDY, RUMBLING RHAPSODY

Of the more than 1,000 volcanoes on Earth, 60 erupted in the year 2000—some violently, with short-lived explosions, others almost passively, grumbling with low-level activity as they have for years. Naturally, scientists are concerned with potentially active volcanoes located near population centers. Their first priority is to monitor and predict eruptions in order to mitigate volcanic risk. One valuable tool is an activity-level color-coding system. A yellow alert level is issued when a volcano is exhibiting intense unrest, such as a swarm of earthquakes or other evidence of magma movement below the volcano, as indicated by inflation of the ground. An orange alert level is given when an eruption is likely within hours or days, and when there is strong evidence of magma movement near the surface. A red alert is given when a volcano is in eruption. While this evaluation system is an important tool for scientists, the overriding concern, of course, is to improve methods of predicting forthcoming volcanic activity in order to save more lives.

"POPO" SETS SCIENTISTS ON EDGE

Ongoing eruptions of Mexico's Popocatepetl—the Aztec term for "Smoking Mountain"—topped the activity list for the year 2000. "Popo" is a steep-sided, 17,887-foot (5,455-meter)-high volcanic cone located only 34 miles (55 kilometers) from Mexico City, and even closer—28 miles (45 kilometers)—to the Puebla metropolitan area. The volcano's potential wrath directly threatens hundreds of thousands of lives. The current period of activity in Popocatepetl began with a small eruption in December 1994, ending five decades of quiescence for this majestic volcano.

Activity intensified in July 1997, when explosions threw ash and lava blocks up to 7 miles (11 kilometers) above the volcano and caused the first ashfall on Mexico City in more than 70 years, temporarily closing the city's airport. This extrusion led to the evacuation of 15 towns, affecting more than 300,000 people living on the volcano's flanks. A lava dome that had begun to grow in the 1,476-foot (450-meter)-deep summit crater in early 1997 is still growing, and periodic explosions have disrupted and ejected parts of it.

Popocatepetl's activity has gradually escalated. Explosions up to 6 miles (10 kilometers) high in December 1998 had caused hot ash to spark brush fires on the flanks of the volcano, and enough ash fell in Mexico City to force a second closing of the city's airport. By mid-2000, a 3-mile (5-kilometer)-radius exclusion zone was enforced around the volcano, and nearby communities were placed on yellow alert. An eruption in May 2000 caused so much ashfall in the eastern part of Mexico City that residents were warned to limit outdoor activities.

By November 2000, the high-risk zone around the volcano had been expanded to a 6-mile (10-kilometer) radius. A significant explosion on November 18 caused heightened concern over landslides and possible slope

Since an eruption in December 1994 ended five decades of calm, activity at Mexico's Popocatepetl has only increased, with billowing ash clouds often looming in the distance.

failure when the glaciers on the volcano's slopes began to melt. Evacuation of towns near the volcano began in mid-December; more than 50,000 people were evacuated from the risk area and placed in temporary shelters. Less dynamic eruptions continued, leading volcanologists to ponder whether Popocatepetl's activity will intensify or if the worst has already passed. Ultimately, only time will tell.

RED ALERT IN GUATEMALA

In Guatemala, in late 1999 and early 2000, frequent Strombolian eruptions—characterized by fountains of fluid basaltic lava rising from a central crater—produced lava flows on the flanks of Pacaya Volcano. Lava fountains, visible from Guatemala City, fed flows that have advanced in three directions several miles from the crater. Associated ash affected La Aurora International Airport and led to evacuations in January 2000. Renewed eruptions in late February 2000 prompted officials to issue a red alert and to evacuate some populated areas. Eruptive activity has since subsided.

UNREST AT YELLOWSTONE CALDERA

A caldera is a large depression formed by the collapse of a volcanic summit. Yellowstone Caldera in Yellowstone National Park, Wyoming, is one of the world's largest, and the eruptions that have occurred there are the largest recorded in the geologic record. Fortunately, volcanic eruptions in Yellowstone are now rare, but any changes in the subsurface "plumbing" are likely to make volcanologists a bit nervous. In early May 2000, Yellowstone's Steamboat Geyser suddenly erupted a plume to a height of 492 feet (150 meters), discharging almost 7,060 cubic feet (200 cubic meters) of steam and hot water. Since such an event is unique in Yellowstone, it makes geologists wonder if the great Yellowstone Caldera is reactivating and getting ready to erupt. Scientists from the U.S. Geological Survey (USGS) and the University of Utah, Salt Lake City, are monitoring and assessing the symptoms of underground turmoil and persistent, but ever-changing, hydrothermal activity.

Haraldur Sigurdsson

ZOOLOGY

RUNAWAY REINDEER

Eskimo in western Alaska are losing their reindeer to a call from the wild. Caribou from rapidly expanding wild herds are wandering onto reindeer ranges and mingling with domesticated reindeer on the state's Seward Peninsula. When the caribou leave, reindeer follow them, usually never to return. Some 3,000 reindeer have run off into the wild over the past 10 years, much to the distress of their owners.

Despite some visible differences, caribou and reindeer belong to the same species, *Rangifer tarandus*. In Europe, all caribou are called reindeer; in Alaska and Canada, only domestic forms of the animal carry that name. For Alaskan reindeer herders, the most important difference is that reindeer meat is a valuable commodity, being rich and tender, in contrast to the stringy and tough caribou meat. And it is not only the meat of the reindeer that is marketable; the animals' fresh, velvet-coated spring antlers have brought herders substantial income from the Asian medicine market.

Some herders have been able to identify and recover their runaways by chasing after them and looking for those with colored ear tags, but recovery is difficult on both humans and the animals. If mixed herds are chased by helicopters or snowmobiles, the comparatively weaker reindeer soon grow exhausted and drop out of the group. And even if animals are retrieved, there is always a chance they will wander off again.

Runaway reindeer tend not to fare well among wild caribou. Reindeer prefer to remain in tight groups, whereas caribou run far and wide, constantly on the move in search of food. Nor do the cousins interbreed, as their mating cycles are not in sync.

A survey conducted by wildlife biologists from the University of Alaska at Fairbanks reported that six of the seven Eskimo who once ran the biggest herding operations on the peninsula saw their herds dwindle from 1,300 or more reindeer a few years ago to zero by the year 2000. Biologist Greg Finstad, who manages the university's reindeer-research program, estimates that there may be fewer than 9,000 reindeer left on the Seward Peninsula, compared with 25,000 a decade ago. Reindeer farmers remain influential, however, since the twice-a-year reindeer roundups generate many jobs and much meat for the inhabitants of this remote and rugged area of Alaska.

In 1998 and 1999, reindeer herders received a total of $250,000 from the U.S. Department of Agriculture for rangeland lost to caribou invasion. In 2000, the rules changed. Now, before any aid can be appropriated, a disaster declaration is required. Based on recent losses, Alaskan herders may receive close to $100,000 for 2001.

HOT-TAMALE BIRDS

Recent studies by a team of three Smithsonian zoologists have located at least five types of poisonous birds in New Guinea. Four of these are various species of *Pitohui*, a blackbird-sized songbird. The fifth and most recent discovery, a blue-capped, nuthatch-like little bird, *Ifrita kowaldi*, represents a different genus altogether. The poison is concentrated mostly in the feathers and the skin of the birds, and although it has a similar chemical makeup, is not as deadly as that of Amazonian "poison-dart" frogs. For the birds, as for the frogs, it is a highly effective deterrent to predators. The Smithsonian scientists recently returned from New Guinea loaded down with every possible food source for the birds. They intend to analyze the food to determine how the birds manufacture the poison. In desperate times, the natives of New Guinea have survived by eating pitohuis, being certain to first carefully remove all of the feathers and skin. Even then, however, they report, the bird's meat burns the mouth like a very hot chili pepper!

PENGUINS DON'T TOPPLE

Members of the British Royal Navy recently completed a mission to Antarctica, where they studied the effects of low-flying helicopters on the king penguin, *Aptenodytes patagonicus*, the second-largest penguin species in the world, weighing in at a stout 77 pounds (35 kilograms). It had been reported by veterans of the Falklands War that king penguins became mesmerized by military helicopters, bending back their heads to watch the craft and swiveling around until they lost their balance and toppled over. Scientists filming the penguins during the recent mission, however, did not notice any toppling penguins during any of their 17 observation flights. The penguins would fall silent at the approach of the helicopters, and some would waddle away. But scientists believe these reactions were more likely a result of the noise, or a response to the hovering aircraft, which the penguins may have perceived as a possible predator. Once the helicopters flew away, or landed and shut down, the penguins would waddle back and resume normal activity—a reassuring sight to conservationists and military alike.

AN EARLY BIRD GETS . . . FROSTBITE?

Ecologists at the Rocky Mountain Biological Laboratory (RMBL) in the West Elk Mountains of Colorado report that robins are returning about two weeks earlier than they did 20 years ago, and that hibernating mammals are emerging as much as a month earlier. They believe these changes in hibernation and migratory patterns partly may be the result of the "differential effects" of global warming at varying elevations. At the Rocky Mountain facility, 9,662 feet (2,947 meters) above sea level, winter duration and severity have remained fairly constant. However, at

An early return to its summer home, combined with the northerly expansion of its range, has left the Virginia opossum above with painful frostbitten ear tips.

lower elevations, the air is warming earlier, prompting the migrating and hibernating species to return to their summer habitats earlier than usual. These species therefore return to scant food supplies, causing depletion of their stored fat and, consequently, delayed or less fruitful breeding.

Shifting wildlife demographics causing a species to encounter climate situations for which it is not prepared have also affected opossums, who have been settling farther and farther north. Opossums, North America's only marsupials, evolved in a mild climate. Their paper-thin ears and scantily furred, ratlike tails are not adequately adapted to withstand frosty temperatures. As a result, those now living in colder northern areas of the United States often suffer frayed ear edges and lose pieces of their tails in winter due to frostbite.

Shrinking Iguanas

Marine biologists are intrigued by recently compiled data concerning a species of seagoing iguana (*Amblyrhynchus cristatus*) native to Ecuador's Galápagos Islands. These vertebrates shrink in size by as much as 20 percent when the El Niño phenomenon causes warming of the ocean and suppresses the plankton on which the reptiles feed.

Following the most recent El Niño event, researchers Martin Wikelski of the University of Illinois at Urbana-Champaign and Corinna Thom from the University of Würzburg, Germany, published a report that covered 25 years of observations. It documented the iguanas' amazing adaptation to changes in their food supply. It is not that young iguanas grew less, but that fully grown iguanas actually became shorter in length during times of food scarcity. The researchers established that if connective tissue alone contracted in the iguanas, it would account for, at the very most, only a 10 percent reduction in length. Therefore, the scientists determined, the skeletal structure of this species of iguana has the ability to shrink and expand its body as needed. Indeed, as the long-term study also demonstrated, these same iguanas regain or exceed their original size once the food supply becomes plentiful again.

Who Gives a Hoot?

Neuroscientists from the California Institute of Technology (Caltech) have determined that an owl locates its prey in the dark by using nearly 1,000 neurons to compute two sound cues from its prey—arrival time and intensity. If a ground-feeding mouse is foraging to the right of the owl, for example, the owl first hears the sound of the mouse with its right ear, and then, a fraction of a second later, with its left ear. Specialized neurons in the bird's midbrain calculate the location of the sound, and thereby help to determine the exact position of the mouse. At the same time, the owl's ears pick up differences in the intensity of a sound, information that is transmitted to the midbrain neurons as well. There, the two cues are "fused," providing an accurate two-dimensional location of the mouse. In other words, the neurons act as switches; the neurons do not respond to time or intensity singularly, but to a combination of both.

To understand the owl's acute ability to locate prey in the dark, Caltech behavioral biologists built on earlier research by neuroscientist Masakazu Konishi. Professor Konishi and colleague José Luis Peña placed microphones in owls' ears to record the differences in time and intensity as sounds reached the animals' ears. The scientists recorded exactly what the owls were hearing as a portable loudspeaker rotated around the birds' heads. What they discovered was that sound that originates at the extreme left of the animal will arrive at the left ear about 200 microseconds earlier than the right.

When the scientists moved the sound source toward the center of each animal's head, time differences decreased. Since an owl's ears are asymmetrical—that is, the left is higher than eye level and points downward, while the right is lower and points upward—the differences in the intensity of the sounds entering the two ears occurred as the speaker moved up and down.

Konishi is now collaborating with computer scientists at Caltech in developing an "owl chip" that will harness the speed and accuracy of an owl's neural networks for promising use in computers.

Cassia Farkas

In Memoriam – 2000

ALDRICH, MICHAEL SHERMAN (51), U.S. neurologist who explored the mysteries of sleep and sleep disorders, and contributed to the understanding of sleep apnea (a condition in which a sleeping person temporarily stops breathing) and narcolepsy (a disconcerting disorder in which the sufferer involuntarily falls into a deep sleep). d. Ann Arbor, Mich., July 18.

ASPINALL, JOHN (74), Indian-born British millionaire and zoo owner who made a fortune gambling and spent it on the creation of country estates for breeding gorillas and tigers. d. London, June 29.

BASCOM, WILLARD (83), U.S. engineer and scientist who supervised pioneering deep-sea exploration in the 1960s, drilling 12,000 feet (3,700 meters) below the ocean's surface to collect the first samples of Earth's "second layer." d. San Diego, Sept. 20.

BLOCH, KONRAD E. (88), German-born U.S. scientist who shared the 1964 Nobel Prize in Physiology or Medicine for the discovery of how cholesterol develops in the human body. Bloch's work allowed researchers to develop drugs called statins that block cholesterol production. d. Burlington, Mass., Oct. 15.

BOYER, L.B. (84), U.S. psychoanalyst who advanced the concept of countertransference in doctor-patient communication. Transference, in psychotherapy, is the unconscious tendency of patients to transfer feelings or attitudes associated with influences in their early lives to their analysts. Countertransference suggests that analysts also reflect their own inner conflicts back to their patients—an unpopular view shunned by the mainstream. d. Walnut Creek, Calif., Aug. 9.

CASIMIR, HENDRIK (90), Dutch theorist of quantum mechanics who predicted that even the seeming emptiness of a vacuum can generate electromagnetic forces to pull objects toward each other—a concept known as the Casimir effect. d. Heeze, Netherlands, May 4.

CHRZANOWSKI, GERARD (87), German-born U.S. psychoanalyst widely regarded as the model for the compassionate psychiatrist in the 1946 novel *The Snake Pit* and the 1948 film based on it. The book, an autobiographical novel by Mary Jane Ward, sheds light on life inside a crowded mental hospital and the common treatments for schizophrenia at the time. d. New York City, Nov. 1.

CLARKE, SIR CYRIL (93), British physician whose fascination with butterfly wings led him to research that helped end infant deaths from blood diseases caused by incompatible Rh factors. As a geneticist, he discovered a parallel between the inheritance of wing patterns on butterflies and the inheritance of blood types in people—a discovery that ultimately enabled women with rare Rh-negative blood to produce healthy babies. He also researched the longevity secrets of centenarians. d. Cheshire, England, Nov. 21.

CROWLEY, GEORGE (80), U.S. engineer and inventor who created the modern electric blanket. Nearly all of his numerous patents belonged to his employers, and when people questioned this, he amiably pointed out that they paid his salary, which he considered sufficient. His other creations included a device for painting and drying golf balls, a tennis-ball bouncer, and electrically heated flight suits for pilots. d. Pinehurst, N.C., Jan. 15.

EPSTEIN, LEON (83), U.S. physician who pioneered treatment of mental illness in the elderly. He developed an early interest in geriatric psychiatry, and introduced the use of psychoactive drugs in treating the elderly—who, before this time, were often neglected. He also helped the U.S. Navy develop profiling methods to determine the suitability of people for combat. d. San Francisco, Nov. 6.

FAVALORO, RENÉ (77), Argentine physician and pioneer in heart-bypass surgery. At Ohio's Cleveland Clinic in 1967, he performed the first heart-bypass surgery to be reported in a medical journal. d. Buenos Aires, July 30.

FESHBACH, HERMAN (83), U.S. nuclear physicist who helped develop the theories underlying the behavior of the nuclei of atoms; then, following World War II, he took an outspoken public stand against nuclear weapons. He was awarded the National Medal of Science in 1986. d. Cambridge, Mass., Dec. 22.

FM-2030 (69), Belgium-born "world citizen" and renowned futurist who changed his name from F.M. Esfandiary to FM-2030. He imagined a future in which people would eventually be made of synthetic parts, wholly provided for, and free from competition. "I am a 21st-century person who was accidentally born in the 20th," he said. "I have a deep nostalgia for the future." Following his death, his body was taken to Scottsdale, Arizona, and placed in a liquid-nitrogen tank at the Alcor Life Extension Foundation; he hoped to be reanimated someday. d. New York City, July 8.

FRIEDMAN, HERBERT (84), U.S. astronomer and pioneer of X-ray astronomy. He conducted much of his research following World War II, putting experiments aboard V-2 rockets sent into the upper atmosphere, where instruments recorded X rays and radiation from the Sun. His work resulted in the discovery of X-ray sources outside the solar system. d. Arlington, Va., Sept. 9.

GARLAND, MILTON (104), U.S. refrigeration expert who earned more than 41 patents, including one for his chief invention, the automatic ice maker. He worked for the Frick Company his entire career, from 1920 until May 2000. d. Waynesboro, Pa., July 27.

GOETZ, ROBERT (90), German-born U.S. cardiovascular surgeon who pioneered coronary artery bypass surgery and created an arterial pump to sustain a patient's heart. He was credited with the first successful clinical coronary operation in 1960. d. Scarsdale, N.Y., Dec. 15.

GROSS, AL (82), Canadian-born U.S. inventor who developed early forms of walkie-talkies, pagers, and cellular telephones. He was credited with giving cartoonist Chester Gould the idea for Dick Tracy's wristwatch radio. d. Sun City, Ariz., Dec. 21.

HAMILTON, WILLIAM (63), Egyptian-born British biologist who offered a genetic basis for altruism, the inspiration for Richard Dawkins' best-selling *The Selfish Gene*. He studied insect survival instincts, defense, and reproduction. He died from malaria contracted during a trip to Africa to study the origin of AIDS. d. Oxford, England, March 7.

KABAT, ELVIN (85), U.S. microbiologist who founded immunochemistry, the study of the chemical reactions involved in immune processes. d. North Falmouth, Mass., June 16.

KEENAN, PHILIP C. (92), U.S. astronomer whose work in the spectral classification of stars later helped astronomers understand the chemical evolution of galaxies. d. Columbus, Ohio, April 20.

KETY, SEYMOUR S. (84), U.S. psychiatrist who delivered the first strong evidence that schizophrenia runs in families. d. Westwood, Mass., May 25.

KNIPLING, EDWARD (90), U.S. entomologist who revolutionized pest control; his methods of rendering the destructive screwworm sterile enabled farmers to banish the insects. d. Arlington, Va., March 17.

LEE, CHESTER "CHET" (80), U.S. Navy captain during World War II who later became a mainstay at the National Aeronautics and Space Administration (NASA), serving as mission commander for the last six *Apollo* Moon landings, including *Apollo 13*. d. Washington, D.C., Feb. 23.

LEPRINCE-RINGUET, LOUIS (99), French nuclear physicist who explored cosmic rays and, in 1944, copublished an article describing evidence of a new subatomic particle—the meson. d. Paris, Dec. 23.

LOCKLEY, RONALD (96), Welsh-born New Zealand naturalist whose work inspired the book *Watership Down*. He established bird observatories in Britain and New Zealand, became intensely interested in the behavior of rabbits, and later wrote the screenplay for one of the first nature films, *The Private Life of the Gannet*, which won an Academy Award for Best Documentary. d. Auckland, New Zealand, April 12.

LORD, FREDERIC (87), U.S. mathematician who developed the process for scoring fill-in-the-bubble examinations. His trailblazing mathematical model, Item Response Theory, altered the course of standardized testing. d. Naples, Fla., Feb. 5.

MONOD, THÉODORE (98), French naturalist who discovered approximately 30 new species of plants and insects, 50 crustaceans, and several fish. He traveled on foot and by camel across the Sahara. d. Paris, Nov. 21.

MORRISON, JOHN S. (87), British professor who created a stunning replica of an ancient Greek trireme, a warship noted for its maneuverability, speed, and fighting prowess. In 1987, after years of intensive research and construction, his re-creation was launched in the Aegean Sea. d. London, Oct. 25.

MURPHY, GERALD (65), U.S. urologist whose research led to the prostate-specific-antigens (PSA) test, widely used to detect prostate cancer. d. Tel Aviv, Israel, Jan. 21.

NEEL, JAMES V. (84), U.S. genetic researcher who helped uncover sickle-cell anemia and who studied the effects of radiation on atomic-bomb survivors. He foresaw the importance of inherited factors in understanding and treating disorders. d. Ann Arbor, Mich., Feb. 1.

ORNE, MARTIN (72), Austrian-born U.S. psychiatrist whose work promoted the field of hypnosis. He was also an expert in the fields of dissociative identity disorder (commonly known as multiple personality disorder) and brainwashing, but hypnosis was his lifelong pursuit. He assisted in a number of major cases, testifying on behalf of heiress Patricia Hearst in her kidnapping case, and against Kenneth Bianchi, the Hillside Strangler, who claimed he suffered from multiple personality disorder. d. Paoli, Pa., Feb. 11.

POLIS, GARY ALLAN (53), U.S. zoologist, desert ecologist, and a leading authority on scorpions. In March 2000, while leading a routine Earthwatch Institute expedition to study lizards, spiders, and other predators on islands in the Sea of Cortez, the group's boat sank, and Polis and three other researchers drowned. d. Sea of Cortez, Mexico, March 27.

PORTWOOD, RAYMOND, JR. (66), U.S. computer-game pioneer credited as one of two principal creators of the popular Carmen Sandiego series of children's computer games. He began his career at age 17 as an artist for Walt Disney, working on a number of animated feature films. d. Windsor, Calif., July 17.

PRINZ, MARTIN (69), U.S. curator of the meteorite collection at the American Museum of Natural History. He was the driving force behind renovation of the museum's Ross Hall of Meteorites, which imported the "largest rock in captivity," a 34-ton meteorite discovered in Greenland and estimated to be 4.5 billion years old. d. Manhasset, N.Y., Dec. 16.

RAUSING, GAD (77), Swedish innovator who invented the Tetra Pak, a revolutionary brick-shaped milk carton made of paper, plastic, and aluminum; people in the United States would recognize the cartons as juice packs. The invention made him one of the richest men in the world, and a target for terrorists and blackmailers. d. Montreux, Switzerland, Jan. 28.

REEMTSMA, KEITH (74), U.S. physician credited with developing cross-species transplants. In 1964, he transplanted a kidney from a chimpanzee to a woman; she survived for nine months after the operation. He performed six more similar kidney-transplant surgeries between 1963 and 1964. He was also considered the model for Dr. Hawkeye Pierce in the movie *M*A*S*H*. d. New York City, June 16.

REIS, DONALD (69), U.S. neurobiologist who explored the brain's role in human emotions, behavior, and disease. He found evidence that brain disorders could produce hypertension, and he contributed to the understanding of dementia, strokes, Parkinson's disease, and schizophrenia. d. Stonington, Conn., Nov. 1.

REISNER, MARC (51), U.S. environmental writer and ecology advocate who authored *Cadillac Desert: The American West and its Disappearing Water,* a seminal work on the environmental cost exacted by water projects. d. San Anselmo, Calif., July 21.

REYNOLDS, JOHN HAMILTON (77), U.S. physicist who refined techniques for cosmic aging—the technique of dating meteorites and primordial rock formations by measuring isotopes of the elements helium, argon, and xenon. His achievements heightened confidence in the perceived chronology of the early solar system. d. Berkeley, Calif., Nov. 4.

RHODES, HAROLD (89), U.S. inventor who created the electric piano. During World War II, he entertained troops with a small portable piano he had built himself. Following the war, he worked with Leo Fender, the electric-guitar pioneer, to develop the electric piano. d. Los Angeles, Dec. 17.

ROSSI, HARALD HERMANN (82), Viennese-born U.S. biologist who developed microdosimetry, a technique that provided the scientific underpinnings for the measurement of radiation. d. Upper Nyack, N.Y., Jan 1.

RUGE, ARTHUR C. (94), U.S. inventor who created the bonded-wire strain gauge, the SR-4, a fingernail-sized gauge that revolutionized how things are weighed and tested for stress. d. Lexington, Mass., April 3.

SANDELL, GEORGE (88), U.S. musician, teacher, and inventor who created the Gee-Bee, a sponge with a plastic handle for washing. d. Santa Monica, Calif., Aug. 26.

SCHILLING, MARTIN (88), German-born developer of the V-2 missile, used against Allied forces during World War II. It traveled at an altitude of 60 miles (100 kilometers) and a speed of 1 mile (1.6 kilometers) per second—faster than the speed of sound. Following the war, he was relocated to the United States, where he and a team of developers eventually helped launch America's first satellite. d. Burlington, Mass., April 30.

SIMPSON, JOHN ALEXANDER (83), U.S. nuclear physicist and astrophysicist who helped to develop the nuclear bomb and developed instruments that have been sending data back from space for nearly 40 years; he also built the first cosmic-ray detectors. d. Chicago, Aug. 31.

SIRKIN, LES (66), U.S. geologist who mapped the ways glaciers shaped North American coastlines from Long Island, New York, to Baja, California. He was an expert in stratigraphy—the layered arrangement of rocks—of the Mesozoic and Cenozoic eras. d. Block Island, R.I., June 25.

SMITH, MICHAEL (68), British-born Canadian chemist who shared the 1993 Nobel Prize in Chemistry for developing one of the basic tools of genetic engineering. His research allowed scientists to reprogram the genetic code, altering its structure and function—a technique that could eventually help battle genetically based diseases. d. Vancouver, British Columbia, Oct. 4.

STEBBINS, LEDYARD G. (94), U.S. biologist and botanist widely credited with bringing modern evolutionary thinking—in line with Darwinian theory—to the study of plants. d. Davis, Calif., Jan. 19.

STRAND, KAJ AAGE (93), Danish-born U.S. astronomer and former scientific director at the U.S. Naval Observatory, whose pioneering work determined stellar distances with reflecting telescopes. He guided the design and construction of the U.S. Navy's Kaj Strand Astrometric Reflector in Flagstaff, Arizona. d. Washington, D.C., Oct. 31.

STRAUCH, KARL (77), German-born U.S. physicist who searched for the basic building blocks of the universe and helped to provide insights into the fundamental structures of matter and energy. d. Boston, Jan. 3.

TANAKA, TOYOICHI (54), Japanese-born U.S. biophysicist who created "smart" gels—polymers linked together with the ability to absorb water and provide elasticity and fluidity. The gels have had a significant impact on chemistry, medicine, agriculture, and in a number of other fields. d. Wellesley, Mass., May 20.

THOMPSON, HOMER (93), Canadian-born U.S. archaeologist who for decades led the excavation of the Agora, the civic center of ancient Athens. He was widely regarded as one of the outstanding classical archaeologists of his generation. d. Hightstown, N.J., May 7.

TITOV, GHERMAN (65), Soviet cosmonaut who in 1961 became the second Russian to fly in space and the first man to sleep there. d. Moscow, Sept. 20.

TRUESDELL, CLIFFORD (80), U.S. mathematician and historian of mathematics who developed the foundation for continuum mechanics—the study of elasticity, the bending of beams and bridges, and the study of vibrations and liquids. d. Baltimore, Jan. 14.

TUKEY, JOHN (85), U.S. statistician and broad thinker who is credited with coining the word "software." He developed important theories about analyzing data and rapidly computing numbers. d. New Brunswick, N.J., July 26.

ULTMANN, JOHN E. (75) Austrian-born U.S. cancer expert who advanced the understanding of how treatment should vary according to the stage of the disease. He developed new drugs to treat cancer and made strides in the use of chemotherapy. d. Hyde Park, Ill., Oct. 23.

WEINSTEIN, LOUIS (92), U.S. physician who made advances in the treatment of infectious disease during a time when there were no antibiotics and few vaccines. Considered a founder in the specialty of infectious diseases, he was a heroic figure during the New England polio epidemics of 1949 and 1955. d. Newton, Mass., March 16.

WHYTE, WILLIAM (86), U.S. gang sociologist who specialized in reform. His 1943 book *Street Corner Society,* which he compiled by living in and spending time with gangs, championed a method he called "participatory action research." d. Ithaca, N.Y., July 16.

WILSON, ROBERT R. (85), U.S. physicist who specialized in the construction of particle accelerators, which smash subatomic particles together at high speeds, allowing for research into their behavior. In 1972, he opened the Fermi National Accelerator Laboratory—Fermilab—which contains the most powerful accelerator in the world. d. Ithaca, N.Y., Jan. 16.

ZINN, WALTER H. (93), Canadian-born U.S. nuclear physicist who played a major role in the Manhattan Project, overseeing construction of the project's nuclear reactor. d. Clearwater, Fla., Feb. 14.

INDEX

ACKNOWLEDGMENTS

Sources of articles appear below, including those reprinted with the kind permission of publications and organizations.

THE WORLD'S MOST ELUSIVE CARNIVORE, page 16: Vicki Croke/© 2000. Reprinted with permission of *Discover* magazine. Originally appeared as "The Deadliest Carnivore" in the April 2000 issue of *Discover*.

RESTORING A NATIONAL TREASURE, page 22: Article originally appeared in the April 1999 issue of *Agricultural Research* magazine.

COLORLESS IN A WORLD OF COLOR, page 25: Reprinted with permission from the author. Article originally appeared in the August/September 2000 issue of *National Wildlife* magazine.

CUTTLEFISH SAY IT WITH SKIN, page 30: Reprinted with permission from *Natural History* magazine, April 2000. Copyright the American Museum of Natural History 2000.

WHERE THE SPITTING COBRAS PLAY, page 35: Reprinted with permission of the author. Article originally appeared in the Spring 2000 issue of *California Wild* magazine.

STINKERS OF THE PLANT WORLD, page 39: Reprinted by permission of the author. Article originally published in the January 1997 issue of *ZooNooz*, published by the Zoological Society of San Diego.

THE TRUTH ABOUT WOODCHUCKS, page 43: Reprinted with permission from *Animals* magazine. Article originally appeared in the September/October 2000 edition (published by the Massachusetts Society for the Prevention of Cruelty to Animals/American Humane Education Society).

BIRD COURTSHIP: THE DANCE OF LIFE, page 46: Reprinted by permission of the author. This article first appeared in *ZooNooz* magazine, February 2001.

CLAW-TO-CLAW COMBAT, page 51: Reproduced with permission from *New Scientist* magazine, the global authority on science and technology news © RBI 2000 www.newscientist.com. Originally appeared in the April 8, 2000, issue.

LIGHT AND MAGIC, page 64: Reprinted by permission of the author. This article originally appeared in the June/July 2000 issue of the *Air & Space/Smithsonian* magazine.

SCOPING OUT THE MONSTER STAR, page 72: Reproduced by permission. © 2000, *Astronomy* magazine, Kalmbach Publishing Co.

SPACE-SHUTTLE IMPERSONATOR, page 78: Reprinted by permission of the author. Article originally appeared in the October/November 2000 issue of *Air & Space/Smithsonian* magazine.

THE DARK SIDE OF LIGHT, page 94: © 2000 Joe Bower. First published in *Audubon* magazine, March/April 2000. Reprinted by permission.

LAKE VOSTOK: PROBING FOR LIFE BENEATH ANTARCTIC ICE, page 99: Reprinted with the permission of the author; article originally appeared in the July 2000 issue of *Smithsonian* magazine.

CREATIVE DESTRUCTION, page 106: Reprinted by permission of AMERICAN HERITAGE Inc.

SPEED LIMITS, page 124: This article is reprinted by permission of *The Sciences* and is from the September/October 2000 issue.

FOR SOME, PAIN IS ORANGE, page 132: Reprinted by permission of the author; article originally appeared in the February 2001 issue of *Smithsonian* magazine.

BUILDING FROM BABY BABBLE, page 139: Reprinted with permission from *SCIENCE NEWS*, the weekly newsmagazine of science, copyright 2000 by Science Service Inc.

MAKING A MODERN MUMMY, page 148: Wendy Marston/© 2000. Reprinted with permission of *Discover* magazine.

ARTIFICIAL ANASAZI, page 155: Reprinted with permission of *Discovering Archaeology* magazine and is from the March/April 2000 issue.

MAKING STUFF LAST, page 162: Reprinted with permission from *SCIENCE NEWS*, the weekly newsmagazine of science, copyright 2000 by Science Service Inc.

THE REIGN OF THE SIERRA STORM KING, page 166: Reprinted with permission from the author. Originally appeared in the January/February 2001 issue of *Weatherwise* magazine.

REFINING THE ART OF MEASUREMENT, page 178: Copyright © 2001 by *The New York Times*. Reprinted by permission.

UNDERHANDED ACHIEVEMENT, page 184: Curtis Rist/© 2000. Reprinted with permission of *Discover* magazine.

HOW SQUIRRELS FLY, page 186: Reprinted by permission of the author; article originally appeared in the February 2001 issue of *Smithsonian* magazine.

JOINING HANDS: THE MATHEMATICS OF APPLAUSE, page 189: Josie Glausiusz/© 2000. Reprinted with permission of *Discover* magazine.

WHAT EDWARD TELLER DID, page 192: Reprinted by permission of AMERICAN HERITAGE Inc. Article originally appeared in the Winter 2001 issue of *American Heritage of Invention and Technology*.

DOUBLE DECKER, page 204: Reprinted with permission from *Popular Science* magazine's October 2000 issue. Copyright © 2000, Times Mirror Magazines, Inc.

SOMETHING'S FISHY ABOUT THIS ROBOT, page 209: Reprinted by permission of the author; article originally appeared in the August 2000 issue of *Smithsonian* magazine.

MICROSPIES, page 215: Reprinted by permission of the author; article originally appeared in the April/May 2000 issue of *Air & Space/Smithsonian* magazine.

THE WEB WITHOUT WIRES, page 229: Copyright © 2001 by *The New York Times*. Reprinted by permission.

Manufacturing Acknowledgments

We wish to thank the following for their services:

Color Separations, Que-Net Media, a member of the Quebecor World Group;
Text Stock, printed on sappi Fine Paper NA 70# Somerset Matte;
Cover Materials provided by Ecological Fibers, Inc.;
Printing and Binding, Quebecor World Book Services.

ILLUSTRATION CREDITS

The following list acknowledges, according to page, the sources of illustrations used in this volume. The credits are listed illustration by illustration—top to bottom, left to right. Where necessary, the name of the photographer or artist has been listed with the source, the two separated by a slash. If two or more illustrations appear on the same page, their credits are separated by semicolons.

3 Courtesy, AeroVironment Inc.;
© Edwin Aguirre/*Sky & Telescope*;
© Tui De Roy/Minden Pictures
8- Courtesy, Javier Garcia-Guinea;
9
10 © Sydney Freelance/Liaison Agency
11 © Laurent Rebours/AP/Wide World Photos
12 © Tom & Pat Leeson; Ciel et Espace;
© Jeff Tinsley/Smithsonian
Institution/AP/Wide World Photos
13 © Alain Compost/Peter Arnold, Inc.;
© James King-Holmes/Science Photo
Library/Photo Researchers;
14- © John Cancalosi
15
16 © Peter Oxford/BBC NHU Picture Library
17 © Peter Oxford/BBC NHU Picture Library
18 © Steven Stankiewicz/Discover Syndication
19 © Peter Oxford/BBC NHU Picture Library;
inset: © Ron Toft/Discover Syndication
20 © Peter Oxford/BBC NHU Picture Library
21 © Peter Oxford/BBC NHU Picture Library
22 © Khue Bui/AP/Wide World Photos
23 © Khue Bui/AP/Wide World Photos;
© Scott Bauer/Agricultural Research
Service, USDA
25 © Tom & Pat Leeson;
© Maslowski Photo/Photo Researchers
26 © Gerard Lacz/Peter Arnold, Inc.;
© Gordon & Cathy Illg/Animals Animals
27 © Sydney Freelance/Liaison Agency
28 © Gary Retherford/Photo Researchers;
© Tom McHugh/Photo Researchers
29 Above, above right, and top: Courtesy of
Belinda Henton, of Olney, Illinois, home of
the white squirrel; left:
© Alvin E. Staffan/ Photo Researchers
30 © Mark Strickland/Oceanic Impressions
31 © Fred Bavendam/Minden Pictures
32 Top and bottom: © Fred Bavendam;
center: © Fred Bavendam/Minden Pictures
33 Both photos: © Mark Strickland/Oceanic
Impressions
35- All photos: © Dong Lin/California Academy
38 of Sciences
39 © Alain Compost/Peter Arnold, Inc.
40 Both photos: © Wayne P. Armstrong
41 All photos: © Wayne P. Armstrong
43 © Lynn M. Stone/DRK Photo
44 © Leonard Lee Rue III/Animals Animals
45 UPI Photo Service/Newscom
46 © Jack Fields/Photo Researchers
47 Top: © Brian J. Coates/Bruce Coleman Inc.;
center and bottom: © Kenneth W.Fink/
Bruce Coleman Inc.
48 © David Gillison/Peter Arnold Inc.;
© Wardene Weisser/Bruce Coleman Inc.
49 © Tom McHugh/Photo Researchers;
© Kenneth W. Fink/Photo Researchers
50 © Frank Lane Agency/Bruce Coleman Inc.
51 © Andrew J. Martinez/Photo Researchers
52 © Andrew J. Martinez/Photo Researchers
53 © Larry Lipsky/Bruce Coleman Inc.
54 © Superstock
56- © 1998 Lynette Cook
57
58 NASA
59 NASA
60 NASA/AP/Wide World Photos
61 NASA; NASA/AP/Wide World Photos
62 NASA
63 NASA
64 © Joe McNally
65 Courtesy ESO
66 © Joe McNally
67 Courtesy ESO
68 Courtesy ESO
69 Ciel et Espace
70 © Joe McNally

72 © Anglo-Australian Observatory/
photography by David Malin
73 Courtesy of the Art Institute of Chicago,
the Alfred Stieglitz Collection
75 NASA/CXC/SAO; Jon Morse/University of
Colorado and NASA; Elisha
Polomski/courtesy, University of Florida;
ATCA image/courtesy Stephen White/
University of Maryland
76 © 2000 *Astronomy* Magazine, Kalmbach
Publishing Co.
78- All artwork: © John MacNeill
83
84 © Superstock
86- © Richard Hamilton Smith
87
88 © Ricardo Mazalan/AP/Wide World Photos
89 © Frans Lanting/Photo Researchers;
© Tui De Roy/Minden Pictures
90 Top and bottom photos:
© Tui De Roy/Minden Pictures; center:
© Gregory G. Dimijian/Photo Researchers
91 © Tui De Roy/Minden Pictures;
© George Holton/Photo Researchers;
© Frans Lanting/Minden Pictures
92 © Tui De Roy/Minden Pictures;
© George Harrison/Bruce Coleman Inc.
93 Both photos: © Ricardo Mazalan/AP/Wide
World Photos
94 © Inaki Relazon Roca
95 © Edwin Aguirre/*Sky & Telescope*
96 © Pat & Rae Hagan/Bruce Coleman Inc.
97 NOAA
99 © Rob Wood/Wood Ronsaville Harlin, Inc.
100 Courtesy, John C. Priscu, Department of
Land Resources and Environmental Sciences,
and Recep Avci, Department of Physics,
Montana State University
101 JPL/NASA
103 © C. Munoz-Yague/Eurelios
104- © B. Malaize/Extra-Pol/Eurelios
105
106 © Nick Ut/AP/Wide World Photos; inset:
© Patrick Magallanes, Texas Shredder
Inc./Image Corps
108 Hulton Getty/Liaison Agency
109 Brown Brothers
110- © Steven Stankiewicz
111
113 © I. Wilson Baker
114 © Superstock
116- ChemSyn Laboratories
117
118 Background and inset: © Biophoto
Associates/Photo Researchers
119 © Patricia McDonnell/AP/Wide World Photos
120 © J. Axamethy/AP/Wide World Photos;
© Chris Hondros/Liaison Agency
121 © Bob Child/AP/Wide World Photos
123 Courtesy, Jonathan F. Day, University of
Florida, IFAS; © Bridget
Montgomery/AP/Wide World Photos
124 © Adam Pretty/Allsport
125 © Scala/Art Resource, NY
126 © Eric Draper/AP/Wide World Photos
127 © Thomas Kienzle/AP/Wide World Photos
129 © Laurent Rebours/AP/Wide World Photos
132- All illustrations: © Kay Chernush
137
139 Clockwise from left: © Michael Newman/
PhotoEdit; © Myrleen Cate/PhotoEdit;
© Myrleen Cate/PhotoEdit;
© Elizabeth Hathon/Corbis Stock Market
141 © Bob Daemmrich/The Image Works
142 © Myrleen Cate/PhotoEdit
144 © Superstock
146- © Tarik Tinazay/Agence France Press
147
148 © Brian Velenchenko/*Discover* Magazine

149 © Pat Remler/*Discover* Magazine
150- Crossover photo: Corbis-Bettmann;
151 all other photos: © Pat Remler/*Discover*
Magazine
152 Corbis-Bettmann; © Sergei Karpukhin/
AP/Wide World Photos
153 © Pat Remler/*Discover* Magazine
155 Machelle Wood and Steven Harrison/
courtesy *Discovering Archaeology*
156 Photo: Paul Logsdon, courtesy of M.L.
Logsdon/photo courtesy *Discovering
Archaeology*; map: Machelle Wood/
courtesy *Discovering Archaeology*
157 Jonathan Haas, courtesy of George J.
Gumerman/photo courtesy *Discovering
Archaeology*
158 The Brookings Institution
159 Both illustrations: The Brookings
Institution
161 Laboratory of Tree-Ring Research,
courtesy of George J. Gumerman/photo
courtesy *Discovering Archaeology*
162 © Jeff Tinsley/Smithsonian
Institution/AP/Wide World Photos
163 © Peter Mauss/Esto
164 Clockwise from top left: Courtesy, Yvonne
Shashoua, private collection; AP/Wide
World Photos; Liaison Agency
165 NASA
166- Photo: © Steven Frame/Stock, Boston
167
168 Brown Brothers
169 The Granger Collection
170 Culver Pictures, Inc.
171 © Mark McLaughlin/Mic Mac Publishing;
inset: Brown Brothers
172 © Mark McLaughlin/Mic Mac Publishing
173 © Mark McLaughlin/Mic Mac Publishing
174 © Superstock
176- Courtesy, Brookhaven National Institute
177
178 © Robert Rathe/National Institute of
Standards & Technology
179 © Robert Rathe/National Institute of
Standards & Technology
180 © Geoffrey Wheeler/National Institute of
Standards & Technology; National Institute
of Standards & Technology Archives
181 National Institute of Standards & Technology
182 © Shelley Michael
184 © Tony Triolo/*Sports Illustrated*
185 © Nigel Holmes/*Discover* Magazine
186 © Richard Alan Wood/Animals Animals
187 © Regis Lefebure
189 © Ed Bock/Corbis Stock Market
190 © Superstock
191 © Marty Lederhandler/AP/Wide World Photos
192 Reuters/Archive Photos
193 © Nat Farbham/TimePix
194 © Ralph Morse/TimePix
195 © Jacqueline McBride, Lawrence
Livermore National Laboratory
197 © Steven Stankiewicz
199 © Charles Tasnadi/AP/Wide World Photos
200 © Superstock
202- © Simon Burt/Apex
203
204- All artwork: © Mike Speigner
205
206 All artwork: Courtesy, Airbus Industrie of
North America
207 Artwork: © Mike Speigner
209 © Peter Menzel
210 © Sam Ogden
211 © Sam Ogden
212 © Peter Menzel
213 © Peter Menzel
215 Photo: Courtesy, AeroVironment Inc.;
art: © John McNeill

216 Both photos: © Chad Slattery
217 © Stanley Leary/Courtesy, Georgia Institute of Technology
218 © Chad Slattery
219 © Courtesy Ilan Kroo/Aircraft Aerodynamics and Design Group/Stanford University
221 © Fritz Hoffmann/The Image Works
222 © Museum of the City of New York/Talfor/Holmes/Archive Photos
223 © Lance Nelson/Corbis Stock Market; © Jose Fuste Raga/Corbis Stock Market
224 © John Zoiner/Corbis Stock Market
225 © Martha Bates/Stock, Boston
226 © John Cetrino/AP/Wide World Photos
227 © Ray Juno/Corbis Stock Market; © Lester Sloan/Liaison Agency; © James King-Holmes/Science Photo Library/Photo Researchers
229 © Seth Resnick/Stock, Boston
231 © Norbert von de Groeben/The Image Bank
232 © Superstock
234 © Simon Burt/Apex; © Neil Brake/*The Tuscaloosa News*; © Suzanne Plunkett/AP/Wide World Photos
235 © Kristiaan D'Aout/Laboratory for Functional Morphology/University of Antwerp; NASA
237 © Keith Weller/Agricultural Research Service, USDA
239 AP/Wide World Photos
241 Both photos: AP/Wide World Photos
243 Image by Howard Lester, MMT Observatory
246 © John B. Carnett/Reprinted from *Popular Science* magazine with permission. © Times Mirror Magazine, Inc.
248 © Toshihiko Sato/AP/Wide World Photos
250 © Doug Mills/AP/Wide World Photos
251 © Adam Nadel/AP/Wide World Photos
253 © Kristiaan D'Aout/Laboratory for Functional Morphology/University of Antwerp; © Mark Moffett/Minden Pictures

254 Courtesy, Touchstone Books/Simon & Schuster; courtesy, Picador USA; courtesy, Free Press/Simon & Schuster; courtesy, Joseph Henry Press
255 Courtesy, Farrar, Strauss & Giroux; courtesy, Pocket Books/Simon & Schuster; courtesy, Taschen America LLC; courtesy, Oxford University Press
256 Westview Press/jacket photograph by Vito Cannella; courtesy, Harper Collins Publishers; courtesy, Harvard University Press; courtesy, Oxford University Press
257 Courtesy, W.W. Norton & Company, Inc.; cover from *Building Big* by David Macaulay, jacket art: © 2000 by David Macaulay. Reprinted by permission of Houghton Mifflin Co. All rights reserved; courtesy, Checkmark Books, an imprint of Facts on Files, Inc.
259 © John Colwell/Grant Heilman
261 © Jockel Finck/AP/Wide World Photos
263 © Simon Burt/Apex
264 © David Weintraub/Stock, Boston
267 © Paul Sakuma/AP/Wide World Photos
270 Courtesy, Six Flags California
271 Courtesy, Global Electric Motorcars, LLC; © Naokazu Oinuma/AP/Wide World Photos
272 Courtesy, Rand McNally; courtesy, Fleishman-Hillard, Inc.
274 © Fred Greaves/AP/Wide World Photos; courtesy, Given Imaging Ltd.
275 © Stephen Nash
277 © Gregory G. Dimijian/Photo Researchers
280 © David McNew/Liaison Agency
282 © Richard Chesher/Photo Researchers
284 © Jane Sapinsky/Corbis Stock Market
286 AP/Wide World Photos
288 © Rick Bowmer/AP/Wide World Photos
291 Courtesy, Javier Garcia-Guinea
293 © Jim Olive/Peter Arnold, Inc.
294 © Jim Olive/Peter Arnold, Inc.

298 National Hurricane Center/AP/Wide World Photos
299 Daniel Wolfe/Environmental Technology Laboratory/NOAA
301 © L.M. Otero/AP/Wide World Photos; © Neil Brake/*The Tuscaloosa News*; © Karel Prinsloo/AP/Wide World Photos
303 All photos: © Roland S. Lundstrom/AP/Wide World Photos
304 © Peter Fownes/Stock South/PictureQuest
305 All photos: © Claudio Bresciani/Reuters/Scanpix/Newscom
307 All photos: © Jan Collsioo/AP/Wide World Photos
309 © Chuck Pefley/Stock, Boston
312 Dave Gray/Woods Hole Oceanographic Institute
313 Jim Page/NCMNS
314 Adapted from an image by Ed Heck/AMNH; inset: 3-D imaging by Paul Fisher/NCSU College of Veterinary Medicine, Biomedical Imaging Resource Facility. CT data courtesy of Ashland Community Hospital
315 Illustration by Kim Reed-Deemer/Northern Illinois University
316 Courtesy, Fermi National Accelerator Laboratory
319 © Steven E. Frischling/UPI Photo Service/Newscom
321 © Edwin Aguirre/*Sky & Telescope*
323 © Tim Crosby/Newsmakers/Liaison Agency; inset: © Bill Greenblatt/Liaison Agency
327 All photos: NASA
329 © Suzanne Plunkett/AP/Wide World Photos
331 Both photos: Courtesy, Los Angeles County MTA
332 © Wesley Boxce/The Image Works
334 © Rod Planck/Natural History Photographic Agency

Cover photo credit for *Encyclopedia Science Supplement:* © John Cancalosi